álvaro siza

Phaidon Press Limited
Regent's Wharf
All Saints Street
London N1 9PA

First published in English by Phaidon Press Limited
© 2000 Phaidon Press Limited

First published in Italian by Electa
© 1999 Electa Milano
Elemond Editori Associati

A CIP catalogue record for this book is available from the British Library

ISBN 0 7148 4004 1

All rights reserved. No part of this publication may be reproduced, stored in a retrieval system or transmitted, in any form or by any means, electronic, mechanical, photocopying, recording or otherwise, without the prior permission in writing from Phaidon Press Limited.

Printed in China

álvaro siza

Complete Works
Kenneth Frampton

Contents

7	**Preface: Álvaro Siza and the Art of Fusion** Francesco Dal Co
11	**Architecture as Critical Transformation: The Work of Álvaro Siza** Kenneth Frampton
66	**Homage to Álvaro Siza** Fernando Távora
69	**Complete Works** 1952–1999

Writings by Álvaro Siza

71	On My Work
82	Leça da Palmeira
160	Évora-Malagueira
252	Living in a House
336	The Museum of Santiago de Compostela
356	The Chiado
377	The Church at Marco de Canavezes
527	Villa Savoye
572	Alvar Aalto
597	On Design

Appendices

607	Biography
608	Bibliography
615	Chronology of Works
618	Index of Works
620	Acknowledgements

Preface

Álvaro Siza and the Art of Fusion
Francesco Dal Co

Few contemporary artists enjoy the prestige, the authority and, above all, the respect that are bestowed upon Álvaro Siza Vieira. The honest coherence of his work is unimpeachable and his merits, travestied though they may sometimes be, are beyond dispute. The success that his work enjoys, as demonstrated by the various distinctions awarded to him both at home and abroad (amongst these, between 1988 and 1998, Siza received the Premio Mies van der Rohe, the Pritzker Prize and the Praemium Imperiale), is the fruit of a long, industrious and lucky career, a life lived with admirable equilibrium. Restraint, on the other hand, is the key to his work, as can be seen even in the plans he drew as a young man, and the first projects he completed in Porto – the city where Siza works and where he graduated in 1955 – and in the neighbouring municipality of Matosinhos, where he was born in 1933.

From the late sixties onwards, the interest of well-informed critics and architectural culture in general turned increasingly towards Siza. He was seen as the leader of the Portuguese architectural world, one which, thanks to the liveliness and originality of its collective work, has become a privileged reference point in the architectural landscape of the past two decades. Since 1974, when Portugal embraced democracy and embarked upon a period of remarkable social and economic development, Siza's work has become a symbol of the country's rebirth.

In the latter half of the fifties, after completing his university degree, Siza worked together with a teacher with a very powerful character, Fernando Távora. From the late fifties onwards, Távora's work and activities, which are not yet adequately appreciated and studied outside Portugal, were crucial in guaranteeing the knowledge and diffusion in Lisbon and Porto of the experiments being carried out in contemporary European architecture – despite the isolationist obscurantism of the dictatorship installed by António de Oliveira Salazar (1932–68). The most recent CIAM Congresses have provided ample opportunities for the study and comparison of these developments. The most important thing that Siza learned from Távora was a working method. Having appreciated Távora's professional attitudes and the refinement of his culture, Siza renewed his commitment on the level of design, as revealed in his more than promising early works: four one-family dwellings in Matosinhos (1954–7), the Boa Nova restaurant (1958–63) and the public swimming baths (1961–6) built in Leça da Palmeira. In parallel with the process of democratic transformation which took place in Portugal from the mid-sixties onwards, Siza made a crucial contribution to his country's attempts to address the issue of popular housing on new principles, with the activities promoted by the SAAL programme. The residential complexes that he built in Bouça and in São Victor (Porto, 1974 onwards), within the context of the SAAL initiatives, anticipated by some years the start of work on the construction of the district of Quinta da Malagueira in Évora (from 1977), which proves that he had reached maturity. This is one of his most accomplished works, one which was able to renew the noblest tradition of twentieth-century European architecture while giving it highly original inflections. These residential districts, which have absorbed the most important experiments carried out in radical architecture in Germany, Austria, Switzerland and Holland in the twenties (in particular the work of such architects as Oud and Stam, May and Taut and, above all, Loos, although additional references might also be cited), also reveal the influence of the culture of Italian neo-realism, with which, as one observer has remarked, they share 'the proud reclaiming of the values of poverty'. When he designed the districts of Porto and Évora, in poor and socially disadvantaged areas, Siza first demonstrated the importance of the idea which has become key to his work: the honest and generous modesty with which he responds to each new professional opportunity, the conviction which he, himself an excellent story-teller, holds that 'an architecture is not ugly in its theme, because there are no beautiful or ugly themes in architecture; there is only good or bad treatment of the theme', to paraphrase Julio Cortázar's definition of the novelist.

The quantity of work Siza designed and built in Berlin, even before the city had been swept by the money and expectations that have been invested there since the fall of the Wall, testifies to his steadfast commitment to the force of his convictions. A number of Siza's works for Berlin, especially for the redevelopment of the then marginal district of Kreuzberg, owe a great deal to the development of his research and the maturity of his poetics. It was in Kreuzberg that he built the residential complex of Schlesisches Tor (from 1980): this work, the first that he completed outside Portugal, with its paradigmatic character and the contemporary nature of its interpretative reading (the configuration of the building being the result of the highly personal dialogue in which the architect engaged with the characteristics of the area), won him the attention of international critics and designers.

Following on from this achievement, Siza's fame and notoriety grew continuously. He was offered more and more distinguished and prestigious projects in various European countries. Invited to participate in major competitions throughout the eighties and nineties, Siza carried out work not only in Portugal, but also in Holland, Spain, Germany and Italy. The most important buildings from this recent phase of his career include the architecture faculty and the Serralves Foundation Museum in Porto, the university library in Aveiro, the church in Marco de Canavezes, the Portuguese pavilion at the 1998 Lisbon Expo, the residential settlements in The Hague, the Vitra factory in Weil am Rhein, the rectory of Alicante University and, above all, the Museum of Contemporary Art in Santiago de Compostela.

Rigorous and eclectic, severe but not without irony, both banal and proud, indifferent to novelty but often surprising, Siza's architecture takes simplicity as a form of richness in itself. A 'builder of gravity', as Fernando Távora has described him (and 'gravity' should be understood in its twin senses of 'serious commitment' and 'physical weight', as we are reminded by the seventeenth-century document from which Távora borrowed the expression), Siza displays his commitment with a hint of a smile. He combines will and reason; his rhetoric is based on subdued ways of speaking; a frugality of expression alternates with flashes of grandiloquence; his culture is such that it justifies the freedom he demonstrates; he checks any vain ambition of ostentation through the exercise of good taste; he nimbly conceals the dextrous thefts with which he enriches his repertoire.

Some people persist in interpreting Siza's architecture as the mechanical product of ideas suggested to him by his peculiar capacity to interpret the characteristics of the places for which his schemes are conceived. They reduce his work to a kind of contextualism of a greater or lesser refinement. To this notion, Siza replies: 'I am not in favour of submitting to the context. The very idea fills me with horror.' The sentiment is best expressed by the grammarian and scholar Servio Onorato: 'Nullus enim locus sine genio est' ('For no place is without its spirit'). Siza has supplied interpretations, which the critics have proceeded to rob of their originality, from his earliest works onwards. In fact, the Boa Nova restaurant and the swimming pool at Leça da Palmeira make it clear how the 'relationships' which, from that point onwards, Siza's buildings seek to define with the environments that they occupy, do not actually seek to heighten their natural tendencies so much as to render all the more apparent the conflicts generated by the act of design, superimposing the appearances of things over the rigours of the geometry which is, as Siza well knows, at the root of architecture. What Siza draws from the places where he builds are chance and challenges, the hidden possibilities which he transforms into the materials of his composition. He does this out of the conviction that what is preserved in those places, in the rocks of the Atlantic coast at Leça da Palmeira and in the Chiado in Lisbon, in Santiago de Compostela and in Berlin, is the work of time. As Siza likes to assert, natural stratifications reveal that work just as clearly as cities offer themselves to anyone capable of seeing the extraordinary wealth of sedimentation that goes into their make-up, making the built environments look like coral reefs, revealed to the eye by the waves of the sea and time itself. Anyone who places undue generic emphasis on Siza's 'minimalist' vein will overlook the centrality in his work (and in this he is a true follower of Loos) of the respect and quest for an economy of expressive means. This is because, as Siza maintains, 'one thing that upsets me terribly in architecture is waste, apparent even in the use of light', and, consequently, one thing that is crucial for him is the distinction between decoration and ornament.

Siza's works are also characterized by a continuous critical dialogue with the tradition of contemporary architecture. His buildings display a non-systematic proliferation of citations and more or less cryptic allusions to Frank Lloyd Wright, Le Corbusier, Loos, Oud, Aalto (above all) and Barragán (in this last case, incidentally, we could make many interesting distinctions between the two architects, despite what one reads in the current literature, starting with their contrasting fascination with everything that 'sullies' the life of buildings). What remains fundamental is the conceptual basis that Siza's works express and which gives them their unity. It takes as its model the study of vernacular and traditional buildings, both Portuguese and Mediterranean, to which Siza has devoted himself since his training. What Siza's work reveals is a different version of modernity, pressing historiography to confront the problem (often overlooked but nonetheless apparent) of the study of the mixture, the fusion of models which underlies the basic experiments of contemporary architecture. It is in fact obvious that, of these models, 'spontaneous' vernacular architecture, the kasbahs of North Africa and the Maghreb, the white Mediterranean settlements and the square stones of the vernacular rural architecture of the Iberian peninsula are just as important as the influence of the ascetic rationality that shapes the formal universe of mechanical production.

A tireless draftsman, Siza has made the sketch his chief instrument of study and communication. It might be described as the place where he stores his restlessness, and above all where he practises the far from innocent art of contamination on which his high manner is based. His drawings, apparently made without ever lifting the pen from the paper, are distillations and deposits of the materials that regularly feed into his designs;

impressions, memories, shadows and traces career wildly after one another. This hubbub of figures reveals the modes of comparison and interrelation which Siza creates from the things that surround him, which attract him or which provoke his curiosity; the emotions and memories communicated to him by landscape and cities, illustrious predecessors and buildings, acting as a fertile starting-point for each of his works. With studied frugality, his buildings restore, in rarefied form (and all the more clearly for that), the essential passages and intersections of the interlacings and dialogues seen in the drawings. In the sketches, in the designs and, finally, in the buildings themselves, Siza expresses a selective attitude originating in the avid and insatiable desire for solitude that marks his poetics. This aspiration is translated into the sad, controlled, curious and generous tone that he adopts in the face of situations and objects; an attitude of resignation, knowing that the desire he mentions to 'build in the desert' has no hope of satisfaction, because in the 'land of architects', 'en esta tierra non hay disiertos' ('there are no deserts in this land').

Bonjour Tristesse, Schlesisches Tor Residential Complex, Berlin, Germany, 1980–4

Enduring the world, Siza uses his wits to confront its inhospitable vulgarity, its swarming haste, its aimless rushing, its arrogant need for conclusions. His buildings demand time and attention; they are surprising in the conflicts they display. Most importantly, they counterpose the abstract and subjective rhythm of the spaces that constitute them with the rapid, distracted flow of everyday life. The disillusioned realism which animates these buildings also makes them capable of expressing vigorous yearnings, and they draw nourishment from the contradictions that they encounter for those reasons. Nevertheless, Siza's works are firmly fixed in life and in the everyday; so much so that each of his works seems to be encompassed within the phrase: 'I am myself and my circumstance, and if I don't save that I don't save myself either', as we read in Ortega y Gasset's *Meditations on Quixote*.

Faintly voicing impossible aspirations, with an elegance that can only derive from the art of subtraction, Siza's works seem to observe the world, and seem each day to wake to the words written in a shaky hand on the rounded corner of the Schlesisches Tor building in Berlin: 'bonjour tristesse'.

Tea House, Boa Nova
Restaurant, Leça da Palmeira,
Portugal, 1958–63

Architecture as Critical Transformation: The Work of Álvaro Siza
Kenneth Frampton

So, what is the answer? There is no answer except reverting to the uncertainty of reality, maintaining 'a total lack of illusions about one's age, yet supporting it relentlessly'. How to revert to enduring reality is, undoubtedly, a very complex theoretical and ideal matter; this becomes apparent as soon as one goes beyond reality's empirical, tangible surface and defines it in terms of deliberate choices and projects, as a 'concrete utopia', a 'principle of hope', to borrow Ernst Bloch's beautiful expression … But it is also a constructive effort, a problem concerning the choice of tools and methods.

In the course of thirty years – during which the obsession with history emerged and developed – the belief has taken root that architecture cannot be a means for changing social relationships; but I maintain that it is architecture itself that needs, for its very production, the material represented by social relations. Architecture cannot live by simply mirroring its own problems, exploiting its own tradition, even though the professional tools required for architecture as a discipline can be found only within that tradition.

Vittorio Gregotti, March 1982[1]

Predisposing Causes: 1910–1954
As in other parts of Europe where the concept of the nation state was fragile and democracy was still a somewhat improvised middle-class endeavour, Fascism was on hand to occupy the power vacuum precipitated by the trauma of transition, enjoined in Portugal with the self-imposed exile of the King in 1910 and the failure of the ensuing Republican regime to improve the conditions of the peasantry and the working class.[2] In the crisis of 1926, the Liberal Government's reliance on the military for the maintenance of social control led to a military dictatorship and, two years later, to the rise of António de Oliveira Salazar, who became the absolute ruler of the country in 1932. In the following year, Salazar's position was consolidated by the adoption of a fascist constitution. As elsewhere, Fascism in Portugal became engaged in the modernization of an underdeveloped and largely agricultural country. This led, in the first few years of the regime, to a certain support for modern architecture, as reflected in a house projected by Carlos Ramos in 1929 and in the Beja High School designed by Cristino da Silva in 1930. Thus during the early years of its rule the Salazar regime seems to have entertained modernity in both a stylistic and a programmatic sense. I have in mind a multi-storey garage realized in downtown Porto by Rogério de Azevedo in 1932 and a number of 'moderne' houses built in the suburbs of Porto by Manuel Marques, Jorge Viana and others, at about the same time.[3]

However, the official polemic of the Estado Nuova after 1935 would proclaim the full reactionary character of Salazar's cultural policy and this would be further reinforced by the totalitarian historicism of the World Portuguese Exhibition staged in Lisbon in 1940. The accompanying official debate as to the authentic form of the Portuguese house – echoing the cult of the *Heimatstil* in the Third Reich – manifests itself in a series of pastiche works, including a number of rather *retardataire* designs by the architects Cassiano Branco and Antonio Varela. This debilitating eclecticism, bordering on kitsch, was countered in 1947 by urgent appeals for a critical interpretation of the specifics of the Portuguese vernacular in all its diversity. The first of these was Francisco do Amaral's proposal in the magazine *Arquitectura* that one should organize a systematic survey into all the different manifestations of the vernacular in Portugal; the second was Fernando Távora's essay, 'The Problem of the Portuguese House,' published in the *Cuadernos de Arquitectura* when Távora was only twenty-three:

The study of Portuguese Architecture, or construction in Portugal is not as yet done. A number of archaeologists have written about and dealt with our houses but, as far as we know, none of them has given a contemporary sense to this study thus making it a participating element in new architecture …

When studying our old or popular houses, the conditions that created and developed them, in relation to the Land or Man must be determined, and the ways the materials were used and satisfied the needs of the time must also be studied. The popular house will supply us with great lessons when properly studied, as it is more functional and less fanciful, or in other words, more in accordance with the new intentions. Nowadays one … stylises it for national and foreign exhibitions:

nothing can be obtained by an attitude of this type which leads to the dead end road of the most absolute negation possible.[4]

This mutual advocacy eventually led in 1955 to a national inquiry into the state of contemporary Portuguese vernacular in all its aspects, thereby documenting a virtually timeless mode of building as this had been determined over time by a specific landscape, climate and *modus vivendi*. This painstaking and exhaustive study, in which Távora and his colleagues played a seminal role through their survey of the Minho region, was first published in 1961 as *Arquitectura Popular em Portugal*.[5] Távora's intense activity during the late forties and early fifties at both a national and international level, together with his faith in the possibility of evolving a 'third way' for modern Portuguese architecture, one that was neither unduly xenophobic nor abstractly cosmopolitan, brought him to the attention of his professor, Carlos Ramos, who invited him to teach in 1950. Six years later Távora's position was reinforced by Ramos becoming director of the Escola Superior de Belas-Artes do Porto (ESBAP) in 1956.[6] In fact, while Ramos and Távora were of different generations they were both equally active in attempting to cultivate a more vigorous culture of contemporary architecture in a rather ambiguous, unpredictable and culturally repressive environment. Thus where Ramos was a founder member of the national Organization of Modern Architects (ODAM 1947–52),[7] Távora would represent the Portuguese wing of CIAM at the CIAM 8 Congress held in Hoddesdon, England in 1951, and again at the CIAM 10 and CIAM 11 Congresses, staged at Dubrovnik and Otterlo in 1954 and 1959 respectively.[8] All these peregrinations would culminate with his participation in the World Design Conference held in Tokyo in 1960, the year in which he would also visit Frank Lloyd Wright's Taliesin in the United States.[9]

As an assistant instructor, Távora played a seminal role in mediating Ramos's tendency towards academic eclecticism and his preoccupation with 'newness' in an exclusively empirical sense.[10] At the same time, in his own early work he seems to have resisted the more sophisticated modernist syntax adopted in the 1950s by such distinguished local architects as Armenio Losa, Alfredo Viana de Lima and Rui Pimentel. After the Breueresque manner of his 1952 graduating thesis, entitled 'A House Overlooking the Sea', Távora began to cultivate a neo-vernacular, quasi-Brutalist approach as we find this in his tennis pavilion for the Quinta da Conceição park and in the Cedro School built in Vila Nova da Gaia – both of which date from the period 1956–60.[11] This partially coincides with the period that Álvaro Siza was working in Távora's office, that is to say from 1955 to 1958, having entered Távora's employ after six years at the ESBAP. It seems that Siza did not formally graduate from the school until 1965, when he already had been in practice for seven years and had over ten buildings to his credit. One year later in 1966 he would become a full professor at the school.

In 1968, when the Portuguese of Siza's generation were finally allowed to travel abroad quite freely, Siza and his Porto colleagues first went to the 'liberal' north, to Holland and Sweden, and above all to Finland, where they spent the best part of their first study tour looking at the work of Alvar Aalto (1898–1976).[12] That Siza was already prepared by publications to assimilate the work of Aalto is suggested by the line that he pursued during the first nine works of his early career, realized between 1957 and 1970.

Although it can hardly be considered a cause, there is surely no doubt that the so-called *Revolution dos Claveles* ('Revolution of the Carnations') of 25 April 1974 had a decisive influence on Siza's life, as it surely had on any other Portuguese who lived through this tumultuous period. The establishment of the SAAL organization – *Serviço Ambulatório de Apoio Local* – by Nuno Portas when he was Secretary of State to the revolutionary Housing Ministry, had an immediate impact on architects and other building technicians in that they were commanded to design housing for the economically underprivileged. They had to do this through open public discussion with the future occupants, a protracted and occasionally abrasive interaction which came to an abrupt end in 1976 with the return to democratic socialism under the leadership of Mario Soares, at which point the so-called Mobile Local Support Services were disbanded. As Siza has remarked: 'Within SAAL, there were very different tendencies, both political and professional, which ranged from the teams that took the processes of participation to their final limits, to the teams based on rigorous town planning discipline …'.[13]

Although this experience was rather troubling for Siza, it is clear that it established his reputation as an architect who was able and willing to work with the urban poor in a discursive way and this seems to have led to his future selection as a housing architect in Portugal, Germany and The Netherlands.

In the Name of the Vernacular: 1954–1979
Siza's early works are inseparable from the larger effort to re-cast the Portuguese tradition in modern terms. Like Távora, Siza sought to reinterpret the Minho vernacular in the light of a neo-Brutalist aesthetic, an approach which seems to have led them both to the work of Alvar Aalto. Despite stylistic tropes borrowed from Távora, this Nordic influence is evident in Siza's second public work of consequence, the Boa Nova Tea House completed in Leça da Palmeira in 1963.[14] We may sense this from the contrapuntal rhythm of the restaurant's monopitched roofs which may have been partly inspired by the roofs of Aalto's Säynätsalo City Hall of 1949–52, or more forcibly perhaps through the stepped podium leading up to the restaurant; an application of Aalto's 'geological' layering to a rather unruly rock formation.[15] Otherwise Boa Nova is Mediterranean in its affinities, as we may judge from the battered, white, plastered chimney shafts and the saddle-backed roofs covered in Roman tiles.

The Orientalism evoked by Távora in the tennis pavilion for the Quinta da Conceição park,[16] completed on his return from Japan in 1960, also recurs here in the timber lining of the restaurant. There

Tea House, Boa Nova Restaurant

is also perhaps a trace of the Near East in the pavilionated character of the double-height internal space that sweeps down over the dining room to culminate in large picture windows giving onto the volcanic rockscape. Be this as it may, the overall exotic image of the roof surely stems from the wood-lined eaves of the over-sailing roofs and the large gutters hung off their ends. (We may

note that a similar aura seems to emanate from the gambrel roof of the parish hall that Siza completed in Matosinhos in 1956–9.)

Monopitched roofs covered in Roman tiles, wooden fenestration and timber boarding, combined with load-bearing granite walls and concrete slabs, play a particularly expressive role in Siza's work during the first sixteen years of his practice from 1954 to 1970. While this palette is only too evident in the detached houses that he built in Matosinhos in the second half of the fifties and in the Carneiro de Melo House realized in Porto in 1957–9, timber first comes to assume a major role in the Boa Nova Tea House, where wood establishes both the external and internal character of the work. This is particularly noticeable in the boarded ceiling of the restaurant, somewhat deceptively suspended beneath a monopitched reinforced concrete slab, a feature which imparts an intimate crafted feel to the space. This atmosphere is primarily induced by the use of red African Afzelia wood, the exoticism of which is enhanced by decorative crenellations, particularly around the downstands of the clerestory lights that occur wherever the monopitched roofs intersect. As Paulo Martins Barata has written:

> This presence of wood in the enclosing membrane is extended both to the window frames and the underside of the slab overhangs. In the latter, a long wood board soffit is only interrupted by the rafters that hold the wood fascia and drainage gutters. These rafters, despite their constructional significance, are profusely ornamental and, like all the other elements of carpentry, are retentive of a symbolic meaning that recalls a kind of weaving … However, on the interior, wood is not circumscribed to the ceiling. It is overtly used as a decorative material that like a wild creeper scrambles from the floors to the bases, doors and casings, while finally reaching the ceilings and column capitals, in an elaborate play of notches and indentations of solid planks.[17]

Aalto emerges more decisively as an influence in the swimming pool that Siza designed in 1958–65 for a flat, wooded hill-top within a park that Távora had just finished in the grounds of the Quinta da Conceição in Matosinhos.[18] This diminutive acropolis, set amid pines and bounded by whitewashed masonry walls that merge with equally whitewashed service buildings, is more subtly layered than the Boa Nova earthwork. The support buildings at the apex of the hill are arranged in an L-shaped formation, adjacent to a triangular declivity at the northern end of the enclosure. As in Greek sacred sites, one gradually approaches this complex through a stepped promenade to eventually arrive at two monopitched single-storey structures, housing showers, lavatories, lockers, a ticket office and a cafeteria. These serve as a kind of *propylea* through which one has to pass in order to gain access to the linked pools. No one has captured the multiple cultural significance of this labyrinthic assembly better than Barata who sees it as a synthesis of agrarian typology and modernist abstraction, and further as a combination of traditional craft with modern concrete construction. As he puts it:

> … Thus, we find thick walls of hand-laid granite masonry on top of which a solid concrete slab and beam was cast. While the whole was blended in a rough sand-finished plaster and painted with white lime, the sheathing marks on the slab were left unplastered as an overt intent to expose the structural system …[19]

Barata goes on to stress the important role played by red mahogany joinery throughout and the way this is offset by whitewashed walls and the cement floors. For him it is a *tour de force* in timber construction that owes a particular debt to Aalto.

This tectonic *temenos* was reworked a few years later on the Atlantic seafront of Leça da Palmeira, where Siza excavated an ocean pool in the rocky foreshore lying to the south of the Boa Nova restaurant. The project was intended to augment the swimming facilities of the Matosinhos beach next to the old port. Once again we are confronted with a topographic conception

opposite
Tea House,
Boa Nova Restaurant

below
Quinta da Conceição
Swimming Pool,
Matosinhos,
Portugal, 1958–65

overleaf
Ocean Swimming Pool,
Leça da Palmeira,
Portugal, 1961–6

below
Alves Costa House,
Moledo do Minho,
Portugal, 1964–71

opposite
Alcino Cardoso House,
Moledo do Minho,
Portugal, 1971–3

orthogonally planned, somewhat neo-plastic house seems to bring Siza's pursuit of the 'vernacular' to a close. The Magalhães House announces this decisive break through its exposed in-situ concrete walls and its introduction of totally glazed, full-height gridded openings, painted white; a further development of the internal conservatory partitions of the Alves Costa House. It is but a step from this house to the Alcino Cardoso and Beires Houses, where similar gridded fenestration will be painted black. Made in this last instance out of extremely thin wooden muntins, the glazing evokes something of the traditional 'curtain walling' to be found in northern Portugal and Galicia.[23]

As a culmination of this series of free-standing, single-storey suburban houses, we come to the house that Siza built for his brother, António Carlos Siza, in Santo Tirso in 1976–8. Here Siza's typical quadripartite cluster plan is wilfully deconstructed and reassembled as a cacophonic conjunction of walls within the confines of an extremely constricted and contorted site. Two countervailing bay windows preserve, as it were, the vestigial axial order of some normative condition, but otherwise the dwelling is rendered as an ingeniously disjunctive patio house. Vertical, horizontal and diagonal axes cut across the plan in order to fix the intersection of subdividing walls and to establish intimate perspectival vistas. Some of the formal ramifications of this operation are perceptively revealed in the following text by Peter Testa:

> Siza does not rely on a fixed type or a finite and stable number of forms a priori. The stress is on the importance of relations rather than the forms themselves ... This is perhaps best illustrated by considering the paired columns in the dining room. Unexplainable from only a structural point of view, they stand between two volumetric zones articulating the circulation space which surrounds the patio. The simple square columns are oriented on different axes. The top of one column is twisted relative to itself, forming a capital ... By pairing columns in this way from a static viewpoint, we may simultaneously perceive oblique and frontal views of the same element ...
>
> This notion of simultaneity is in fact furthered through the superposition and transparency in the cross-views which cut transversely through the constructed area. These cross-views associate rooms not normally seen together, and allow an observer to see right through several interior and exterior spaces while maintaining a sense of enclosure. Here the use of regulating lines serves to define visual axes which distort every object within their path and construct alignments relating elements by inflection. In a strategy that both suggests and subverts dominance, these sight lines depart from or converge on a single vanishing point fixed on the center of the dining room window.[24]

Siza's constantly changing counterpoint between walls and volumes that either circumscribe patios or articulate sectional displacements, or which, on occasion, combine both procedures, attains a subtle if barely inflected application in the Alcino Cardoso House completed in an old vineyard in Moledo do Minho in 1971–3. Here the spatial layering assumes a temporal dimension so that both building and enclosure are articulated in such a way as to express the passage of time. Thus the dominant profile of the existing rubble stone farmhouse, consisting of two prisms capped by shallow-pitched tiled roofs, is sustained by recessing a new single-storey bedroom wing into the ground. Tied into the main house by a low rubble wall, the horizontal profile of this triangular plan-form is reinforced by a band of double-hung sash windows painted black. The resulting neo-Wrightian continuity is covered by a flat metal roof with standing seams. This contrasting dialectic between old and new is reiterated in the details, in the light wooden furnishing and plywood lining of the interior, and in the old stone props for the pergolas of the vineyard that find themselves reused to form a portico opening onto the steps of a stone-trimmed

swimming pool. Such improvised transformations may be found elsewhere, above all in the barely noticeable sliding iron gate that closes the main driveway or in the stairway leading down to a narrow lane bounding the site on its southern edge, a full floor below the level of the vineyard. Where the one looks like a rickety iron contraption, hastily wrought by the local blacksmith, the other proclaims its sophistry through a gridded timber frame set against a rubble stone retaining wall that looks as though it has always been there. Of this interplay between old and new Siza has written:

> The existing and new elements are in deliberate contrast and stand out sharply overlapped, although a swimming pool projected afterwards, was designed as a sort of ruin, invented from the memory of so much that belongs to the Minho and also other landscapes. It was oriented according to the sun and aspires to be connected with everything else, new and old, as if it were an intermediate or an impossible synthesis.[25]

Siza was so insistent on maintaining this subtle interaction between old and new that he successfully resisted the client's suggestion that the old vines be uprooted and replaced by maintenance-free orange trees. For him such a *nouveau riche* gesture would have completely ruined the *genius loci* of the site.

One year before he had alluded directly to the architect's responsibility of sensitively reinterpreting the spirit of any site in terms of its intrinsic genealogy. Thus in his 1979 prose/poem entitled 'To catch a precise moment of the flittering image in all its shades,' he wrote:

> Most of my works were never fulfilled;
> some of the things I did were only carried out in part,
> others were deeply changed or destroyed.
> That's only to be expected.
> An architectonic proposition, whose aim is to go deep
> into the existing transformation trends,
> into the clashes and strains that make up reality;
> a proposition that intends to be more than
> a passive materialization, refusing to reduce
> that same reality,
> analysing each of its aspects, one by one;
> that proposition can't find support in a fixed image,
> can't follow a linear evolution.
> Nevertheless, and for that same reason,
> that proposition can't be ambiguous,
> nor restrain itself to a disciplinary discourse,
> however sure it seems to be.
> Each design is bound to catch,
> with the utmost rigour, a precise moment
> of flittering image in all its shades
> and the better you can recognize
> that flittering quality of reality,
> the clearer your design must arise.
> It is the more vulnerable as it is true.
> That may be the reason why only marginal works
> (a quiet dwelling, a holiday-house miles away)
> have been kept as they were originally designed.
> This is the outcome of a participation in a process
> of cultural transformation of construction-destruction.
> But something remains. Pieces are kept here and there,
> inside ourselves, perhaps gathered by someone,
> leaving marks on spaces and people,
> melting in a process of total transformation.[26]

With these words Siza categorically redefined contextuality, arguing that the architect had a responsibility not only of harmonizing with the context but also of opposing it or even, on occasion, of pursuing both options at once, articulating the first operation from the second in different parts of the same work. For him this contrapuntal process of action and reaction can only be determined on a case-by-case basis. The implications of adopting such a critical stance ought to be self-evident, namely, to represent the moment in time in which a work is realized and at the same time to link this instant with the past, thus fusing both into a process of continual transformation that, while momentarily arrested, waits in its turn to be transformed. As in the writings of the Portuguese poet Fernando Pessoa, this stance is as existentialist as it is realistic and the combination of these two seemingly contradictory attitudes can at times be disconcerting, since they require an ethical stoicism that is rare in a society increasingly transfixed by commodification.

Towards an Organic Architecture: 1969–1982
A dramatic shift towards the organic first became evident in Siza's practice in his unrealized urban proposals for an office building in the Avenida D. Afonso Henriques in Porto (1968) and the Caxinas housing scheme projected for Vila do Conde (1970–2), both being under various stages of development from 1969 to 1973.[27] Designed as a curtain-walled structure to be added to an historical fragment on a steeply sloping urban site, the Avenida D. Afonso Henriques project demonstrated a completely opposite stance to the one that Siza adopted at the same time for the bankers Borges & Irmão, who wanted to enlarge an existing bank on the river front in Vila do Conde. In order to incorporate a segment of the adjacent frontage, Siza proposed a second facade that would be capable of unifying both the existing and the new frontages. The resulting relatively blank external and internal elevations rising to the full height of a three-storey banking hall would have been unified on the interior by an elaborate *poché* and by a lantern light affording oblique views of the convent of Santa Clara, situated on the high ground above the bank.

As in the house for his brother in Santo Tirso, Siza again employed 'regulating lines' here as a means of engendering the form of the internal space. Recalling Marcel Duchamp's use of *stoppages etalons* as an instrument for constructing the *malic moulds* in his *Large Glass* of 1919, this device comes to be more developed in Siza's second free-standing bank commission, this time for the firm of Pinto & Sotto Mayor in Oliveira de Azeméis (1971–4). This contextual 'breakthrough', realized at a major intersection in the town, subtly reflects the specific form of the surrounding context while simultaneously developing a totally fresh language, based on a reinterpretation of certain *tropes* inherited from the pre-war modern movement, most notably perhaps features drawn from Erich Mendelsohn's Rudolf Mosse Pavilion designed for the Cologne Press Exhibition of 1928. (This is most evident perhaps in the pylon carrying the name of the bank and in the sweeping ground floor glazing emphasizing the horizontality of its steel transomes.) At the same time the interior evoked the organicism of Aalto or even that of Hans Scharoun although, as Siza informs us, 'the fundamental reason for those distorted geometries is to permit the entry of light into the patio of the adjacent house, a magnificent house of the XVIII century bought by the bank along with the site.'[28]

While radial lines and seams, emanating from points beyond the confines of the building, determine the volumetric sweep of the banking hall, together with the dramatically stepped section of the ceiling, the main volume is further animated by organically shaped toplights and amorphous corner intersections. This bank,

Alcino Cardoso House

Villa Cova Housing Complex,
Caxinas, Vila do Conde,
Portugal, 1970–2

completed in 1974, established Siza's reputation on an international scale, a status that was broadly acknowledged at the time in the critical writings of Nuno Portas, Vittorio Gregotti, Oriol Bohigas and Bernard Huet.[29]

The theme of ruination, first broached in the Alcino Cardoso House of 1971–3, is returned to in the Beires House (1973–6) erected on a small suburban plot in Póvoa do Varzim. Referred to as the *Casa Bomba* because it resembles the remains of a cubistic modern house which has been bombed, the Beires House is again based on an irregular cluster of rooms grouped around an enclosed court, although in this instance the volumes will be separated from the nearby street by nothing more substantial than a wall of medium height. This tight cluster formation was an effort, on a restricted terrain, to meet the client's request to have an arrangement like that of the Rocha Ribeiro House where the dwelling had been focused about a large tree. Siza responded to this eccentric brief with a subtle deconstruction of the classic nine-square plan. This operation is most evident on the ground floor where three of the original squares have been erased by a faceted curtain wall. This feature is repeated on the first floor where a slightly different plan configuration is adopted, while the central square of the original paradigmatic plan has now been rotated through thirty degrees. Both floors are faced by a somewhat unusual triple-hung curtain wall in which only the upper two tiers of the glazing operate as sash windows, while the lower tier, where not fixed, is side hung, opening out into the garden at grade or onto the balcony above. As in the Alcino Cardoso House the delicately profiled window sections make a direct allusion to the coastal vernacular of the north. As we have already noted, the black finish so accentuates the delicacy of these profiles as to lead one to assume that they are of steel, which is indeed the material employed for the horizontal glazing bars of the semi-circular bay window to the rear of the building. This differentiation between front and back seems to imply a transhistorical reference in terms of window details; that is to say a critically regionalist[30] timber vernacular expression on one side and full-blooded modernist steel-framed glazing on the other. This opposition seems to be paralleled here by Siza's load-bearing granite walls that, by virtue of being plastered and rendered in an ochre wash, impart an ambiguous reading to the masonry enclosure that is simultaneously old and new; old in terms of the actual mode of construction and new, or at least abstract, in terms of both plaster finish and colour. To this is added the subtle subdivision of the internal space by full-height glazed screens that ingeniously slide into the faceted facade, either to subdivide the rooms or, alternatively, to open them up so as to permit a continuous spatial movement.[31] The modernist ideal of flexible space seems to make itself ironically manifest here in an interior that, shrouded in sun blinds, could hardly be more bourgeois in its furnishings and atmosphere. Sequestered before a lush overgrown courtyard garden, the Beires House, despite its modernity, seems to be nostalgic for a lost golden age.

Siza's rhetorical excursus into organicism ends as it began with a bank; this time a totally new branch for Borges & Irmão in Vila do Conde (1978–86). Facing onto a tree-lined market square, close to the Matriz Church and to the site of his earlier project for the same client, this three-storey, narrow-fronted structure mediates between two different levels in the city fabric. Due to this sectional displacement, the building is not only treated as a *megaron* that incorporates a stairway (cf. Le Corbusier's Citrohan House of 1922) but also as a double-fronted structure serving both upper and lower street frontages. Thus while the first floor, opening off the main market street, accommodates the principal banking hall, the lower ground floor is exclusively dedicated to the safety deposit section and is accessed directly from the lower level, along with the external public stair. The second floor, devoted exclusively to offices, is accessed by an elevator and by a private internal stair and external ramp. Thus the mass comes to assume the form of a compressed three-dimensional *yin-yang* figure with exactly the same curve terminating the parallelepiped at its northern and southern ends.[32] This curve, once more reminiscent of Mendelsohn, is echoed in the curved plan-form of the marble-covered banking counter and in the equally curved continuous lighting strips in the ceiling of the first floor. Siza's copious use of matched marble revetment in this building, first on the facing of the stairs and then as a protective dado to all the public areas, that is to say to the lower wall surfaces of the banking halls and the counters, follows almost to the letter Adolf Loos' contention that thin marble cladding is the cheapest wallpaper in the world since it never wears out. Even though Siza had used light marble facings in his bank interiors for Pinto & Sotto Mayor in Lamego (1972–4) and again, for the same clients, in Oliveira de Azeméis, there is a decisive shift towards *luxus* here in that he now indulges with consummate skill in the symmetrical matching of heavily veined panels in spectacular black and white marble. It is a level of luxury that we will not encounter again until the Duarte House of 1980–4.

Existenzminimum: 1973–1977
Siza's familiar play between received typology and its adaptation to the context assumes a rather controversial and contradictory character in the housing that he designed for the workers' councils that were formed under the auspices of the short-lived SAAL organization in the heady days of the so-called 'Portuguese Spring' that followed the left-wing bloodless revolution of 25 April 1974. The first of these schemes, the Bouça housing quarter in Porto (1973–7), was projected as four parallel blocks comprising some 128 three-bedroom maisonettes, stacked one above the other to yield a four-storey slab. Only half of the initial scheme was actually realized, although now, after more than twenty years of benign neglect, the government appears to be committed to completing the scheme and restoring the existing blocks.[33] A man of the Left[34] both then and now, this was Siza's first experience with participatory democracy, and the difficulty that he experienced in arriving at a design which was capable of meeting the demands of

left
Borges & Irmão Bank,
Vila do Conde,
Portugal, 1969

opposite, above
Borges & Irmão Bank

opposite, below
Pinto & Sotto Mayor Bank,
Oliveira de Azeméis,
Portugal, 1971–4

both architect and client took its toll, as we may gather from the following retrospective assessment about the workers' committees from a 1983 interview with France Vanlaethem:

> ... their attitude was sometimes authoritarian, they denied all awareness of the architect's problems, they imposed their way of seeing and conceiving things. The dialogue was very contentious. In front of such a situation the architect can assume two attitudes. He can acquiesce in order to avoid tension. But this stance is purely demagogic and in this case the intervention of the architect is in vain. On the contrary, he can confront the conflicts; they are inevitable given the means of distributing information being controlled, distorted or not even provided at all. Such was the situation in Portugal. Consequently, to enter the real process of participation meant to accept the conflicts and not to hide them, but on the contrary to elaborate them. These exchanges then become very rich although hard and often difficult.[35]

Certain conflicts must surely have arisen over the different modes of access adopted in the upper and lower maisonettes, judging from the spontaneous modifications that the buildings have since undergone. One senses that the participatory process ended in an impasse that must have been equally disturbing for both the architect and the future occupants. In fact the scheme was at its best at the level of site organization; first, because it was closed on its northern boundary by a four-storey high wall that served as an acoustical shield against the adjacent railway and, second, because the four blocks were to have been terminated at their southern ends by *bâtiments d'angles*, respectively a library, a laundry and two corner shops. These elements would have bonded the new quarter into the existing urban fabric, not only physically, but also programmatically.

Of the two Porto housing schemes that Siza designed under the auspices of SAAL, São Victor was possibly the more successful, perhaps because it was simpler.[36] At the same time it was the more polemical of the two schemes in as much as the architect cunningly inserted his two-storey block of maisonettes into the ruined, half-demolished, pre-existing residential fabric that had once occupied the site. Two a priori stances seem to have determined the character of this archaeological layering; first, the architect's refusal to accept that a *tabula rasa* approach was an essential precondition for urban renewal and, second, his implicitly existential attitude towards the interface between his brand new whitewashed dwellings and the disintegrating, partly demolished stonework of the houses that had once stood on the site. Siza's sketches for São Victor seem to envisage the casual occupation of this ruined hinterland by somewhat malevolent figures, by latter-day noble savages in scanty delinquent attire, lounging against the fabric or throwing the occasional stone. We may see this as an evocation of Albert Camus' *L'Etranger* of 1941 brought up to date. On the one hand the 'Other' par excellence; on the other, an extreme sophistication evident in the full-height gridded glazing on the ground floor taken straight from the detailing of the Manuel Magalhães House.

Siza's housing paradigm was fundamentally recast with the 1977 commission to build in-fill housing on a large scale in the Malagueira district of Évora, a town situated in the Alentejo region close to the Spanish frontier some 140 kilometres south-east of Lisbon. Over the past twenty years, this twenty-seven hectare site has undergone a number of transformations, Siza having been commissioned with different housing complexes by successive Communist administrations as sites became available for development. To date around 1,200 houses have been realized, together with related social facilities and an extensive public infrastructure, including roads, sewers and a rather unusual provision of elevated 'aqueducts' carrying water and electrical energy.[37] Aside from their infrastructural function these concrete block and in-situ concrete structures also provide covered walkways through some of the new housing sectors. Orthogonal vehicular access roads, running in a predominantly east-west or north-south direction, divide the various sites into blocks made up of 8m x 11m housing lots. Two L-shaped patio house types were developed for use on either the front or the back of these lots. The individual units are so devised that each of the two-storey dwellings may gradually expand from one to five bedrooms.

Siza's Malagueira housing represents a total departure from the row house (*Zeilenbau*) paradigm of the pre-war Modern Movement. Instead of continuing to pursue the minimum, row-house standards of the Weimar Republic, Siza turned to the low-rise, high-density housing models of the late forties and early sixties, as we find these, say, in Le Corbusier's Roq et Rob housing scheme projected for Roquebrune in 1946, or in Atelier 5's Siedlung Halen, realized outside Berne in 1960. However, unlike the Corbusian stepped *megaron* prototype, as evident in both Roq et Rob and Halen, Siza's Malagueira house derives its format from Roman or Arab patio types, however much these may have been transposed from their original form. The net result is a castellated continuity of white, two-storey, L-shaped patio houses pierced, in a syncopated fashion, with single or paired windows that are referential not only to the Mediterranean tradition as we find in the Cyclades and elsewhere, but also to the critical architectural manner evolved by Adolf Loos in the twenties (particularly as we encounter this in his villa for the actor Alexander Moissi, projected

for the Venice Lido in 1923).

Without any doubt, the Malagueira settlement is the most accessible and readily amenable low-rise housing that Siza has realized to date, although even here aporia arise, such as the perennial contradiction between individual identity and the presence of a collective form which gives priority to the city rather than the automobile. In the last analysis, this is a civic vision which fails to privilege the consumerism that the mass ownership of a car inevitably implies.[38] Thus, while neither garages nor car ports were incorporated into the design, the subsequent infiltration of parked cars into the streets of the new quarters leaves one uncertain as to the character of civic life that will eventually prevail in these extensions to the city. This returns us to the 'value split', between architect and his generically collective client, that was perhaps as much of a factor here as it had been twenty years before in Porto; for as Siza was to remark of the participatory process at Évora:

From my experience I have come to realise that if public participation is to be neither mystifying nor mystified, it must necessarily include conflicts. From these the project was worked out. The concept of the plan, the methods adopted, the design were commented on in varying and contradictory forms, and I believe this was so even before myself and others began to define them.[39]

One of the most remarkable things about the Malagueira development is the way in which it appears to be ancient and modern at the same time. It begins to look as if it had always been there or as Pierluigi Nicolin would put it:

… we realize, with a sense of dizziness, that the image of the building site can be converted into that of an archaeological excavation. And it is perhaps through this inversion of a constructive activity into a de-constructive one that we begin to notice the transition in the project's aim towards a hermeneutic tendency.[40]

As Nicolin points out, the 'weak' philosophy of Gianni Vattimo afforded a particularly compelling model for the part/whole relationship in late modern architecture, bringing the contemporary architect to recognize that the position of the urban designer is *situational* rather than *foundational*. As Vattimo was to put it in his essay 'Project and Legitimization' of 1986:

The problem then becomes a problem of the politics of planning, of how to ensure that the social subjects concerned are not merely kept in mind but are actively consulted … (in this case) the act of building signifies the modification of the environment to which one has always belonged, more than the foundation of a structure from scratch. And today architecture … thinks of itself more as a restructuration of the environment than as the laying of a building in a tendentially neutral site … a labour of modification rather than the placing of a container in the world …[41]

Whether or not Malagueira measures up to the standards of socio-political legitimacy that Valtimo suggests, there is little doubt that by virtue of being progressively assembled as a number of discrete matrices separated by wide spaces, it has allowed for a certain fluctuation within the limits dictated by topography. As Nicolin informs us, while Malagueira is permeated by everyday life at every conceivable scale, it can in no way be simplistically perceived as a popular working class settlement. On the contrary it seems to be fully consummated by the 'bourgeois' bougainvillaea that spontaneously cascades down from one terrace to another, and by the bucolic park sequences that seem to be almost casually inserted into the housing quarters: a greensward together with an ornamental lake edged by bulrushes; a drainage canal crossed by a footbridge, along with a small weir; or, finally, a diminutive performance space enclosed by low walls, with each piece falling into place along the lines of the age-old picturesque tradition.

opposite
SAAL Social Housing Residence, Bouça, Porto, Portugal, 1975–7

right
Malagueira Residential District, Évora, Portugal, 1977–97

Spoken into the Void: 1979–1985

Loosian syntax enters into Siza's architecture in the late seventies, engaging a range of affinities one can only call neo-classic, despite the persistence of Siza's organic manner that will be resorted to when necessary. Apart from the IBA Fränkelufer Housing project of 1979, where Siza first adopted the 'almost nothing' of Adolf Loos' Michaelerplatz building of 1910, the Loosian mode announces itself in another Berlin competition of the same year, his second prize-winning design for the Görlitzer Bad swimming complex, where a 40m-diameter dome was to have been set down into the middle of an 80m x 80m block aligned with the surrounding street pattern. Of the three 3-storey high cubic volumes that surround the dome, two house a pair of swimming pools each, while a third accommodates mechanical plant and support services. The fourth quadrant is filled with a covered ramp and entryway orientated on a diagonal towards the adjacent Lauritzer Platz; a gesture that was to have been echoed on the opposite corner by a flat rotated cube housing a sauna. In addition to the Loosian fenestration and a passing possible reference to Étienne-Louis Boullée, another antecedent is also present, namely Alexander Nikolsky's domed swimming complex projected for a park in Moscow in 1928, where significantly enough the changing spaces beneath the pool were located in the same position. All of this goes to confirm what Peter Testa has repeatedly contended, namely that Siza's architecture is as much nourished by paradigms drawn from the history of architecture doubling back upon themselves over time, as it is inspired by topographic and other historical features embedded in the site itself.

This proto-illuminist mode reappeared in a warped cylinder for the Dom headquarters that Siza projected for Cologne in 1980. In this instance a number of different historical references are combined. On the one hand there is again an allusion to Boullée in the central zenithal light and in the infinitude implied by the receding scale of the spiralling fenestration; on the other, the helicoidal organization of the office floors as a continuous ramp running around an inclined cone surely recalls Wright's Guggenheim Museum of 1959. Over the next decade, Siza projected further circular plans and cylindrical forms; first in his memorial to the victims of the Third Reich, where an enormous grass-covered bowl is shown ironically crowned by a giant empty Doric column (an allusion to Loos' *Chicago Tribune* competition entry of 1922); and second, in a meteorological station, realized for the Olympic Village port in Barcelona in 1990–2. This six-storey, 33m-diameter cylinder[42] functions as a kind of kaleidoscopic labyrinth, wherein the subject is placed in a faceted corridor that opens at the cardinal points onto eight perimeter light slots. In fact since there are few windows opening to the outside, most of the rooms are either obliquely lit or they open onto the internal cylindrical court. Thus the circulating subject perceives the outside environment in terms of framed views, affording fragmentary glimpses of the sea and land. Appropriately reminiscent of a Martello tower,[43] the neo-classical connotations of this cylinder in its heterogeneous maritime context have been precisely captured by Siza's assistant, Joan Falgueras:

> The volume's central nucleus is open to the sky through a courtyard nine metres in diameter. This provides illumination for the interior areas and is reached via the central distribution ring. The windows are set well back and at a slant, and at midday are transformed into the clerestories of an imaginary temple, through which the sun seeps as the day moves on …
>
> The seemingly unworked concrete base course emerges from the cement up through the sand, like a ruin that has been partially excavated.
>
> With calculated force, a subtle, circular screen of Dolomite marble sits atop this rip in the geometry and topography.
>
> The same stone is used within the building for the flooring and wall surfacing in the entrances, stairs and terraces. The other floors are finished in linoleum, with the walls and ceilings in white plaster that joins the varnish on the skirting board, panelling, doors and wooden window frames.[44]

Loos is more directly present as an influence in the three-storey Avelino Duarte House completed in Ovar in 1980–4. This house deployed a number of disjunctive devices first used by Loos and later elaborated on by Le Corbusier. The frontalization of its cubic mass and the 'space-planning' of its interior are among the more obvious Loosian devices at work here, although perhaps the most striking feature is the alternating A-B-A-B-A bay spacing which recalls Le Corbusier's use of a similar syncopated neo-Palladian rhythm in his canonical Villa Stein of 1927. In the Duarte House this rhythm is arranged so as to omit the last A-bay (it is registered solely by the boundary wall) and to reduce the adjacent B-bay to a single-storey addenda. Thus the principal mass of the house is structured about a symmetrical A-B-A system, with the central B-bay serving as the main entry. Thereafter, Loosian features seem to abound throughout the house, particularly in the full-height entrance hall, where a monumental stair faced in marble rises towards the first floor, recalling, amongst other things, the sumptuous marble revetment of the main living volume in Loos' Müller House built in Prague in 1930. The same marble is applied elsewhere in the house; above all in the free-standing column and the 'fractured' fireplace surround in the main living room. Where the first makes an allusion to the single marble column in Loos' Strasser House of 1918, the second treats the chimney breast as an archaeological fragment set adjacent to a typical Loosian mirror.

The net effect of this approach is to transform a modest suburban house into a *palazetto*, combining a sense of domestic intimacy with a feeling for high bourgeois grandeur rarely to be found in a contemporary dwelling. Siza's marble revetment is complemented as one enters the house by finely wrought joinery, an element which serves as a threshold to every cabinet and chamber, imparting not only a sense of comfort and convenience, but also a feeling of intimate depth. This is particularly true on the

Malagueira Residential District

left
Malagueira Residential District

opposite and overleaf
Avelino Duarte House, Ovar, Portugal, 1980–4

first floor of the house where the first and second bedrooms are connected to form a continuous suite with the principal bathroom and terrace, and where the twin bedrooms designated for the children are similarly linked with the aid of a common study and a second bathroom. It is significant that both bathrooms are equipped with two means of access, through the provision of pivoting doors set at right angles to each other, thereby permitting discreet individual use without passing through either the semi-public or private circulation space.

To analyze the Duarte House in terms of Loos' *Raumplan* is somewhat misleading since the floor levels themselves are never broken. Instead the sense of rupture arises from the way in which the stone revetment is applied in relation to the sectional profile which surrounds the first floor perimeter of the stair hall. Here the stepped soffit of the open gallery, leading to the bedrooms, is echoed by the profile of the marble veneer to the threshold of the second floor staircase, which gives way, as it penetrates further into the interior, to wood-lined treads and door reveals. This spatial and material progression loses its intensity on the top floor where a study/library opens simply into the triple-height volume of the stair hall and where an emblematic window sits symmetrically in the curved upper profile of the central bay to the rear of the house. At the same time, the street front of the Duarte House is rendered even more 'silent' than the garden facade of Loos' Steiner Villa of 1910, largely because of its full-height central recess whereby the first and second floor rooms are lit entirely from the slot. Other Loosian references may also be found in the Duarte House, above all in the vaulted ceiling over the stair hall which recalls the roof of Loos' Horner House of 1912.

This subtle abstract syntax is combined with more open figurative form in the project for the Mário Bahia House in Gondomar of 1983–93, where a steep river front site afforded the occasion for a split between a barrel-vaulted entry platform at the top of the cliff and a Loosian mass-form at the river's edge; the two being linked by a free-standing elevator shaft, possibly reminiscent of Lisbon's classic elevator. Due to the fact that parking is not allowed at the top of the cliff, the suspended platform, accommodating the garage, entails an ironic play in which the car occupies the ultimate belvedere position.[45] Peter Testa has called this eccentric work 'a post-cubist model of topological space' in which both surface and space are simultaneously manipulated in independent and interdependent ways. It is this last, perhaps, that is exercised with ever-increasing facility over the following decade, above all in the Figueiredo House built in Gondomar in 1984–94, and with more liberative consequences in the Teacher Training College completed in Setúbal in 1994.

Urban Infill: Berlin and The Hague: 1979–1993

In his work for Internationale Bau Austellung (IBA) in Berlin, Siza accepted the perimeter block as an instrument with which to repair the pre-existing nineteenth-century city fabric, while still acknowledging the extent to which this fabric had been irrevocably damaged by bombardment in the Second World War and subsequently undermined by speculative development in the postwar years. Thus, while remaining committed to his generic principle that very few buildings may be legitimately differentiated as monuments, he none the less resisted the idea that the normative nineteenth-century European city could be, or should be, simplistically reconstructed as though nothing traumatic had happened. Hence, in his Berlin infill projects, first for the Fränkelufer embankment (1979), and then for a large perimeter block in Kreuzberg (1980–4), Siza adopted a critically contextual approach based once more on the Loosian paradigm of an 'architecture degree zero', an architecture of civic silence such as we find in Loos' Michaelerplatz building; that is to say, largely blank facades pierced at regular intervals by rectangular openings.

In 1979, Siza designed six separate interventions for the Fränkelufer quarter, with each one assuming a somewhat different character while employing the same basic language. Thus each building was projected as being six storeys in height with a high parapet set above some five floors of punched rectangular openings, plus a ground floor dedicated to semi-public use where the window openings are extended to the ground. While this was the basic Fränkelufer format, each block was inflected according to its location. This is at once evident from the two corner buildings inserted into the general frontage; that is to say, a prow-like building coming off the adjacent Kohlfurter block versus a clipped diagonal cube that ends a particular section of the frontage. In both

instances the Loosian fenestration is interrupted by long windows and by an appliqué plaster mantle that helps establish the main entrance, producing a blade-like corner in one instance and a blunt front in the other. As Peter Testa has pointed out, a quasi-Mendelsohnian, expressionistic strategy is adopted in these instances, one which is allowed to erode the Loosian format, and this also applies in the other interventions that were sited back from the frontage, with the intent of occupying the voids left within the fabric. These infill pieces in depth are 'rationally' realigned with a fictitious grid lying within the larger grain of the block, thereby commenting on the two kinds of reason that prevailed in nineteenth-century urbanization; the split between the picturesque rationalization of the street facade versus the congestion of the multiple light courts situated to the rear. Where the Fränkelufer intersects with Kottbusserstrasse, Siza designed an infill block capable of participating in both systems at once; a tripartite structure that, while aligned on one face with the street, would confront the interstices of the block on its other two facades. Of this unbuilt prototype Peter Testa has written:

> The small residential building on Kottbusserstrasse suggests the manner in which these intentions are synthesized into an architectural form. Along the street front of Kottbusserstrasse a highly irregular void has developed, exposing the backs and sides of existing buildings to the street. In this case Siza suggests the continuity of the street wall by inserting a planar facade more or less in the center of the open lot. The body of the building, however, develops by interaction with the adjacent buildings, assuming their alignments. Siza's building appears to be constructed and deconstructed through a dialogue which sustains itself on the tension which exists between the interior and the exterior of the block and between the individual building and the city. In the proposal for Kottbusserstrasse, complementary and conflicting aspects of urban space, building and dwelling are set in motion. From this perspective, the formal articulation of each building reflects a search for a figure capable of holding these conflicting worlds together.[46]

This Wittgensteinian insistence that 'what is torn must remain torn' reappears in Siza's Schlesisches Tor redevelopment project in Kreuzberg, Berlin, under realization for IBA from 1980 to 1988 and comprising three separate interventions within the body of a large urban block: a corner residential infill building, popularly known as *Bonjour Tristesse*, a kindergarten and a senior citizens' clubhouse inserted into the interstitial fabric. The seven-storey corner apartment building adopts a Loosian syntax throughout, with an 'expressionistic' inflection at the corner; a wave-like homage to the organic distorting the regular beat of the punched rectangular openings. Siza's habitual play between the organic and the orthogonal assumes a more sculptural character in the senior citizens' club and the kindergarten (particularly in the former which recalls the pre-war seminal work of Hans Scharoun).

This capacity to maintain a Loosian language yet modify its affect in the light of local traditions, comes strikingly to the fore in Siza's Schilderswijk and Doedijnstraat housing in The Hague, under development from 1983 to 1993. In Schilderswijk, as in his Kreuzberg housing, Siza was once again working for a largely Islamic population for whom he designed two four-storey perimeter blocks within a nineteenth-century fabric. Based on a standard floor plan throughout the apartments which were accessed in pairs from a staircase fed by a portico on the street, Siza's Schilderswijk housing followed the local brick-faced tradition almost to the letter save for the fact that the windows were larger and more horizontal. The only break to this rhythm was the clipped corners of the perimeter blocks introduced to permit semi-public entry into the internal courts and to provide a location for the corner shops. The 238 equally street-orientated apartments built in the nearby Doedijnstraat complex had a somewhat different window proportion. The apartments in both developments were fairly flexibly planned so as to accommodate both occidental and oriental patterns of living, with regard to the differentiation between public and private space.

Siza's work in The Hague is more normative and less critical in tone than his infill housing in Berlin, no doubt due in some measure to the continuity of the Berlagian brick tradition and to the Dutch penchant for large areas of glazing, both of which seem to have enabled Siza to modify the abstract severity of his civic language. However, even here there were difficulties in getting a traditional local paradigm accepted, largely because the perimeter blocks were seen as being antiquated and even the use of brick was regarded as reactionary.[47]

Siza's susceptibility to local tradition, more forcible on some occasions than others, is further proof, if any were needed, that his own architecture has always been, in some measure, a critically didactic interpretation of other cultural traditions mixed in with his own idiosyncratic sensibility. This hybrid operation is dramatically evident in the two houses and shops that he built in Van der Vennepark in The Hague in 1988, close to his Schilderswijk-West development. Here, two animated forms at one end of an existing park recapitulate in microcosm the two main traditions of the Dutch Modern Movement; on the one hand, a three-storey house, boat-shaped in plan, that alludes to the brick-faced expressionism of Michel de Klerk, on the other, a rotating rectilinear structure, L-shaped in plan and finished in white plaster with wire mesh balustrades that recalls the received syntax of Dutch Constructivism. Since this double-house also articulates the entry to an underground parking garage, it also implies a certain play with time in another sense in that it unites, however momentarily, the two received meanings of the word 'park', the municipal park in which the building is situated and the car park that now lies concealed beneath.

The New Monumentality: 1985–1989

In the mid-eighties, the scope of Siza's practice changed abruptly as he began to receive one public commission after another, beginning with the first phase of the faculty of architecture in the University of Porto which, starting in 1985 with a single, free-standing pavilion, eventually took a full decade to realize. A year later he received the charge to design a teacher training college in Setúbal which took almost as long to complete, and this was

followed in 1988 by commissions for the main library at the University of Aveiro and the Galician Centre of Contemporary Art in Santiago de Compostela. These four civic works seem to embody the apotheosis of his maturity to date, without in any way prejudicing the equally rich spectrum of commissions that he has since received.

Aside from the fact that Siza was not only an alumnus but also a former faculty member of the ESBAP, the commission for the new architectural school in Porto was particularly fitting; above all, perhaps, because of the initial building that was dedicated to the memory of Carlos Ramos. Conceived as an annexe to the garden of the Quinta da Póvoa villa – a villa that had been previously deeded to the school – this two-storey, first-year building studio was a prelude to the second phase that would be built over the ensuing decade on an adjacent site overlooking the River Douro. Situated at one end of a formal parterre, this patio structure, completed in the space of a year, was subtly inflected so as to respond to the existing villa and its outbuildings, together with the attendant walks and walls that make up the grounds. Thus where one wing of this U-shaped pavilion points towards the villa, the other is orthogonally aligned with a principal path. The resultant building is a sculptural *tour de force* that warrants extensive analysis since it contains the seeds of a typological inflection that will be further developed in the Setúbal Teacher Training College. In fact, the building exemplifies the principle of transformation as a creative method, as a proof of Siza's aphorism, 'architects don't invent anything, they transform reality.' However, since reality for Siza always means in some degree a typological point of departure, we may recognize at once the presence of an a priori type; namely, an open-ended cortile enclosed on three sides. Once this type is overlaid on the topography, we may surmise that the following sequential adjustments had to be made: (1) the initial type was distorted by inclining its north-western wing towards the villa, while aligning its southern wing in such a way as to engender symmetrical re-entrant angles between the two wings. As a result of this manipulation the southern wing became aligned with the principal east-west path running down one side of the parterre; (2) the intersection between the north-western and north-eastern wings was transformed into an entry/stair hall through the superimposition of a cubic block facing north, its central axis bisecting the angle subtended by the two wings; (3) the opposite corner was then clipped at grade, along a tangent to the axis that bisected the intersection between the opposing southern and north-eastern wings; (4) in the middle of the north-eastern wing, opposite the central axis of the patio, a trapezoidal bay window was introduced and its front face aligned with the existing path system; (5) a double interlocking hall in each re-entrant corner was also introduced to provide lobbies and services for the studios that make up the three sides of the patio; (6) the end elevations of the two extended wings were each treated symmetrically about a central window and a door, despite the asymmetrical overhang of the roof which inflected the wings towards the honorific status of the central space; (7) a syncopated A-B-A fenestration system in steel, spanning between structural piers, was introduced to articulate the courtyard glazing on the ground and first floors. This was predicated on a central top-hung A-bay of glass at the first floor, while the equivalent bay at grade comprised a pair of side-hung, steel-framed glass doors that gave access to the court; (8) a subtle manipulation of levels brought the court two steps below the main entry which in turn permitted the creation of a 'baroque' stair on the north-south axis of the cube. This stair fed into the centre of a curved landing, the shape of which was mirrored by a wall separating the upper studios from the stair hall; (9) free-standing elliptical columns on the bisecting axes (one within the stair hall and one without) established the honorific status of the first floor, while judicially placed picture windows of different proportions provided for diverse vistas across the ground floor studio space; (10) lastly, a dedicatory silver-plated bust of Carlos Ramos was placed on a pedestal to one side of the central axis on the upper landing.

Teacher Training College at Setúbal: 1986–1994
As I have already intimated, this building seems to recapitulate some of the transformational operations performed in the Carlos Ramos pavilion. We encounter once again a courtyard as a point of departure; a plan-figure that recalls the Uffizi in Florence or more recently Giorgio Grassi's Student Dormitory for Chieti in Italy (1976), with all the romantic-classical references that this, in turn, entails, ranging from Karl Friedrich Schinkel's Wilhelmsstrasse Extension, Berlin (1818) to Heinrich Tessenow's Klotsche Sächsische Landesschule (1925); and here, of more local provenance, as Madalena Cunha Matos has pointed out, the convent of Our Lady of Cape Espichel dating from 1560. Of the potential role of this last, Matos informs us:

opposite
Luís Figueiredo House,
Gondomar,
Portugal, 1984–94

below
Bonjour Tristesse, Schlesisches
Tor Residential Complex,
Berlin, Germany, 1980–4

left and opposite
Kindergarten, Schlesisches Tor Recreational Centre, Berlin, Germany, 1980–90

below
Senior Citizens' Clubhouse, Schlesisches Tor Recreational Centre, Berlin, Germany, 1980–90

Uffizi, Espichel. Separated by different degrees of erudition and centrality, by two hundred years of history and by distance (although from a human and physical/geographical standpoint, both are part of a Mediterranean world and culture), each consists of two parallel, carefully proportioned volumes encompassing a communal space. In both cases this is the most important space, the one given the greatest attention in terms of proportion and rhythm. As emptiness that has direction, an *open-air* scene that resembles a street but is also reminiscent of a square; of an urban room hewn from compact surrounding material ... the Setúbal building is a work that deals with the concrete memory of architecture, a reworking of spaces that possess a high degree of sociability, precisely because architecture affords the opportunity for a common, shared lifestyle ...[48]

One notes that there are in fact two courts; a formal, all but symmetrical, arcaded courtyard facing north-east and an informal elevated podium facing south-west. The two vertical bars of the H-plan are linked by a foyer that provides internal access to all four wings of the school. The north-eastern court is made up of individual classrooms facing onto an arcaded space, while these rooms are linked via a long corridor on the north-western wing to the gymnasium, music room and amphitheatre. The opposing south-western court is flanked by a cafeteria to the south-east and a library to the north-west. The library and cafeteria flank an informal terrace that is slightly elevated above the surrounding agricultural land.

Perhaps the most surprising and lyrical aspect of the entire composition is the approach to the complex from the parking area situated on a loop road to the east of the H-plan. One enters the main cortile via a loosely assembled, walled-in walkway which restricts one's outlook, until one reaches the canted volume of the *propylea* at the end of the arcaded south-eastern wing. Once under this sloping roof one is confronted by a topographical displacement of astonishing dynamism. Thus, while a declining granite ramp falls away from the entry across the open end of the court, a narrower brick-paved ramp climbs up simultaneously towards the high ground to the right hand side of the portico upon which the caretaker's house is situated. This last is a relatively high and narrow oblong with minimal fenestration and a high *porte fenêtre* facing south-east.

The formal court itself affords the visitor his second surprise, for while it is flanked on three sides by a generous loggia and first floor access galleries on the two facing sides, its end facade is rendered as an opaque plane enlivened by an occasional picture-window and by two projecting forms, one housing the entry lobby and the other amounting to a boat-shaped, dog-leg stair projecting under the loggia into the court. Of these cryptic forms Matos has written:

In stark contrast to whiteness, number and reason, forms emerge that are negative, threatening; a sombre face anthropomorphically designed on the facade of a projecting staircase; a slowly uncurling sea creature that might at any moment retreat back into its shell, closing off access to the interior; a structural collapse, freeze-framed in a given moment of its fall ... The contorted, knotted branches of a cork tree rising to meet the sky.[49]

As Matos observes, this last is framed by the court so as to stand as the aboriginal Portuguese tree, singled out from the surrounding cork plantation by being so honoured and therein establishing the conjunction of loggia and tree, reminiscent, as Matos remarks, of the way in which the Erectheum protects a sacred olive tree, a relic of the goddess Athena on the Acropolis. Matos ascribes to this classical conjunction a critical significance that transcends antique lore. She sees it as a double sign testifying to both the durability of the society and a parallel commitment to the cause of ecological resistance; in a phrase, a symbol that seeks to re-establish 'a link with people that are not blinded by the possession of land, a people that know how to rebuild, restock, without leaving too many scars'.[50]

The third and most discrepant feature of all is the loggia itself which, while it first appears to be compounded of nothing more than a regular rhythm of supports, cylindrical at the corners with square piers in between, is in fact much more inflected, involving three different column profiles in plan – circular, square and ogival; a variation which responds to light in different ways at different times of the year.

There are other features here which, while derived in part from Loos, also owe much to Siza's sculptural propensity; the twin cubes that surmount the cafeteria and the single square window on the axis beneath them, plus the canted and hooded openings that animate the blank plasticity of the addenda. These return us not only to the Carlos Ramos pavilion, but also to the Maria Margarida Aguda House in Arcozelo (1979-87) and the cultural centre projected for Sines (1982-5) where, as in Loos' Steiner House of 1910, dualities abound.

Apart from the elegant, airy deportment of the courtyard, we may say the interior is more expansively developed than the exterior, beginning with the *canon à lumière* in the curved ceiling of the atrium that Matos characterizes as an 'amoeba' of light; one

below
Housing and Shopping Complex, Schilderswijk, The Hague, The Netherlands, 1984–8

opposite
De Punkt and De Komma Social Housing Residence, Schilderswijk-West, The Hague, The Netherlands, 1983–8

that runs the gamut between the wall and the floor of the atrium in a varying diurnal trajectory of sunlight that assumes the form of a distorted circle, depending on the angle and the surface on which it falls. A comparative lightness of touch is to be found in the staircase that gives access to both the first floor and the cafeteria, furnished, in Siza's typical Scandinavian taste, with chairs of light bent plywood, cantilevered off painted tubular metal supports. A light, creamy tone prevails throughout, stemming from the vivacity of the fenestration and the light timber handrails, window and door surrounds, plus plywood wall linings up to dado height. This overall tone prevails throughout the building, where it seems to attain its apotheosis in the top-lit gymnasium with its plywood lining taken up to the full height of the climbing frames attached to the walls.

In retrospect, it becomes clear that Setúbal was a seminal building in Siza's career in that it exploited the cortile type for its representational and normative attributes. Thus, while the monumental peristyle could be readily brought to accommodate the repetitive units, 'the spaces with particular features (auditorium, music room, gymnasium and others) define volumes attached to the U-shaped structure like boats moored in a quay.'[51] This is the essential *parti* adopted in the case of the new rectory designed for the University of Alicante in 1995-8, where the H-plan, double-courtyard type is rendered as a long, narrow, column-less cortile in order to protect the two-storey administration building and its attendant lecture hall against a torrentially hot climate. Thus a Graeco-Roman type is tightened up, as it were, to bring it closer to an Hispano-Arabic sense of enclosure.

Faculty of Architecture, University of Porto: 1986–1996

The new faculty of architecture in Porto is handled as a Piranesian assembly that occupies the best part of a triangular site located to the north-west of the Quinta da Póvoa and the Carlos Ramos pavilion.[52] The facility divides into two wings that converge in a *propylea* located at the north-western extremity of the triangle. The lower of these wings, facing west over the River Douro, is broken up into four separate five-storey studio buildings, with a foundational terrace for a possible fifth to be added at a later date. Comprised of virtually the same components on every floor above the grade, that is to say, a service core plus two offices and two studio spaces, the actual plan arrangement varies slightly from one building to the next, which accounts in part for the different fenestration adopted in each block. Long windows are invariably used on the sides, not only to provide virtually the same level of light to each studio, but also to afford constantly changing bracketed views of the environment as one looks across from one studio through the next to the framed landscape, or alternatively to yet another studio lying beyond. This kaleidoscopic effect depends upon one's precise position in any particular studio, with the slightest shift in one's viewpoint totally transforming the overlaid and framed perspectival view. Appropriately enough, where similar windows are employed on the end elevations of the studios they are covered with a sun visor. With the exception of the angled, L-plan block that begins the sequence, each block presents a literal 'face' to the river on its end elevation. This varying physiognomy depends upon duality for its mask-like image and on the introduction of central windows above the first three floors. The separate studio buildings are connected at the lower ground floor by a corridor three metres below the general datum of the campus. This gallery is linked below ground to the three-storey cafeteria building at the north-western end of the complex. This pavilionated structure, with a covered roof terrace (Edifício A), is effectively the foyer of the northern wing which comprises administrative offices, a semi-circular exhibition gallery, various auditoria, large and small, and a library. The largest auditorium opens out into a large flat, clerestory-lit review space. A diagram indicates how regulating lines were used to control the convergence of the two wings. While the angle of the northern block lines up with a corner of the Carlos Ramos pavilion, the leading edge of the belvedere of the Quinta da Póvoa determines the line of the four studio blocks. Thus ingeniously sited in relation to the contours and the boundaries of the terrain, the northern wing opens up on its interior to accommodate a complex *promenade architecturale*, extending from the ramp that feeds the exhibition gallery to the half-cylindrical form of the gallery itself. A second, narrower ramp wraps around the drum of a semi-circular inner gallery to lead eventually to the stair hall that in turn provides access to the library.

The two-storey space of the library is patently the volumetric *tour de force* that culminates the entire sequence and, as in all of

opposite and right
Teacher Training College,
Setúbal, Portugal, 1986–94

Siza's more complex spaces, we are immediately made aware of its genealogy. While this is surely one of the most sublime spaces of the school, it is also compounded, at the same time, of illustrious precedents that contribute to the cultural resonance of its form. In terms of autonomous invention, it may be seen as a book-lined galleria where the toplight of the historical type is provided through a keel of obscured glass that drops down along the axis of the space like a knife, but it also takes its overall ambiance from the Scandinavian modern tradition and, in particular, from the two canonical libraries designed in sequence by Gunnar Asplund and Alvar Aalto: the Stockholm Public Library of 1926 and the Viipuri Library of 1935. Prison, galleria, bridge, fuselage – a number of typological and structural metaphors spring simultaneously to the mind as one enters the service catwalk between the symmetrical lower chord of the triangular lay-light in obscured glass and the clear glass asymmetrical lantern light that covers the slot in the roof.

Siza, like Auguste Perret, has always regarded staircases as the indispensable touchstones of architectural culture (as in the remarkably expressive stair that he designed for an art gallery in Porto in 1973) and in no single work has he pursued this expressive element more assiduously than in the faculty of architecture where, in the company of ramps of varying length and trajectory, the generic stair passes through numerous permutations as it dramatically punctuates the progression along the architectural promenade. Here one may perceive how the changing character of a successive series of stairs depends upon the interaction of certain plastic elements, such as: (1) the relation of the stair to its threshold or landing; (2) the revetment of the staircase where, of the same stone as the floor, it rises to varying heights depending on the circumstances; and (3) the equally variable figure of the ubiquitous timber-clad, metal handrail set in specific relation to the going of the stair. Thus, in the cafeteria-cum-entrance block (Edifício A), the open marble-faced stairway to the twist floor descends into a monumental marble encasement, while within this case a curved stair-rail springs up into the vomitory in a continuous sweep. By a similar token, the stair leading to the first floor secretariat (Edifício B) is similarly clad in marble but has no handrail since it passes between two reveals. Thereafter we come to the outer and inner semicircular drums, with their perimeter handrails, that make up the exhibition gallery (Edifício C). These are followed at the end of the spatial sequence by a main stair giving access to the library block (Edifício D). In each instance the expression is different; the marble revetment is either riding high or low against the plaster, there is or is not a handrail and so on, including the threshold to the library itself where two short flights of marble-clad stairs, without handrails, placed symmetrically back to back, are set against a marble wall that rises to the full height of the space.

The Galician Centre of Contemporary Art: 1988–1993
Integrated into an irregular site that, aside from sloping in different directions, was also overlaid with historical traces going back to the Middle Ages, the low-profiled mass of the museum had to reconcile four different topographies: the convent gardens rising up the hill to the north-east (the redesign of which was an intrinsic part of the commission), the residential grain of the city to the south-west, a large public garden extending due west, and last but not least, the large brooding mass of the Convent of Santo Domingo de Bonaval. The museum had to be inserted into this context in a subtle and precise manner, with its north-eastern wall being aligned with the wall of the Bonaval Cemetery and its south-western face running parallel to the residential street. As a result of these vectors, the structure emerged as a largely windowless wedge, which echoed the zigzag terracing of the gardens.

In Kahnian terms, we may say that the building consists of a three-storey orthogonal gallery block that is *served* by an equally orthogonal three-storey *servant* block. The latter, L-shaped in plan, intercepts the former in such a way as to enclose a three-storey triangular atrium. Above the lower ground floor, this atrium serves as the main foyer of the institution. A central circulation spine flanking one side of this converging volume accommodates the public and staff staircases, together with passenger and freight elevators that occupy the length and the height of the spine respectively. After ascending the ramp to the top of the podium and passing through the portico, the main circulation route divides about the circulation spine. From the portico, the most direct itinerary leads one to the atrium where one immediately encounters the coat counter, faced in marble as though it were contiguous with the floor. At this point the route splits into two alternatives. One either proceeds into the next foyer that leads directly to the auditorium, and then to the administration wing and the library on the upper floors, or one turns right to enter the circulation spine in order to ascend to the permanent collection above. Alternatively, one passes through the spine into the temporary exhibition galleries running along the eastern flank of the building. A secondary route opens off the portico to pass behind the spine in order to access the bookstore, the café and the café terrace looking obliquely past the Convent to the gardens running up the hill. Below these facilities are public services adjacent to the lower ground floor galleries, while the remainder of the podium is given over to storage and conservational activities of various kinds, ranging from the reception of art to restoration and exhibition preparation, etc. It is one of the ironies of this work that, while it is ostensibly an extension of the topography of the gardens, the circulation spine cuts across the plan in such a way as to interrupt the labyrinthic movement of the space.

At the top of the building one attains the permanent galleries, which are rather traditional in character inasmuch as they depart from the modernist principle of flexible space. Here, the visitor encounters an enfilade of axial rooms, the walls of which are lit from a dropped ceiling and clerestory which ensures that any wall-mounted pieces are more brightly lit than the observer. Of this

Faculty of Architecture,
University of Porto, Porto,
Portugal, 1986–96

Faculty of Architecture,
University of Porto

return to nineteenth-century convention in the name of character and light Siza has remarked:

> … Many directors want buildings to have no character. They think it is better to have big spaces without partitioning and with flexible lighting. The model for this might be Beaubourg in Paris. You have a big machine supposedly with a lot of flexibility so that artists and directors can come and make their own decisions of how exhibits can be created within the available square metres.
>
> I offer another perspective. That is, even with an installation it's nicer to have a dialogue with a particular space. I think that is good for the work of the artist … In the end, I would argue that even Beauborg is not so easy to organize for exhibitions. It seems to be flexible. But in the end there are extreme difficulties. So in my opinion a museum must have its own character …[53]

Here, as elsewhere, Siza's architecture depends as much upon the materials and the general tone of the ambient light as it does upon the specific nature of the space. White marble revetment and light timber floors and furnishings, plus walls and ceilings finished in plaster and painted white above the dado level, jointly assure that the entire museum is filled with scintillating light that, in places, becomes muted as the day unfolds. This internal luminosity is occasionally offset by the external granite facing and by the timber lining of the recessed lecture hall, the seating of which is upholstered in black leather. Light, both natural and artificial, penetrates the spatial continuity in various ways; not only through dropped ceilings but also through side lights, lighting strips and various displacements, such as the atrium clerestory that enables one to glimpse the sculpture garden on the roof. The fluidity of the internal circulation may be modified throughout by the sliding doors, while the main stair has a generous landing at mid-point opening onto the atrium, thereby alleviating the claustrophobic character of the circulation spine.

Here Siza oscillates between the *tectonic* and the *atectonic*, a play that is particularly evident in the granite revetment of the concrete and steel substructure which both simulates load-bearing masonry and denies it at the same time. Thus, in the end plane to the portico, Siza goes out of his way to employ L- and U-shaped pieces, 50mm-thick, in order to convey the impression that the wall is of solid stone. The architect enters here into the Semperian game of both *concealing* and *revealing*, that is to say both covering the steel-framed structure that carries the stone and indicating its latent presence. We are presented *de facto* with the *concealed* reality of the steel frame upon which the stone is hung, and at the same time with the *revealed* rhetoric of the steel lintels, which appear to support the stone. This ambiguous expression is equally fictive on the street facade where a 'long-span' steel lintel presumes to carry the granite above. This counterpoint is even more subtly articulated in the portico, where the load of the free-standing end wall is apparently conveyed to the ground through a wide, built-up box beam made out of two steel channels, back-to-back, welded to a base plate and held clear of the stone-paved podium by two short, cylindrical steel columns. The integrity of this masonry wall is called into question by a reduction in thickness at the very point where the compressive stress would be at its highest. However, we can hardly dismiss this as 'cardboard architecture', for nothing could be further from the idea of the decorated shed. The stone and steel are there in all their materiality and are palpably handled in terms of craftsmanship. What is not convincing is their supposed interaction and we may say that it is this ambiguity that allows the ethics and the aesthetics of the situation to co-exist; for the steel framing does in fact carry the masonry, but not in the manner that is suggested by the exposed structural members.

Obviously, we cannot think of Siza as a consistently tectonic architect, for the referential character of his work plays fast and loose with structure – a trope borrowed from Loos here, a figure taken from Aalto there, neither of whom were particularly tectonic. At times, the earthwork comes to be unequivocally expressed, as in his João de Deus nursery school at Penafiel (1984–91) or in the factory for Vitra, near Weil am Rhein (1991–4), where a concrete undercroft is faced in stone. In many instances, as Paulo Martins Barata points out, the cladding seems to imply a wish-fulfilment. It testifies to a material that the architect would have preferred to have used, had he been able to afford it; solid stone in the case of the museum in Santiago de Compostela, or a solid brick superstructure in the case of the Vitra factory. In both instances, masonry appears as a veneer. On occasion, a material may momentarily appear in all its fullness, as in the main stair of the Duarte House where the thin stone revetment of the treads and risers gives way to a single, solid stone step at the beginning of the flight.

In Santiago de Compostela, Siza is at his most tectonic in the small-scale details, in his windows and door-casings, his handrails and light fittings, and in his use of flush, all-but-seamless polished stone that rises up the walls to envelop countertops and other free-standing objects, creating a magma of luxus that provides a tactile counterpoint to the fluidity of the space. Here the hair-line seams and butt-joints seem to be indispensably expressive in that they emphasize, through their delineation, the changing character of light. This last is typical of Siza's hypersensitive meditation on the

opposite and right
Galician Centre of Contemporary Art, Santiago de Compostela, Spain, 1988–93

below and opposite
Galician Centre of
Contemporary Art

precise interaction of material and form that runs throughout the work. We learn, in a recent interview, how the sharp converging edges of the granite cladding was prized for its capacity to offset the arboreal proliferation by which the museum will come to be surrounded, just as Siza vacillated for equally delicate reasons about the choice of the revetment itself.

> I remember that when I began the museum, I had the idea of making it in white marble – for many reasons. One reason was that in Santiago, like all of the cities in northern Portugal and that part of Spain, including Galicia, it is traditional to build everything out of granite. Even the houses that were originally made of stucco have since been replaced with granite, destroying the historical patrimony. In old photographs and in leftover areas of Santiago, you can see how everything was once white. I also thought that there was a case to be made for introducing a non-local material to an exceptional building in an exceptional part of the city. We shouldn't be afraid of that. When a city is developed, or wants to renew its institutions, it makes an open city. And using non-local materials is in a way a reflection of that opening up, to communication, to context of exchange with history. This was my idea, but as you can imagine, everyone was horrified by it. The fact is that I, myself – maybe even out of shyness or a certain sense of responsibility – abandoned the idea that I thought could have been a tour de force. Maybe it was a little too strong for the context, and so I opted for the traditional granite of Santiago.[54]

University of Aveiro Library: 1988–1995
Influenced by Aalto's Viipuri Library of 1935, this concrete prism, clad in limestone and red brick, is enriched by re-entrant walls in plaster, painted white, and by a folded, monumental, stone-faced concrete apron hovering mysteriously over the entrance. Despite this dramatic exterior, one would be hard pressed to find a more sublime and serviceable work from the last decade of the twentieth century than this university library which, irrespective of its poetic character, is an exceptionally human facility from the point of view of its appropriation and use. It seems to be one of those rare modern buildings in which the users seem to have occupied the place without any effort. On the one hand, it is simply a repository of books which appear to be evenly distributed throughout a largely introspective, top-lit, four-storey orthogonal container, where the principal entry is at the elevated campus level; on the other hand, the entire volume is articulated through the reiteration of an eight-person, double-sided reading desk, arranged in an orderly but occasionally ad hoc fashion throughout the three main reading levels. These tables, flanked by bookshelves so as to form alcoves, impart a rhythm to the space that sets up a two-part counterpoint; first, in relation to the rhythm of the structural bays as these are denoted by free-standing cylindrical columns and, second, in relation to the offset double- and triple-height voids – square and double-square in plan – that create spatial displacements along the central axis, thereby illuminating and unifying the entire library, including even a lounge double-square in plan, situated on the ground floor at the north-western end. The library is lit by conical skylights let into the curved ceiling of the top floor, in addition to receiving a boost from side lights at the entry level. Unexpected diagonal and longitudinal views proliferate along the central axis, focusing on picture windows at the end of the 'nave'. Like the recessed side windows on the undulating south-western facade, the unobstructed plate-glass openings frame spectacular views over the salt marshes and the river that flank the building on this side. These belvedere effects, combined with the wooden furniture and the timber flooring, framing, shelving and panelling up to dado height (not to mention the occasional episode in marble), impart to the entire volume a sense of unparalleled calm and generosity; a space in which to concentrate or freely wander without any obligation. The near personification, in fact, of Siza's lost library of which he writes:

> I like the order of the shelves, the brass labels and the individual lamps in bronze and silk, anonymous, intimate; the ship's stairs and the narrow iron galleries, where going to look for a book can be a journey – not without its dangers.
>
> The modern library has lost this 'attic-like' atmosphere and also the symbolic value, glorified by domes, by cylinders, by high modulated ceilings. It has lost that atmosphere of golden light – materialised by dust in the air – coming from unexpectedly high windows, always inadequate for efficient lighting, which needs the support of small green lamps …
>
> Everything has become practical, ergonomic, hygienic, codified in Neufert, uniformly lit, lined up – shelves like the wagons of an abandoned train, upholstery which is washable and comfortable.
>
> But 'something' has gone missing.

The design of the Aveiro Library reflects – and was not able to resolve – the quest for this 'something' …⁵⁵

Here, as in a great deal of Siza's work and thought, one is forcibly reminded of Walter Benjamin's 'angel of history' who is propelled backwards into the future by the storm of progress which continues to pile up the debris of the past before his feet. The angel, as Benjamin puts it, would like to restore what has been smashed, but the storm is blowing from paradise with such force that he cannot close his wings.⁵⁶

Santa Maria Church, Marco de Canavezes: 1990–1996

Siza's increasingly honorific practice came to a kind of monumental crescendo in two works, the mutual realization of which would take him into the late nineties: the modest Santa Maria Church in Marco de Canavezes and the monumental Portuguese Pavilion built for Expo '98 in Lisbon. The symbolic and syntactical demands made by these institutional commissions – the domain of the spirit versus the protocol of the state – pushed Siza to the very limit of his evolving architectural culture. Some of the difficulties that he encountered, particularly in the case of the church, were outlined in a 1998 interview with Yoshio Futagawa:

> I wanted to make a church that felt like a church and not a building with a cross in it. I wasn't interested in this primitive notion of how a symbol could determine the character of a building. It was too superficial an approach and wouldn't work for me. So I tried to achieve something I would call the character of the church … This is particularly difficult today. The liturgy has been changed a lot by the Vatican. I can give you a simple example, in early times the priest did not face the celebrants. The celebrants looked at his back. This explains the generous space of the apse that was in turn always projected onto the exterior of the building. Of course this apse is part of the character we associate with a church. But as the priest turned to the assembly, the space behind him no longer has a logic … [yet] The burden of tradition is heavy. And new iterations are rarely successful. You can see this when you go to see contemporary exhibitions of religious art. You find nothing that is moving; nothing touches you. It is very difficult. If you try to think of a good cross in modern architecture, I can only think of the ones designed by Le Corbusier in Ronchamp or La Tourette, or the one of Barragán and not much more. There are very few contemporary churches that have this atmosphere that is difficult to describe, that make you feel that you are in a sacred building. I think that the purpose of this project should be to insert this fraternal relationship between men and this atmosphere …⁵⁷

However much recent liturgical changes may have rendered the traditional ecclesiastical model obsolete, Siza would none the less turn to tradition in his attempt to recover the elusive spiritual character; above all, through treating the building as though it were a windowless barn, much as in Le Corbusier's chapel in La Tourette, and further by handling the entry to the south-west as a symmetrical composition, with two square towers enclosing the entrance portal to the nave. As we have already seen, Siza habitually returns to Loos' symmetrical Steiner House format, which we find in one work after another from the Duarte House to the back of the Aveiro Library. It is this format, with its recessive centre plus the narrow, double-leaf, panelled wooden door in the centre of the portal, that imparts to the front of this building a unique and unforgettable Gestalt that is particularly striking as one approaches it obliquely from the village fabric. Both the door and the 16.5m-high towers to either side, the one accommodating a baptistry and the other containing the stairs to the belfry, are the essential dualistic elements that embody the inaugural key to the entire building. As Luigi Spinelli reminds us:

> There is a time of day in which, when the two, ten-metre tall leaves of the main entrance door are flung open, a shaft of sunlight from the south-west floods the single nave right up to the altar. The spaces inside the absolutely vertical (16.5 metre) high volumes of the church, the bell tower and that of the christening font, and the apse chimney in communication with the mortuary chapel below, are served by a diffused light. The two apertures that bring light to the font are lateral and not visible from the front: one brings the light pouring down from very high up along the white ceramic walls; the other comes straight across the surface of the church square paving. This light polishes the granite font, as does the water that overflows and collects at its feet. The sound of this water is one of the materials that contributes to the character of the church's inner space.⁵⁸

With this, Siza returns us to the spirit of the early Christian church which we proceed to encounter in the preternatural character of the nave, stemming in large measure from the billowing presence of the south-eastern inclined wall (illuminated by three inset windows at some 15 metres from the floor), that finds its plastic response in the symmetrical bulging forms of the 'anti-apse' flanking the altar. It is significant that these last should be constructed by inverting the very quadrants that made up the

opposite
João de Deus Nursery School,
Penafiel, Portugal, 1984–91

below and overleaf
Library, University of Aveiro,
Aveiro, Portugal, 1988–95

semi-circular geometry of the traditional apse. Between these embrasures are two oneiric rectangular slots let into the reredos. These slots are illuminated by an unearthly light that serves to evoke a sense of primordial, not to say pagan form. They suggest a kind of Manichaean duality such as may be found in the neolithic sacred sites in Malta or the Balearic Islands, or even in

the remote stone burrows of northern Portugal. It is hardly a coincidence that this same light should illuminate the 'altar' in the mortuary chapel asymmetrically situated some 6 metres below the nave of the church. This plan shift is carried up from the basement in order to accommodate all the other auxiliary spaces that invariably attend a church; the vestry, the sacristy, various offices, etc.

As in Le Corbusier's Ronchamp, light was a key factor in the orchestration of the nave, particularly for the way in which it resembled the light admitted through the thick walls of early Christian structures. This largely accounts for the incline in the north-eastern wall of which Siza has remarked:

> You have this angle that gives some depth to the windows. You can see the light comes in but you don't see the actual windows in perspective. This was obtained in old churches naturally with the thickness of the construction, but today we do make walls about 40 cm so I tried to reintroduce this quality of thickness and density.
>
> This space resulting from the curve is also accessible upstairs to clean the glass. A lot of old churches have this kind of veranda, and I remember when I was a child I was baffled by the mystery of this veranda. I would look up at it, and there would never be anyone there, and I would wonder how it was accessed and who goes there. I projected this sense of wonder here.[59]

The Portuguese Pavilion for Expo '98, Lisbon: 1995–1998

The Portuguese Pavilion for Expo '98 had to address two different levels of state representation at once; on the one hand, it had to serve as the container for a temporary exhibition, on the other, it had to function as a prestige reception pavilion for distinguished foreign visitors. Although it was left unclear as to what its future use would finally be, it was none the less certain that it would ultimately house a state institution of some kind or other. Thus Siza had sufficient reason to treat this commission as a palace, state protocol bringing him to adopt a monumental syntax deriving in part from the programme of the New Monumentality of 1943.[60] Foregoing his earlier excursus into the language of the Italian Tendenza, as we find this in Setúbal, Siza seems to have been drawn to the pre-war Rationalist architecture of Giuseppe Terragni, particularly his unbuilt Palazzo dei Ricevimenti 'E 42, designed with Cataneo and Lingeri in 1938. This is confirmed by the syncopated pier spacing in the two stone-faced screen facades which vary slightly from front to back, with the front screen setting up the basic eight-part rhythm A-A-A-B-A-C-A-A and the back screen echoing this with the variation A-A-A-B-A-C-A-B. Siza chose to mediate this humanist syncopation with a bold gesture drawn from the tectonic modernism of the Brazilian architect Oscar Niemeyer – the long-span catenary roof of Niemeyer's Cavanelas house of 1954. In this typological transposition, the body of the building lying behind the free-standing screen-facade of Terragni's palazzo project is substituted by a concrete catenary roof spanning 75 metres between two free-standing facades. In this way, Siza succeeded in fusing two antithetical imperial images: an allusion to the occidental peristyle of the Roman forum, and a reference to the Oriental nomadic canopy of the Mughal Empire. The colossal scale of this last creates a vast honorific portico open to the sea, reminiscent of the canopy covering the forecourt of Jørn Utzorn's Kuwait Parliament of 1982, and recalling in parallel both Le Corbusier's Assembly Building in Chandigarh of 1961 and Niemeyer's Palace of the Dawn in Brasilia of 1959.

Siza's palace turns its 'side' elevation towards the sea through a two-storey colonnade, similar in its modulation to the peristyle lining the forecourt in Setúbal, complete with an inset, cantilevered access gallery and tall french windows at the first floor. This sixteen-column colonnade returns along the building's northern face for three bays, thereby rotating the full mass away from the ceremonial square to which it remains attached by virtue of the colonnade and the continuity of the quay. Orientated north-south, this last is countered by a plaza running east-west and paved Coppacabanca style in a wavy pattern of black and white stone sets, in accordance with the venerable Lisbon paving tradition.

Santa Maria Church and Parish Centre, Marco de Canavezes, Portugal, 1990–6

Internally, this two-storey structure amounts to a relatively flexible enfilade of orthogonal rooms planned around a central atrium. It remains to be seen how these rooms will be finally appointed and occupied, since the government remains uncertain as to how much of the space will be eventually devoted to honorific purposes and how much will be used to accommodate a national museum.

Appropriately honoured but without illusions, Siza runs forward into history with one more remarkable project after another, works which, whether realized or not, point in much the same direction, namely to the deconstruction of the H-plan *parti* of Sebútal into a series of stratified assemblies, the sculptural concatenation of which is invariably brought to an unexpected resolution through some form of truncation borrowed from Le Corbusier's work at La Tourette. This formal yet functionally modulated freedom first announces itself in the abandoned project for the Manuel Cargaleiro Foundation designed for a difficult urban site in Lisbon in 1991–5. The theme reappears in the recently realized Museum of Contemporary Art in Porto (1999) and as an orthogonal *redent* formation in the Faculty of Media Sciences, projected for Santiago University in Santiago de Compostela in 1993. It assumes a totally disaggregate character – a cancellation of the theme almost – in the Manzania del Revellín Cultural Centre projected for Ceuta, Spain in 1997. In each instance, the formulation of the programme is a task unto itself, the substance in most instances of a struggle between the society and the architect. In this process, as Siza would put it, with reference to a lifetime of struggling but also listening to his beloved *fado* singer – I am alluding to his 1995 essay 'Singer, Architect and Spontaneity' – the voice of the architect becomes hoarse.[61] In the interim, hoarse or not, the architect can hardly now complain of lack of opportunity.

Critical Theory
There is perhaps no contemporary architect who has done more not only to elucidate his practice, but also to expatiate at length, with subtlety and precision, on the general predicament of architecture at the end of the twentieth century. Aphoristic and laconic rather than didactic, Siza has elaborated his thoughts in a series of occasional pieces written over the past twenty-five years and in countless interviews, these last being the preferred mode which he finds to be as convenient as it is stimulating. For Siza, the dialogue is the discursive method par excellence, as much for the creation of architecture as for reflection and the elaboration of theoretical concepts. This dialogical modus obtains as much with the essay form as with the interview, although in the former, of course, it is one's alter ego that has to play the protagonist, as in the heteronymic writings of Siza's beloved poet Fernando Pessoa, with his paradoxical insistence that a Portuguese who is only a Portuguese is not a Portuguese.

In all of this, as in most of Siza's architecture, the ultimate model remains the Finnish architect Alvar Aalto, the one modern master who was popularly assumed to have practised without any theory whatsoever; a myth partially served by Aalto's latter-day provocation that all writing was nothing more than a misuse of paper. In an absolute repudiation of this myth, since Aalto wrote many intriguing and revealing texts throughout his life, Siza was to remark in 1983: 'I know of no more accurate and penetrating analysis of the mental process of designing than what is summarised … in Aalto's writings and discourses, which are no less illuminating for being brief.'[62]

After this, we ought not to be surprised to learn that much of Siza's own discourse will be devoted to his design method in all its circumbulatory effects. Thus we may read, in an early text accompanying an exhibition of his work at the Venice Biennale of 1978:

> The frustration of my early years at school and in my profession is still with me, when a supposedly exhaustive (static) analysis of a problem was followed by a forlorn encounter with a sheet of blank paper.
>
> Since then I have always taken care 'to look at the site' and do a drawing before calculating the square metres of the construction area. The process of designing comes from the initial confrontation of these two gestures.
>
> For this exhibition I have tried to select the materials which might document what I feel to be essential in this process: the endless patient search, the slow approximation of the design which corresponds to the complex objectives and circumstances which are involved in each piece of work …
>
> Witnesses to this search, rather than the design found. Witnesses to the daily doubts, to the small advances and to the mistakes, to the abandonment of an idea and to the recovery of something different from the same idea, …
>
> As a working tool, [these sketches] help to establish a permanent dialectical relationship between intuition and precise examination, in a progressive process of full understanding and visualisation. In this progressive visualisation, in a provisionally final image, the all important *almost nothing* beyond what is already there gradually takes shape …[63]

Topography and the passage of time at a micro scale or in a more extended sense, geography and history, are the two absolutely fundamental points of departure for Siza's *transformational* method as we may judge from his short disquisition on drawing and building in 1995.

> Learning – the acquisition of the ability to keep on learning – is still based, in my opinion, on drawing – on learning to see, to understand, to express – and on history in the sense of taking on an awareness of the present as it evolves.
>
> The learning of building – of the ability to build with other – is not separable from Architecture, because different disciplines should not exist, but instead there should be a convergence, a constant awareness that no creative act can be

Portuguese Pavilion
at Expo '98, Lisbon,
Portugal, 1995–8

separated from the material fact of its happening.

No idea of opposition between landscape – perception and construction of the land – and object – fragment of the land – has any place in the teaching of Architecture.[64]

This simple, rather incisive declaration summarizes, in short order, many of Siza's irreducible principles, from his assertion that the architect is not a specialist (or more ironically, that he is a specialist in non-specialization) to his concomitant insistence on the crucial importance of teamwork and on communication in all its interdisciplinary aspects, for as he puts it, 'in the society we live in, design without dialogue, without conflict and encounter, without doubt and conviction by turns, in our search for simultaneity and liberty, is unthinkable.'[65] For Siza, architecture means to absorb the opposite and go beyond the contradiction, to seek the Other in each of us. In this regard, he is categorically opposed to the growing division of labour in the building industry, to the isolation of the architect from the client and the craftsman alike, through the increased bureaucratization of the building process. He has in mind, surely, the emergence of the construction manager as a further sub-divided countervailing authority having the mandate to overrule the architect's on-site supervision. On the other hand, he is equally antithetical to autonomous architectonic intervention, particularly where it is indifferent to both the site and the building process, and where it wilfully ignores the socio-cultural purposes to which the building is ostensibly dedicated. As he puts it, with regard to the collective nature of design and construction:

Those who try hardest, in the situation of isolation, are sooner or later accused of elitism – a concept which is not always clear, and which is often used to make ignorance acceptable.

I have to not be me if I want to participate, pushing aside the old insecurity which frequently, fortunately, has led me to work in a team – a team of designers.

Working in a team is like working alone, but with a capacity for analysis and invention multiplied by X. Each person's discoveries, each hypothesis launched into the flow, generate further hypotheses and further discoveries on their part and other's – as happens with my ideas when I work alone – but here at a giddy rate....

It is therefore urgent, not least for the work of these agents, that we extend information early on and to everyone, to bring to an end the myths of specialisation, of the incommunicable complexity of all the different specialisms.[66]

As opposed to the art of architecture wilfully masquerading as fine art writ large, Siza provocatively insists that architects do not invent anything; that instead of a priori, value-free creation, the task of the architect is to transform reality. For Siza, formal complexity must be largely derived from real complexity and not from gratuitous invention. Thus we find him writing: 'It will have to be recognized that a language is not being invented, just as a way of life is not invented. It will have to be recognized that language is transformed in order to adapt it to reality or shape reality.'[67]

Siza concedes elsewhere that there is none the less an irreducible tension in his architecture between the relative autonomy of architectonic form and the unity of the topographic whole. Nevertheless he finds it disturbing how, in a great deal of contemporary practice ...

Certain cliches emerge that construct a type of exuberant monotony, incapable of production tissue. In the historical centres, the houses are practically all the same and nobody seems to find them boring. The difference occurs more subtly, on another scale. That is why I am so interested, lately, in proportion as an alternative to the contemporary obsession for the total innovation of the image ...[68]

Siza recognizes that, even in his own work, it is at times necessary to modulate the sculptural impulse in order to save the work from becoming socially indecipherable – the great shortcoming, in fact, of the modern avant-garde at its most extreme. In short, there is a need to maintain a balance between the vitality of the figurative on the one hand and the normative regularity of the received type on the other; the dialectic that is between innovation and tradition that finds its philosophical parallel in the hermeneutics of Hans Georg Gadamer.[69] As Siza puts it, if the 'transfiguration' is not properly understood, the architecture becomes monstrous; however, if it becomes too constrained it cannot survive.[70] At the same time, an architect is unable to create a legible monument, a significant institutional difference without a compact and repetitive urban fabric against which it may be read.[71]

By a similar token, but at a median scale, it is evident that for Siza the poetics of construction, that is to say tectonics at the level of the intimate fabric, remains an essential factor in rendering architecture accessible in the socio-cultural sense. Thus, as Vittorio Gregotti wrote now nearly thirty years ago at the beginning of Siza's architectural maturity:

Siza does not use detail as decoration or technological ostentation but as an intimate dimension which makes architecture accessible: a way of tactilely verifying the consistency and the uniqueness of the thing made in a certain place at a certain moment in time; a means of coming into contact with the construction by feeling one's way round it. A technology of detail which is made of the unexpected distances between parts introducing spatial tension between the smallest, commonest elements through their reciprocal positioning, overlapping and interrelating.[72]

There is a melancholia in Siza's writing that is no less elegiac for being leavened with irony, and this brings his *Weltanschauung* close to that of Walter Benjamin or even Ernst Bloch, as we may

left and opposite
Portuguese Pavilion
at Expo '98

judge from the following remarkable passage touching, however obliquely, on the ecological responsibility of architecture:

> After years of passionate invention, of separation from History, of glory and failure, after the Modernist movement, a reading, albeit transitory, of the huge amount that we received from the previous generation seems fairly clear to me. In spite of new materials and new techniques, of the growth and the death of cities, of the breaking down of frontiers and of setting up of new frontiers, of solidarity and of extinction, of euphoria and of frustration, of the conquest of space and of the death of the forests, the essence of Architecture has not changed.
>
> No tree uprooted for building and no stone taken from the mountain is restored to us. No yellowed photograph brings back the Beauty that is gone. It remains to us to attempt – to continue – the construction of Beauty ... Natural or constructed, we transform everything with too much eagerness, with too much ambition or dissatisfaction. The liberty gained, endlessly necessary, also paralyses, or reduces to dust. And so we live in a period without style, in other words, objectively without any centre.[73]

Among other morbid symptoms, Siza surely has in mind the destruction that mass tourism has wrought on large parts of the Atlantic and Mediterranean coasts, along with the chaotic spread of the megalopolis across vast tracts of former agricultural land; but he also knows that this cataclysm 'does not exclude the will to intervene and even hope – hope in the endurance and grandeur of nature evident from an aeroplane window at great height.'[74]

Transfixed before a vibrant archaeology, where the unfinished always remains open to further elaboration, and where a site is valued not so much for what it is as for what it might become, Siza pursues an architecture of resistance. The global has always to be offset by the local at every level, not in terms of some categoric rejection of universal technology, but rather in recognition of the need to mediate technique through culture – a gesture always broaching that melancholic gap between the realization of form and the ruination of time.

Portuguese Pavilion
at Expo '98

Notes

1. Vittorio Gregotti, 'The Obsession of History', *Casabella*, no. 478, March 1982, p. 41.
2. The Portuguese Republic was proclaimed on 5 October 1910, after a three-day insurrection at Lisbon had forced King Manuel II to flee to Britain. Republican sentiment sprang from resentment at the extravagance shown by the monarchy in the previous half-century, from acute poverty among the workers and from hostility to the reactionary policy of the Church. The new regime carried through a number of anti-clerical measures and adopted a liberal constitution, but it was not able to improve conditions among the workers and relied upon military rule to prevent violence. In the early 1920s the democratic government became notorious for its corruption and inefficiency; Portugal remained a poor and backward country with a high rate of illiteracy (see A.W. Palmer, *A Dictionary of Modern History 1789–1945*, London: Penguin, 1962).
3. Both Carlos Ramos and Cristino da Silva designed works in the early 1930s which could be considered as falling under the rubric of the 'moderne', that is to say they adopted a stripped, stylistically modern manner deriving from such exponents of Art Deco as Robert Mallet-Stevens. The same may also be said of Cassiano Branco in Lisbon and of J. Marques da Silva, Antonio Varela, Jorge Viana and Januario Godinho in Porto. See *Architectures à Porto*, Liège: Mardaga, 1987, pp. 36–46.
4. Fernando Távora, 'The Problem of the Portuguese House', in Luis Trigueiros et al., *Fernando Távora*, Lisbon: Blau, 1993, p. 13.
5. For a full transcription of the Távora study see Alfredo da Mata Antunes, *Arquitectura Popular em Portugal*, 2nd edn, Lisbon: Associação dos Arquitectos Portugueses, 1980, pp. 3–111. His collaborators on the survey were Rui Pimentel and Antonio Menéres.
6. See Álvaro Siza, *Siza: Architecture Writings*, Antonio Angelillo (ed.), Milan: Skira, 1997, p. 59. In his 1995 homage to Távora, Siza wrote: 'Fernando Távora started as a teacher in the Faculty of Architecture – then the Porto School of Fine Arts – in 1950, newly qualified and without a salary, at the invitation of Professor Carlos Ramos. Out of militancy and solidarity.' Other teachers at the time were Carlos Loureiro, Octávio Figueiras, Agostinho Rica, João Andresen and Mario Bonito.
7. See Manuel Mendes, 'Porto: The School and its Projects 1940–1986', in *Architectures à Porto*, op. cit., pp. 54–5. Mendes writes: 'In 1947, several architects who had been trained at the School of Porto between the beginning of the Spanish Civil War and the end of the Second World War, and forming part of the CAM doctrine, founded the Organization of Modern Architects "with the confidence, youthful enthusiasm and wish to take part, by their own means, in solving the urgent technical and social problems facing the country" (C. Barbosa). The ODAM was dissolved in 1952. During this period, there were exhibitions, a number of written texts and collective opposition to the ideas used in low-cost housing projects and to the town council's attempt to impose an official "style of Porto".

'At the end of the decade, the "New State" once again restated its aggressive and doctrinaire policy by organizing in 1948 a large documentary exhibition devoted to public building policy. At the same time the National Union of Architects organized its First National Congress of Architecture. The compromises and contradictions resulting from the devotion to "Modernism" were debated, and the Congress organized a well-timed discussion on the existing qualities of architecture and the conditions and limits of professional work. On the problems raised by the ODAM group of architects and a number of others, it was considered necessary to work for an aesthetic revolution in order to resolve urban and housing problems. The idea that the evolution of architecture should be accompanied by the basic liberties of individual and collective life was also put forward. The right for creative liberty was associated with social

8   problems arising from spatial organization. Theories of Le Corbusier and the Athens Charter were quoted in order to emphasize the urgent need for a new urban and architectonic rationality. There was a need to reintroduce natural qualities into the lives of the Portuguese – sun, space and trees. Instead of asking questions about "style", it was the architect's particular knowledge and the public respect for his creative autonomy that were in question.'

8. Bernardo Ferrão writes: 'Távora attended the CIAM/Hoddesdon, at which his concerns regarding the identification of modern architecture with formal and spatial traditional values were confirmed; he later stated that this was the Congress of "Le Corbusier of Chandigarh, of Hindu Architecture, of that huge area brimming with spontaneous displays; when Tange presented his buildings, (Ernesto) Rogers claimed they were intensely Japanese".' in *Fernando Távora*, op. cit., p. 27. Ferrão is citing from an interview in Spanish between Javier Frechilla and Fernando Távora published in the Madrid review *Arquitectura*, no. 261, April 1986, p. 24.

9. Frank Lloyd Wright's Taliesin in Spring Green, Wisconsin made an overwhelming impression on Távora when he visited the United States in 1960 on a joint grant from the Calouste Gulbenkian Foundation and the High Culture Institute. In his as yet unpublished diary he wrote in an entry dated 9 April 1960: 'Taliesin impressed me for all it represents as a whole, for its cosmic strength, for all that existed there besides the stones, the timber, and this or that refinement of the form… Time at Taliesin favours architecture and landscape that I believe cannot happen with 90 per cent of modern architecture.' See *Fernando Távora*, op. cit., pp. 95–6.

10. A detailed study of the role of Carlos Ramos in the formation of the Porto School, in both senses of the term, has yet to be made. In lieu of this Manuel Mendes affords us some indication of the evolution of the ESBAP curriculum in the 1940s and 1950s. He writes: 'During this period, two events are of decisive importance concerning the direction and evolution of the School of Porto: Ramos became Director of the Art College and the publication of a study of Portuguese vernacular architecture … Under Ramos's direction a new dynamic was introduced to educational methods, but of greater importance was the new energy he gave the School's community life. From a teaching point of view, although he still directed the Department of Architecture, he invited four members of the ODAM group to join him: Agostinho Ricca, Jose Carlos Loureiro, Mario Bonito and Fernando Távora … with the setting up of the study curriculum in 1957 and the clarification of teachers' status, which now accepted the idea of a career, the State police forced Ramos to change his team. Mario Bonito and Agostinho Ricca were replaced by Octavio Filgueiras and Arnaldo Araujo, and Joao Andresen returned to his town-planning courses. Filgueiras and Araujo had obtained their diplomas after working on town-planning and on the rural habitat: "Town-Planning: a rural concept" (1953) and "Forms of rural habitat in North Bragança: a contribution to community structure" (1957). Both belonged to the Porto CIAM group founded by Viana de Lima and including Andresen, Távora and Antonio Velloso. They both took part in the 10th CIAM Congress in 1956 with a project called "A rural community plan".'
See 'Porto: The School and its Projects 1940–1986', in *Architectures à Porto*, op. cit., pp. 54–6.

11. Távora's architecture is both complex and variable during the early 1950s as is evident from his 1952 diploma project *Casa Sobre o Mar*, which was not only influenced by Breuer but also by figures as diverse as Oscar Niemeyer in Brazil, and even possibly Giuseppe Terragni (for his *Casa Sul Lago* project of 1934). Távora surely became aware of Niemeyer's work through G.E. Kidder Smith's *Brazil Builds* of 1952. The proposed use of *azulejos*, traditional brightly coloured ceramic tiles, as partial cladding for the *Casa Sobre o Mar*, also suggests this influence. A few years later after working on the vernacular survey he moved towards the Nordic influence of Alvar Aalto while making subtle references to the Portuguese vernacular, as in the summer house he realized in Ofir in 1958.

12. See interview with Pe'era Goldman in *Technology, Place and Architecture*, Kenneth Frampton (ed.), New York: Rizoli, 1998, p. 150. Siza remarks elsewhere on visiting Spain and Paris somewhat earlier, but in general it is clear that travel was somewhat restricted until the liberalization of the regime in the late 1960s.

13. See Siza's interview with Alejandro Zaera in *El Croquis*, no. 68/69, 1994, pp. 24–5: 'SAAL was the opportunity for a generation of architects to work in the historical centre. In Oporto most of the operations were incorporated on the half circle surrounding the historical centre, where workers were living in poorly built houses.' For a detailed account and analysis of SAAL see Alexander Alves Costa, 'The SAAL Operation', in Álvaro Siza, *Professione poetica*, Quaderni di lotus 6, Milan: Electa, 1986, pp. 71–6.

14. In fact the Boa Nova Tea House is a hybrid work as its plans somehow suggest. It was the outcome of a competition held in 1956 and won by the partnership of Fernando Távora and Francisco Figueiredo. After choosing the specific location where the building would be erected, Távora turned the project over to his young collaborator Álvaro Siza. (I am indebted to Paulo Martins Barata for this information.)

15. Of this early Aalto influence Siza has recently stated that: 'I had only seen [Aalto's work] in magazines when I made Boa Nova. Aalto had already had a strong influence in Europe and in Portugal in particular, because his architecture related to this new interest in vernacular architecture in Portugal … there was a natural connection to his work. There was a connection in terms of the political and economic climate in Finland and Portugal. The yet undeveloped industries of Finland after the war etc. His work exemplified the importance of high

16 craftsmanship of woodwork and other crafts … And this relationship with Alvar Aalto … was important to maintaining a line which didn't have traditionalism or regionalism as its goal.' See Siza's interview with Yoshio Futagawa in *Álvaro Siza, GA Document Extra*, no. 11, 1998, p. 20.

16 In his 1986 interview with Javier Frechilla (*Architectura*, op. cit.) Távora remarked: 'I visited Japan after designing the pavilion but before its construction. There are certain details that are a result of the trip … It is possible that [the project] contains a certain remote oriental influence as does traditional Portuguese architecture from the XVIth century onwards.' Cited in Bernardo Ferrão's essay in *Fernando Távora*, op. cit., p. 31.

17 Paulo Martins Barata, 'Building Art in Our Time', in *Álvaro Siza 1954–1976*, Lisbon: Blau, 1997, pp. 61–2.

18 Távora worked continuously on refurbishing and modifying the park from 1956 to 1960. In 1980 Távora wrote: 'The park was a monastery of monks who settled there in the XVth century and later, it became private property … I worked there as if I were the prior of the monastery. I walked about with the stone masons and gardeners telling them what to do.' See *Fernando Távora*, op. cit., p. 66.

19 Paulo Martins Barata, description of the Quinta da Conceição Pools, 'Building Art in Our Time', op. cit., p. 44.

20 Paulo Martins Barata, description of Leça Swimming Pool, ibid., p. 82.

21 'I remember that when starting the project I bought a book on Frank Lloyd Wright, and certain aspects, certain parts of his work … exercised a positive influence on my work. In the swimming pool is present the power of its geometric essentialness, made clear in the use of the underlying 45°. I remember that Wright was a kind of path to freedom.' *Álvaro Siza: Opere e Progetti*, Pedro de Llano and Carlos Castanheira (ed.), Milan: Electa, 1995, p. 22. Cited by Paulo Martins Barata in his description of the Leça Swimming Pool, op. cit., pp. 81–2.

22 Martin Heidegger, 'Building, Dwelling Thinking', in *Poetry, Language and Thought*, trans. by Albert Hoffstadter, New York: Harper Row, 1971, p. 154.

23 Vitoria and La Coruña are two towns in Galicia where this form of curtain walling employing sash windows predominates. See Bernard Rudofsky, *The Prodigious Builders: Notes Towards a Natural History of Architecture With Special Regard to those Species that are Traditionally Neglected or Downright Ignored*, New York: Harcourt Brace Jovanovich, 1977, pp. 322–3.

24 Peter Testa, 'The Architecture of Álvaro Siza'. *Thresholds, Working Paper 4*, typed manuscript issued by the Department of Architecture, Programme in History, Theory and Criticism, MIT, Cambridge, 1984, pp. 21, 25, 27, 29. In 1979, Bernard Huet writes of the same work as achieving a categoric 'dichotomy between the container (solid, opaque, static) and the contents (fragile, transparent, dynamic).'

25 See text by Álvaro Siza in feature on the architect, *Architecture & Urbanism (A + U)*, no. 123, December 1980, p. 41.

26 Ibid., p. 9.

27 The housing was situated in a fishing village some thirty kilometres from Porto on the coast. It comprised some twenty houses and a few shops, some of which were realized.

28 See Siza's interview with Alejandro Zaera, op. cit., p. 22.

29 Portas and Gregotti were among the first to acknowledge the importance of Siza's work in their respective essays that appeared in *Contraspazio*, no. 9, September 1972, although Portas had first written on Siza's work as early as 1960. Bohigas wrote his appraisal in March 1976 in *Arquitecturas Bis*, no. 12, while Bernard Huet followed in 1979 with his essay, 'Álvaro Siza, architetto 1954–79' written for the Padiglione d'Arte Contemporanea, Milan, in 1979 and published in Álvaro Siza, *Professione poetica*, op. cit. Portas acknowledged the marginalized 'critical aestheticism' of Siza's work and its self-conscious distanciation from large-scale corporate practice, as this was epitomized at the time by the realistic productive capacity of such concerns as the American firm of Skidmore, Owings and Merrill. Like Bohigas, Portas went on to stress the doubly dialectical character of Siza's architecture, that is to say, on the one hand, its disruption of received, rational prototypes through its stress on the fluidity of the *promenade architecturale*, and on the other, the potential split between the given continuity of the topographic context and the oppositional character of Siza's autonomous form. Huet on the other hand would see this form as potentially catalytic as in Siza's unfinished art gallery for Porto, of which we read: 'As usual Siza used the concrete features of the "site", that is the building's rather ordinary structure, which he made "react" and which he invested with new meaning by introducing a sculpturally "cubist" stairway whose formal instability redefined and brought into play the inert space of the basement.' (See Álvaro Siza, *Professione poetica*, op. cit. p. 179.)

30 This term was coined by Alex Tzonis, Liane Lefèvre and myself at the beginning of the 1980s. See my essay 'Towards a Critical Regionalism: Six Points for an Architecture of Resistance', in *The Anti-Aesthetic: Essays on Postmodern Culture*, Hal Foster (ed.), Port Townsend, Washington: Bay Press, 1983, pp. 16–30.

31 I have argued elsewhere that something of Pierre Chareau's Maison de Verre in Paris (1932) is detectable in the interaction between the curtain wall and the sliding glass screens of this house. We have little evidence for this save for Siza's passing interest in the work of Chareau which we find in his collected writings of 1997 (Álvaro Siza, *Siza: Architecture Writings*, op. cit.).

32 In his interview with Alejandro Zaera (op. cit., p. 23), Siza provided a particularly interesting explanation for these curves, namely that because they fused with the lateral wall, they magnified the apparent scale of the narrow-fronted form. This responded to the client's request for the bank to have a certain presence with regard to the urban space.

33 Ibid., p. 24, Siza remarks: '… But the project was never finished because the SAAL were dissolved and the work being done was abruptly interrupted. The houses were not finished, but the future tenants, afraid of losing them, occupied the building. This led to a degradation that was even promoted by the politicians themselves, up to the point that the same situation continues today. The tenants periodically call me to try to find solutions and the local politicians periodically promise to finish the complex after the elections and then nothing happens.'

34 Despite Nuno Portas' misgivings arising out of his own populist prejudices, there is little doubt as to the critical socialist stance of Siza's practice as we may judge from Alejandro Zaera's observation that Siza's retrospective explanations are often decidedly Marxist and materialist in tone rather than poetic or humanist. See *El Croquis*, op. cit., p. 22.

35 See interview with France Vanlaetham published as 'Pour une architecture épurée et rigoreuse', in *ARQ Architecture/Quebec*, 14 August 1983, p. 18.

36 In his interview with Alejandro Zaera (*El Croquis*, op. cit. p. 24), Siza remarks that this project was initiated by the Housing Ministry before the Revolution and that the SAAL asked him to rework it to lower standards after April 1974.

37 We see such a stone arcaded aqueduct (probably of Roman provenance) interacting with an eighteenth-century city fabric in Vila do Conde. See Alfredo da Mata Antunes, *Arquitectura Popular em Portugal*, op. cit., p. 35.

38 Of this, Siza has remarked, 'I remember when I presented the plan for the patio houses in Évora, everyone was saying: it's horrendous, no one can live between those walls. But if you go to the historical centre of Évora, where everyone wants to live, it is full of high walls. Nobody sees them. This loss of objectivity is connected to the consumerism which affects urban culture and which forces us into that artificial construction of differences. See *El Croquis*, op. cit., p. 17.

39 See Pierluigi Nicolin's introduction to the Quinta da Malagueira, Évora, in Álvaro Siza, *Professione poetica*, op. cit., p. 93.

40 Ibid., pp. 93–4.

41 Gianni Vattimo, 'Project and Legitimization', in *Lotus*, no. 48/49, 1986, pp. 123–4.

42 Legend has it that Siza slightly reduced the diameter of this cylinder when its site was changed after the design had been fully developed.

43 Martello towers were built along the southern coast of England as a deterrent against invasion during the Napoleonic Wars. They were named after a tower of this type in Corsica captured by the British in 1794.

44 Joan Falgueras, descriptive text of the Meteorological Station, in *Álvaro Siza 1986–1995*, Lisbon: Blau, 1995, pp. 132–8.

45 Brigitte Fleck, *Álvaro Siza*, Basel: Birkhauser Verlag, 1992, p. 40.

46 Peter Testa, *The Architecture of Álvaro Siza*, op. cit., p. 63–5.

47 Siza informs us that 'the solution I proposed aroused much interest among the residents, but was radically rejected by the co-operative that had to build the houses. The proposal of an *old fashioned* typology and the use of brick was interpreted as a reactionary attitude … I believe that the fundamental reasons for the rejection were mainly due to the fact that the proposal did not fit perfectly into that construction machinery, of which, as you know, the Dutch are in possession. Anyway [Alderman] Duivenjstein had to take the conflict to the Dutch parliament where it was passed. In the second phase that I was assigned afterwards, the typology was immediately accepted by the co-operatives.' *El Croquis*, op. cit., p. 28.

48 Madalena Cunha Matos, 'Analysis of a Project: The Setúbal College of Education', in *Álvaro Siza 1986–1995*, op. cit., pp. 11–6.

49 Ibid., p. 11.

50 Ibid., pp. 9–10.

51 Álvaro Siza, *Siza: Architecture Writings*, op. cit., p. 196.

52 As William Curtis suggests, one may usefully compare Aalto's plan for the Institute of Technology in Otaniemi (1949) to Siza's more irregular juxtaposition of similar elements in the Faculty of Architecture. However, one may also note Siza's ingenious mannerism in this regard, for here Aalto's semicircular auditorium has been transformed into a concentric gallery space. See William Curtis, 'Álvaro Siza: An Architecture of Edges', *Álvaro Siza 1958–1994*, in *El Croquis*, no. 68/69, 1994, pp. 32–45.

53 Álvaro Siza (Interview with Yoshio Futagawa), op. cit., p. 53.

54 Interview with José Antonio Aldrete-Haas in *Bomb*, no. 68, Summer 1999, pp. 50–1.

55 Álvaro Siza, *Siza: Architecture Writings*, op. cit., p. 195.

56 Walter Benjamin, 'Theses on the Philosophy of History, 1940', in *Illuminations*, New York: Harcourt, Brace and World, 1968, pp. 259–60.

57 Álvaro Siza (Interview with Yoshio Futagawa), op. cit., p. 56.

58 Luigi Spinelli, 'The Parish Church Complex of Marco de Canavezes, Portugal', *Domus*, no. 802, March 1998, pp. 19–21.

59 Álvaro Siza (Interview with Yoshio Futagawa), op. cit., p. 45.

60 While monumentality is the latest theme that runs throughout the evolution of the modern avant-garde, it emerges as a consciously revisionist approach after the Second World War in the 'Nine Points on Monumentality'; a polemic written by Siegfried Giedion, Jose Luis Sert and Ferdinand Léger in 1943, published in S. Giedion, *Architecture You & Me*, Cambridge, MA: Harvard University Press, 1958.

61 Álvaro Siza, *Siza: Architecture Writings*, op. cit. p. 43.

62 Ibid., pp. 102–3.

63 Ibid., pp. 23–5.

64 Ibid., pp. 29–30.

65 Ibid., p. 29.

66 Ibid., pp. 27–8.

67 Ibid., p. 40.

68 *Álvaro Siza 1958–1994*, *El Croquis*, op. cit., p. 18.

69 Modern hermeneutics took a particular turn with the publication of Hans Georg Gadamer's *Truth and Method* in 1960. To the extent that architecture is inseparable from the concerns of practical reason, Gadamer's discourse seems to have a particular relevance to the field at the end of the century. As Georgia Warnke writes at the end of her study, *Gadamer: Hermeneutic Tradition and Reason* (Stanford, CA: Stanford University Press, 1987, p. 174): 'The "cultured" individual is one who can place his or her life and concerns within a larger perspective or, to use Gadamer's term, "horizon" … Similarly, the *gebildete* culture is one that understands its place within a larger world community … In becoming cultured we do not simply acquire better norms, values, etc., we also acquire the ability to acquire them. In other words we learn tact, taste and judgement. Perhaps we cannot codify what we have learned as a method for adjudicating between beliefs; nonetheless, through the historical experience and conversation with others that are part of a self-formation … we can learn to think. And this practical reason thus substitutes for the dogmatism of the Enlightenment'.
70 Álvaro Siza, *Siza: Architecture Writings*, op. cit., p. 51.
71 Ibid., p. 88.
72 Vittorio Gregotti, in Álvaro Siza, *Professione poetica*, op.cit., pp. 187–8 (first published in *Contraspazio*, no. 9, September 1972).
73 Álvaro Siza, *Siza: Architecture Writings*, op. cit., pp. 32, 34.
74 Ibid., pp. 45–6.

Homage to Álvaro Siza
Fernando Távora

Porto, 1992
I like to use the expression 'builder of works of gravity' which, in a seventeenth-century Portuguese document, referred to the master of architectural practice. It is a very felicitous expression: the 'master' is the one who builds with stone or with another material; the work is a work of 'gravity', serious, important, significant, thoughtful.

It is not by chance that I take a particular interest in the question of gravity in architecture: just as we only become aware of our breath when we are short of air (as our great writer, Fernando Pessoa, put it), in the same way we become aware of gravity at the moment when it disappears.

Let us reflect on the term for a moment. 'Gravity' applies, precisely, to behaviour – a grave man, a grave action, a grave word. However, in its physical sense, 'gravity' refers to a force which locates us, which gives us weight and ensures that we stand vertically (Aristotle wrote that man is the only animal whose axis meets the centre of the earth).

This means that behavioural, moral or intellectual gravity must be placed in relation to physical gravity, in that the two meanings of the term are complementary, and when we use the word we evoke both the notion of weight and of intelligent and thoughtful action. Let us not forget that gravity, physical or plastic, contributes significantly to the temporal or symbolic stability of architecture.

I have said that the question of gravity in architecture interests and preoccupies me because it strikes me that in our own time gravity is beginning to be in short supply, like breath.

There are plenty of 'builders': more and more of them and they are more ambitious, but there are few 'builders of works of gravity'.

We live in a difficult and complex world, in which the rulers and the ruled, grandiose projects and petty actions, stand in opposition to one another.

In the case of Portugal, the issue is aggravated by apprehension and by the claims with which we confront the modern world. We have engaged in a bitter struggle, running after a train which left long ago without waiting for us, and which we will not easily climb aboard, notwithstanding the few million escudos of funding set aside for the purpose. Personally, I maintain that our capacity to understand the meaning of gravity, as Portuguese people and, in this specific case, as architects, is under threat. Much of our architecture, in the broadest sense, is wearing itself out in its unsuccessful attempts to conquer the problem. The references, the proper gravity, have vanished; the axis no longer touches the centre of earth, not even the heart of man. It acquiesces in the sad and facile adventure of form for form's sake, the guaranteed success of images, the pleasure produced by facile sensations. It ignores the essential and cultivates the accessory, it chooses individual fame over the defence of human, social and spiritual values. It prefers bombast to eloquence, ornament to structure, error to intelligence. It seems to me that, like astronauts, we are walking in an atmosphere without gravity, without weight or references, indifferent to top or bottom, horizontal or vertical, without north or south. Deceived by a facile simulacrum of richness, we forget our deepest thoughts, our social obligations, our values, whether they be those that our fathers have handed down to us or those that still remain to be created. And all of this occurs even if we never stop talking about it, but lack any conviction or desire to act.

We might, for example, consider our own land; the autocrats lovelessly tear it to pieces, burning forests, killing rivers, polluting dwellings. The madness of men, and the madness of the spaces they make, try to outdo one another; speculation, ugliness and discomfort are all the rage.

But in that case is it right, on this 1 July 1992, World Architecture Day, for an old professional – perhaps disillusioned, perhaps mistaken, perhaps superannuated – to describe the Portuguese situation in such pessimistic terms? Maybe it isn't, but even my proverbial and well-known optimism are not enough to prevent me from seeing what is happening, nor to make me change, in the slightest, my description of the situation that has come about in Portugal.

It remains the case, however, that we still have Portuguese people and a particular architecture in our country. Let us now applaud Álvaro Siza, who is an example of that architecture, and who practises this art in an excellent way.

A genuine 'builder of works of gravity', he is a committed professional, who has given wholeheartedly of himself. His work deserves gratitude on an international level for the integrity that he demonstrates with his capacity for both deep roots and transformation, animated by a superior intelligence and an almost unique sensibility. 'Builder of works of gravity', I repeat, is an expression that applies perfectly to Álvaro Siza, a great builder of spaces and magnificent images, the creator of an extremely complex body of work (because it is always identical to itself, and always different), but one which is profoundly simple and endowed with a great creative force.

So I am paying homage to him: a homage that is simple, direct, grateful, friendly, emotional. So, today, in Porto on 1 July, let us perform a much-needed duty and express a hope: that his work (even beyond its own value, and on condition that it is properly understood and interpreted, and that it is not subject to facile and gratuitous imitations) may represent a sure alternative 'to the base and cocooned sadness' that surrounds us. Álvaro Siza is an architect 'of gravity', powerful and Portuguese.

Originally published in Italian in M. Faiferri (ed.), *Álvaro Siza Progetti e Opere*, Rome: Edilstampa, 1998.

Complete Works
1952–1999

1952 Kitchen for Grandmother's House *Matosinhos, Portugal*

Most of my designs have never been realized. Some of them have only been partially completed, others have been profoundly altered or even abandoned. One must make allowances for this.

An architectural study that seeks to take its place within existing innovative trends, among the conflicts and tensions that characterize reality – a study that tries to be more than a purely passive transcription of reality, refusing to place limits on that reality, and analysing each of its aspects, one by one – cannot be based on static images, it cannot follow a linear evolution.

For the same reason, such a study cannot be ambiguous, it cannot be reduced to a disciplinary discourse, however correct it might seem to be.

Each of my designs seeks to capture, with the utmost rigour, a single concrete moment of a fleeting image, in all its nuances. To the extent to which one manages to capture that fleeting quality of reality, the design will emerge more or less clearly, and the more precise it is the more vulnerable it will be.

These reasons must be why only marginal works (a residence in a quiet place, a holiday home far away from everything) have been realized as they were originally designed.

This is the result of participation in the process of cultural transformation which includes construction and destruction. But something of all this remains. Fragments realized here and there, kept within us, marks left in space and in people, pieces which someone will later pick up, which will melt into a process of total transformation.

Then we put those pieces together, creating an intermediate space and transforming it into an image, and we give it a meaning, so that each image has a significance in the light of the others.

In this space we can find the final stone and the final conflict. We transform the space in the same way as we transform ourselves: through pieces confronted with 'others'.

The landscape – as the dwelling-place of man – and man – as the creator of the landscape – both absorb everything, accepting or rejecting that which had a transitory form, because everything leaves its mark on them. Starting off with isolated pieces, we seek the space that supports them.

I have been asked to speak about my professional work. I have written a few lines, eight points, almost at random.

1. I start a design when I visit a site (the schedule and the conditions are vague, as almost always happens). Other times I start earlier, from the idea I have of a site (a description, a

photograph, something I have read, something I have overheard). This does not mean that much is kept from a preliminary sketch. But everything starts somewhere. A site is valid for what it is and for what it could be or wants to be – sometimes these are opposing things, but they are never unrelated. Much of what I have designed in the past (as much of what others have designed) rises and falls within the first sketch. In a confused way. So much so that little remains of the site which evokes it all. No site is a desert. I might always be one of the inhabitants. Order is the bringing together of opposites.

2. It is said that I design in cafés, that I am an architect of small works (having had a go at the other kind I think: if only it were not so, they are the most difficult). It is true that I design in cafés but I do not do so like Toulouse Lautrec in cabarets, or for some Prix de Rome, amongst the ruins. The atmosphere of a café neither inspires nor transports you. But it is one of the few places – here in Porto – where you can remain anonymous and concentrate. It is not a matter of avoiding the conference table, avoiding interdisciplinary discussions, the telephone, the regulation forms, the catalogues of prefabricated components or facilitating tools that make so many things so much easier, the computer or the neighbourhood meeting. It is to overcome – and that is the word – the bases for working with this and for this. (How many cafés I have frequented; I move on when I notice I am getting special attention along with my tea and coffee.)

3. Some of my latest projects have involved lengthy discussions with organized groups of residents or future residents. There is nothing new about that. I have worked like that in other circumstances, or I have wanted to. In the Portugal which emerged from the revolution of 1974 it was not however a case of wanting to or not. Once the prisons had been opened, the struggle for housing in Porto, in Lisbon, or in the Algarve went far beyond the limits of the house, the district and the cooperative. It took possession of the city. A brief episode. Once it is taken on as a method, what is a movement degenerates into a comfortable alibi, an alienating moderator, reluctant to take the plunge into the reformulation of the desire – our desire or that of others.

4. It is said that my works, both recent and those made some years ago, are based on the traditional architecture of the region. Yet even with these works I encountered the resistance of workmen and the anger of passers-by. Tradition is a challenge to

innovation. It consists of successive inserts. I am a conservative and a traditionalist – that is to say, I move between conflicts, compromises, hybridization, transformation.

5. They tell me that I do not have a supporting theory or method. That nothing I do points the way. That it is not educational. A sort of boat at the mercy of the waves which inexplicably does not always get wrecked (which is another thing they tell me). I do not expose the boards of our boats too much, at least not on the high seas. Excesses tend to smash them to bits. I study the currents, eddies, I make sure I know where the inlets are before taking a risk. I can be seen alone, walking the deck. All the crew and the equipment is there, the captain is a ghost. I dare not put my hand on the helm, when the pole star is barely visible. And I do not point out a clear way. The ways are never clear.

6. I would not like to make what I design with my own hands. Nor design all on my own. That would make it sterile. The body – hand and mind and everything – does not end at the individual's body. And no part is autonomous.

7. My unfinished, interrupted, altered works have nothing to do with the aesthetics of the unfinished, nor with a belief in the open work. They have to do with the enervating impossibility of completion, with the obstacles I cannot manage to overcome.

8. I discuss with a workman how to lay a 30 x 30 mosaic on an irregularly shaped floor: on the diagonal (as I propose) or parallel with one of the walls. He tells me: 'In Berlin we do not do it the way you say.' I return to the site the next day. 'You were right. It is easier to do it this way,' the workman tells me. We agree on the same point: to build in the most practical and rational way, as happened – if only we could fly back in time – at the Parthenon or at Chartres, or at the Casa Milá. And today: to rediscover the magical strangeness, the peculiarity of obvious things.

1954–7 Four Houses *Matosinhos, Portugal*

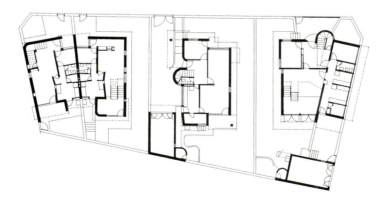

73 plan

1956–9 Parish Centre *Matosinhos, Portugal*

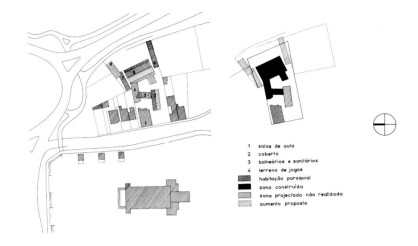

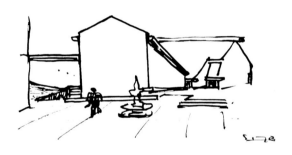

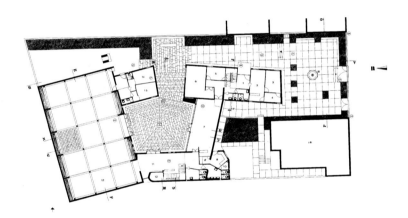

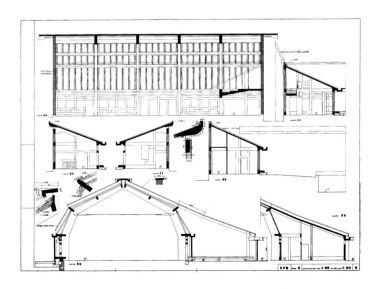

76   site plan, sketch, plan, long and cross sections

1956   Design for Low-Cost Housing *Matosinhos, Portugal*

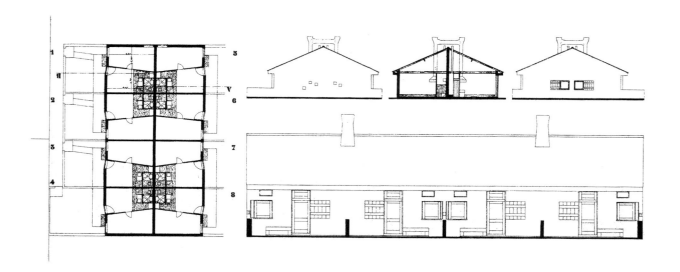

1957–9   Carneiro de Melo House *Porto, Portugal*

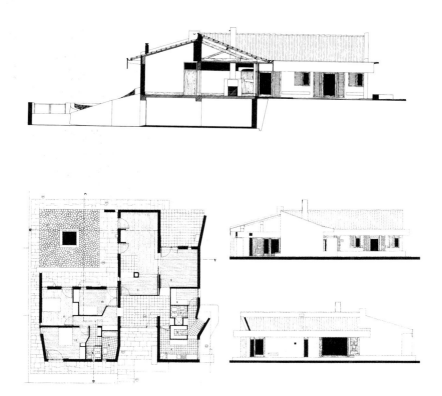

above plan and elevations *below* section, plan, south and north elevations

Leça da Palmeira
Álvaro Siza

I remember going to Valencia as a child: I felt the sensation of reaching the limits of the city and being embraced by an orchard of orange trees. Today, on the other hand, in South America there are vast cities that give the sense of having no limits at all. Anyone travelling through Buenos Aires and moving away from the centre will experience the sensation that the city is interminable. What disappears is the sense of continuity of the landscape in relation to the city; it is a terrible phenomenon and one that is becoming increasingly apparent, particularly in developing countries. This otherness, however, is fundamental to any project.

The anxiety that arises from this is expressed in my first buildings along the coastal road of Leça da Palmeira. This area was actually characterized by the presence of an edge. A retaining wall surrounds the beach and the cliff, facing the Atlantic. The landscape was almost untouched, because a decree issued by the coastguard prevented any building work.

The first project, for the Boa Nova Restaurant, was developed for a competition held by the town of Matosinhos in 1956. The site was chosen because of its rocky promontory. The place is in a sense predestined, apart from anything because in the memory of the inhabitants it is connected with the life of the local poet Antonio Nobre. The extraordinary beauty of the location is likely to intimidate an architect who is, as I was, just starting out. As recent experiences have demonstrated, to build in a particularly beautiful site is often to destroy that site.

The project developed out of the attention paid to the natural equilibrium of the area, which stretches between a small church and a lighthouse further away. However, the restaurant is not a tall building, whether because of the nature of the building, or to avoid clashing with the dimensions of the church. The objective of the project was not to compete with this presence, at the same time ensuring that the building was not without character, and reconciling the autonomy of the new building with its pre-existing surroundings. In its initial phases, the building was to follow the contour of the rocks, almost as though anchored to them. Only subsequently, after we had noticed the excessive, perhaps immature, discontinuity of its profile, I opted for a practically horizontal roof, while the articulation of the various functions was adapted to the contour of the rocks. This initial experience turned out to be important in refining my sensitivity to the coherence of architectural expression and its context. A few years later, the municipality of Matosinhos decided to build a swimming pool a few hundred metres south of the restaurant, still along the coast. They selected a site where the rocks formed a small lake and the project was given to an engineer, the brother of Fernando Távora. Having understood the impact that the building was liable to have on the landscape, he decided to collaborate with an architect and suggested my name to the council. Távora's brother had designed a swimming pool closed in by four walls. My project, however, sought to exploit as far as possible the natural conditions which had, so to speak, already started to design the swimming pool, making use of the cliff and complementing its natural basins with such walls as were strictly necessary. In this way we managed to integrate the landscape and the building, but the ensemble, thanks to our earlier experience, was clearer and more autonomous in its definition.

An architecture of taut lines and long walls sought to achieve an encounter with the rocks; the aim was to draw a geometry out of the surroundings, or rather to determine its predisposition to accommodate a particular geometry. Architecture is about making geometry.

One crucial factor lay in resolving the problem of the entrance. There was very little depth because the road ran close to the coastline and a wall of plastered stone, a kilometre and a half long, separated the level of the road from the beach. The solution was found by designing zigzag paths so as to give the entrance to the complex a sense of great depth. At the same time, the variations in light produced by a gradual passage through the dimly-lit zones served as an introduction to the final stretch, in the open air. Here, high walls shielded the bathers against the light coming from the beach and a small bridge led along the shore to the sea, concluding the stretch modulated by the controlled use of light.

The shallowness of the area meant that the project favoured a longitudinal configuration, which is why, despite the fact that it stands a kilometre and a half away, the building becomes the ideal extension of the Boa Nova Restaurant. At this point it became clear that we would have to coordinate the development of the area. For that reason, in 1974, I developed an overall plan, although it was never adopted. Now that a great deal of time has passed, Boa Nova is a building marked by its age. If it does not seem at all dated, this is due to the fact that the character of the landscape inspires respect and prudence. Analysing its architectural configuration, one will see the clear influence of Alvar Aalto and, in particular, of the Viipuri library.

1958–63 Tea House, Boa Nova Restaurant *Leça da Palmeira, Portugal*

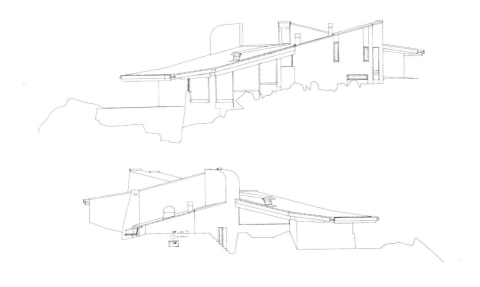

84   elevations

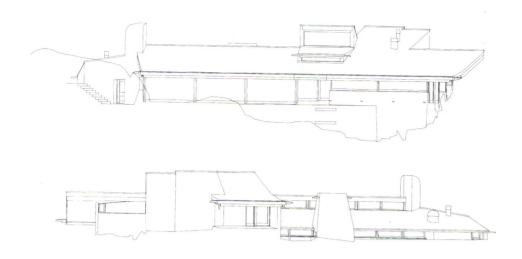

85   elevations

87

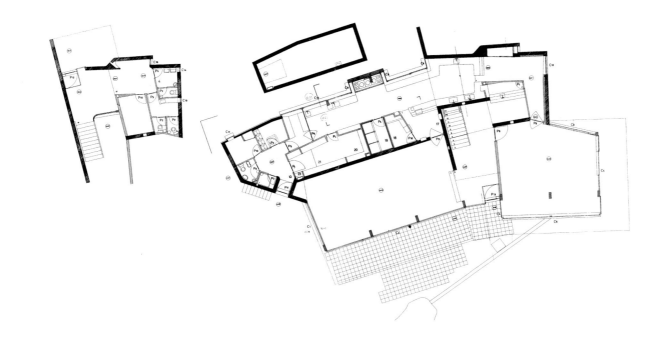

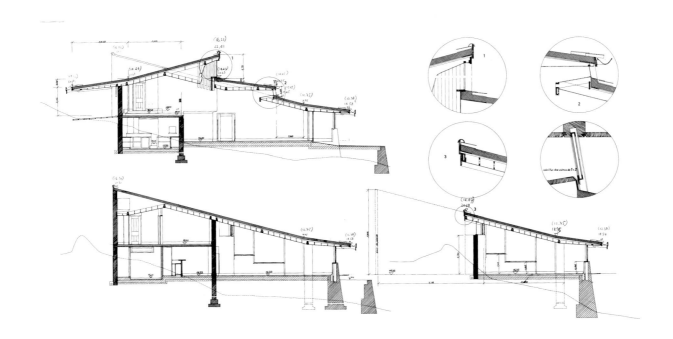

plans, cross sections and construction details

1958–65 Quinta da Conceição Swimming Pool *Matosinhos, Portugal*

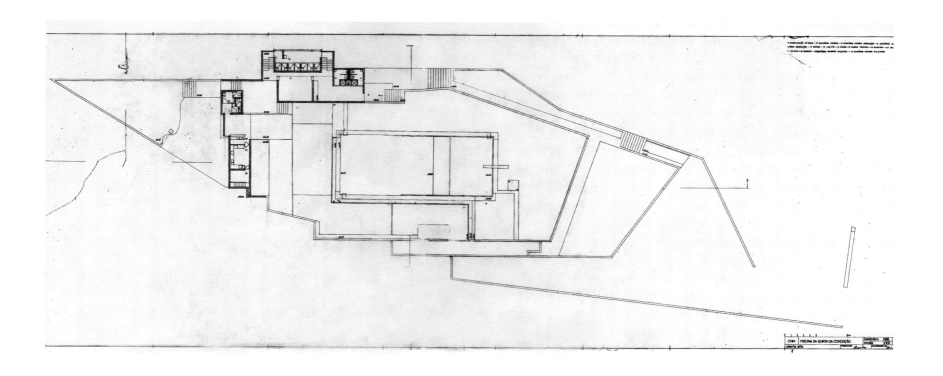

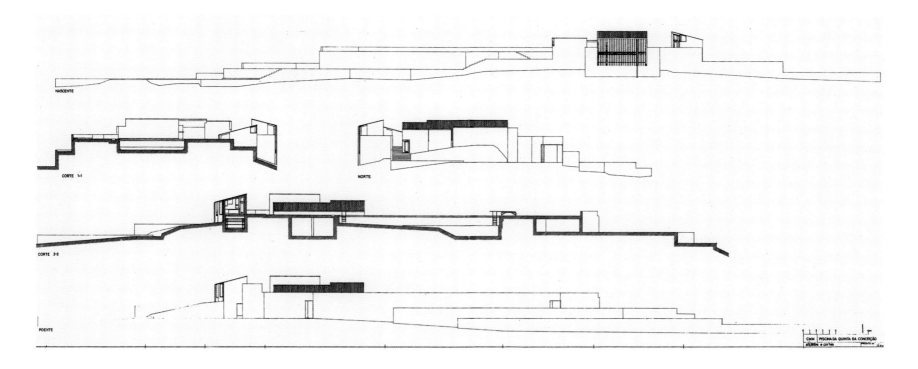

89 plan, elevations and sections

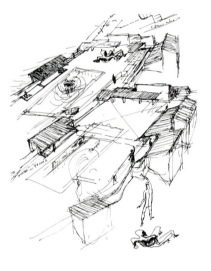

1959   Design for Monument to Aos Calafates (boat builder) *Foz, Porto, Portugal*

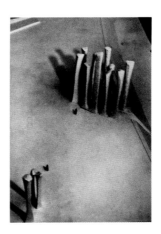
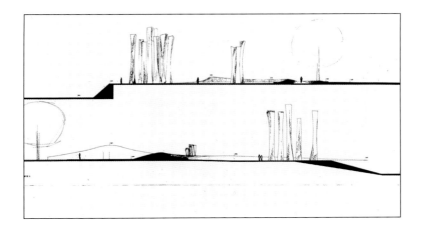

1960   Restaurant Design *Perafita, Matosinhos, Portugal*

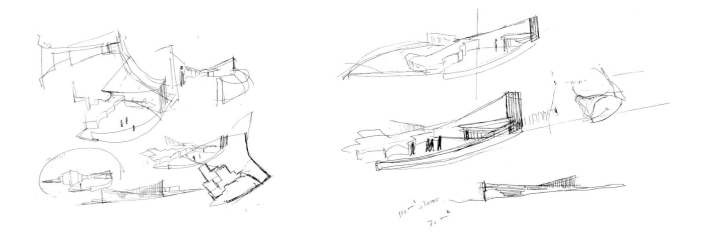

1960   Martins Camelo Family Grave at the Sendim Cemetery *Matosinhos, Portugal*

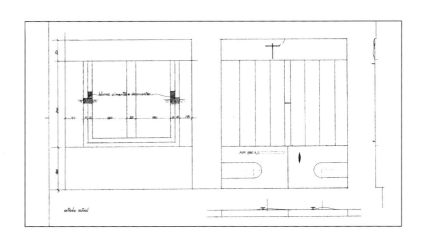

92   *above* sections and building details *centre* sketches *below* plan and sections

1960 Angola Oil Refinery Cafeteria *Matosinhos, Portugal* (demolished)

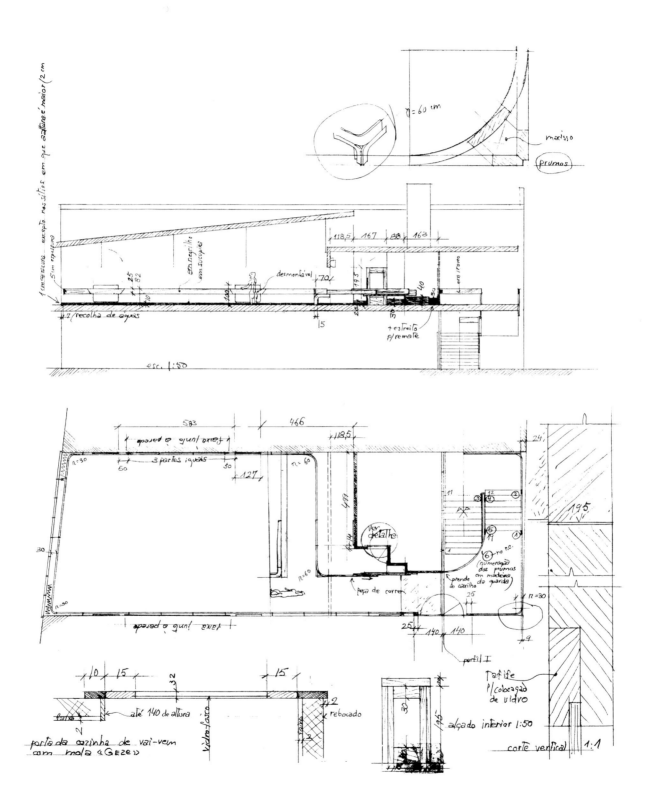

plan and sections

1960 Remodelling of Parents' House *Matosinhos, Portugal*

 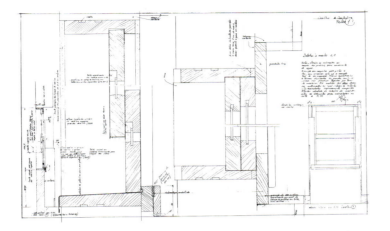

1960 Tennis Court Design for Senhora da Hora *Matosinhos, Portugal*

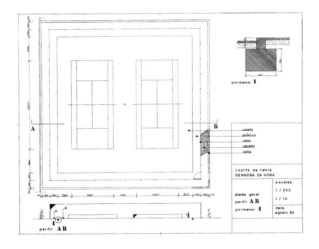

1961 Design for Doctor Júlio Gesta's House *Matosinhos, Portugal*

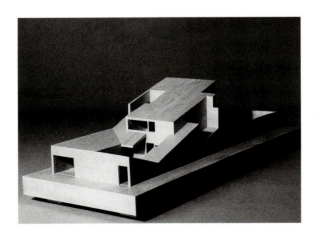 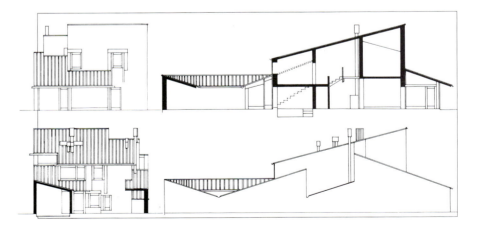

above building details *centre* plan and section *below* sections and elevations

1960–9 Luís Rocha Ribeiro House *Maia, Portugal*

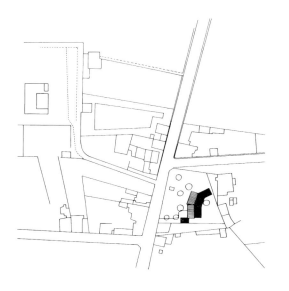
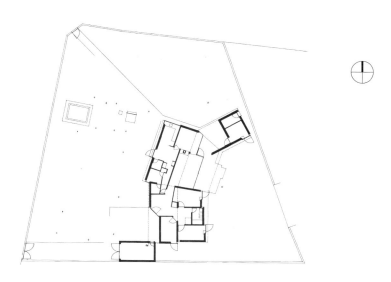

95 site plan and plan

1960–3 Lordelo Co-operative *Porto, Portugal*

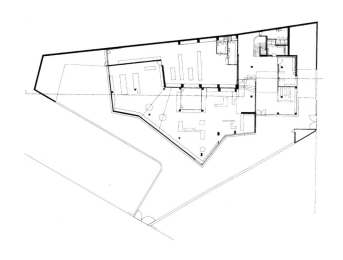
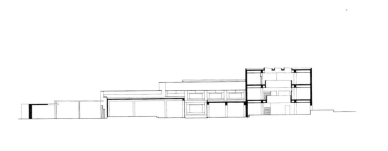

96 plan and section

1961–6 Ocean Swimming Pool *Leça da Palmeira, Portugal*

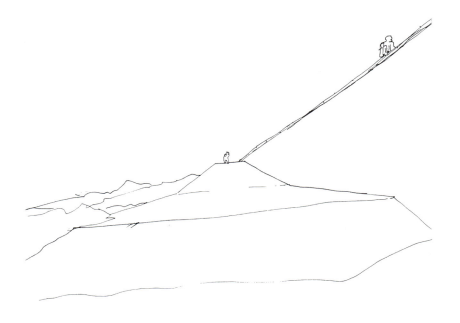

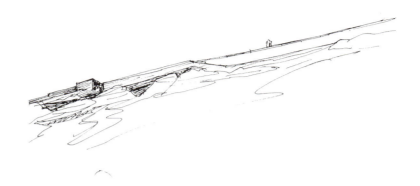

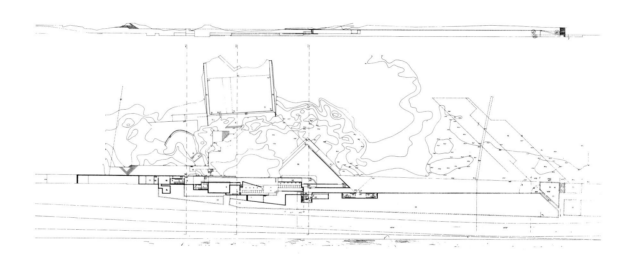
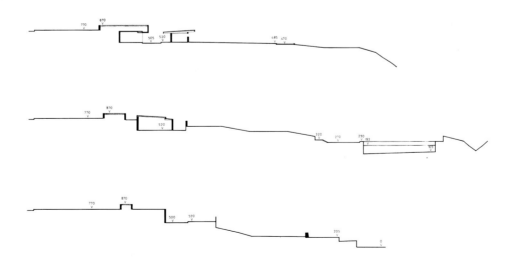

site plan, plan and cross sections

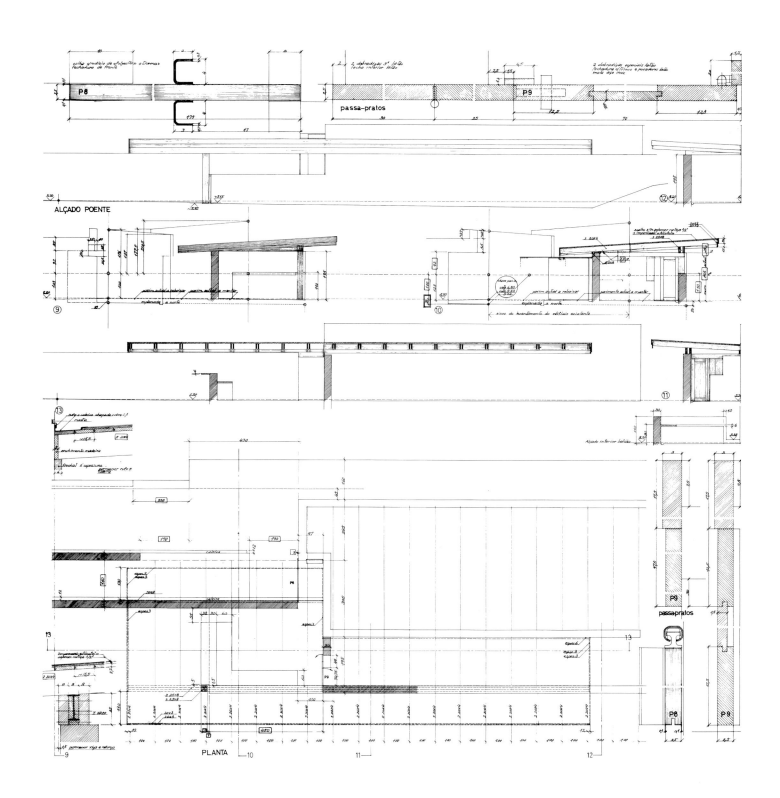

plans, sections and elevations

1962–5   Ferreira da Costa House *Matosinhos, Portugal*

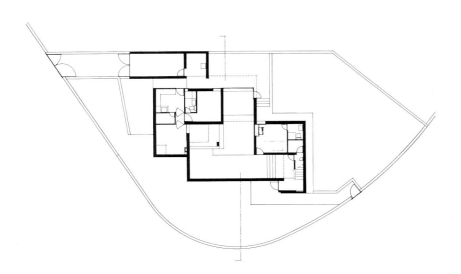
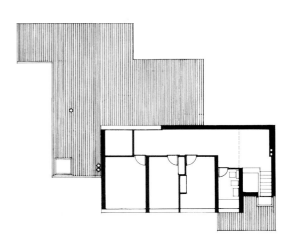

1963   Design for Rui Feijo House *Moledo do Minho, Portugal*

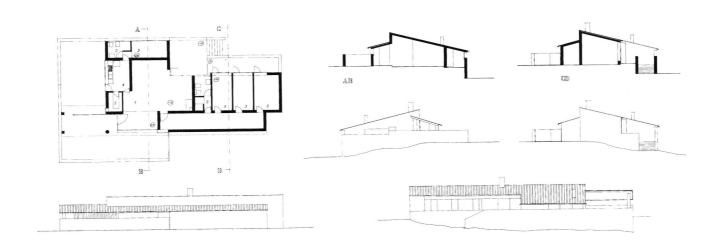

above plans *below* plan, elevations and sections

1964–70 Alves Santos House *Póvoa de Varzim, Portugal*

1965–74 Leça and Boa Nova Coastal Development Plan *Leça da Palmeira, Portugal*

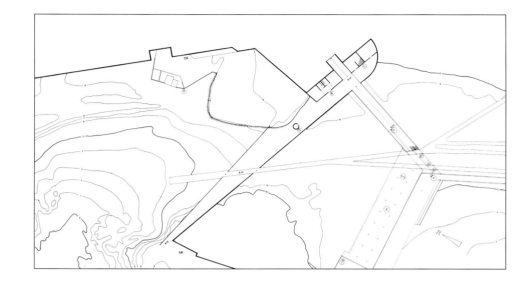

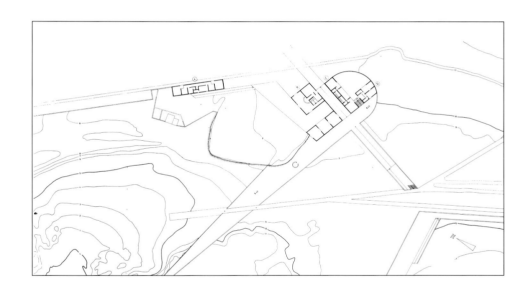

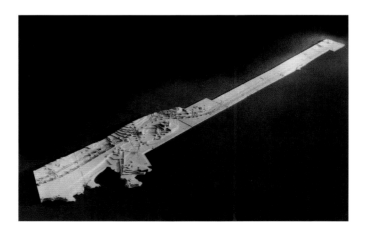

109   site plans

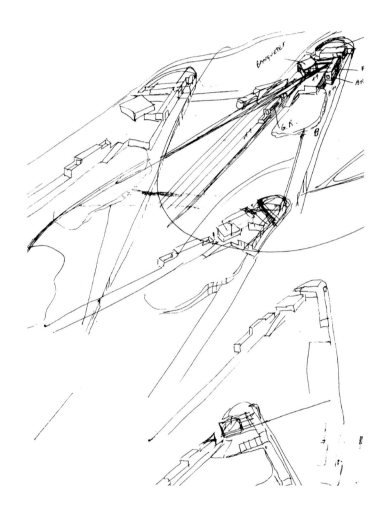

1966   Design for Adelino Sousa Felgueira House *Marco de Canavezes, Portugal*

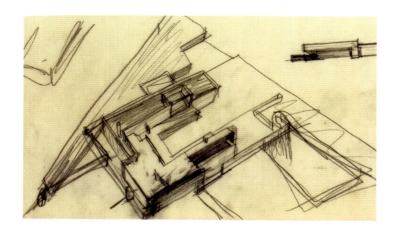
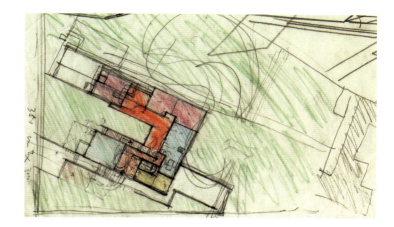

1966–70   Design for Sacor Petrol Station *Matosinhos, Portugal*

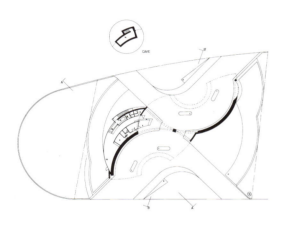
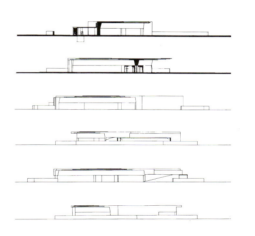

1966   Warehouse *Matosinhos, Portugal* (demolished)

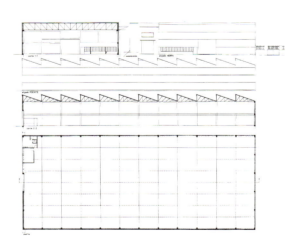

111   *above* sketches *centre* site plan, sections and elevations *below* plan, sections and elevations

1967 Hotel Design *Vale de Canas, Coimbra, Portugal*

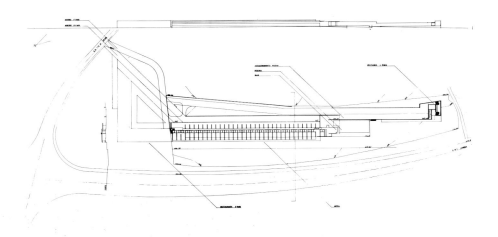

1966 Study for Ocean Swimming Pool Restaurant *Leça da Palmeira, Portugal*

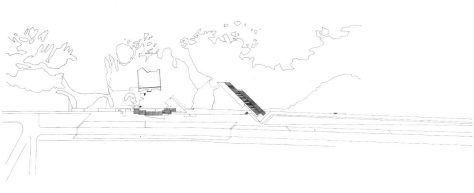
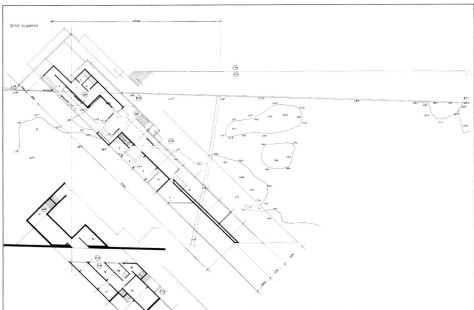

above site plan *below* site plan and plans

1967–80   Monument to Antonio Nobre (poet) *Leça da Palmeira, Matosinhos, Portugal*

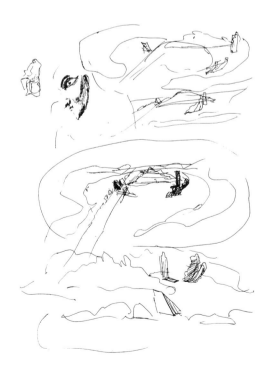

1967–70 Manuel Magalhães House *Porto, Portugal*

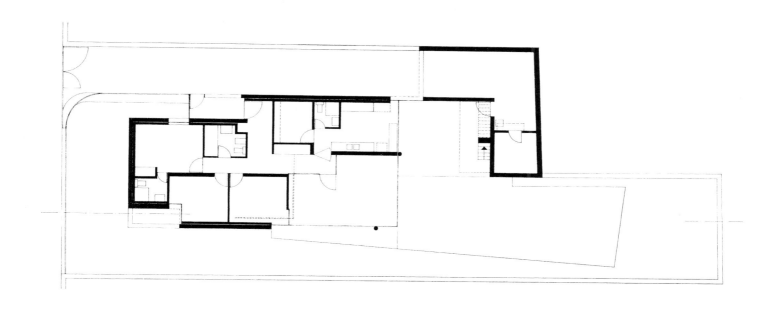
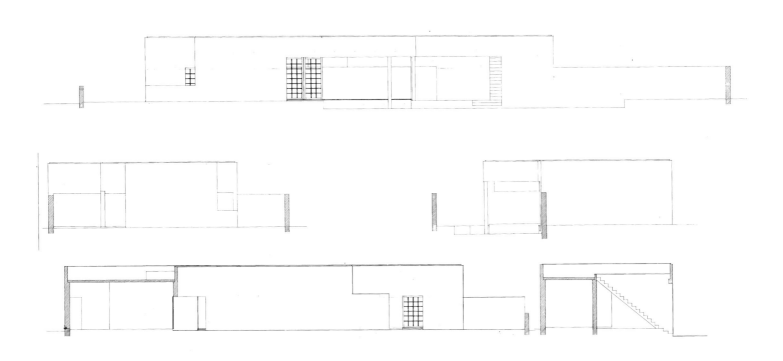

115 plan, elevations and sections

above view of Manuel Magalhães House from street

1968   Urban Development Plan for Avenida D. Afonso Henriques *Porto, Portugal*

1968   Studies for Carlos Vale Guimarães House *Aveiro, Portugal*

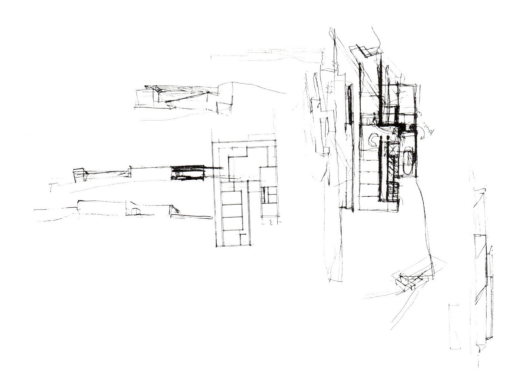

117   *above* site plan *below* plans

1968–74 Design for Office Building, Avenida D. Afonso Henriques *Porto, Portugal*

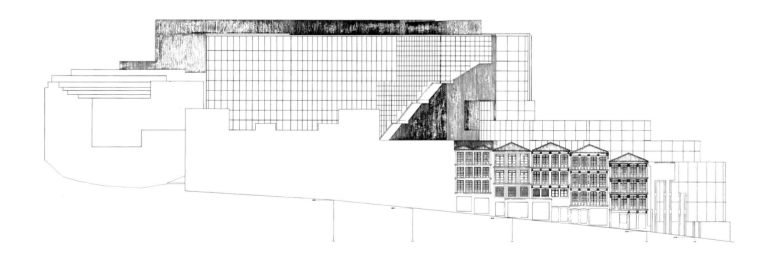

118   north elevation

1969–74 Borges & Irmão Bank I *Vila do Conde, Portugal*

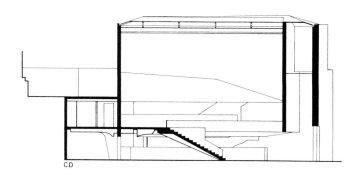
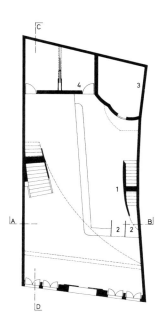
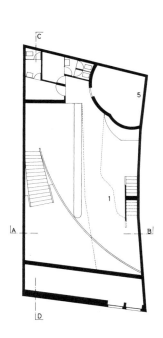
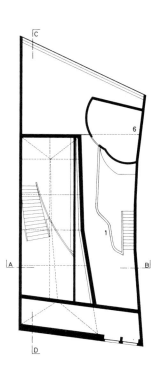

sections and plans

1969 Shop Facade Remodelling and Interior Design *Porto, Portugal* (modified)

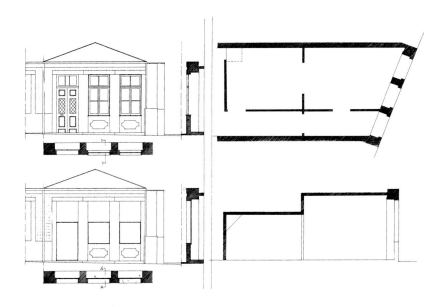

1970 Interior Design for Domus Co-operative *Porto, Portugal* (modified)

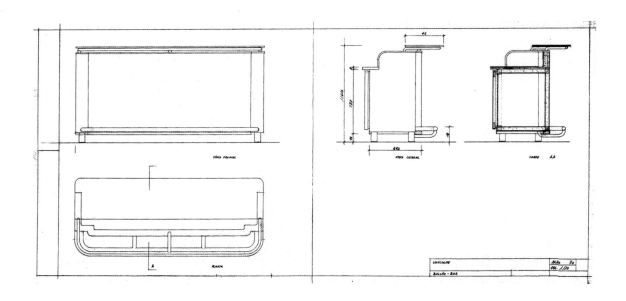

above original elevation and design elevation, plan and long section *below* plan and sections

1970–2 Study for Álvaro Bonifacio Housing Scheme *Ovar, Portugal*

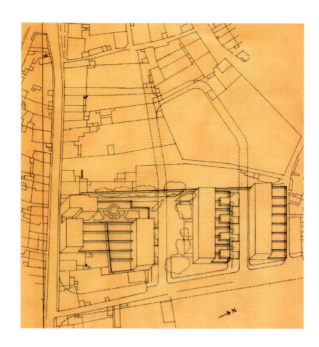

1971–2 Study for Mobil Oil Housing Complex *Matosinhos, Portugal*

123 *above* site plan *below* elevation

1970–2 Villa Cova Housing Complex *Caxinas, Vila do Conde, Portugal* (partially constructed and then modified)

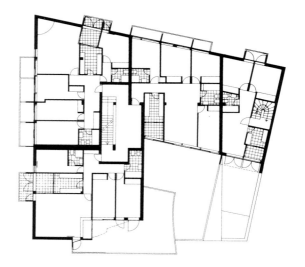
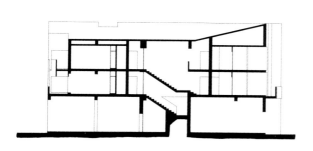
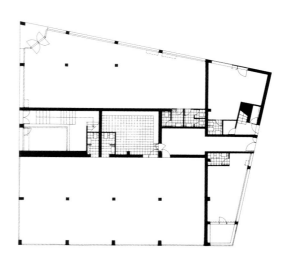

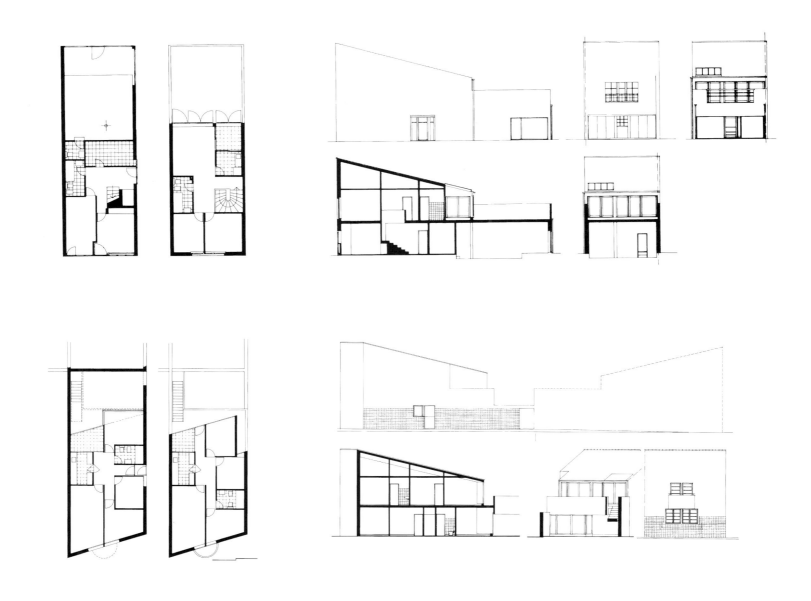

125 ground and first floor plans, elevations and sections

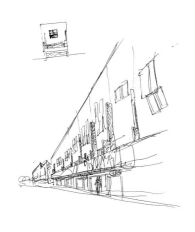

1971–3 Alcino Cardoso House *Lugar da Gateira, Moledo do Minho, Portugal*

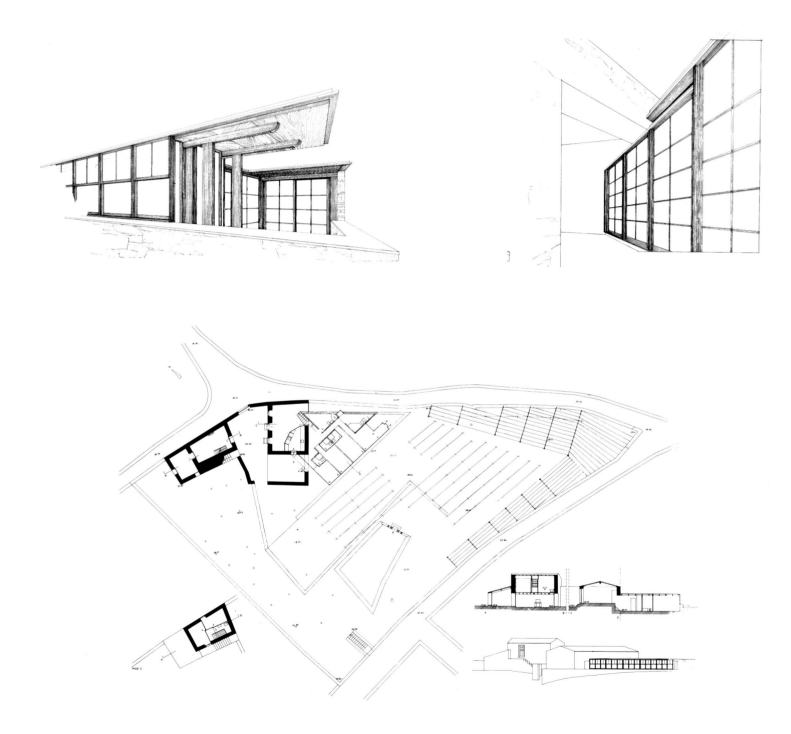

127 *above* perspectives *below* site plan, long section and elevation

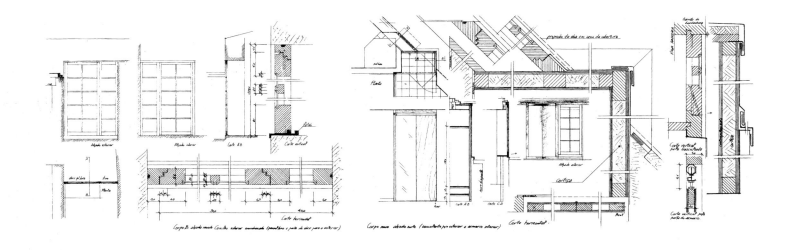
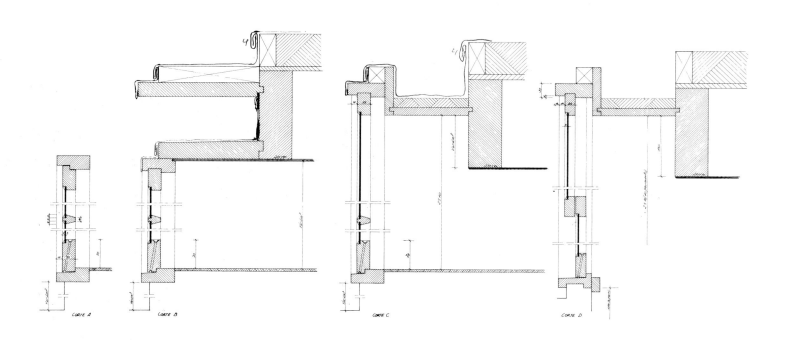

128　construction details

1971–4 Pinto & Sotto Mayor Bank *Oliveira de Azeméis, Portugal*

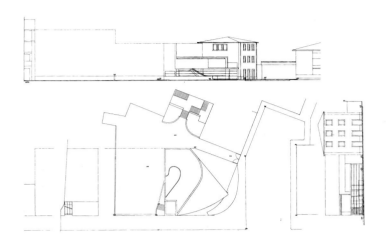

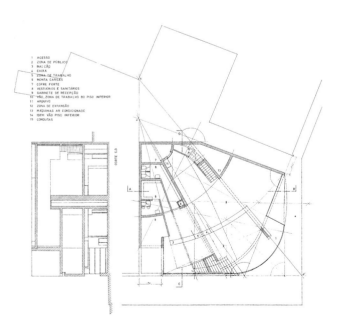
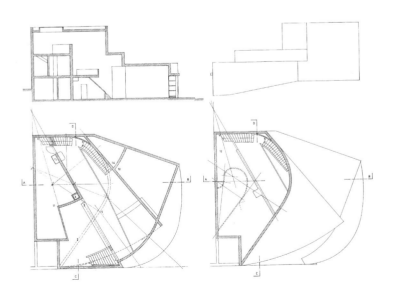

above plan and sectional elevations, roof plan and elevations *below* ground, first and second floor plans, sections and elevations

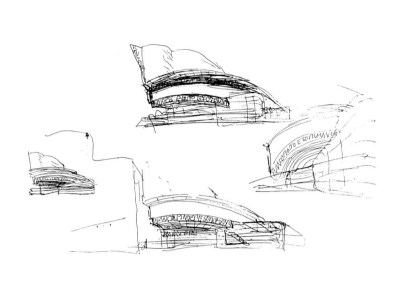
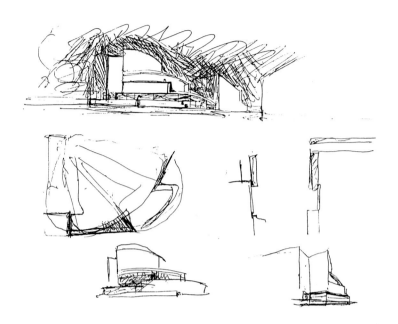
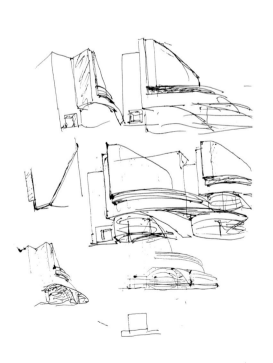

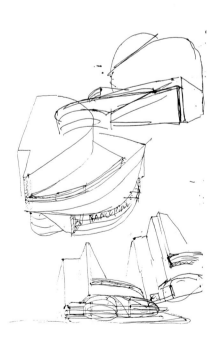

1972   Domus Co-operative Supermarket *Porto, Portugal* (modified)

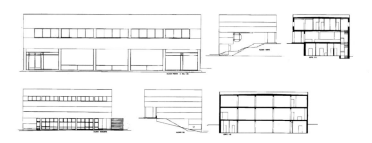

1972   Design for Marques Pinto House *Porto, Portugal*

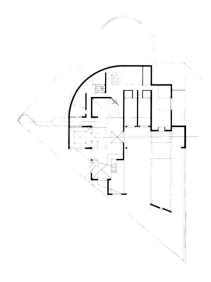

1972   Studies for Barbara de Sousa Housing Scheme *Ovar, Portugal*

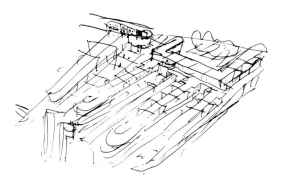

above ground, first and second floor plans, elevations and sections *centre* plans *below* sketches

1972–4   Pinto & Sotto Mayor Bank *Lamego, Portugal* (modified)

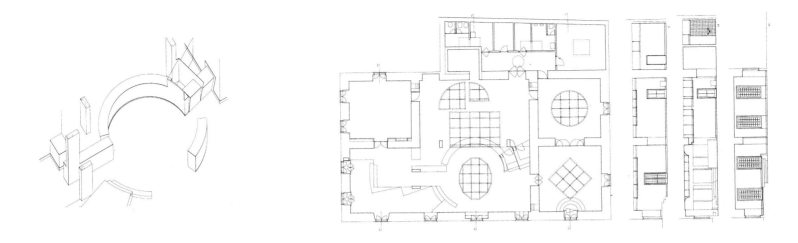

1972   Lamego Club *Lamego, Portugal*

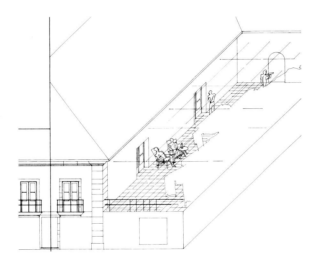

1972–3   Design for Pinto & Sotto Mayor Bank *Régua, Portugal*

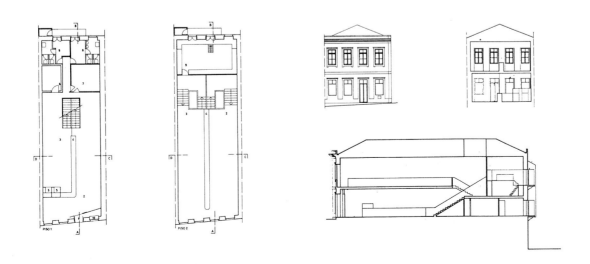

137   *above* axonometric, plan and sections *centre* axonometric *below* ground and first floor plans, elevations and section

1973   Study for Chapel in Rio Tinto *Gondomar, Portugal*

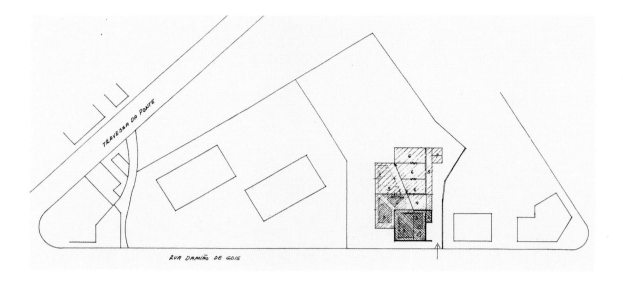

1973–4   Design for House in Azeitão *Setúbal, Portugal*

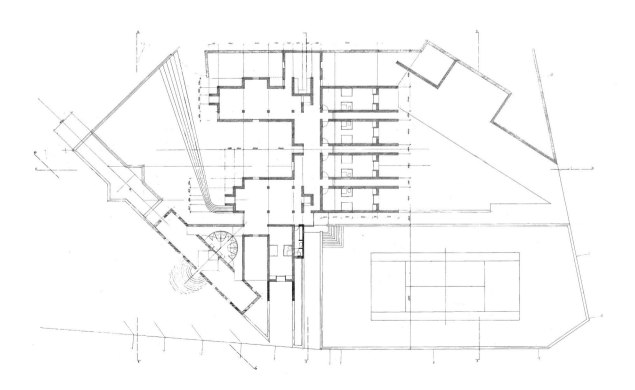

138   *above* site plan *below* plan

1973–4 Art Gallery *Porto, Portugal* (modified)

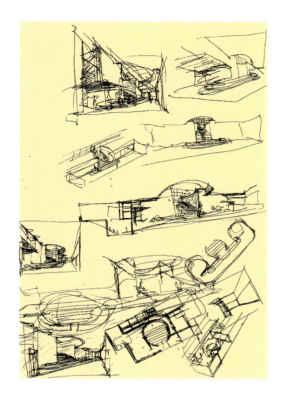

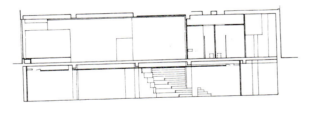
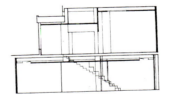
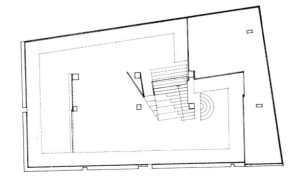
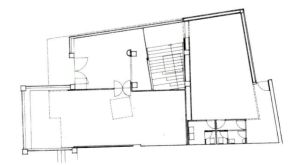

139 sketches, long section, cross section, ground and first floor plans

1973 Studies for Residential Complex for Housing Development Office *Bouça, Porto, Portugal*

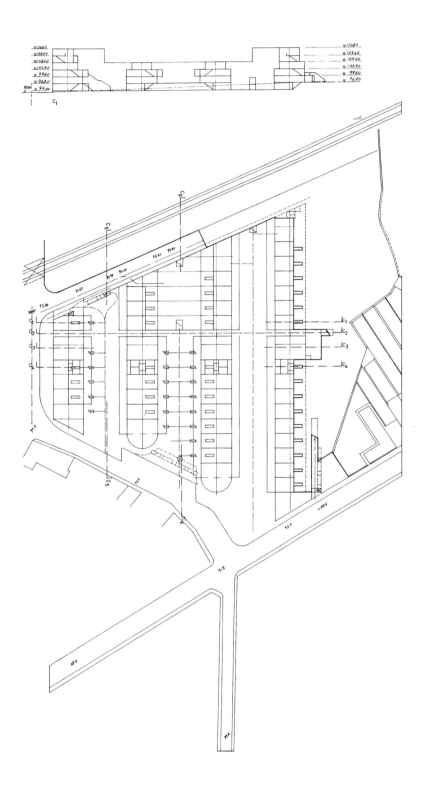

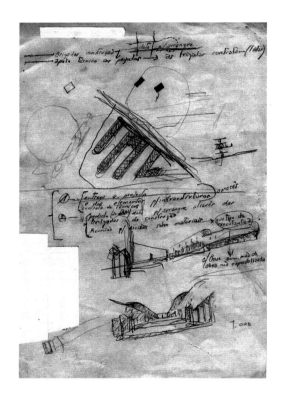

sketch, section and site plan

1973–6 Beires House *Póvoa de Varzim, Portugal*

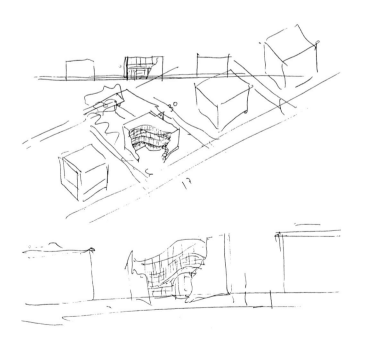

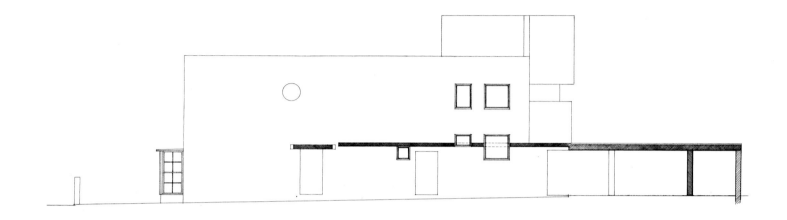
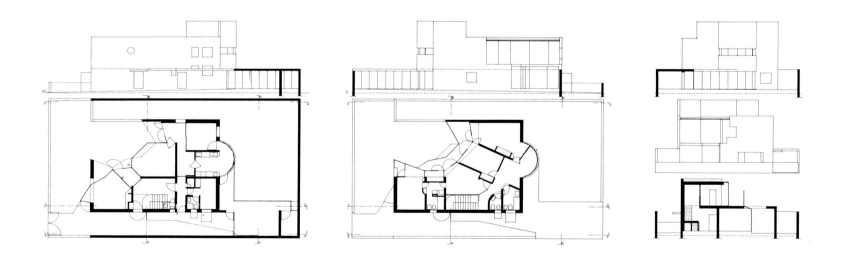

144 elevations, plans and sections

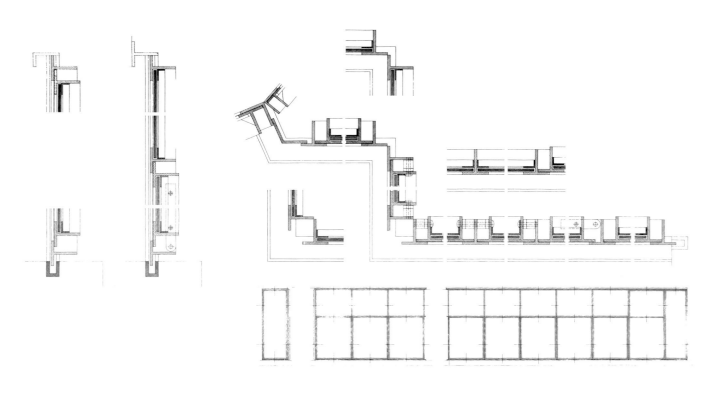
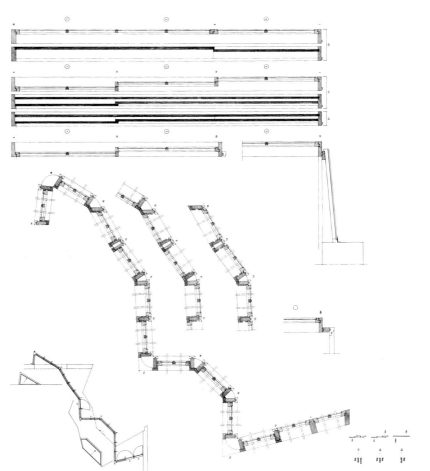

145 wall construction details

1974–9 SAAL Residential Complex *São Victor, Porto, Portugal*

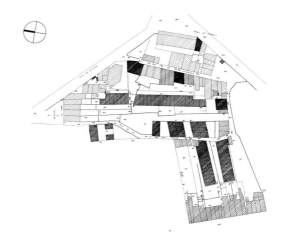

site plan

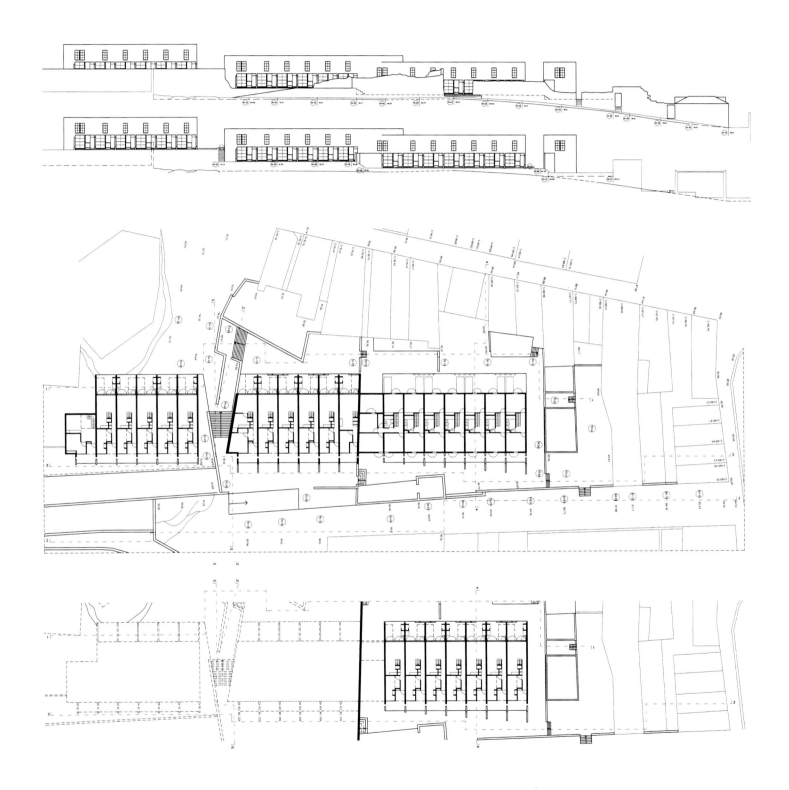

147 elevations and plans

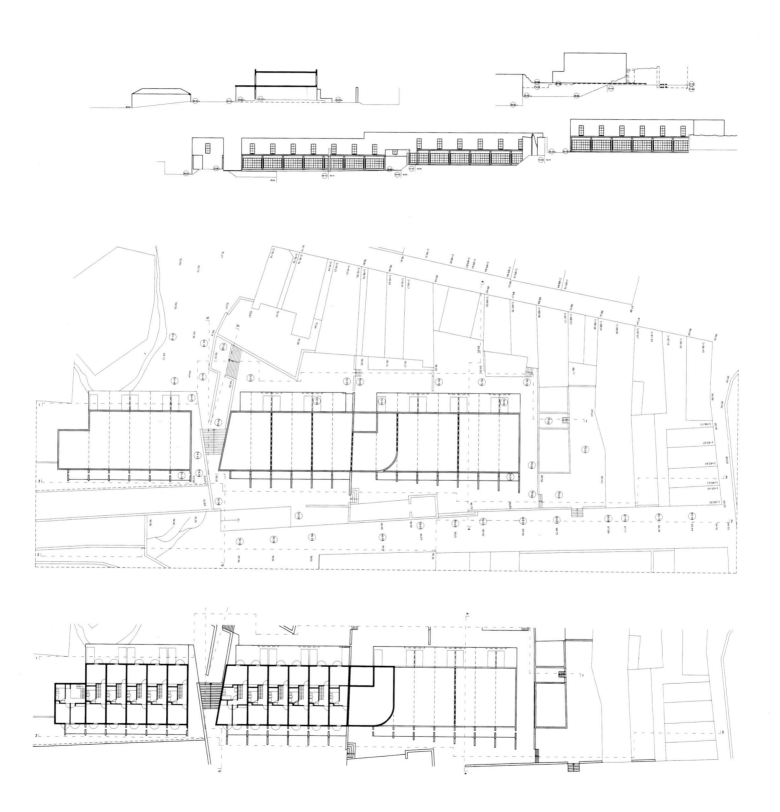

148　sections, elevations and plans

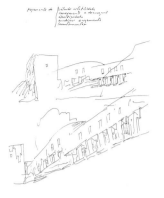

1975   External Staircase and Remodelling of Cálem House *Foz do Douro, Porto, Portugal*

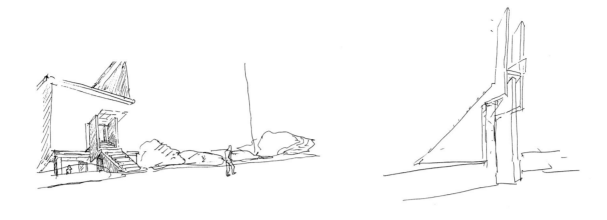

1975   Design for Paula Frassineti School *Porto, Portugal*

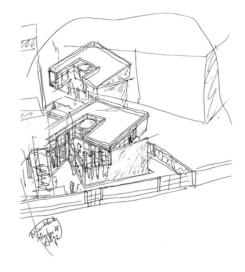

1975   Design for Pico do Areeiro Restaurant *Madeira Island, Portugal*

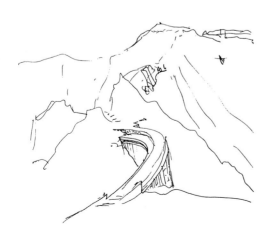 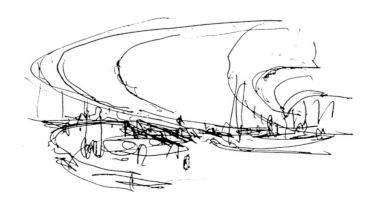

1975–7 SAAL Social Housing *Bouça II, Porto, Portugal*

152

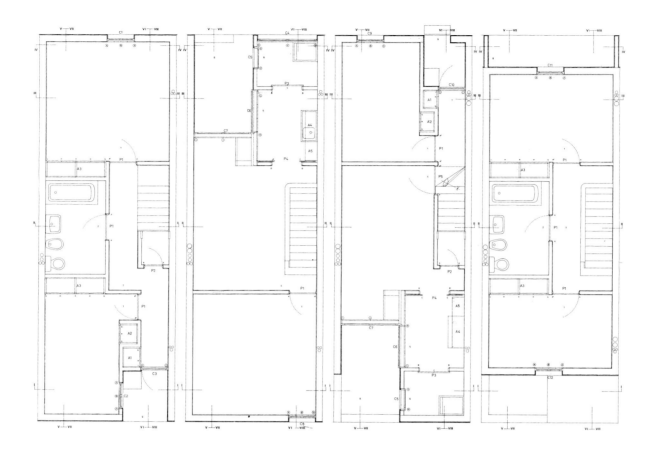

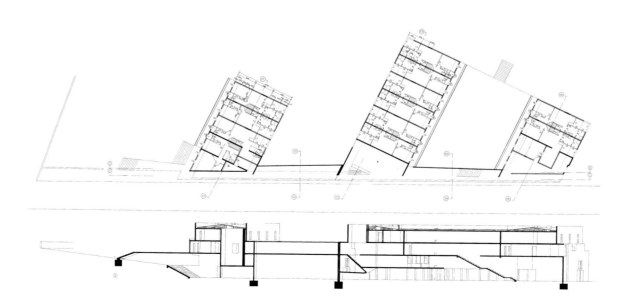

154 *above* ground, first, second and third floor plans *below* second floor plan and long section

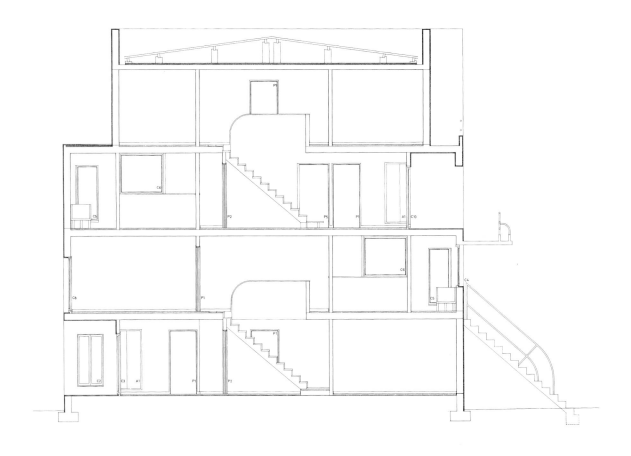
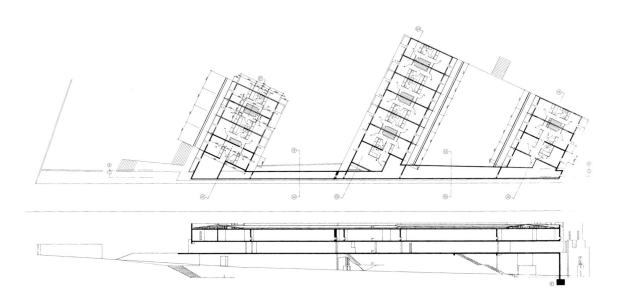

above cross section *below* third floor plan and long section

1976 Studies for Ribeira Market Stall *Porto, Portugal*

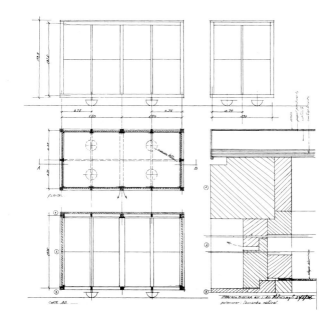

1976 Design for Reconstruction of Two Houses in the Barredo Quarter *Porto, Portugal*

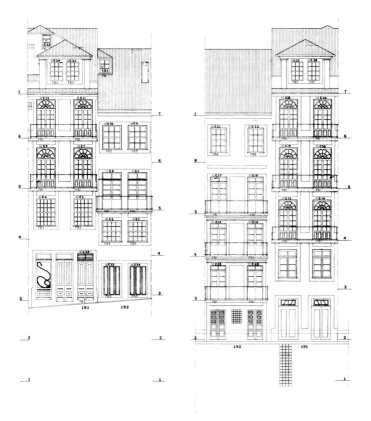

above construction details *below* elevations

1976   Urban Development Plan for Lada Square and Redevelopment of Barredo Quarter *Porto, Portugal*

1976   Design for Francelos House *Vila Nova de Gaia, Portugal*

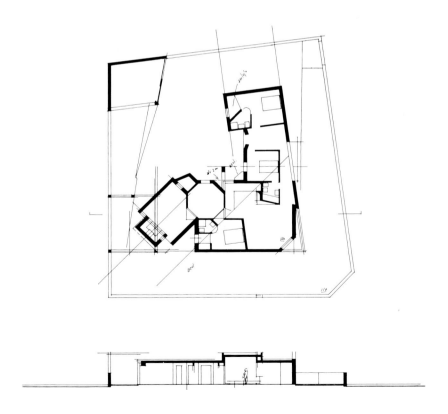

below plan and section

1976–8 António Carlos Siza House *São João de Deus, Santo Tirso, Portugal*

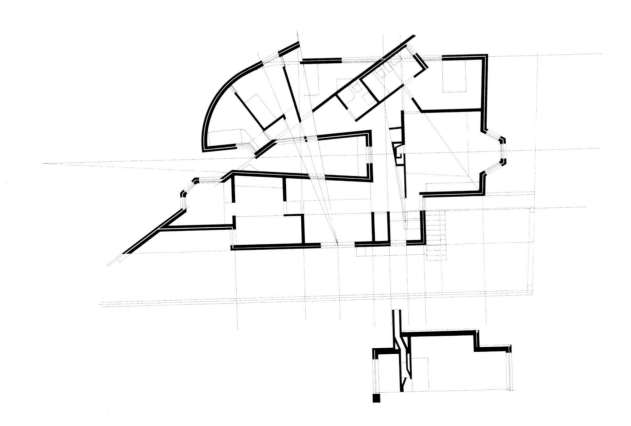

plan and section

Between the blocks and the aqueduct, I set aside some open spaces, intended for commercial activities at a later date. I wanted to avoid the location of new functions being alien to the neighbourhood's structure. The intersection between the principal and the secondary pipes thus allowed the creation of a series of interstitial spaces that multiply the possibilities of the project. Paradoxically, the most violent criticisms came from the interpretation of these spaces as incomplete places and I was accused of being incapable of finishing the work. In reality, my morphological concern with the complex was very real and these places are now beginning to be occupied.

A domed building will play a decisive role in this difficult definition of the dimensions of the buildings. Like the aqueduct, this building will occupy an intermediate area between the built fabric and the open spaces, and will be a privileged site of community life and an essential part of the city's development. It has not yet been built and, although the structural calculations have already been made (and are not expensive), any guarantee of its construction remains remote. Nevertheless, in a sense this domed building already exists, and slowly assumed its form during the design of elements of the small park, which will serve as its backdrop. At that point, the pipe is not separated from the urban grid, but is integrated with the houses. All these elements, together with the shape itself of the plot of land, help to distinguish the half-dome with precision. This space housed the tank and the cork oak, later destroyed by the bulldozers during construction. Both are still present in the memory and when the half-dome is built, will return to their positions.

The difficult construction of this second scale is essential for the integrity of the project. Recently, for example, it was suggested that the East-West axis be widened to accommodate traffic. This intervention, however, would destroy the integrity of the complex and the question of whether or not I continued my work in Évora rested upon the approval of this proposal. Any work must be prepared for changes and transformations, but cannot accommodate those which will lead to its destruction. There are certain interventions that a city cannot withstand; indeed, many contemporary cities demonstrate that, beyond a certain limit, resistance is no longer possible. Only someone aiming for finished and immediate readings of a city, someone who is incapable of reading between things, could believe that Malagueira is incomplete, with ill-defined or abandoned areas.

I have read many interpretations that generally associate vernacular Portuguese architecture with rationalism. I consider myself alien to this outlook and do not find it important. I think it is, first of all, necessary to study the economic and technical reasons of the context in which one intervenes. Apart from the limited funds which I mentioned before, the local building conditions in Alentejo were also a determining factor. In this region in southern Portugal, sparsely inhabited and characterized by large estates, most work has, until very recently, been seasonal. In Alentejo, local production progressed at a very slow pace, depending on manual techniques and materials, with the sole exception of public housing buildings, of which there were very few. This situation, in fact, thoroughly explains the excellent state of conservation of Évora and of the entire Alentejo, where there was no construction and no destruction: a kind of landowner's jewel. Houses were built with bricks fired in the sun, which are still made and used today. For my project, this method could not be used given the extent of the programme and, for this reason, traditional production was out of the question.

The last controversy was related to the flat roofs. Nevertheless, one of the reasons for the choice was the shortage of roofing tiles. Besides, to build the first hundred houses, the City Council of Évora had to co-sponsor an existing small factory that produced cement blocks. This explains the deficiencies in the building, since there was a shortage of skilled workers and technical know-how. From this perspective, the patio, which is certainly the result of historical influences, is explained by the need to create a micro-climate between the climactic conditions of the exterior and the interior, since the materials used did not give adequate protection to the rooms. The project cannot be understood if you ignore these facts. On the other hand, it must also be pointed out that the first hundred dwellings were designed for people who came from the country and who therefore still had rural values. Consequently the design of the house with a patio was influenced by many different models, not merely those which could be reduced to vernacular architecture or the modern movement.

1977–97 Malagueira Residential District *Évora, Portugal*

164　　site plan

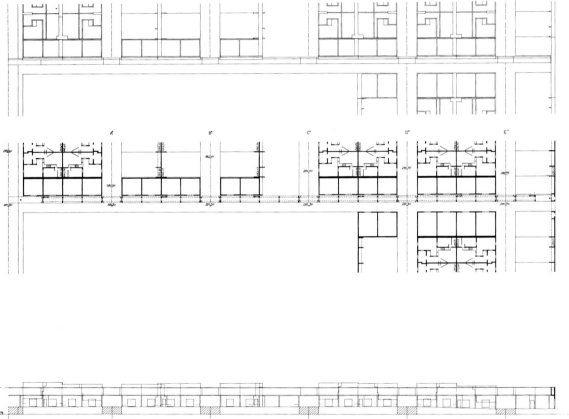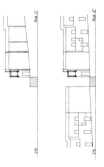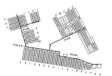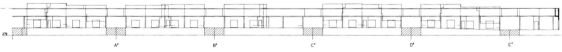

plans and elevations

1994 Design for Residential Complex *Malagueira, Évora, Portugal*

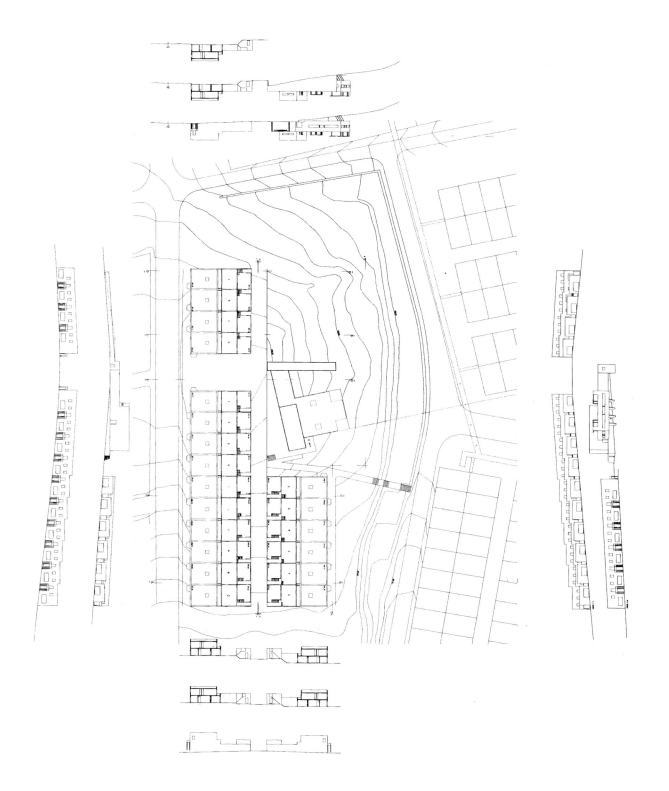

177 site plan, elevations and sections

1997 Design for Social Centre *Malagueira, Évora, Portugal*

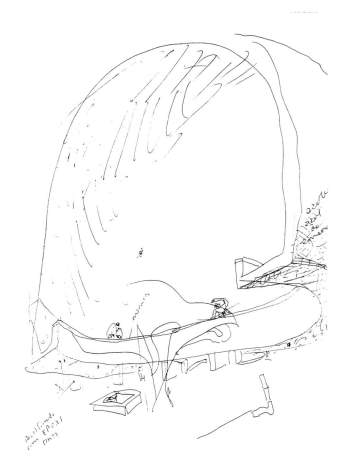

1977 Design for Borges & Irmão Bank *Vila do Conde, Portugal*

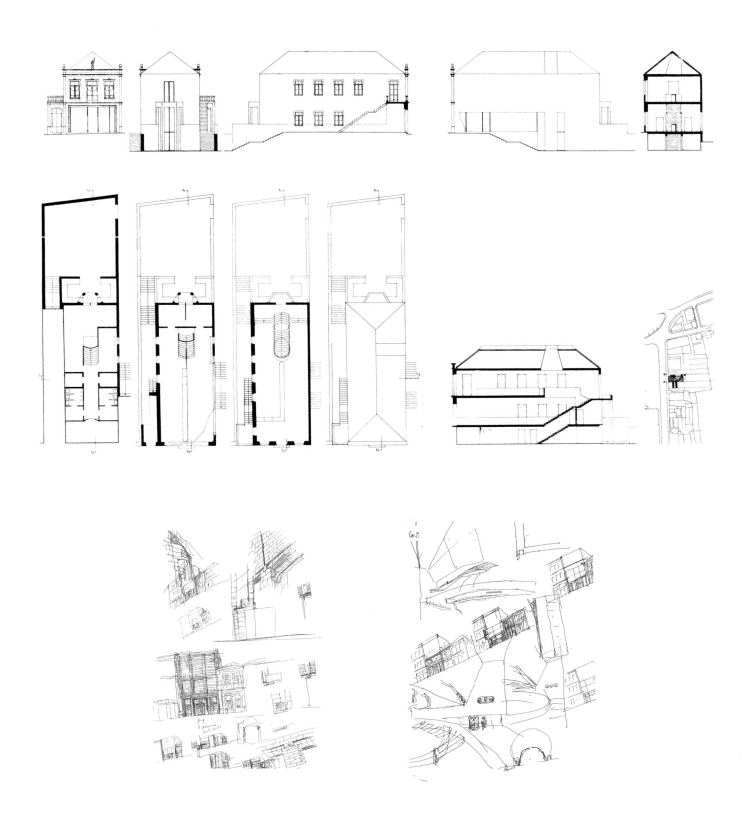

ground, first, second floor and roof plans, elevations and sections

1978–86 Borges & Irmão Bank *Vila do Conde, Portugal*

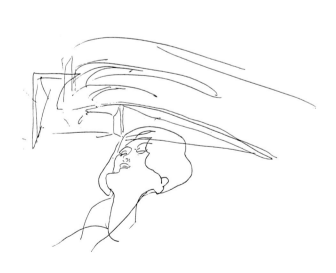

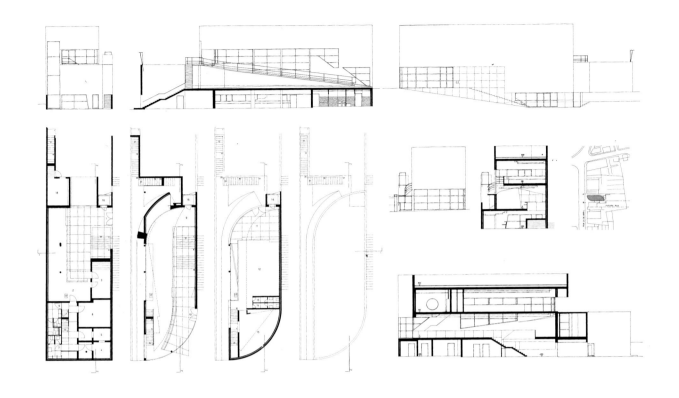
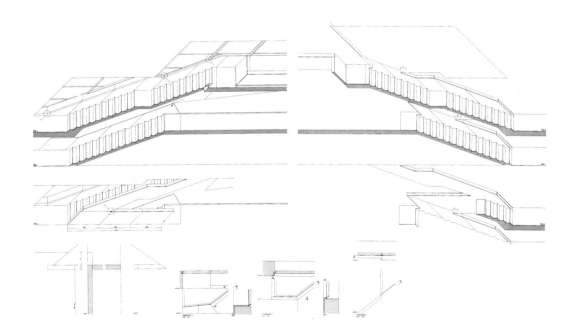

above ground, first, second floor and roof plans, elevations and sections *below* construction details

1979–86 J. M. Teixeira Apartment *Póvoa de Varzim, Portugal*

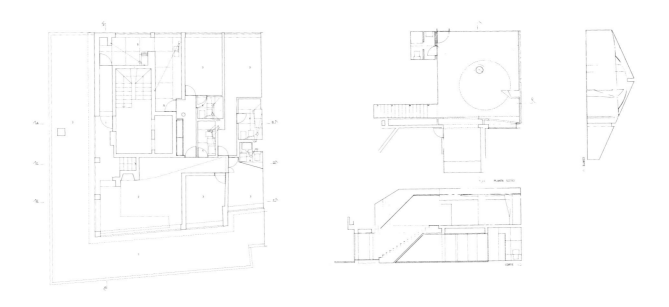

187 plans, long section and cross section

1979–87 Maria Margarida Aguda House *Arcozelo, Vila Nova de Gaia, Portugal*

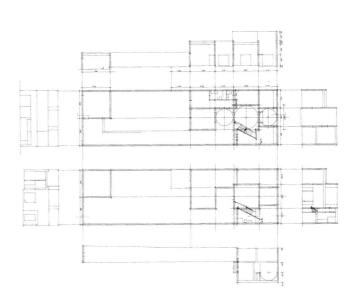

189 plans, sections and elevations

1979 Design for Fränkelufer Residential Complex *Berlin, Germany*

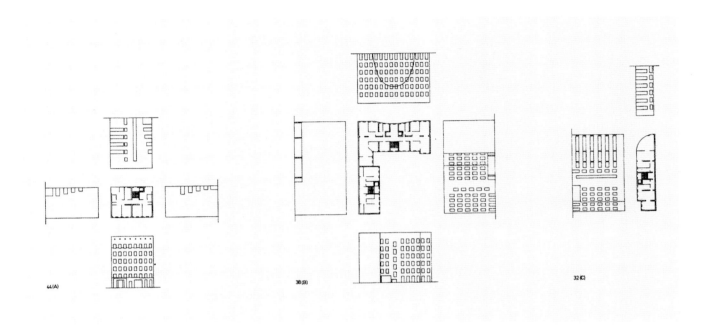

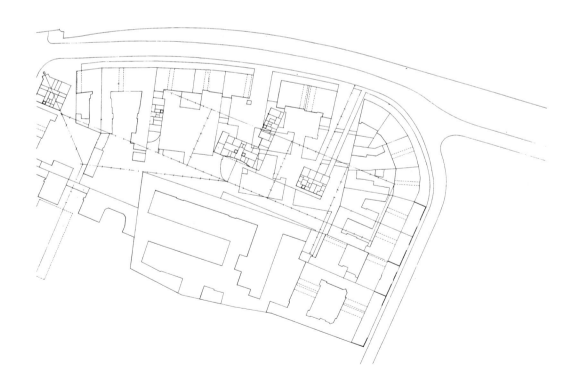

above plans and elevations *below* site plan

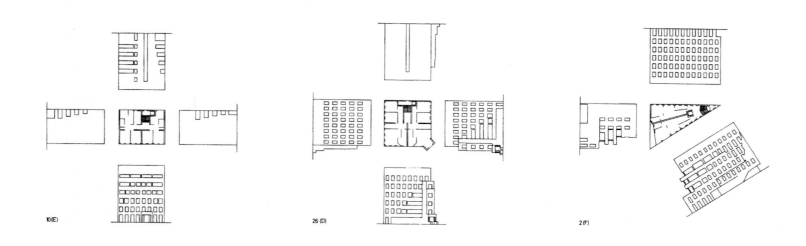

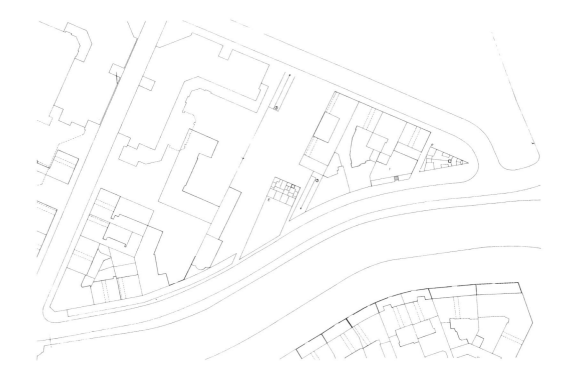

above plans and elevations *below* site plan

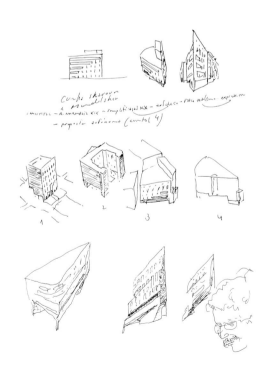

1979 Design for Görlitzer Bad Swimming Pool *Berlin, Germany*

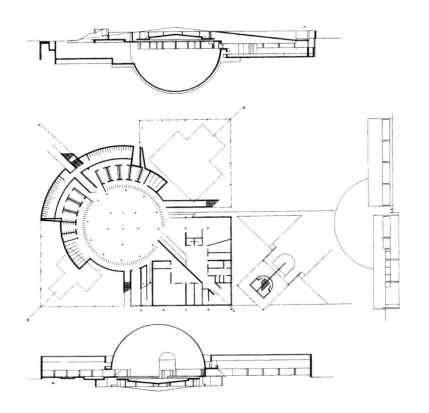

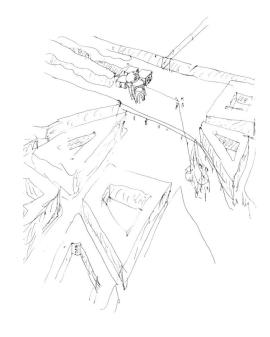

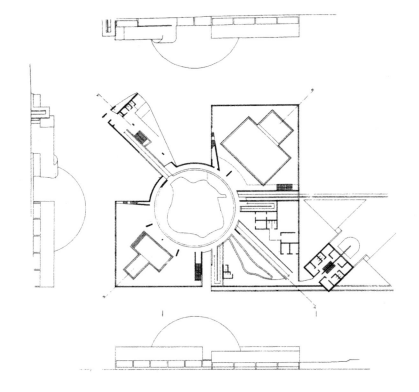

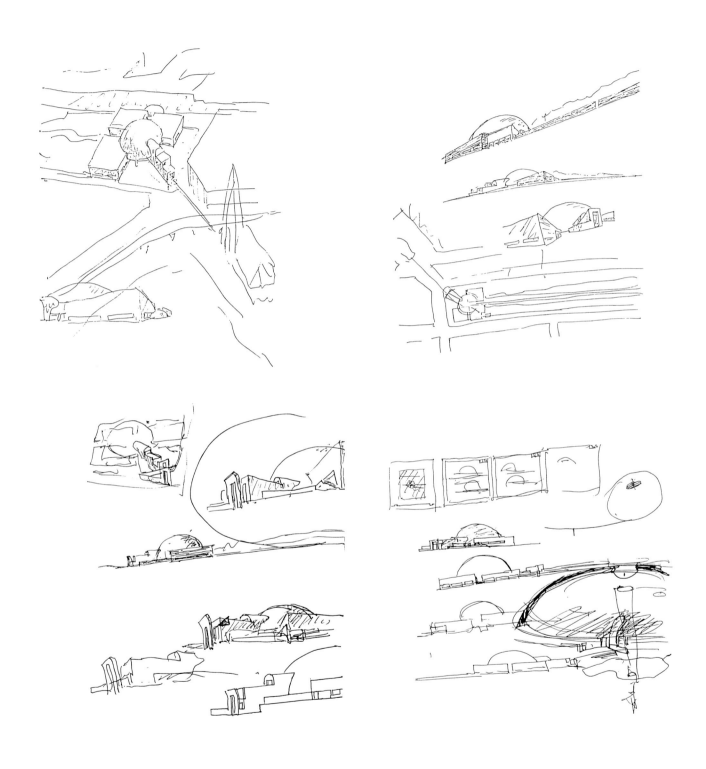

1979–81 Design for Habiflor/Florbela Espanca Co-operative Residential Complex *Villa Viçosa, Portugal*

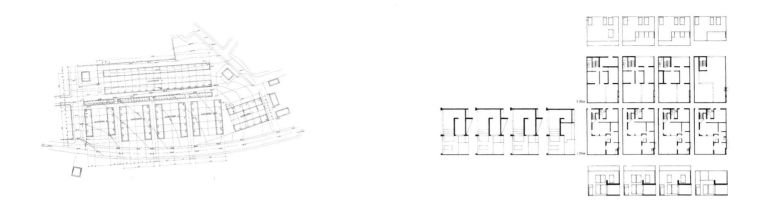

1979–81 Design for A Riconquista Co-operative Residential Complex *Aviz, Portugal*

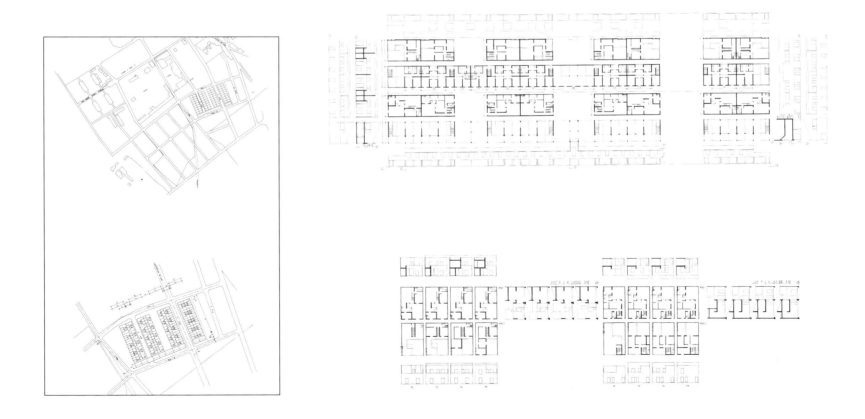

195   *above* site plan, plans and elevations *below* site plans and plans

1980 Design for Caixa Geral de Depósitos *Matosinhos, Portugal*

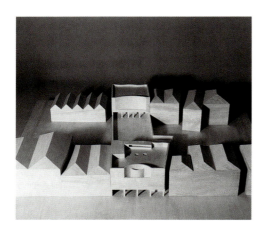
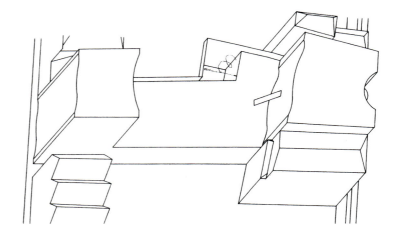

1980 Competition Design for Schlesisches Tor Residential Complex *Berlin, Germany*

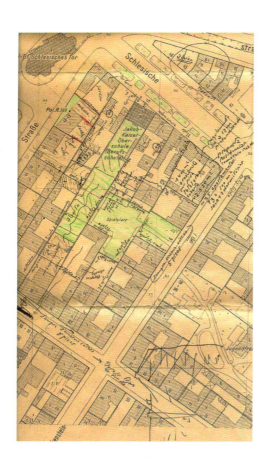
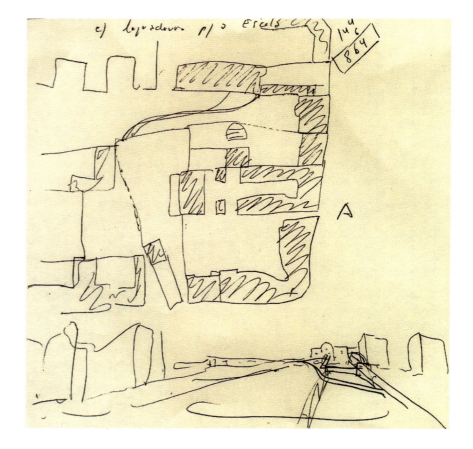

above model and bird's eye perspective *below* site plan and sketch

1980–4 Bonjour Tristesse, Schlesisches Tor Residential Complex *Berlin, Germany*

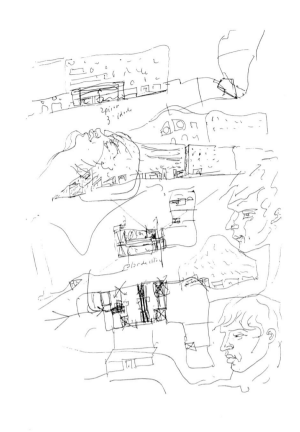

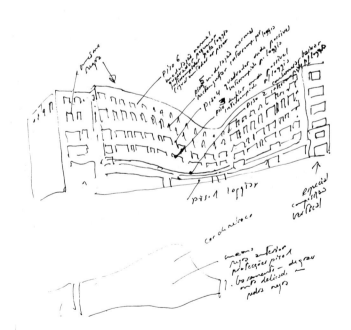
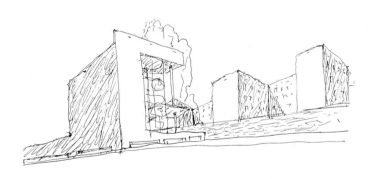

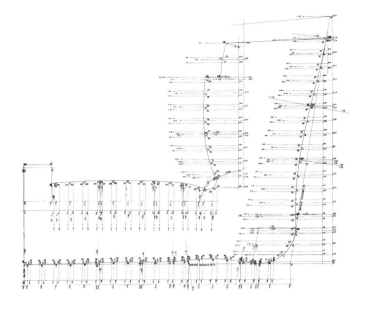
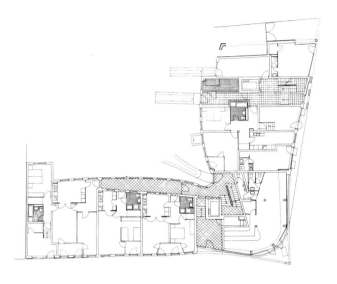
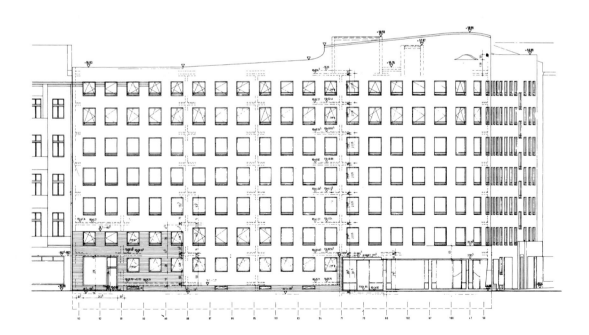

202   diagramatic study, plan and south-east elevation

1980–91 J. M. Teixeira House *Taipas, Guimarães, Portugal*

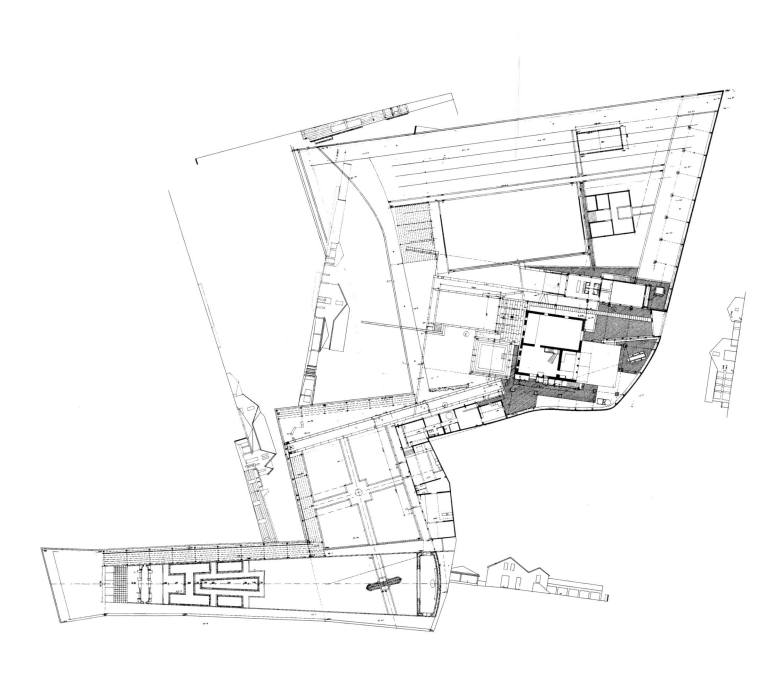

205 site plan and elevations

1980 Design for Dom Company Headquarters *Cologne, Germany*

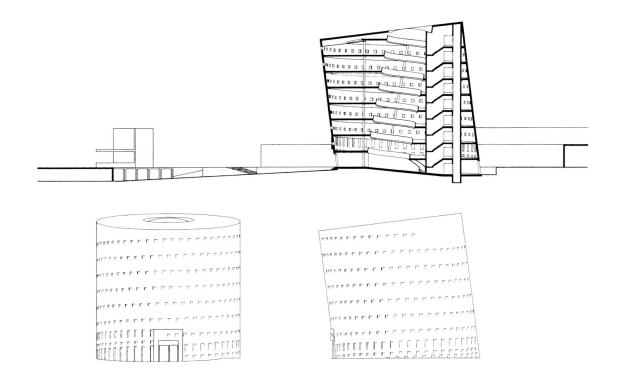

1980 Apartment Building, 11–12 Kottbusser Dam – IBA Competition – Finalist *Kreuzberg, West Berlin, Germany*

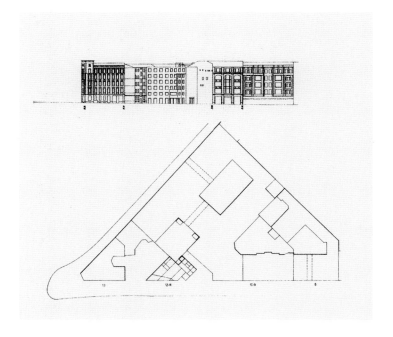

210   *above* Dom section and elevations *below* site plans and elevation

1980–4 Avelino Duarte House *Ovar, Portugal*

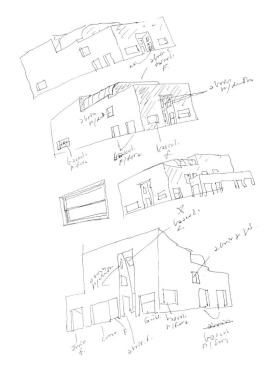
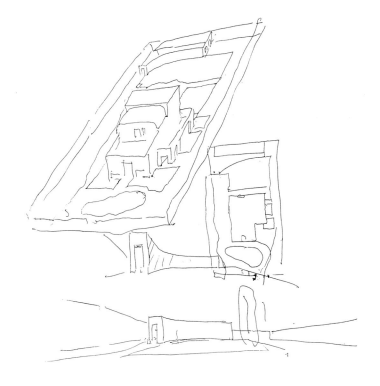
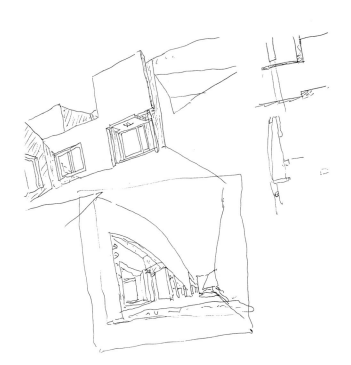

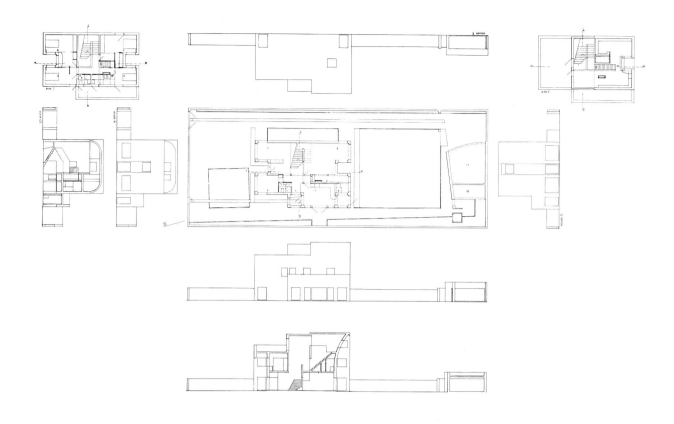
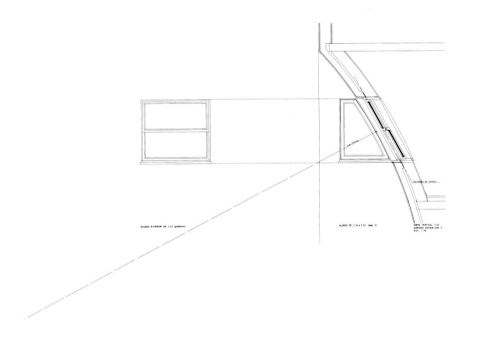

215 *above* plan, sections and elevations *below* curved wall construction detail

1980–90 Kindergarten and Senior Citizens' Clubhouse, Schlesisches Tor Recreational Centre *Berlin, Germany*

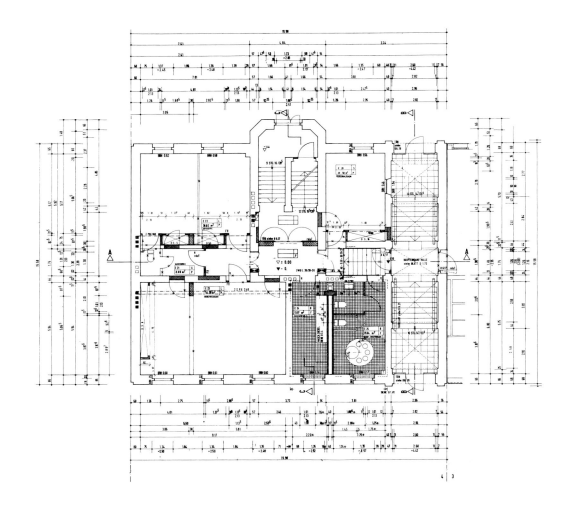
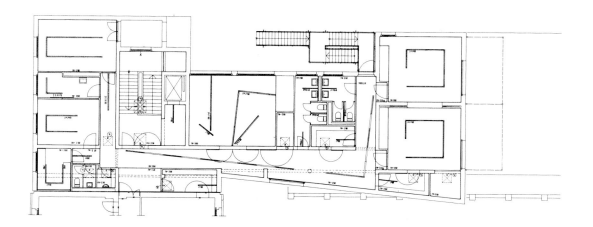

Kindergarten – plans

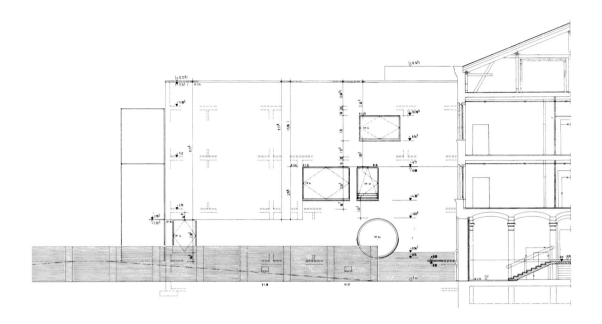
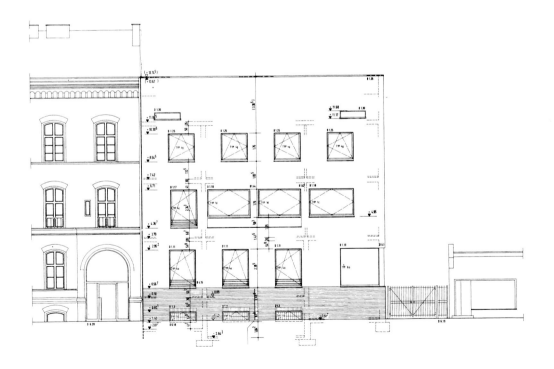

1981   Design for Fernando Machado House *Porto, Portugal*

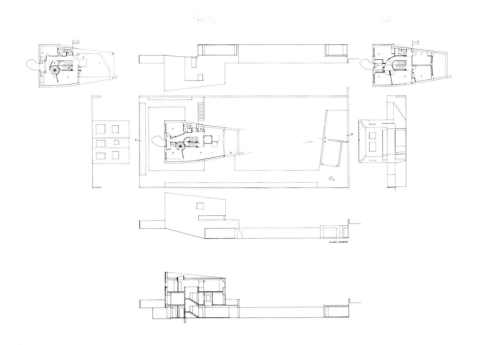

1981   Design for Hotel and Restaurant in Monte Picoto *Braga, Portugal*

221   *above* ground, first and second floor plans, sections and elevations *below* site plan

1982–5 Design for Cultural Centre *Sines, Portugal*

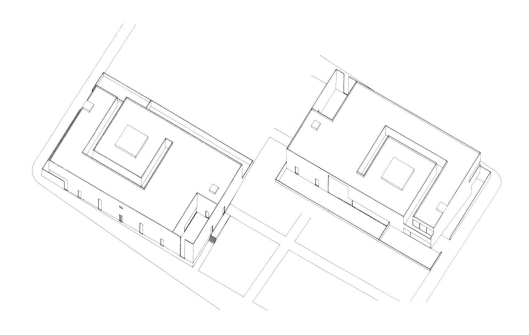

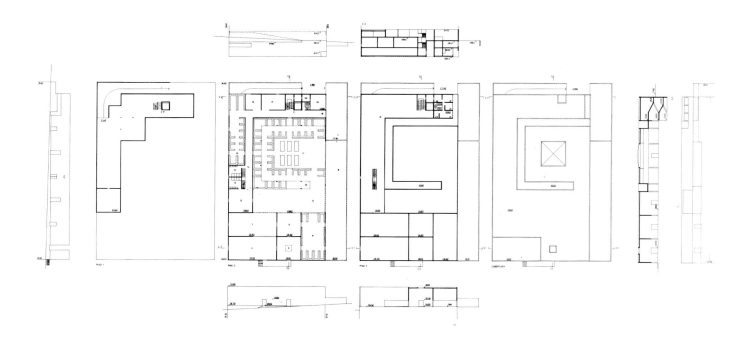

222 *above* axonometric *below* ground, first, second floor and roof plans, sections and elevations

1982   Study for Coach Station *Guimarães, Portugal*

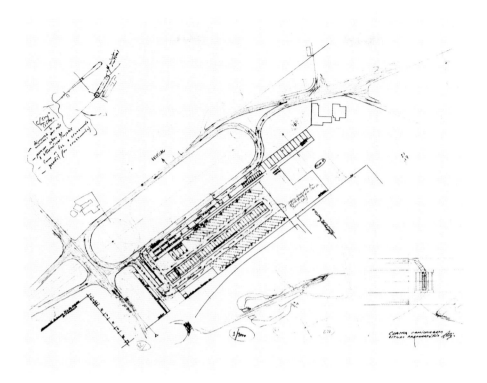

1982   Design for Aníbal Guimarães da Costa House *Trofa, Portugal*

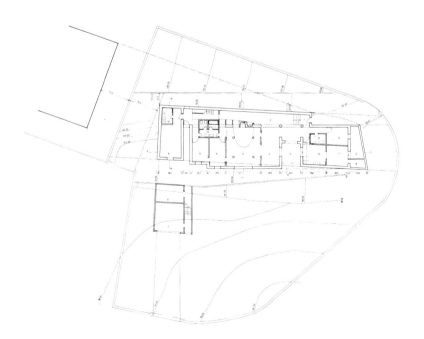

above site plan *below* plan

1982–8 Shopping and Office Complex *Guimarães, Portugal*

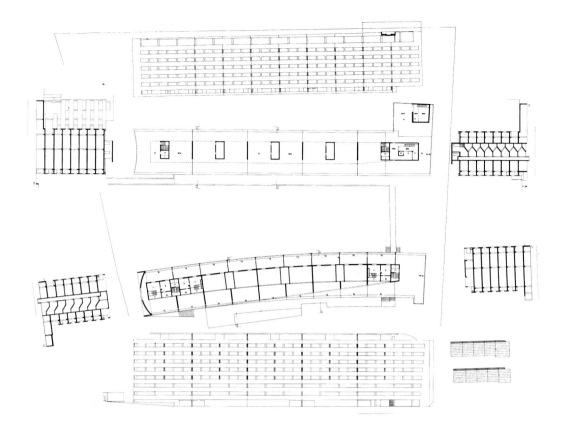

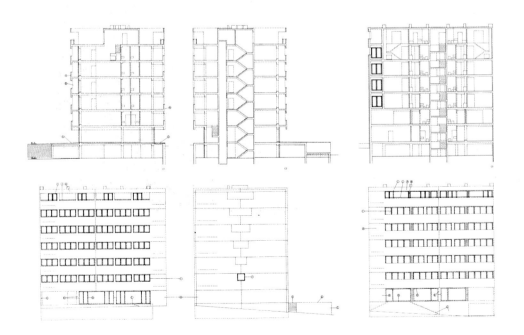

225   *above* plan, sections and elevations   *below* sections and elevations

1983–93 Design for Mário Bahia House *Gondomar, Portugal*

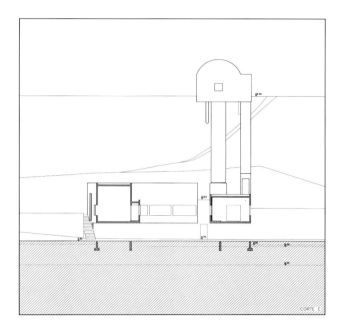
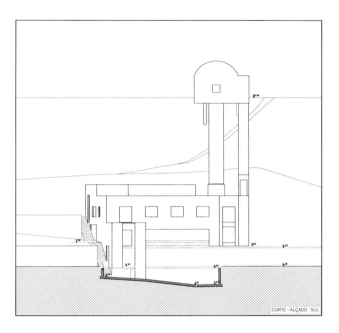
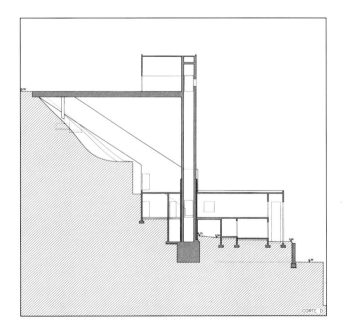
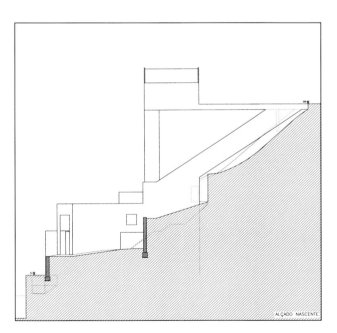

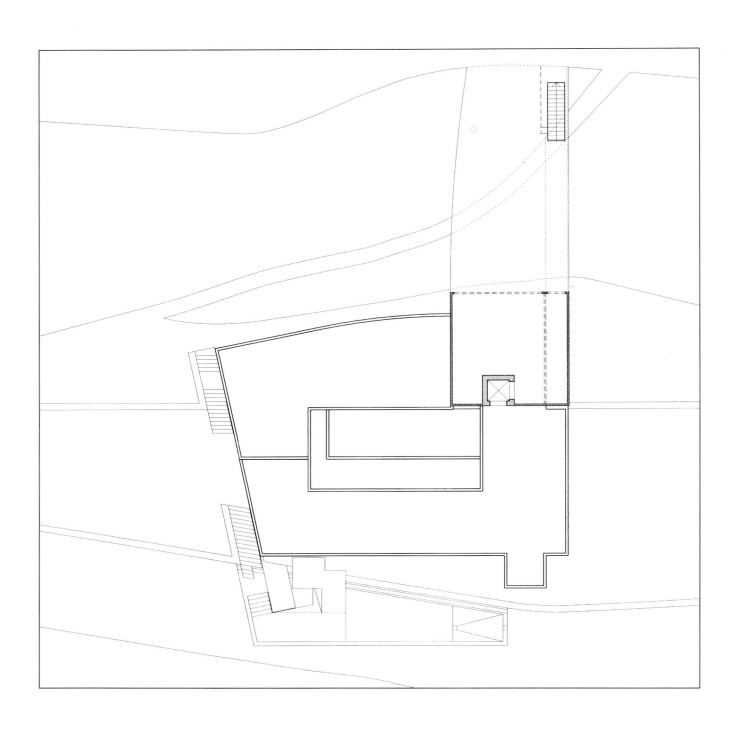

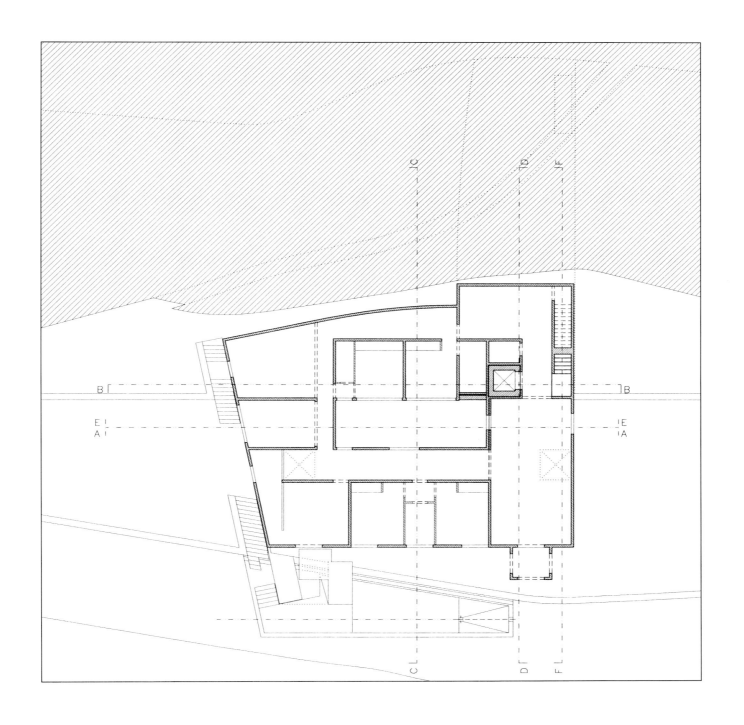

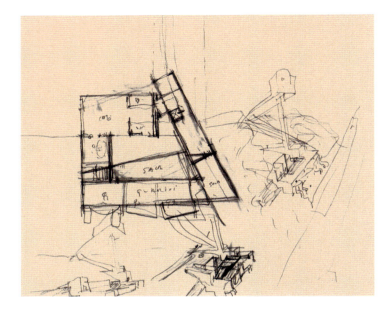

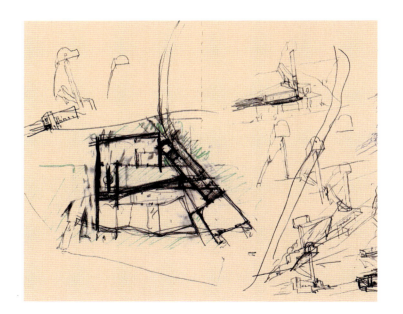

1983 Nina Shop *Porto, Portugal* (modified)

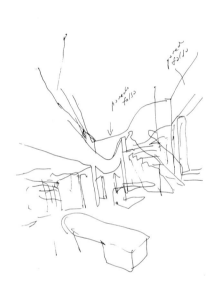
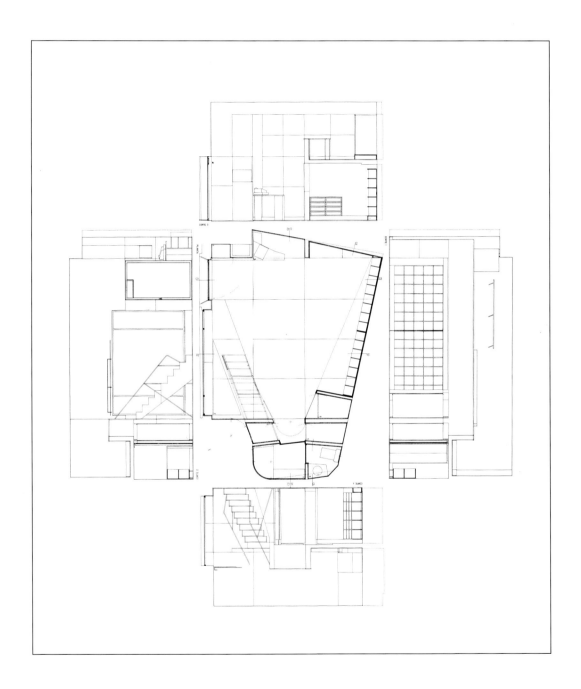

sketch, plan and sections

1983–4 Macau City Expansion Plan *Macau, China*

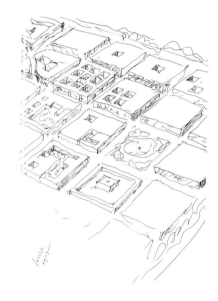
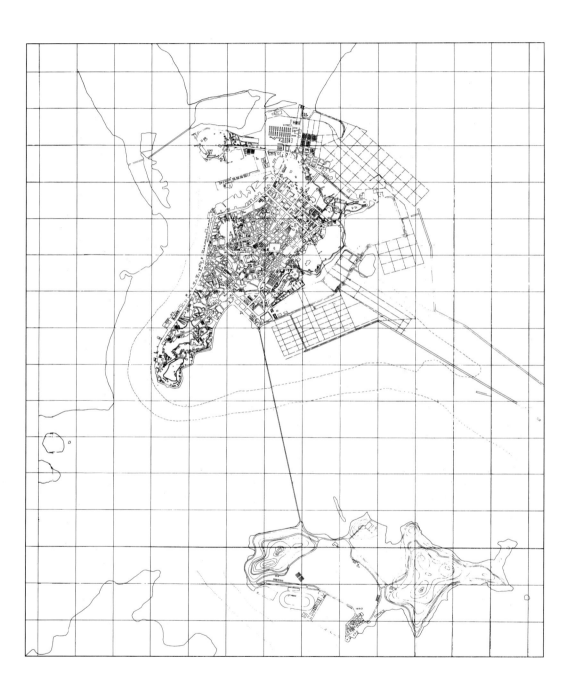

232 sketch and site plan

1983   Design for Kulturforum *Berlin, Germany*

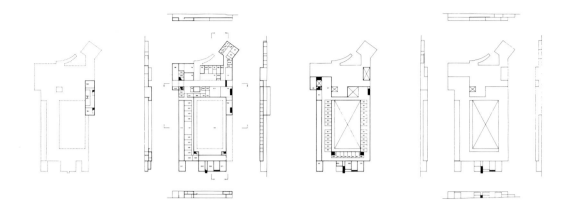
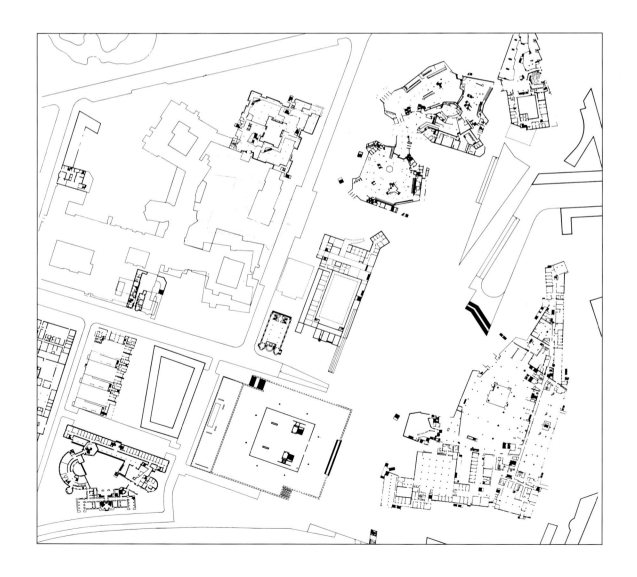

234 lower ground, ground, first floor and roof plans, sections, elevations and site plan

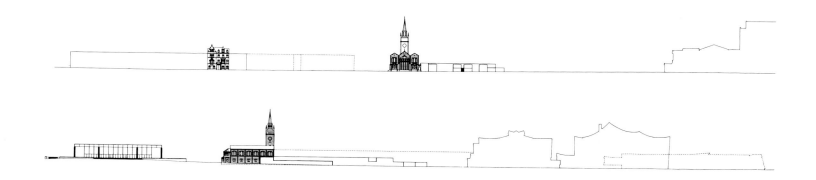

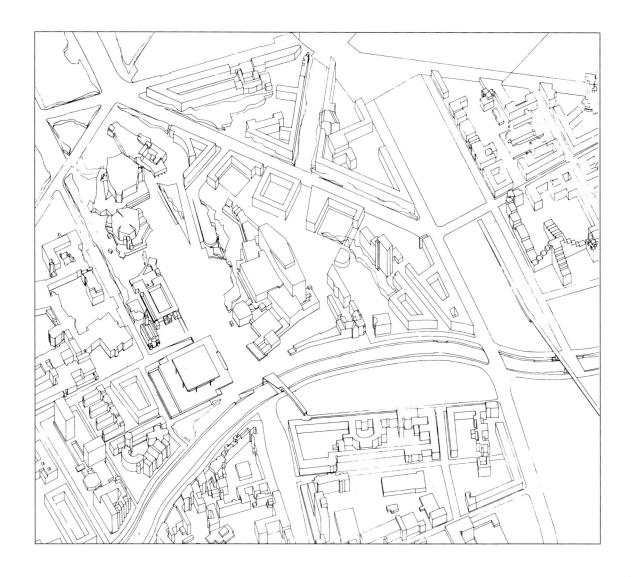

235 elevations and axonometric

1983–97 Design for Restoration of Church *Salemi, Italy*

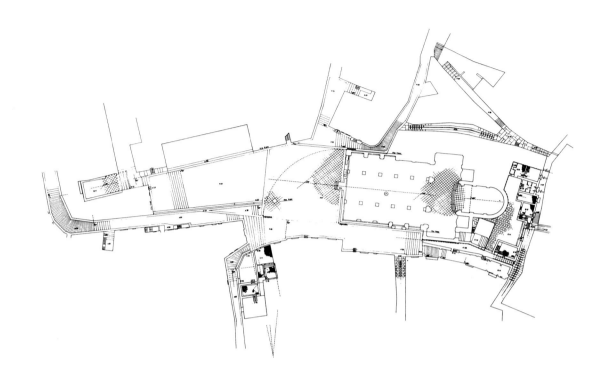

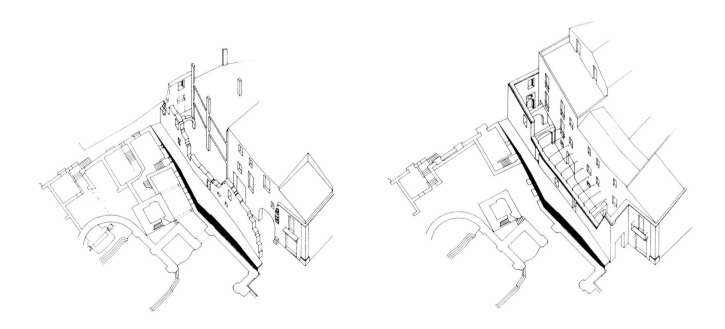

site plan and bird's eye perspectives, before and after

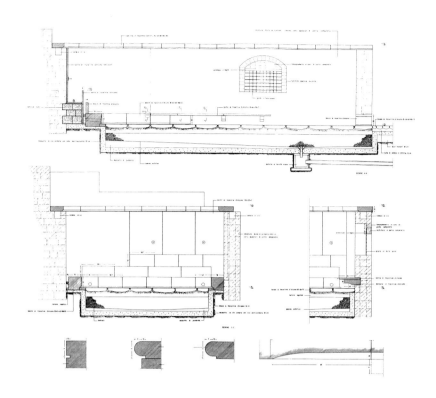
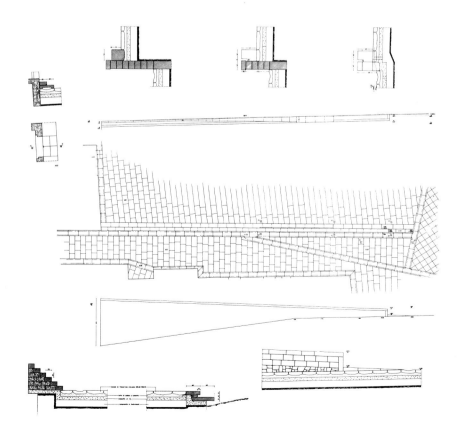

237 construction details

1983 Design for Monument to Gestapo Victims *Berlin, Germany*

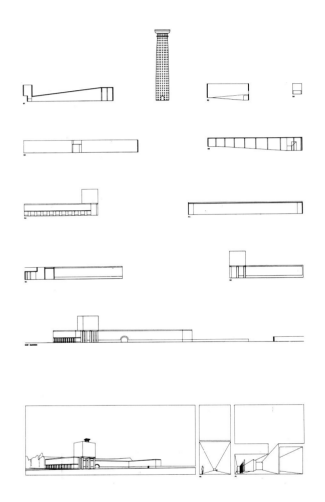
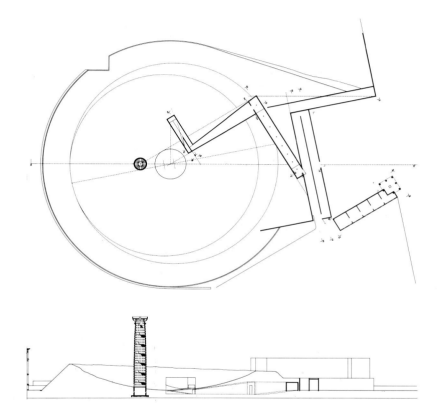

238   plan, sections and elevations

1983–9 Design for Hotel *Malagueira, Évora, Portugal*

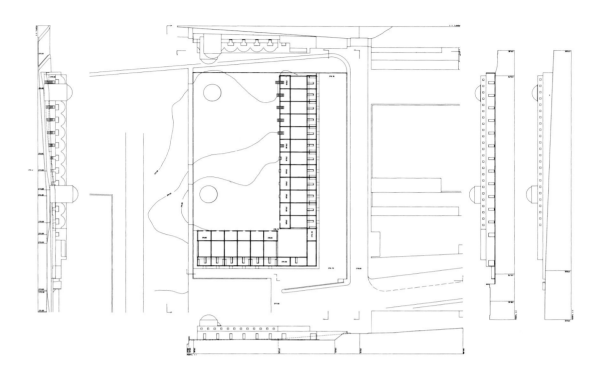

1983 Design for Extension of French Institute *Porto, Portugal*

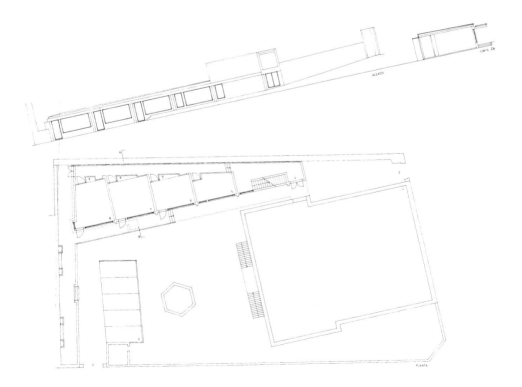

239   *above* plan and sections *below* plan, section and elevation

1983–4 Urban Plan, Schilderswijk-West *The Hague, The Netherlands*

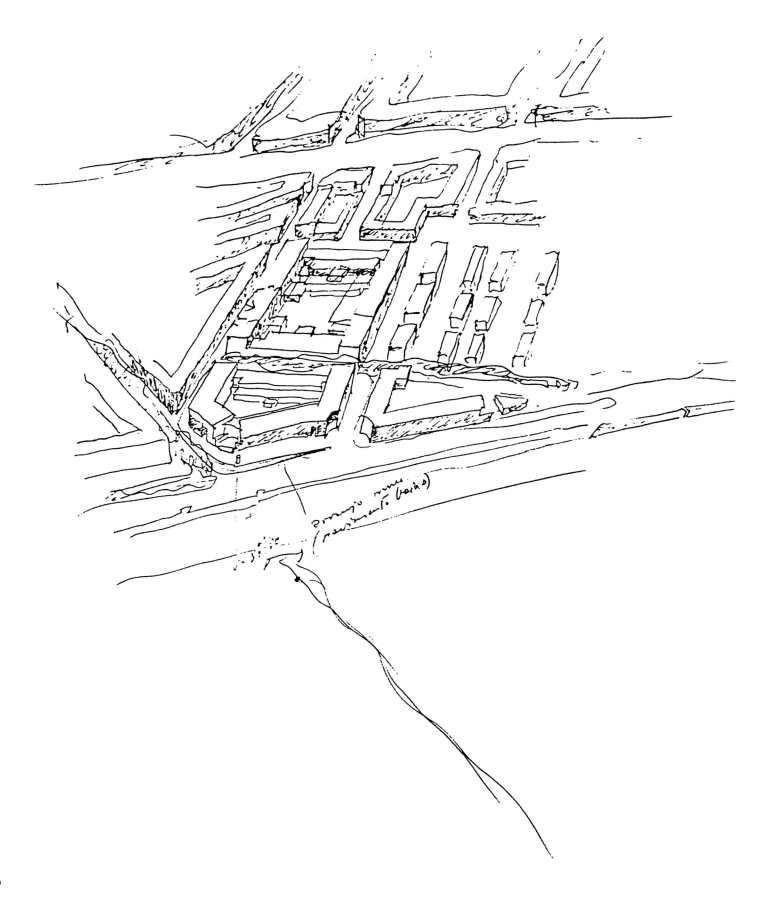

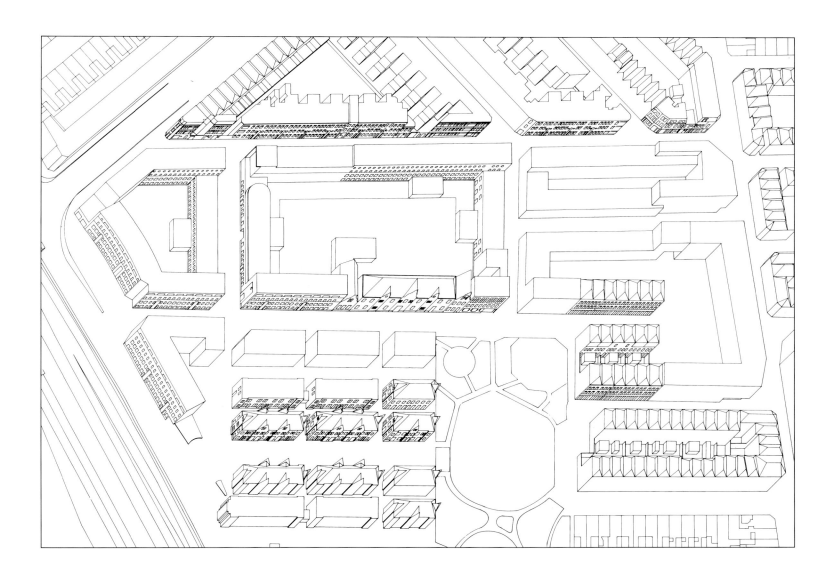

241 site axonometric

1983–8 De Punkt and De Komma Social Housing, Schilderswijk-West *The Hague, The Netherlands*

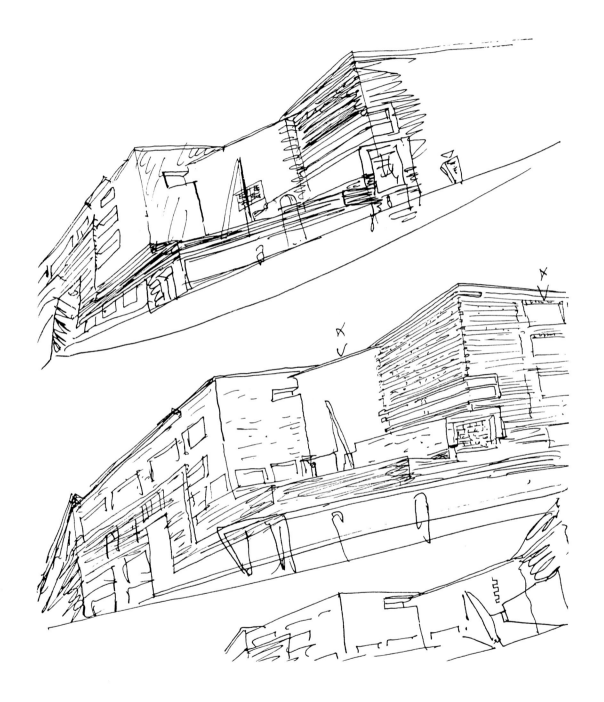

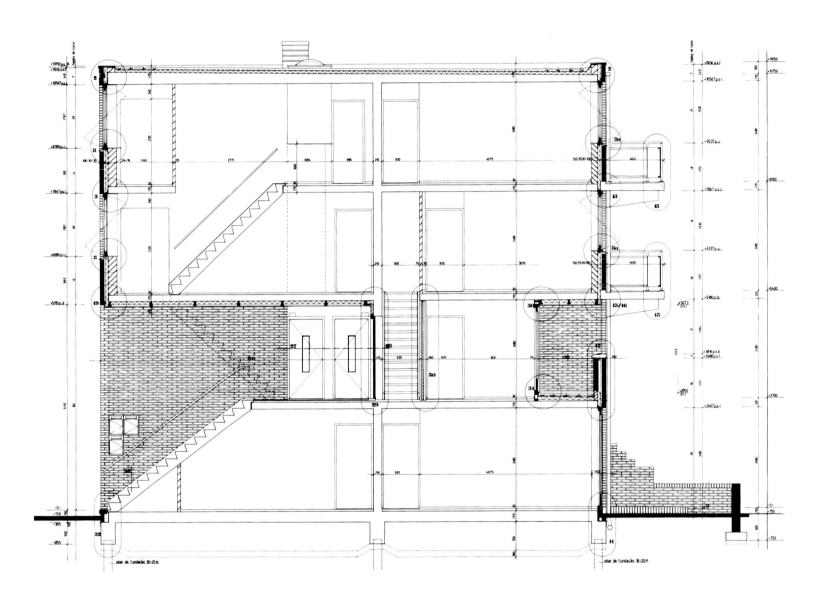

248   cross section

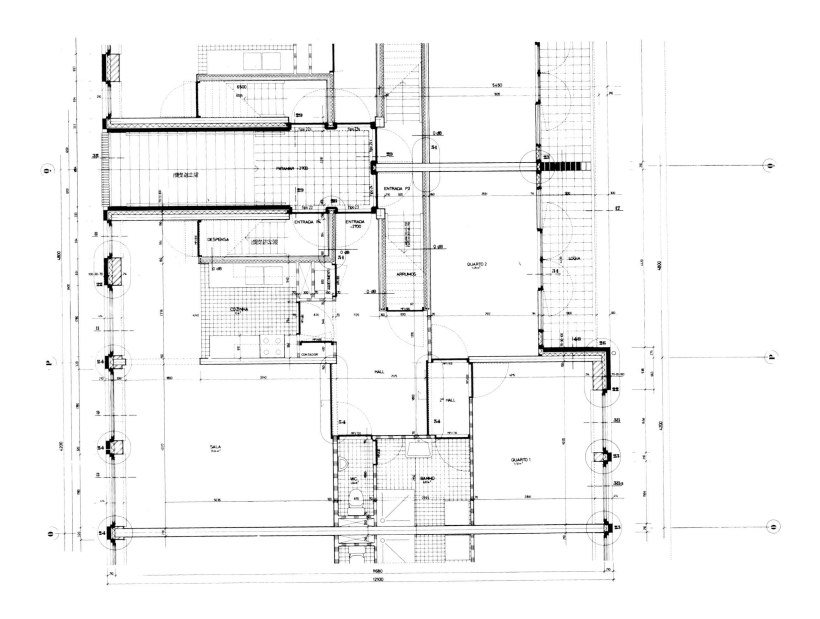

first floor plan

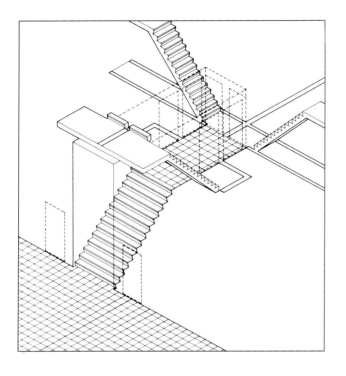 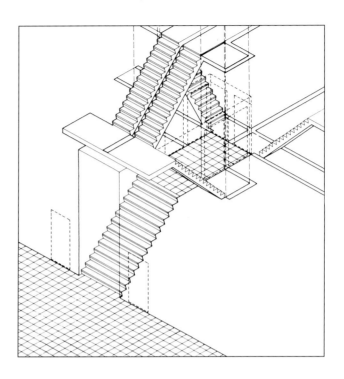

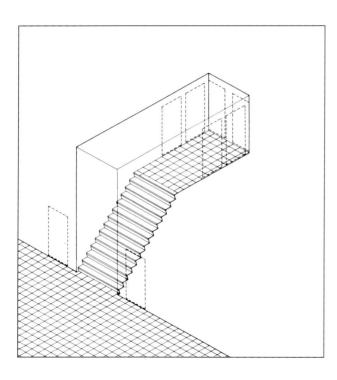 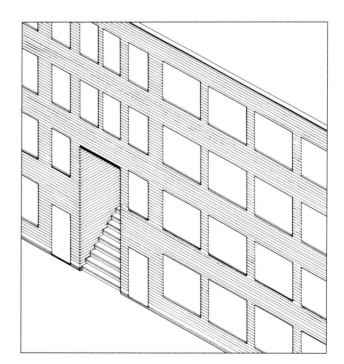

250 *above and below left* axonometrics showing internal circulation *below right* axonometric of facade

1984   Urban Redevelopment Plan *Caserta, Italy*

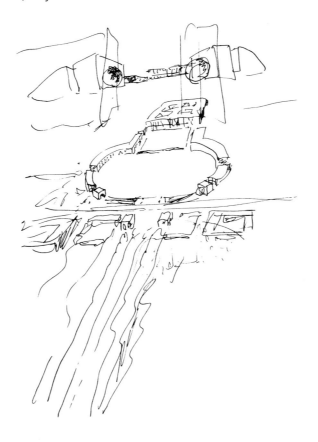

1984   Design for Erhard Josef Pascher House *Sintra, Portugal*

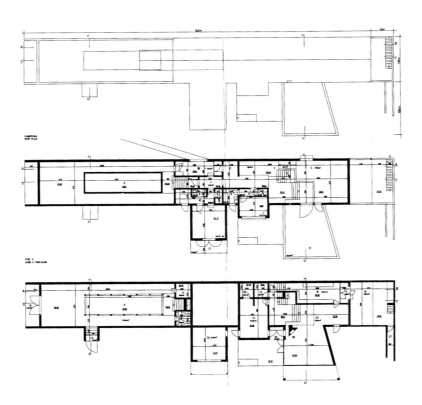

below roof, first and ground floor plans

Living in a House
Álvaro Siza

March 1994

I have never been able to build a house, a real house. I don't mean designing and building houses, a minor thing which I can still manage to do, although maybe not very well.

The idea I have of a house is the idea of a complicated machine, in which every day something breaks down: a lamp, a tap, a drain, a lock, a hinge, a socket, and then a cylinder, a stove, a fridge, a television or video; and the washing machine, or the fuses, the curtain springs, the security bolt.

The drawers jam, the carpets rip, as does the padding of the dining-room sofa. All the shirts, socks, sheets, handkerchiefs, napkins, table-cloths and kitchen-towels are lying torn beside the ironing-board, whose protective cover is in a parlous state. Water is also dripping from the ceiling (the neighbour's pipes have burst or a roof-tile has fallen off, or the waterproofing has come loose). And the gutters are full of rotten brown leaves.

When there is a garden, the grass grows menacingly and whatever free time you have is not enough to deal with the madness of nature: fallen petals and legions of ants invade the thresholds of doors, there are always the dead bodies of birds, mice and cats. The chlorine of the swimming pool has run out, the robot is broken; there is no suction apparatus to restore the clarity of the water or suck up the legs of insects, fine as hair.

The granite flagstones or floors are getting covered with a perilous slime, the varnish is darkening, skins of paint are peeling off and revealing the knots of wood reduced to a facade. An old man's finger could go through the frames, the panes of glass are cracked, the bitumen has fallen out, the silicone is coming off the surfaces, there is mould in the cupboards and in the drawers, beetles are becoming resistant to the insecticides. The polish has always run out even if you can find the tin you are looking for, the joints are coming apart, the tiles are falling off, first one, then the whole wall.

And that is the least of it.

Living in a house, in a real house, is a full-time job. The house owner is at the same time a fireman (houses are always burning down, or flooding, or gas escapes silently and usually explodes); a nurse (have you seen the splinters of wood from the bannisters getting stuck under your nails?); and a lifeguard, he is in full command of all the arts and professions, he is a specialist in physics, in chemistry, he is a lawyer, or he does not survive. He is a telephonist and receptionist, he calls at all hours, getting hold of plumbers, carpenters, bricklayers, electricians, and then he them submissively. And then it is necessary to sharpen blades, buy accessories, to oil, to rearrange, to dehumidify; the dehumidifier immediately breaks down and after that the air conditioning and the heat pumps.

But there is nothing worse than the torture of books which move about mysteriously by themselves, muddling themselves up on purpose, attracting dust. The dust penetrates the upper edge of the pages, tiny creatures eat them with an indescribable noise; the pages stick together, the leather stains, drops of water trickle from vases of dying flowers onto engravings and spread through the cloths in a furious process of dissolution. The doormat is falling apart and there is a deep gash in the wood, the hairs of the brush are coming out, precious objects are cracking, the boards of tables and of furniture are coming apart in terrifying cracks, the cistern no longer flushes, the stove is filling with soot – any day now it will catch fire. Great-grandmother's glasses are cracking in the glass cabinet, the bottles of *vinho verde* given life with the tiniest amount of sugar are bursting, the corks are popping out, or rotting, even the best vintage is going off.

When for the first time a fused light is not replaced immediately the whole house is in darkness, and this invariably happens on a Saturday, at the same time as one of the tyres of the only available car gets a puncture.

This is why I consider owning, maintaining and renovating a house to be a matter of heroism. In my opinion there should be an Order of the Guardians of Houses and every year the appropriate honour and a high financial award conferred.

But when all this effort of maintenance is not apparent, when the wholesome aroma of wax in a house, which is otherwise well-ventilated, is mingled with the perfume of flowers from the garden; and when in it, we, irresponsible visitors who are not particularly aware of moments of happiness, feel happy and forget our worries as barbarian nomads, then the only possible prize is one of gratitude, of silent applause – a moment of pause, looking around, losing ourselves in the golden atmosphere of an autumn interior at the end of the day.

1984–94 David Vieira de Castro House *Famalicão, Portugal*

253

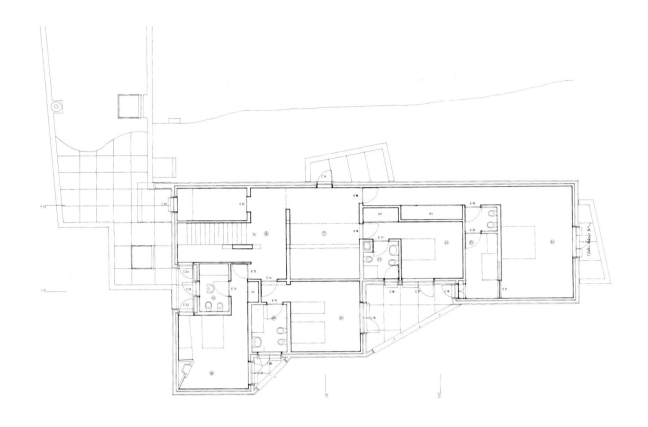
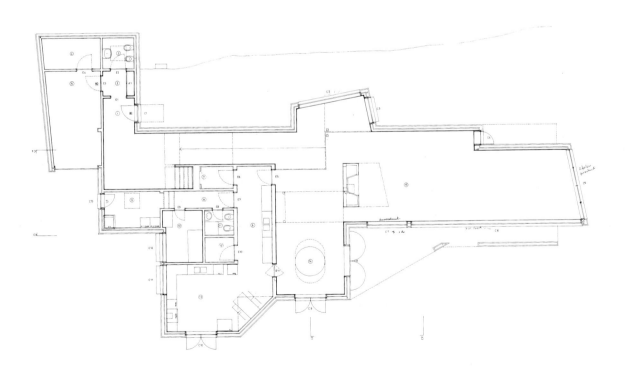

257 ground and first floor plans

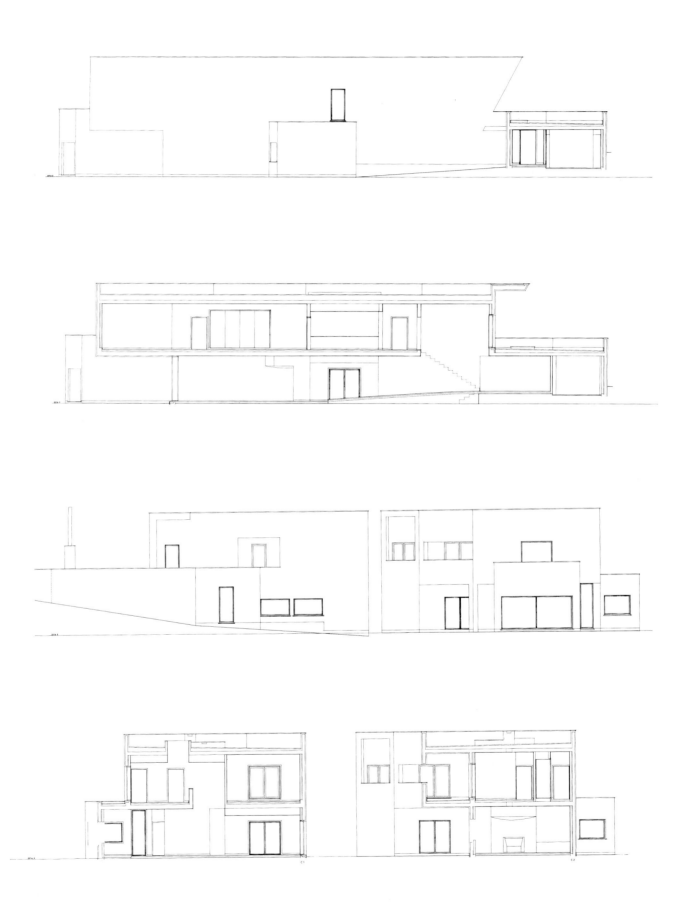

258　elevations, long sections and cross sections

1984–94 Luís Figueiredo House *Gondomar, Portugal*

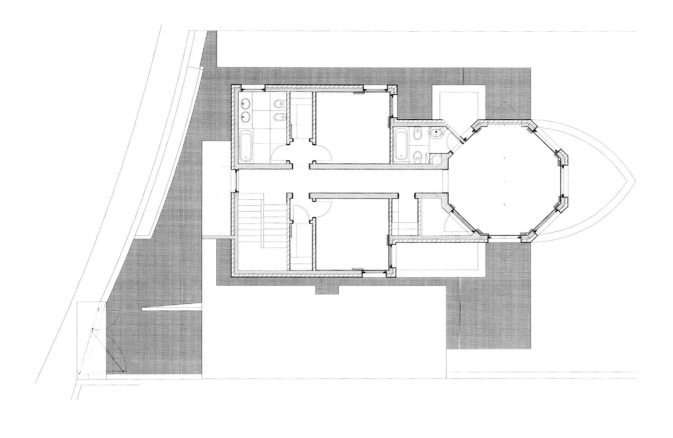
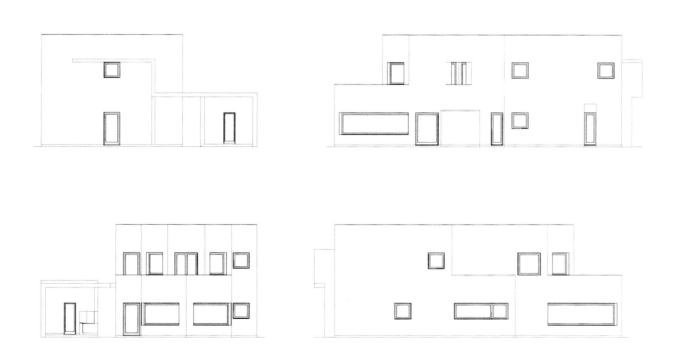

plan and elevations

1984–91 João de Deus Nursery School *Penafiel, Portugal*

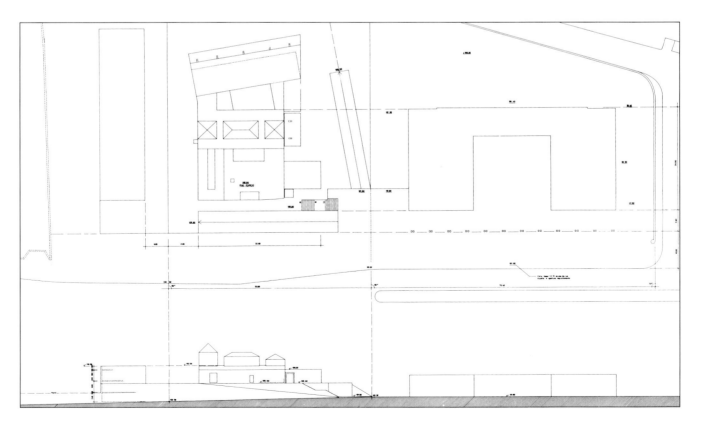

267   *above* elevations *below* site plan and elevation

1984–6 Restoration of Póvoa House, Faculty of Architecture *Porto, Portugal*

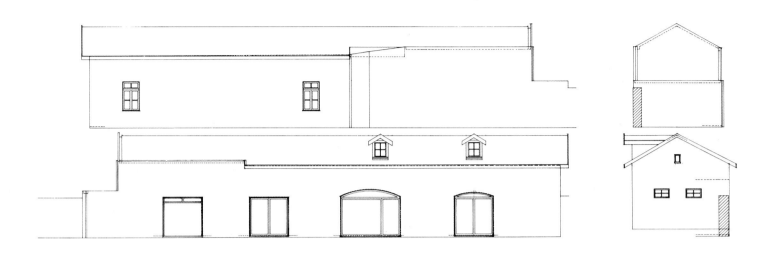

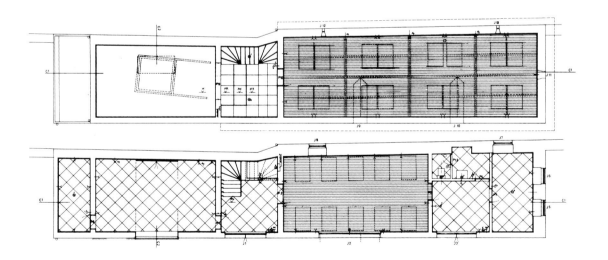

269   elevations and plans

1984–8 Housing and Shopping Complex, Schilderswijk *The Hague, The Netherlands*

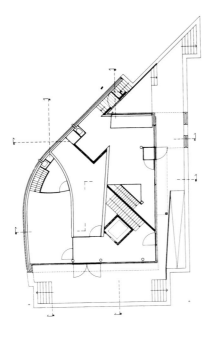
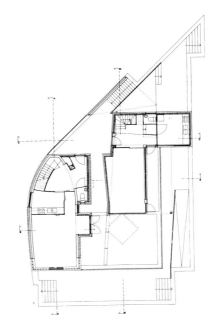
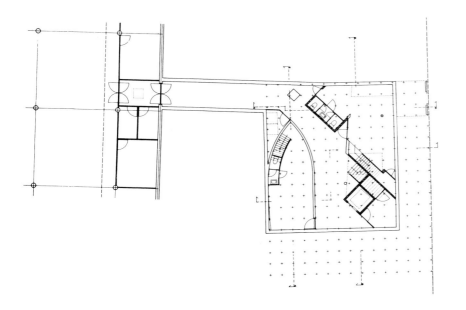
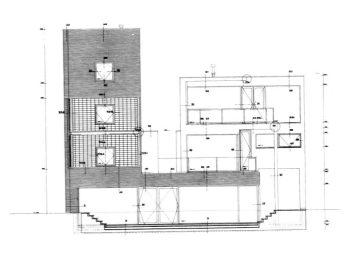

271   first, ground and lower ground floor plans and south-east elevation

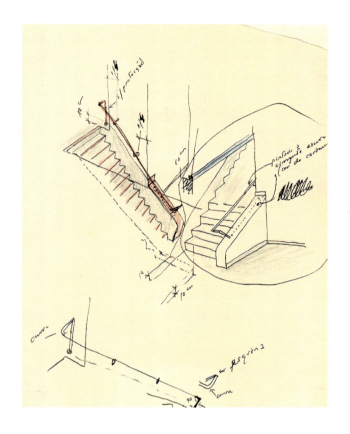
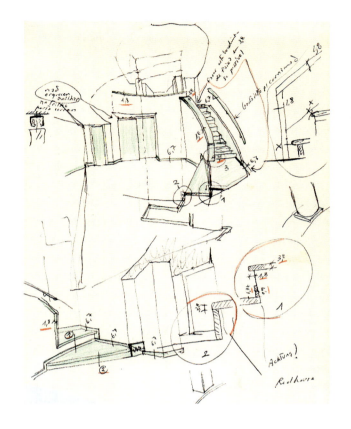

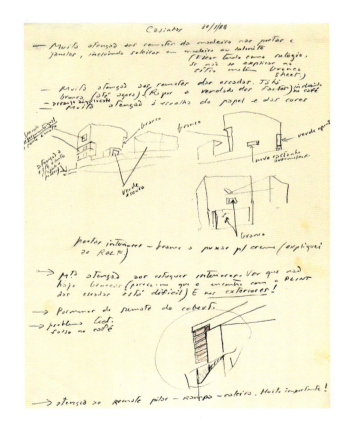

1985–8 Van der Vennepark Garden, Schilderswijk-West *The Hague, The Netherlands*

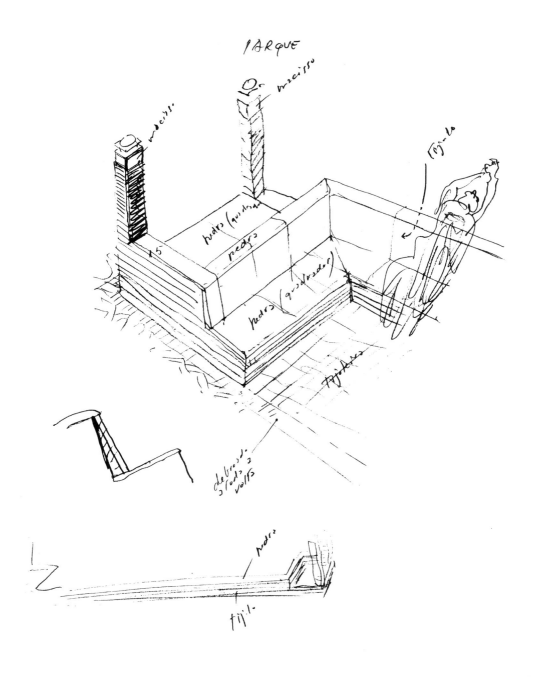

1985 Restoration of Campo di Marte, Giudecca *Venice, Italy*

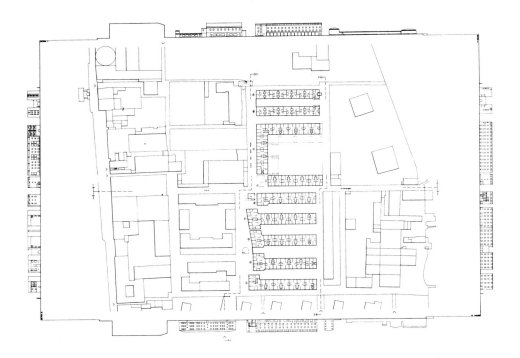

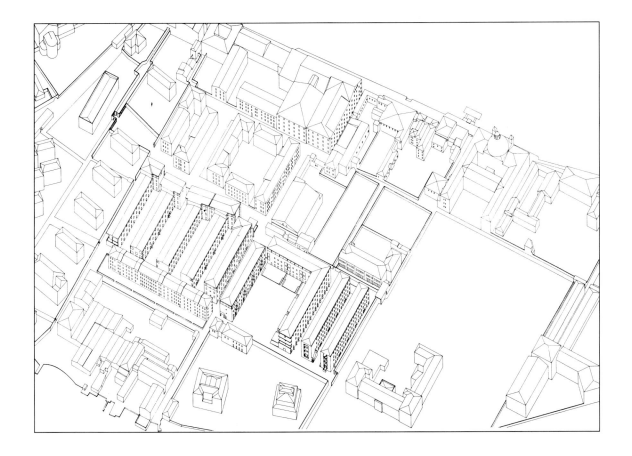

above site plan and elevations *below* axonometric

1985 Study for Espertina Housing Scheme *Águeda, Portugal*

above Campo di Marte sketch *below* elevation and site plan

1985–6 Carlos Ramos Pavilion, Faculty of Architecture *Porto, Portugal*

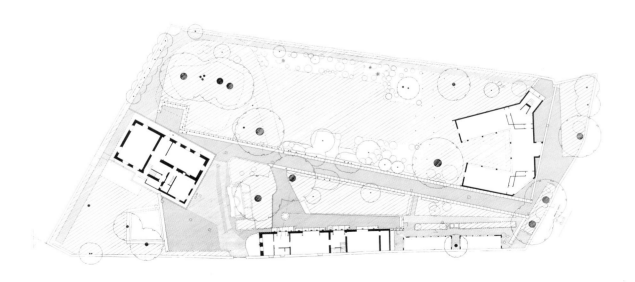

site plan

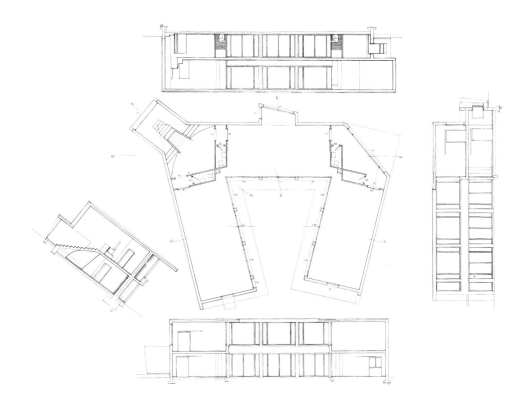
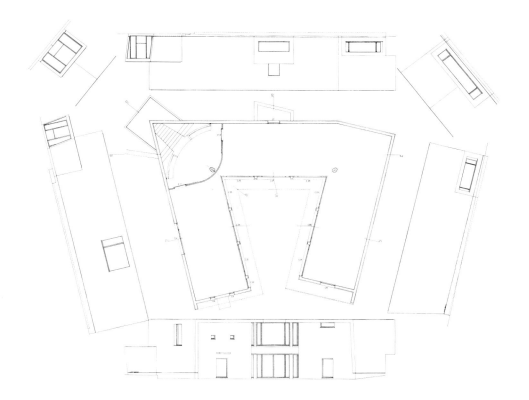

283   ground and first floor plans, sections and elevations

1986   City Park Design *Salemi, Italy*

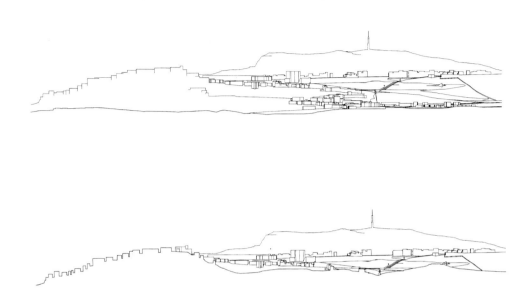

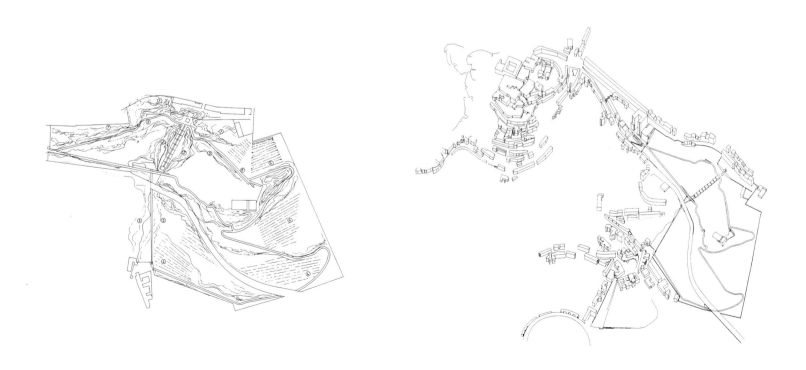

285   perspectival elevations and site plans

1986 Expo '92 Master Plan – Competition *Seville, Spain*

1986 Design for Hydrographic Institute *Lisbon, Portugal*

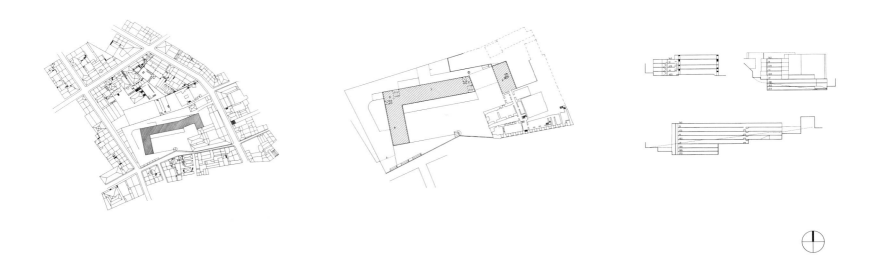

1986–7 Urban Plan *Monterusciello, Naples, Italy*

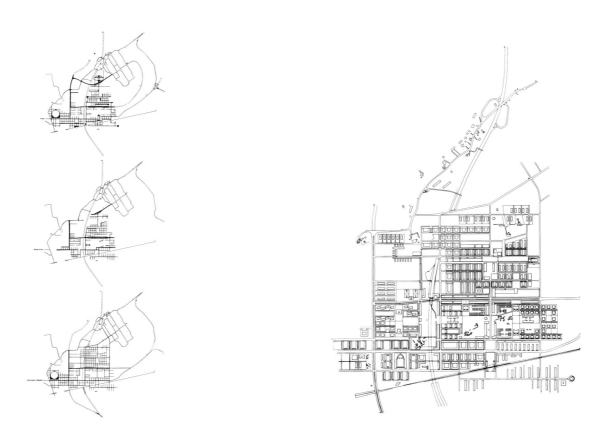

above site plan, fourth floor plan and sections *below* circulation studies and site plan

1986 Design for Extension of Winkler Casino *Salzburg, Austria*

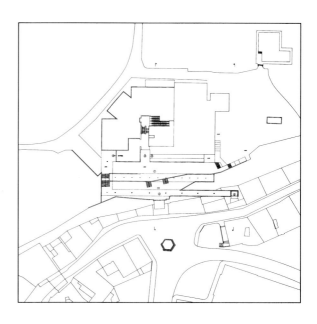
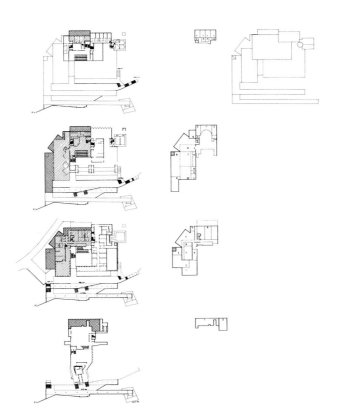
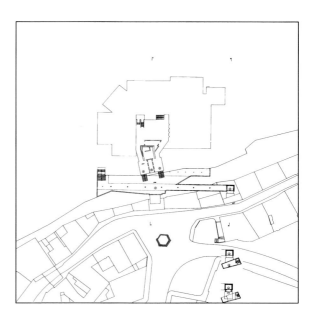

sketch, plans and site plans

1986–7   Urban Plan for Pendino Quarter *Naples, Italy*

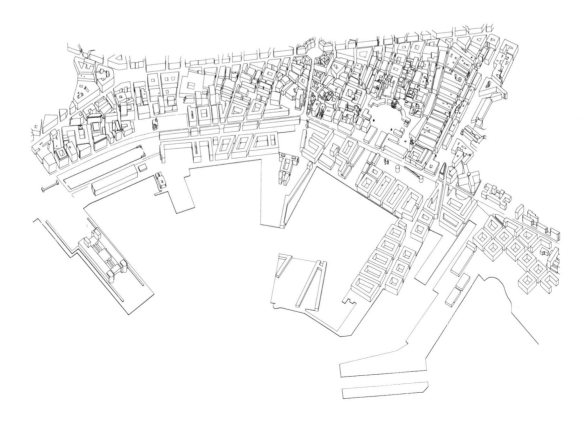

site plans and axonometric

1986–94 Teacher Training College *Setúbal, Portugal*

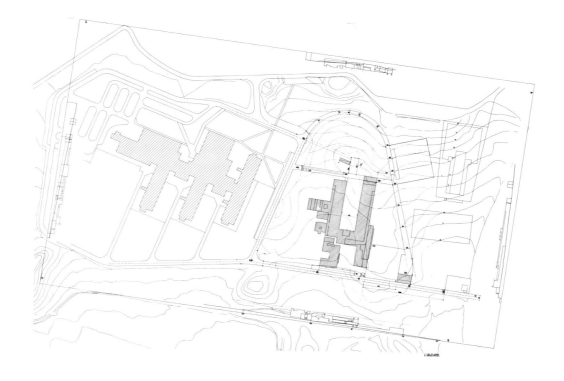
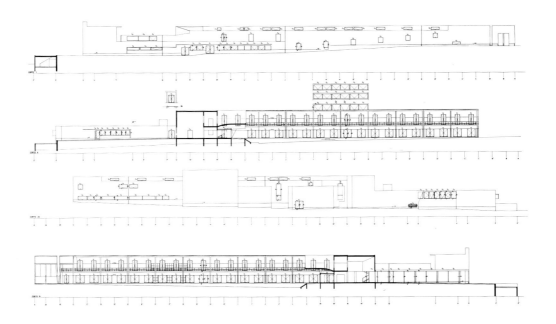

295   site plan, sections and elevations

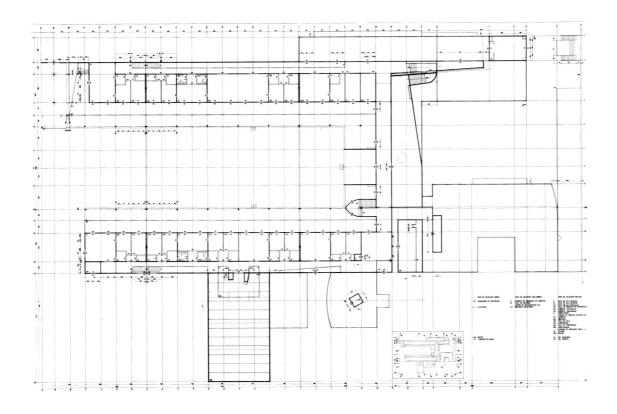
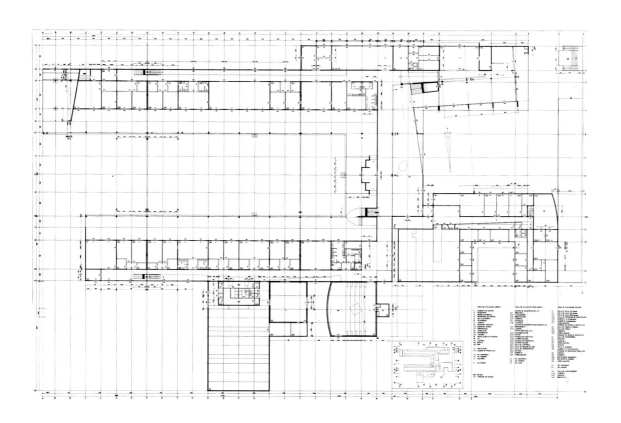

1986–96 Faculty of Architecture, University of Porto *Porto, Portugal*

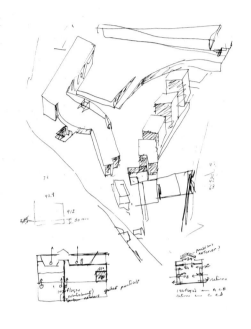
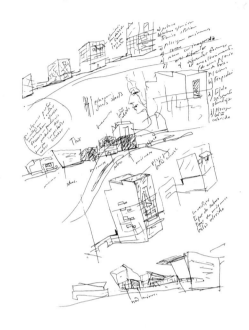
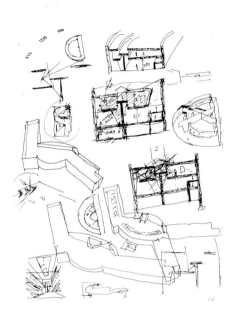
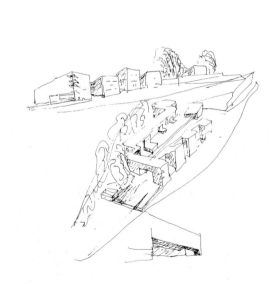

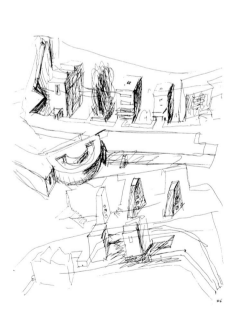

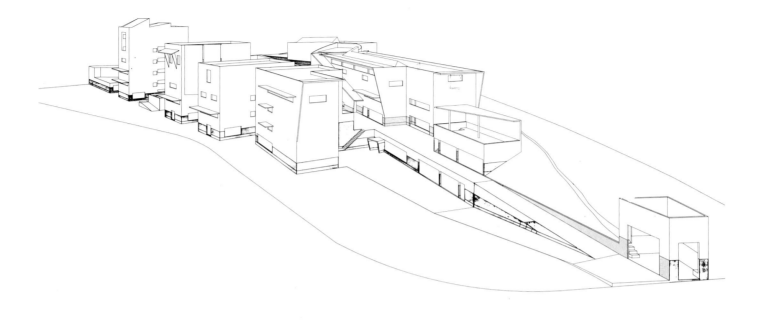

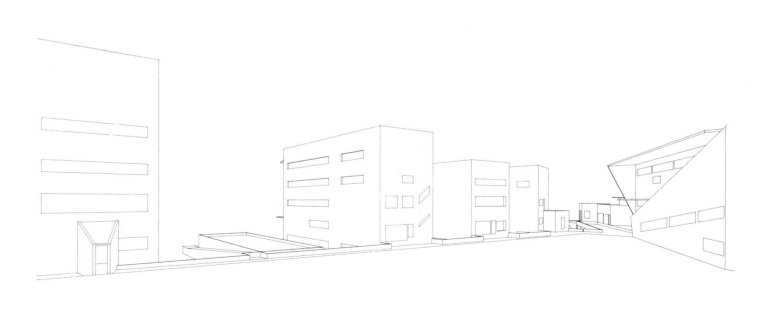

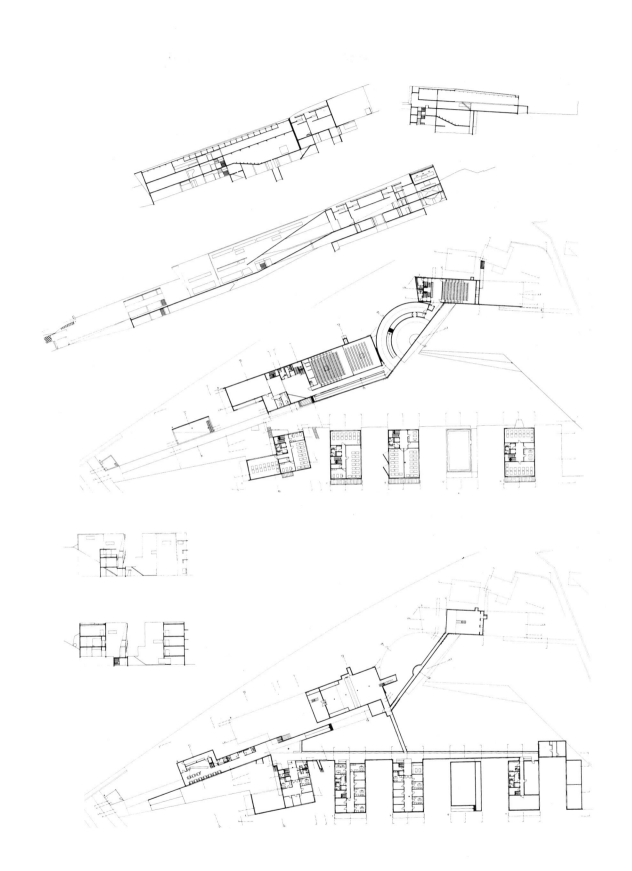

311   ground and first floor plans and sections

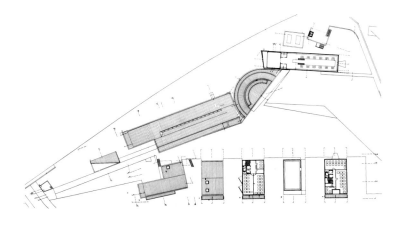

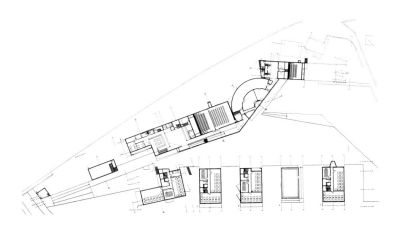

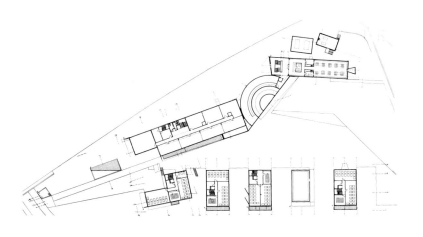

first, second and third floor plans, elevations and sections

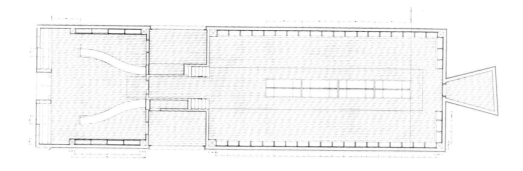
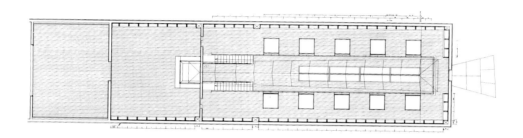
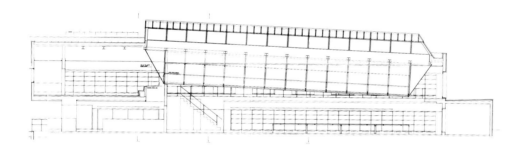
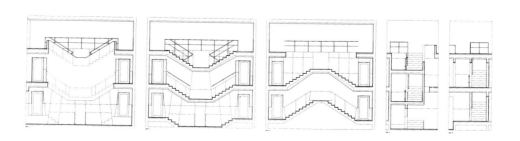

313 ground and first floor plans and sections

1987–96 César Rodrigues House *Porto, Portugal*

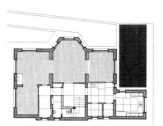
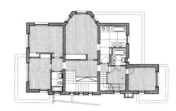
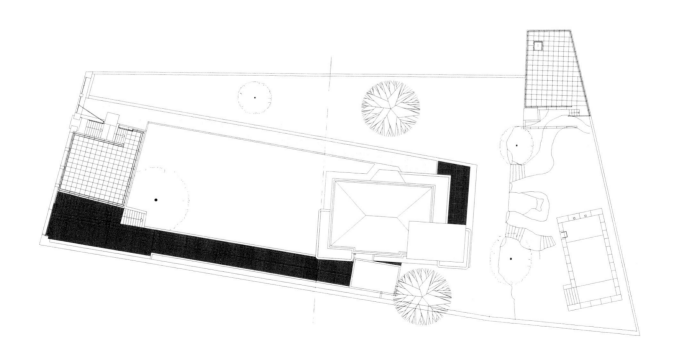

318   stair detail, ground and first floor plans and site plan

1987–96 Design for Remodelling of Miranda Santos House (Ferreira da Costa) *Matosinhos, Portugal*

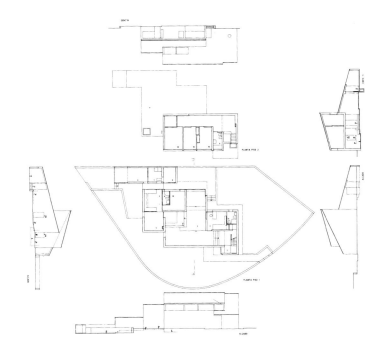

1988–9   Design for La Defensa Cultural Centre *Madrid, Spain*

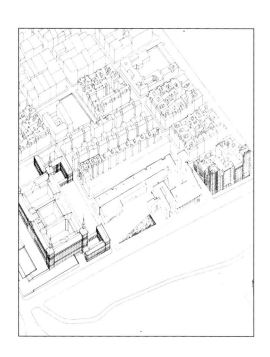
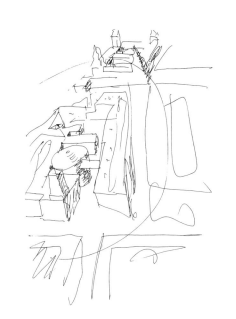

320   *above* ground and first floor plans, sections and elevations of Miranda Santos House *below* axonometric and sketches for La Defensa

1988 Design for Matteotti Piazza *Siena, Italy*

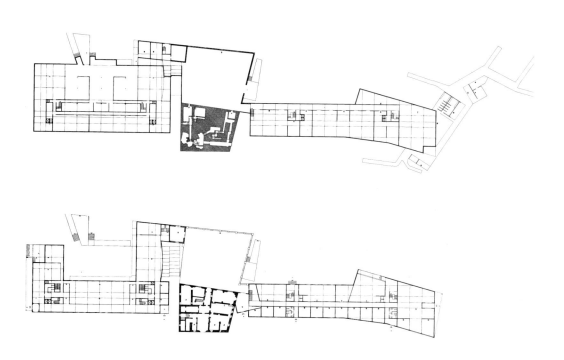

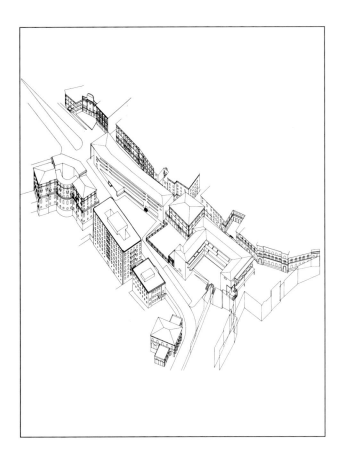
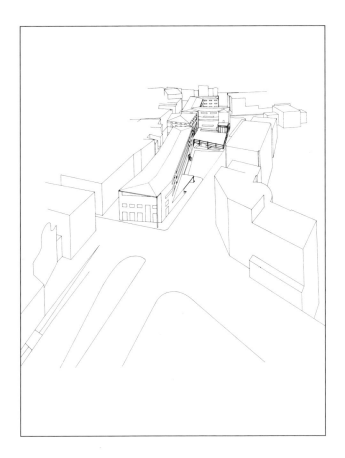

321   *above* lower ground and ground floor plans *below* axonometric and perspective

1988 Design for Malagueira Housing *Évora, Portugal*

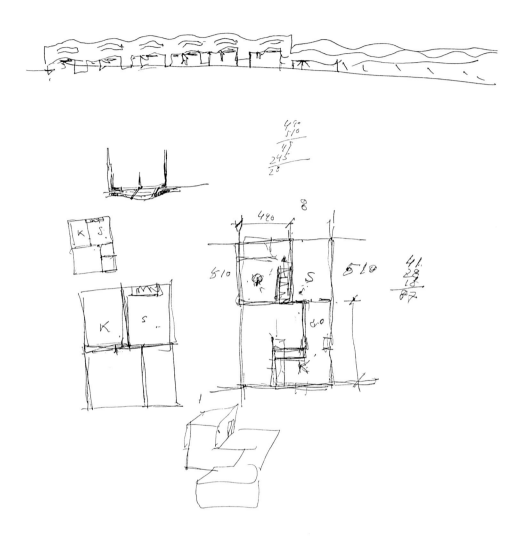
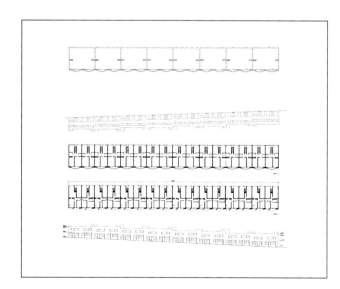
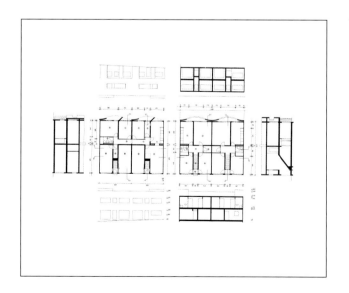

322   plans, sections and elevations

1988–9 Piezometric Tower, University of Aveiro *Aveiro, Portugal*

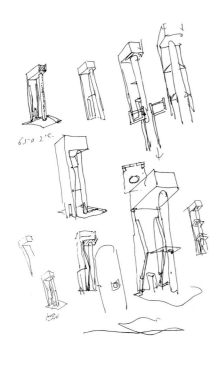
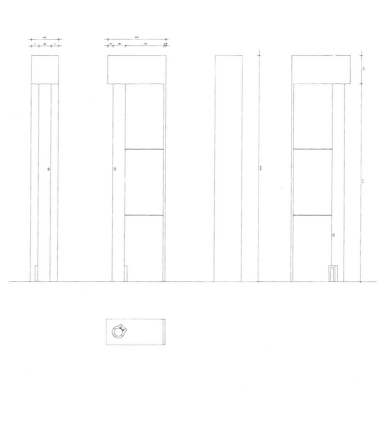
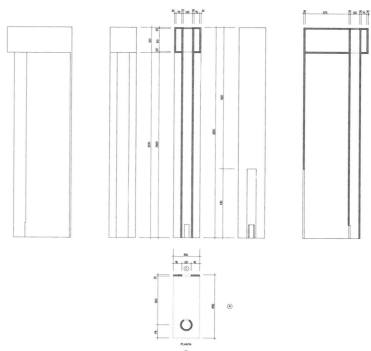

324 plans, sections and elevations

1988–95 Library, University of Aveiro *Aveiro, Portugal*

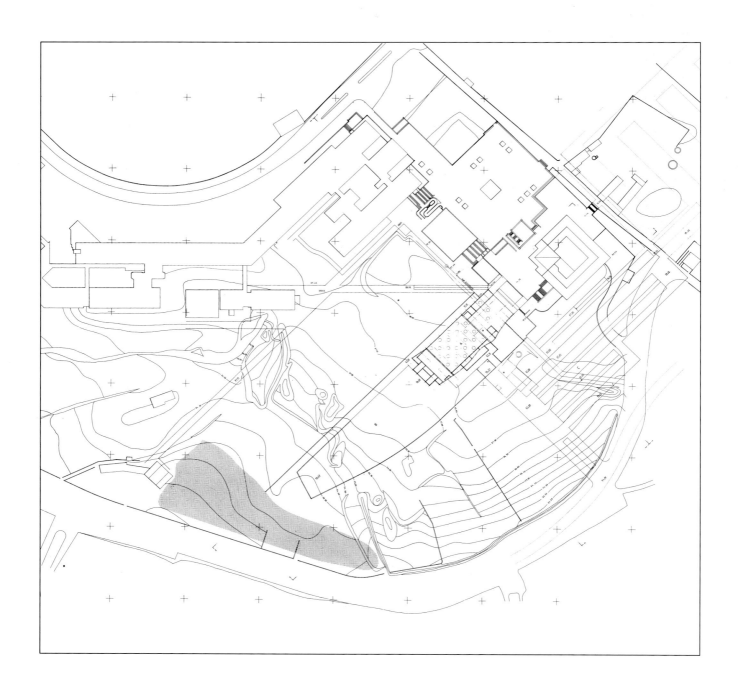

332　site plan

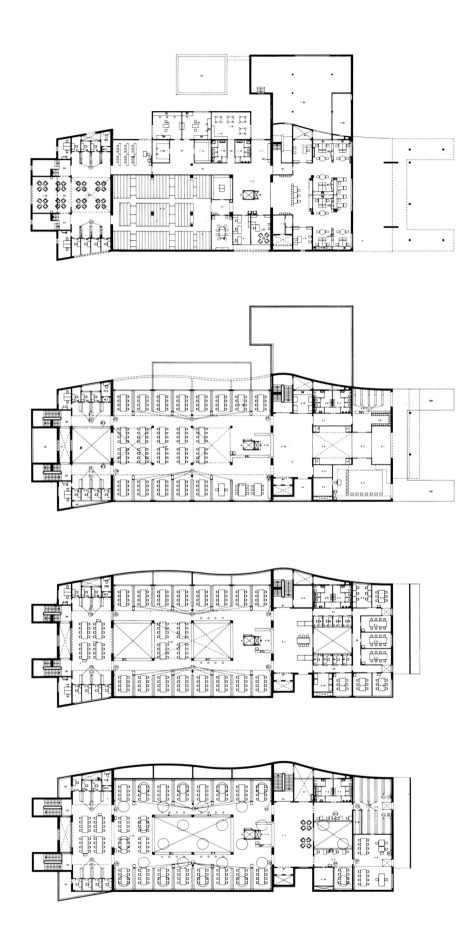

333   ground, first, second and third floor plans

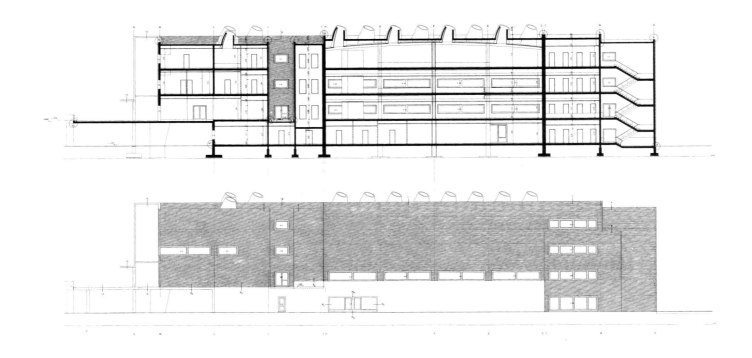
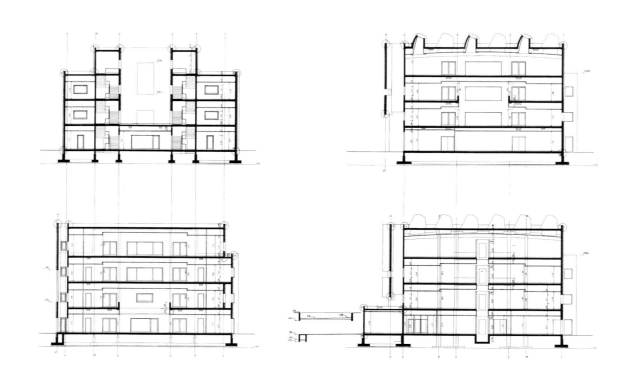

sections and elevations

The Museum of Santiago de Compostela
Álvaro Siza

When I was commissioned to build a museum in Santiago de Compostela, I was specifically asked to place it far from the road. The request revealed the widespread fear that architecture can sometimes arouse, not without reason. When one is building only a few metres away from a building classed as a national monument, as is the case with the Convent of Santo Domingo de Bonaval, one is apprehensive of compromising its integrity. For this reason I was asked to 'hide' the new museum. I argued that a cultural centre would be such a meaningful building for the city that it could not simply be thought of as an annexe to the convent. In addition, I managed to show that the convent had never been entirely visible due to the presence of a high granite wall that divided the property. I was able to work on the essential relation that the new building would have with the road. Thus, once the site of the museum was defined, the task of bringing it closer to the convent became necessary.

In the new museum, in harmony with the entrance, two areas define a small open space which interacts with the raised square opposite the facade of the convent. Facing one another, these two urban spaces define the access to the garden, which thus becomes the central element on which all the other buildings depend, something which had already occurred when the convent was being built. Immediately after this entrance to the garden there is a modest construction which I have preserved, and which articulates the routes along the terraces. The plan of the museum opens up to follow the course of the green spaces. The relation with the exterior, the road and the garden, was studied to take into account the needs of the interior, with a view to finding a harmonious relation between form and function, and guaranteeing transparency among the various parts. From this three areas were developed, each corresponding to three categories of function: the atrium and the offices, the auditorium and the library, and the exhibition halls. The first of these areas insists on proximity to the road, unlike the second, which moves away from it, whereas the third borders the garden. In the plan, this articulation translates into two triangles which could not only appear as residual spaces, but which claimed a major role in their own right because they were situated at key points. The first of these spaces lies between the auditorium and the atrium, along the outer perimeter of the building. This solution, which was reached very slowly, derives from the arrangement of the buildings on the other side of the road. The second triangle is located inside the building, and receives and distributes the light in the heart of the museum. This clear configuration of the spaces was supported by two routes identified as 'clarity' and 'liberty', exploiting the opportunity that no precise programme had ever been defined for the museum,

and that there was no properly defined collection of works, a problem still to be resolved. But the museum's flexibility has been thoroughly proven, since its exhibition halls have not suffered from the uses to which they have been put.

The design of the green spaces concludes the museum project. Since my initial contacts with the committee, I had understood that I would also be responsible for the design of the garden. From an eighteenth-century map I was able to understand the organisation and articulation of the convent space, and the study of these pre-existing relationships acted as the spur for the museum project. The constant search for connections with the surrounding built environment found expression in a solid building, whose final configuration was defined by the work on the design of the garden, which proved to be a perfect instrument for the 'use' of nature. The great wisdom in building has distinctive roots in Galicia, passed down from the Celts to the Arabs. Because the plan I have mentioned could not supply all the information that was needed, additional research was undertaken and we finally discovered the ancient irrigation system of the area. The old granite canals were brought to light, along with the half-destroyed fountains and walls, and the garden is designed on the basis of zigzag ramps and flights of steps. The paths within the museum follow a similar course.

In the project for the Serralves Museum in Porto, one of the chief problems lay in restricting the impact of the new building on a beautiful garden from the thirties, the extension of an art deco house. Exactly as had happened in Santiago de Compostela, in this museum the form and organization of the spaces required by the programme derive from the special relation with the garden. This green area, miraculously preserved in the centre of Porto, is characterized by the interesting sequence of the house, the formal garden, a wood and an area of farming land. The encounter between the different dimensions of the museum and the house is one of the most interesting aspects of the project. The museum develops out of an atrium that makes reference to the art deco house and then branches off in a 'U' from a large central hall.

1988–93 Galician Centre of Contemporary Art *Santiago de Compostela, Spain*

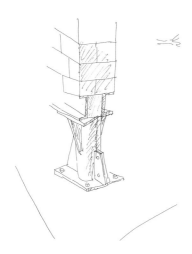

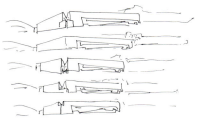
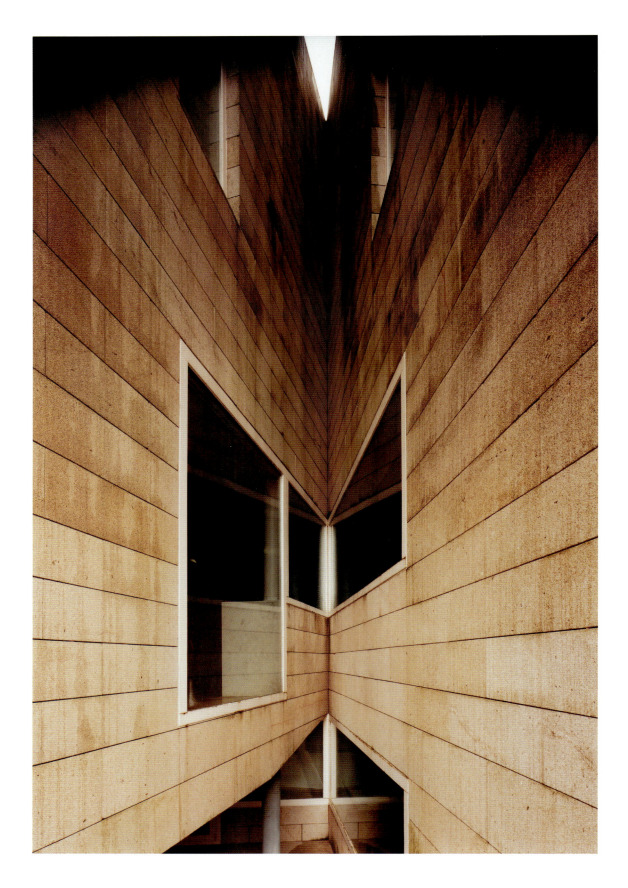

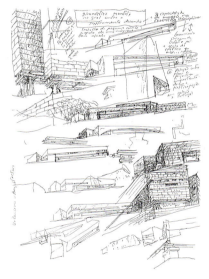

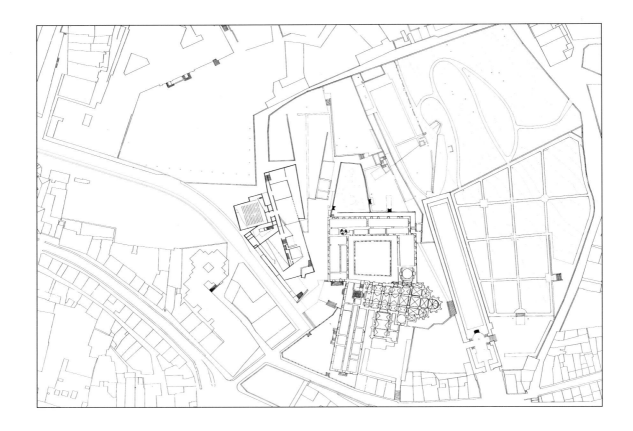
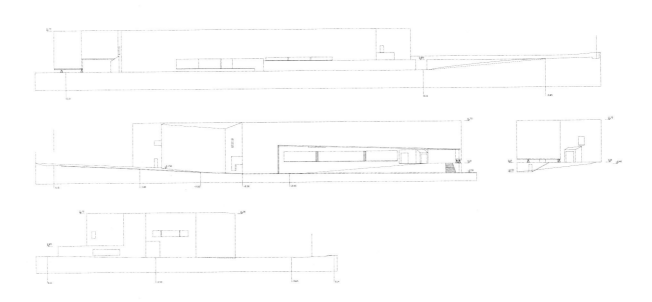

site plan and elevations

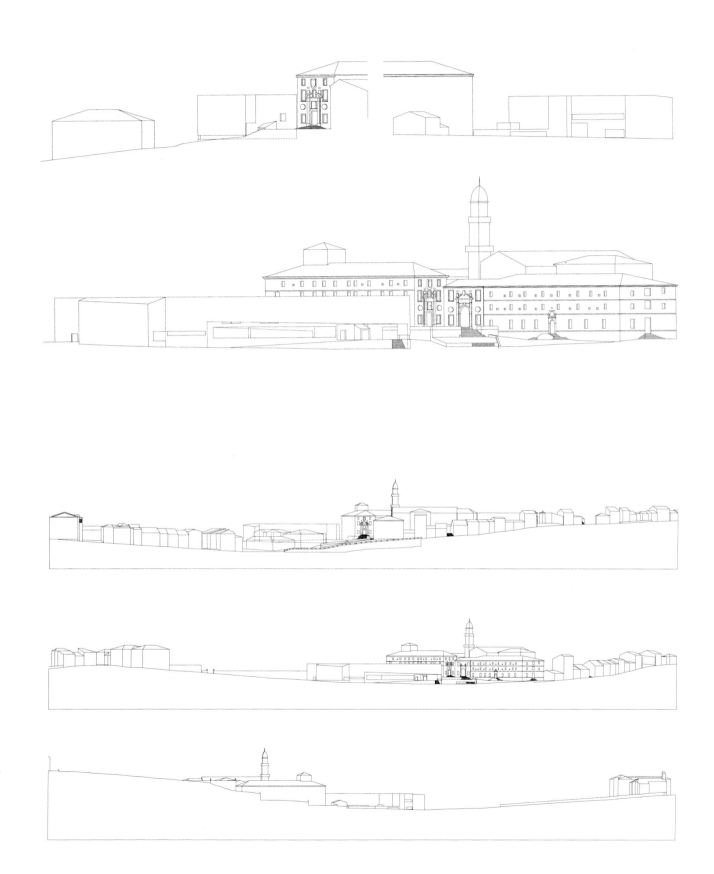

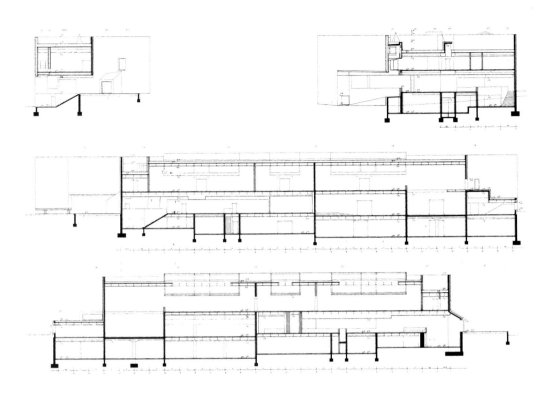
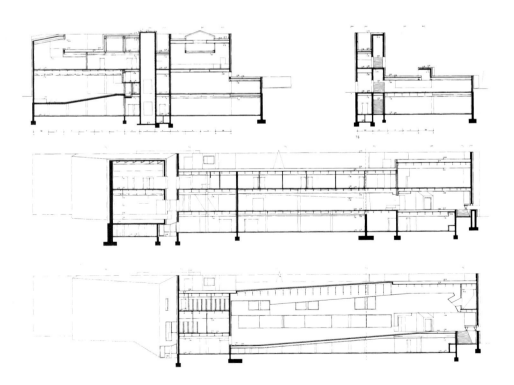

long and cross sections

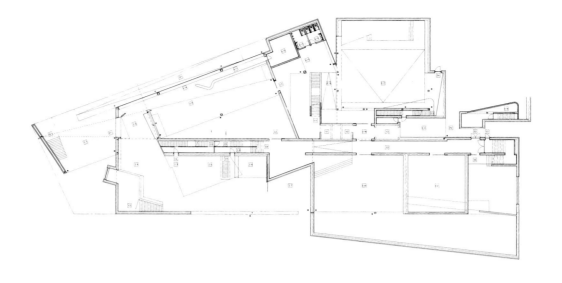
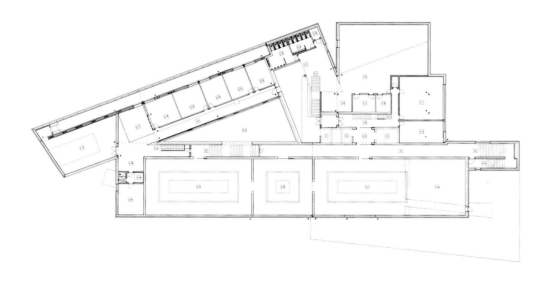
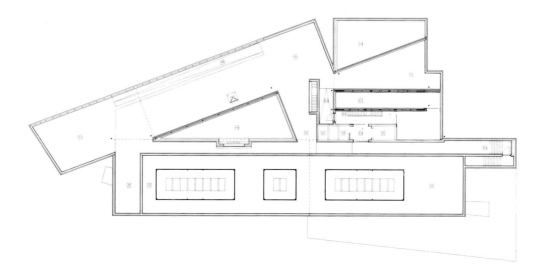

346   lower ground, ground, first/second floor plans

1990–4 Santo Domingo de Bonaval Garden *Santiago de Compostela, Spain*

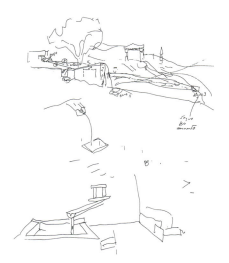

351　site plan, plan and fountain details

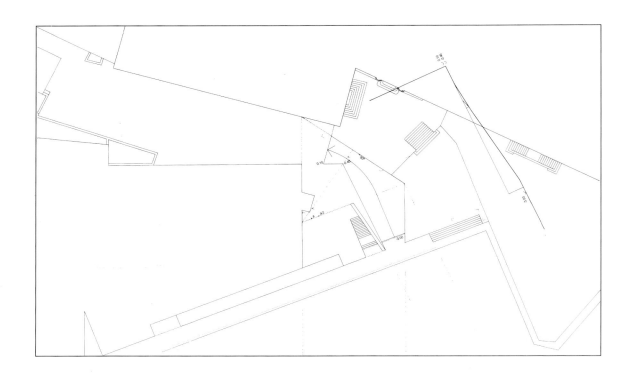

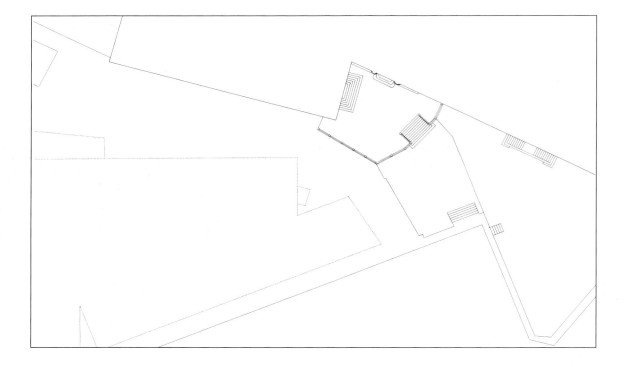

above existing plan *below* new plan

1988   Design for Sports Complex *Villanueva de Arosa, Spain*

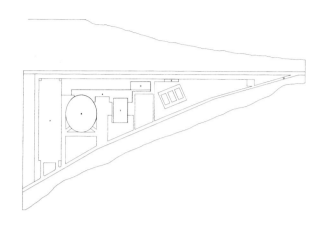
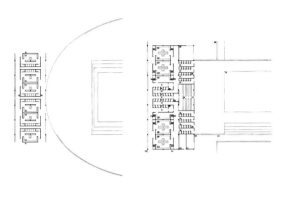

1988–91   Design for Alcino Cardoso House *Moledo do Minho, Portugal*

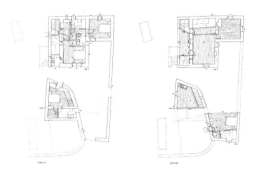

1988–9   Carvalho Araújo Shop *Lisbon, Portugal*

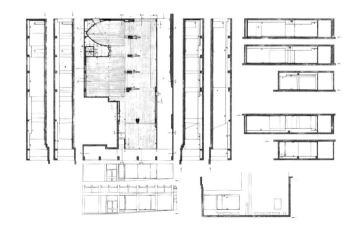

354   *above* site plan and plan   *centre* elevations and plans   *below* plan and sections

1988 Design for Guardiola House *Seville, Spain*

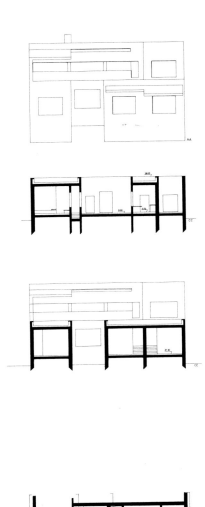
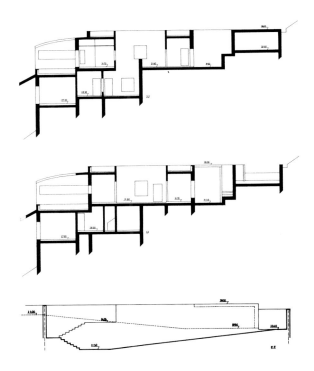
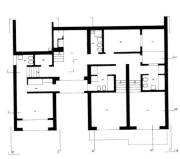
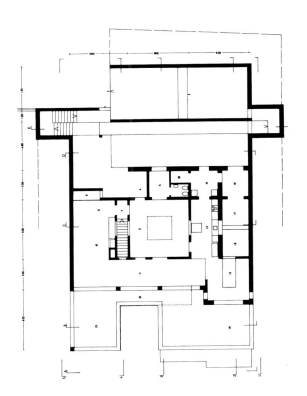

elevations, sections and plan

What it cannot be any more. A moving, fascinating machine in which the past is present, in which everything has the charm of an alley, golden dust at the close of the day, worn graffiti, gleams and fractures, the enchantment of the kitsch and things that have passed out of fashion, of garbage, a suffocating atmosphere, of drugs, and a glimpse of the Tagus. Tombstones with forgotten names, collages of ambiguous style, an abandoned courtyard with little animals and rare plants, decadence. Nostalgia for something I have hardly known.

What it will be. The same as it was? There is an inevitable touch of falseness. The air of a model exposed to time, premeditated, liable to dissolution. In Rua Garrett, on the left and as far as the Carmo Hotel, one can see a magnificent gateway built out of limestone, metal, wood, glass and mirrors. This gateway opens onto a tall gallery, with light at the far end. It invites you to enter, even though there are no neon lights, advertising signs, loudspeakers, or popular marches. The light is natural, breaking up the facade with its rigid Pombalino design, while people are silhouetted against the light as they walk through the gallery: half-light and reflections.

At the end, the facade of the hotel reappears, hybrid in appearance and recently modified, without much conviction, as it was years ago. It opens its arms and raises its head, once that of a church. Beyond the curtains, one catches a glimpse of peaceful rooms. The rows of windows struggle on equal terms with the limestone-faced wall. There are uniformed doormen, tenants, businessmen, married couples, foreigners, pornographic booksellers, bars, restaurants, upholsterers and gilders, music underneath the silence. On the upper floors the windows reveal nothing, apart from the occasional guest drawing a curtain and peering out with an anxious gaze. And the space is filled with this gaze.

The crowds pass through Rua Nova do Almada, a multitude in movement links the Escada de São Francisco to the Escada do Carmo – large windows amidst the sculptures done up by the people from the neighbouring Beaux Arts.

Is it all the same? Some people are disappointed: the shop windows are boring, it is said, a bit of modernism is needed. Anyone who looks closer notices the double glazing and other things, especially the people who live there. Those who live in better conditions notice nothing. Nor do they need to.

And this gateway? A stark hole, without frontage or molding, an unexpected hole, a sort of incomplete funnel that embraces a splendid flight of steps, before the great deterioration that has produced incomparable rotundities and strange patches of plaster. In the air, the bridge of the elevator, a foretaste of the upper city. And the light at the end of the gallery, full of green and lilac, like a painting by Malhoa; and shadows, bamboo chairs and exquisitely-coloured drinks, the weight of the supporting walls. At sunset, the people living at the top open their windows or cross the courtyard of the Carmo, climb the flights of steps and pause on the landings. The city rises slowly, first peers out and then suddenly bursts through the curtains – the Tagus, Paço, working-class districts, Castelo, Rossio. The arches of the Convent explode. Someone recalls, in amusement, a different expectation.

1988 Reconstruction of the Chiado Area *Lisbon, Portugal*

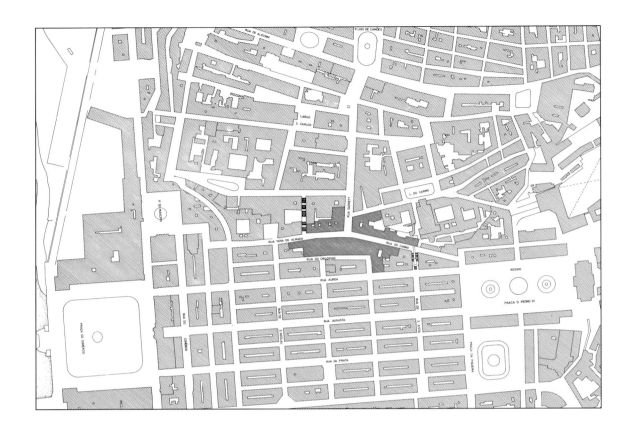
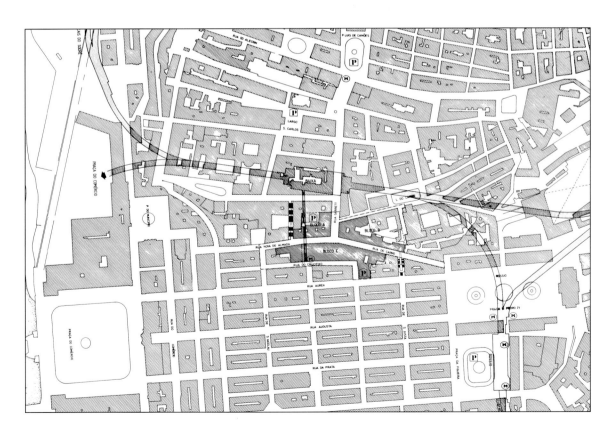

site plan and intervention plan

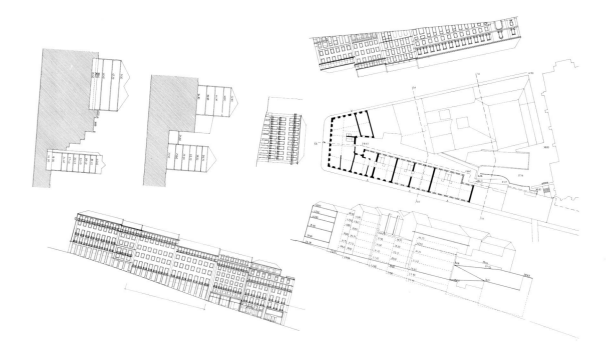

perspective, site plan, sections and elevations

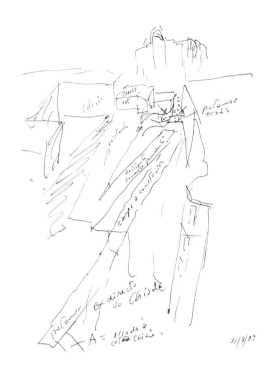

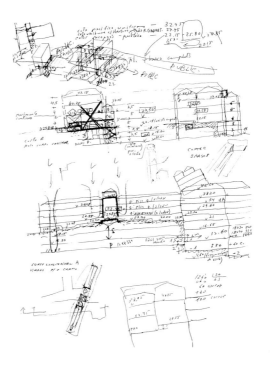
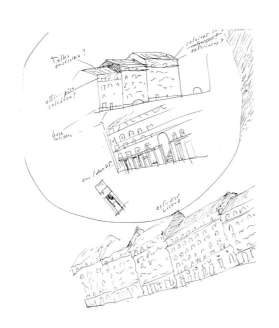
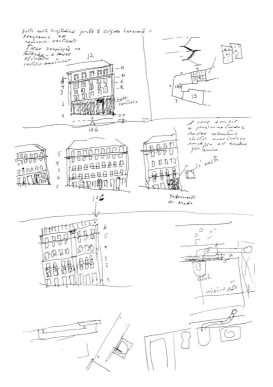

1988 Design for Reconstruction of Portal di Riquer *Alcoi-Valencia, Spain*

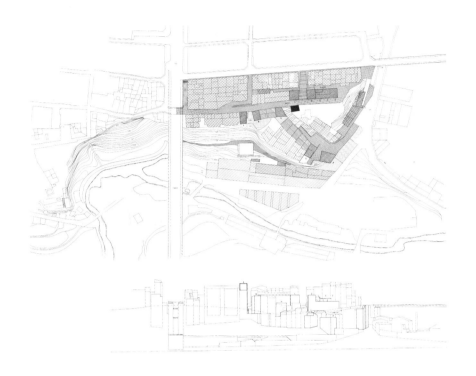

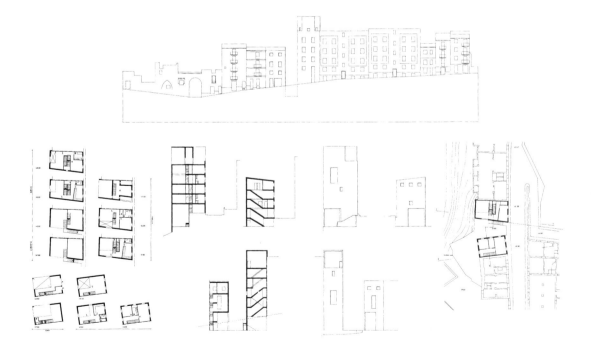

above site plan and perspective *below* plans, sections and elevations

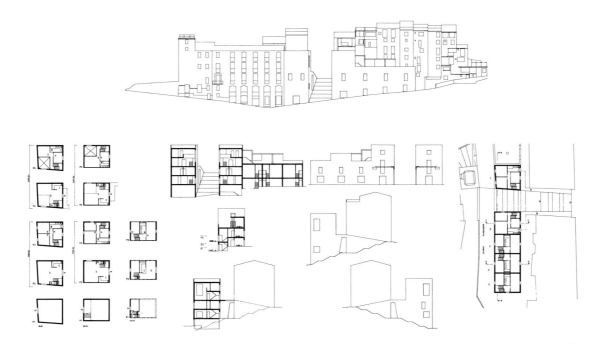

1989 Housing in Concepción Arenal *Cádiz, Spain*

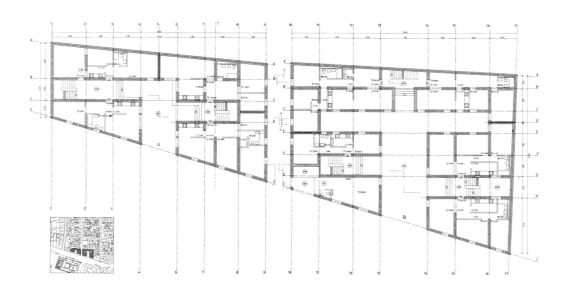

366 *above* Portal di Riquer plans, sections and elevations *below* site plan and plan

1989   Competition Design for National Library of France *Paris, France*

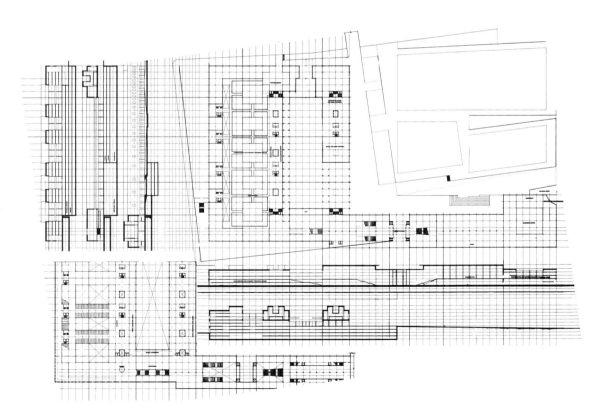

367   plans and sections

1989–93 Residential Settlement, Schilderswijk *The Hague, The Netherlands*

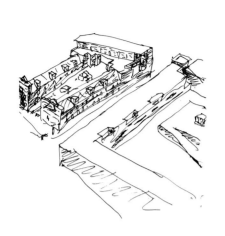 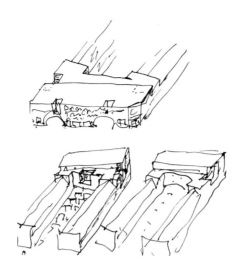 

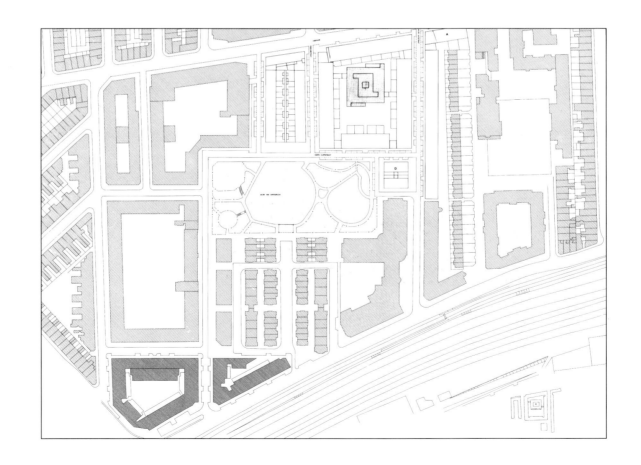

369   site plan

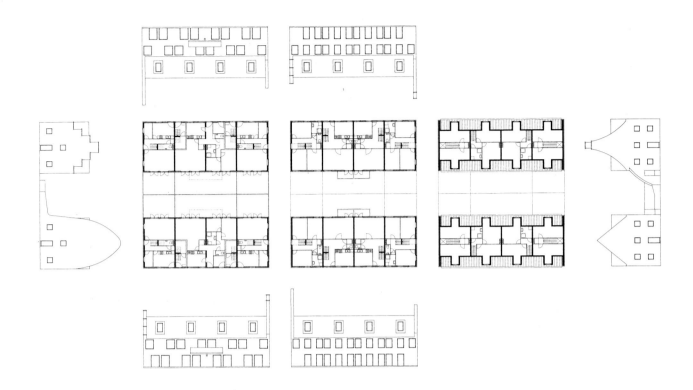

370   *above* plans and elevations *below* elevations

1989 Design for S. João Bosco Church and Parish Centre *Malagueira, Évora, Portugal*

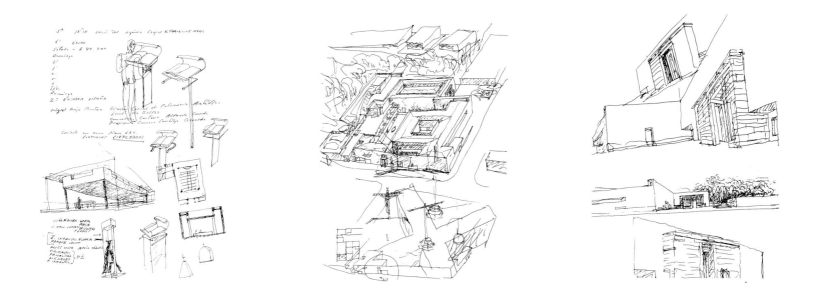

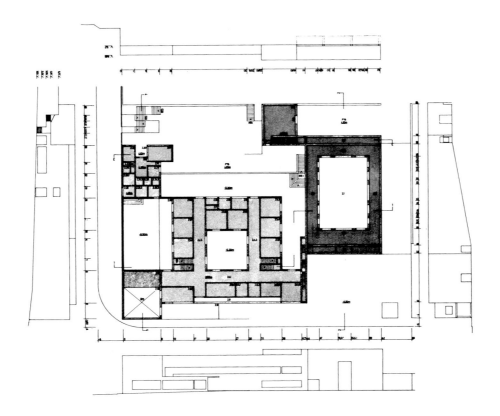

first floor plan and elevations

1989–95   Ferreira de Castro Office Building *Oliveira de Azeméis, Portugal*

1989   Urban and Circulation Study for Praça de Espanha *Lisbon, Portugal*

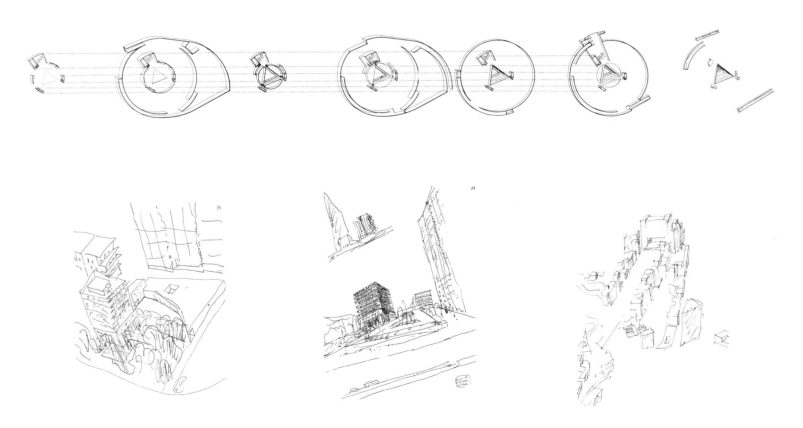

373   *above* sketch *below* exploded circulation diagram and sketches

1989–95 Ana Costa and Manuel Silva House *Santo Ovidio, Lousada, Portugal*

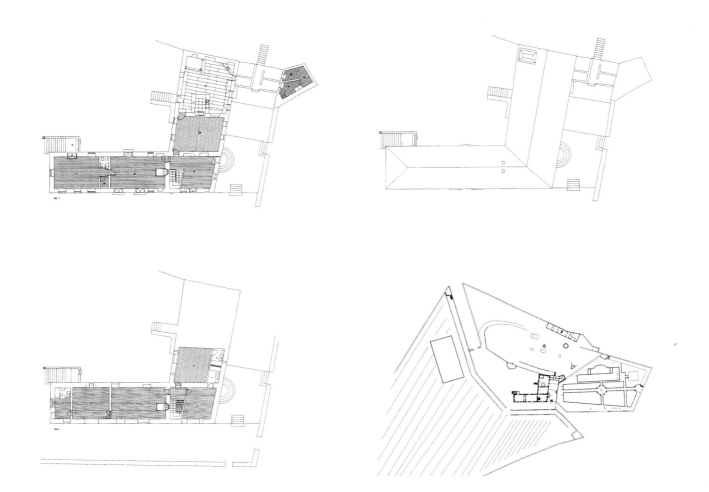
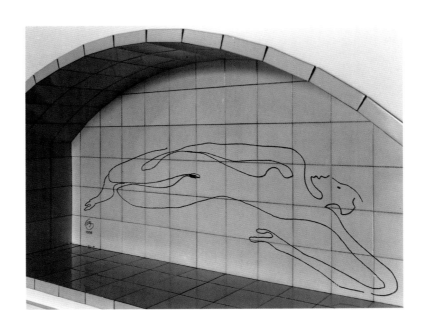

375   ground, first floor and roof plans and site plan

1990 Design for Pereira Ganhão House *Tróia, Portugal*

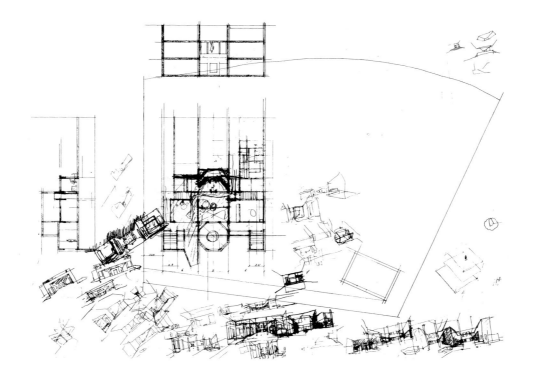

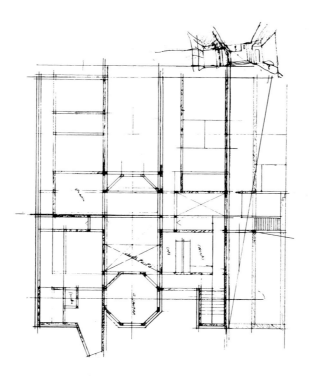

The Church at Marco de Canavezes
Álvaro Siza

The church that rises out of the little town of Marco de Canavezes, some distance east of Porto, is part of a religious complex that will eventually comprise an auditorium, a catechism school and the parish priest's residence. I had been profoundly disturbed by my visit to the area selected for the building; it was a difficult site with a very uneven terrain, immediately above a busy road. In addition, this part of the city is marked by buildings of dreadful quality. That is why the complex aims to define a *place*, instead of an insignificant slope.

The church is articulated on two levels: the upper level accommodates the congregation, the lower is a mortuary chapel. The two spaces have very different characteristics, as their respective access routes demonstrate. The mortuary chapel effectively acts as the base of the building: it defines a levelled slope with the church resting upon it. Its granite walls and cloister establish the distance from the road. This inhabitable platform was intended to have the appearance of a 'constructed landscape'. No less important is the location, facing the main entrance, of the parish centre and the parish priest's residence; their areas define a large 'U' facing the smaller 'U' formed by the bell-tower and the baptistry. This in turn defines the space that is able to accommodate the large area of the main facade and establishes a rapport with the small-scale buildings surrounding this 'acropolis'.

The initial reference point for the project was a pre-existing building, an old-people's home, correct and orderly in style, which stands on the upper part of the slope and extends to the road. The rest of the complex was articulated from this new level, in response to the confusion of the existing buildings, and finally permitting the definition of the churchyard, which looks out over the beautiful valley of Marco de Canavezes. The large portal of the church, ten metres tall, is justified in relation to this great vista. Normally, in order to enter the church, a glass door beneath the right-hand tower is used; the main entrance is opened only on very special occasions. Once inside the church, one becomes aware of the presence of a long, low window to the right which, once again, gives a view outside, and one does not notice the diffuse light coming down from the openings in the curved and inclined wall on the left. What one sees is the valley and the buildings in the foreground. The window does not encourage the atmosphere of contemplation that we expect from a church, and this has created a degree of controversy, as did the placing of the statue of the Virgin. But this effigy occupies an intermediate position, it is strongly lit in its position at the end of the window, and serves as an introduction to the space occupied by the altar, which people entering do not immediately see. The plane of liturgical celebration is elevated to a height of three steps and complemented by two openings through which a clear light enters, filtered by a high chimney. The layout interacts with the light that bathes the curved forms of the apse and the overall space of the church. The natural lighting varies over time depending on the position of the sun, from the projection of a single shaft of light to the silence of dispersal. All the elements have been composed coherently but the order that emerges from them, which introduces objective and deliberate contradictions, was constructed in a slow and laborious way. There are no preconceived ideas at work here; what we see is the product of the distillation of a series of reflections on the nature of religious space. These reflections have been made difficult today by the major reforms that the liturgy has undergone, as evidenced by the fact that the priest now celebrates mass facing the congregation. This transformation has altered the character of the celebration and rendered the traditional organization of the liturgical space irrelevant. However, this new situation does not allow us to consider the church as an auditorium and almost all recent projects have failed to address the problem in the appropriate way. By reflecting on the 'functional' implications defined by this situation, and holding conversations with theologians, I have identified the need to guarantee the communion between the celebrant and the congregation, avoiding the separation typical of an auditorium. For that reason, in the apse, I have adopted convex rather than concave walls, without following any hypothesis simply drawn from liturgical reforms, although with the aim of maintaining a connection with the objects and movements that form a part of the celebration. Around the altar, the ambo, the tabernacle, the seats and the cross have been slowly defined, and have contributed in turn to the configuration of the space, being organized according to the established movements of the mass. In this way the church has acquired its shape as a negative sculpture, and tensions and connections of continuity have been defined between the various parts.

The design of the route which leads from the exchoir to the mortuary chapel, on the lower floor, is the result of the study of what happens in these spaces, and an awareness of the significance of funerals for the people of the Minho region of northern Portugal. Here during funerals, families and close friends are close to the departed, while many other people follow the ceremony from some distance away. This has suggested the definition of a sequence of spaces with different characteristics, and for that reason I thought of the cloister, a place where people can retire to smoke, chat or even talk business – a way of reacting to the grief produced by such a direct encounter with death.

The cloister is followed by a first, fairly wide gallery marked, after the entrance, by the prolongation of the curved wall of the apse. On the left, a few metres along, is another gallery at the end of which there is a vertical window providing a view of the road. I don't know precisely the connection between this opening and the horizontal one inside the church, but I believe that the horizontal form in the base is intended to convey the sensation of weight and the gravity of the building. The route concludes in the mortuary chapel, which communicates with the first gallery through a window. In this way, anyone inside can observe the people coming in or going out, just as, on the upper level, the congregation can see the road. In the chapel, the path of light that illuminates the altar on the upper plane concludes with an opening that gives a view of the cloister. A flight of steps leading from the cloister to the upper level is an important presence here, because the unity of the project derives from the configuration of the routes leading in a circle back to the starting-point, to suggest the sensation of being in a closed and confined place.

I have always been impressed by the fact that churches tend to impose an atmosphere of contemplation; for that reason the openings are often so high that it is impossible to look out, and the use of polychrome glass stands in the way of transparency. It seemed to me, however, that recent liturgical reforms are at odds with this closed and segregated conception of space. So, when I began to study the project, I became aware of the importance of this break with the continuity of tradition, one which barely touches on the relations between church and society in everyday life. For that reason, in spite of the adaptations, I tried to preserve continuity with tradition, and if one pays close attention to the

character of this church, it soon becomes apparent that the conception behind it is substantially conservative. The design of the highly axial plan is an expression of this, as is the vertical nature of the interior. In fact, although the nave has a square section, the articulation of the various elements, like the openings behind the altar, aim to create a vertical effect. Tiles were used on some of the internal walls. Due to the fact that it was necessary to adopt a surface that could be easily cleaned and maintained, I had originally thought in terms of a wood covering, but this would have compromised the verticality of the walls and the reflections of light. So, instead, I thought of using hand-made tiles with a slightly irregular surface, which give off particular reflections, as do the gaps that underline their discontinuity with the plastered wall. At first I thought of using them throughout the whole of the church but, given the problems involved in the curved walls and the doorways, I restricted their presence. One of the objectives I had been set was to ensure that the details should not be so obvious as to compete with the spatial structure. For that reason I paid a great deal of attention to studying the relations between the various materials used.

Outside one becomes aware of the considerable presence of granite, a material which is typical of the natural and built landscape of the region. The base emerges as the necessary counterpoint to the lightness and geometrical conciseness of the white volume above. At some times of the day the church seems to dematerialize, while at others it stands out starkly against the sky: for this reason, too, we needed to adopt a base that would 'anchor' it to the ground, as in some of the pre-Columbian buildings that I have been able to study in Peru.

1990–6 Santa Maria Church and Parish Centre *Marco de Canavezes, Portugal*

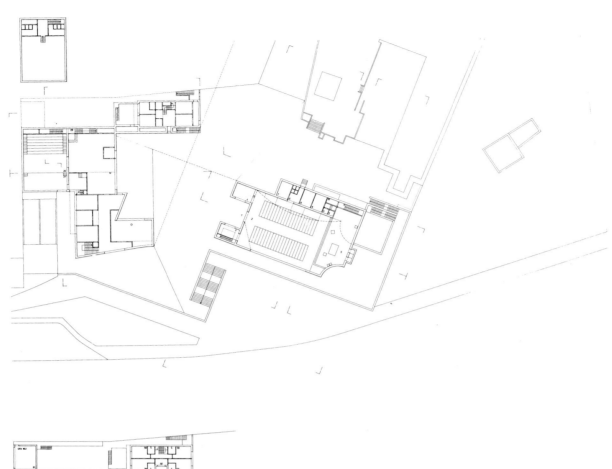
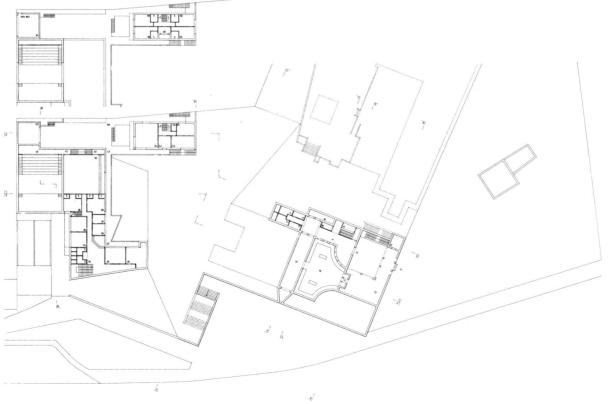

382 plans

383

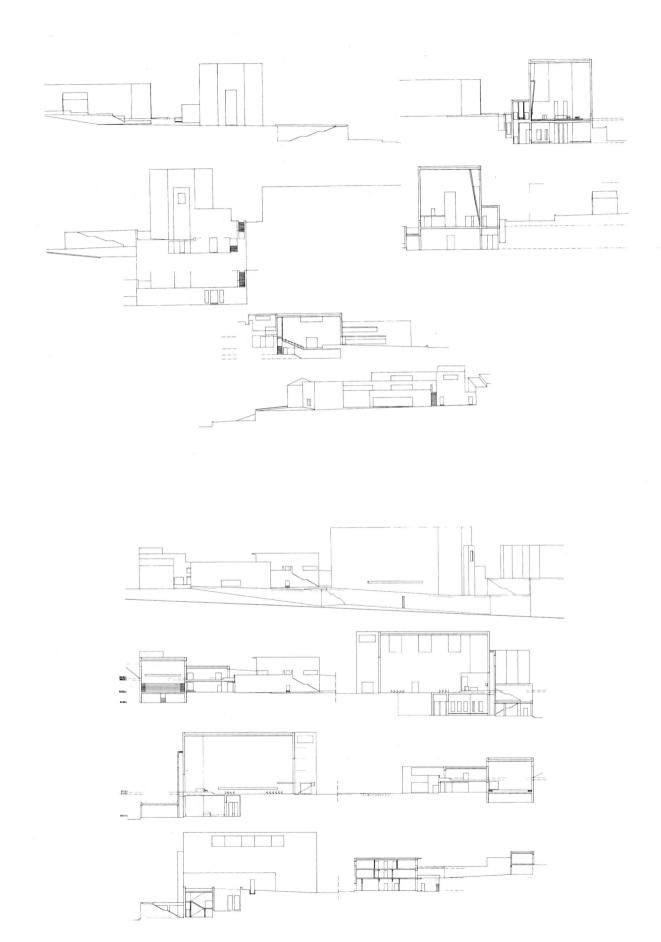

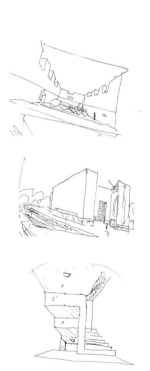

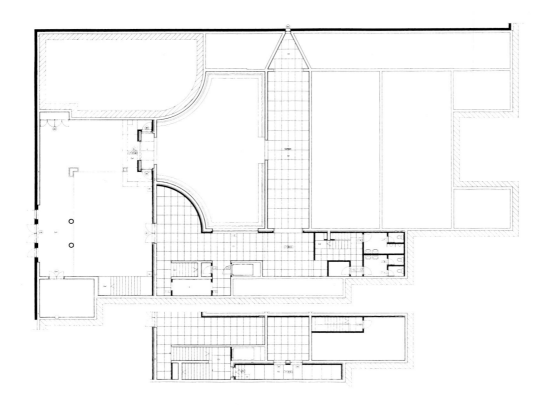

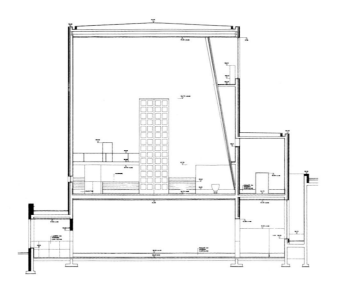

plan and section

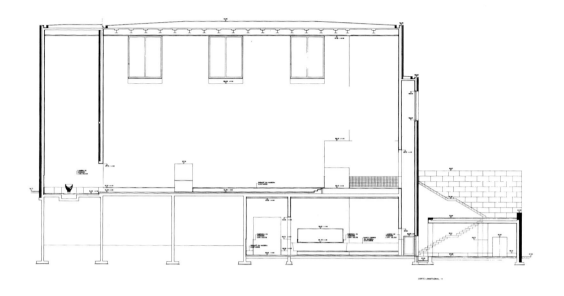
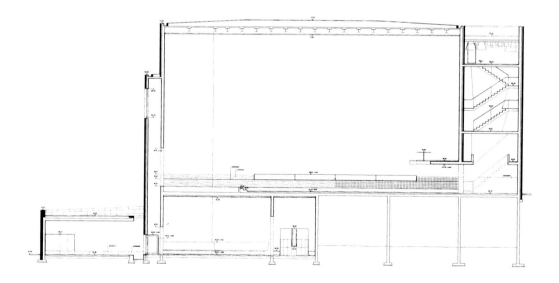

388 long section and cross section

1990 Ceramic Terrain Housing and Offices *Maastricht, The Netherlands*

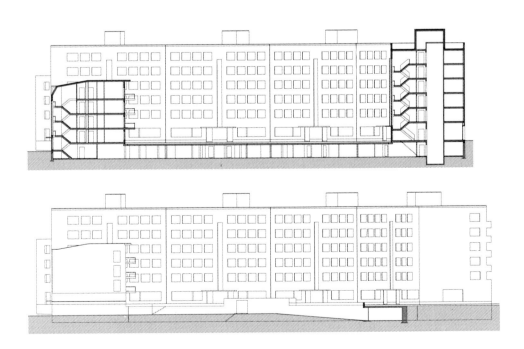

site plan, section and elevation

1990–3 Design for Santo Domingo de Bonaval Restaurant *Santiago de Compostela, Spain*

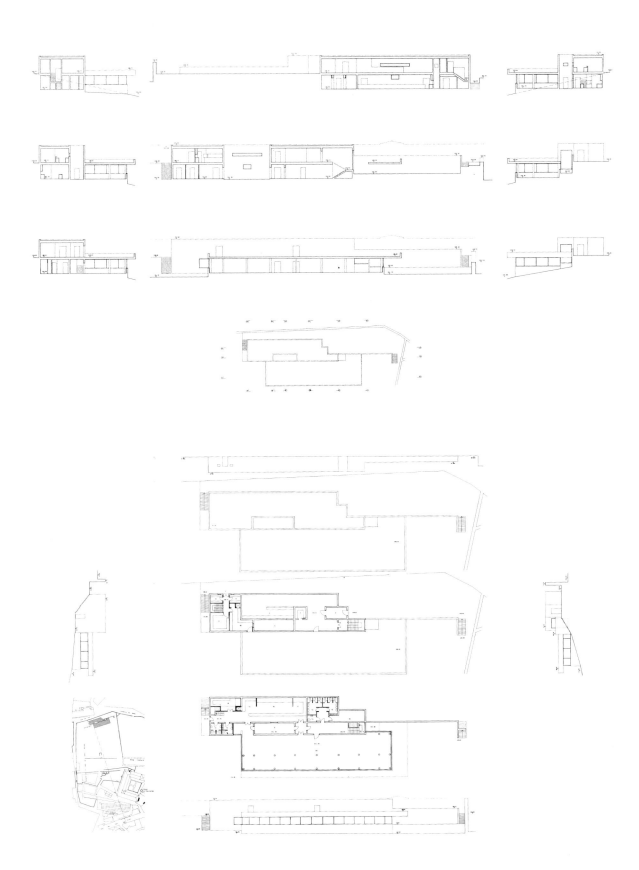

above long and cross sections *below* site plan, plans and elevations

1990–2 Olympic Village Meteorological Centre and MOPU Delegation Headquarters *Barcelona, Spain*

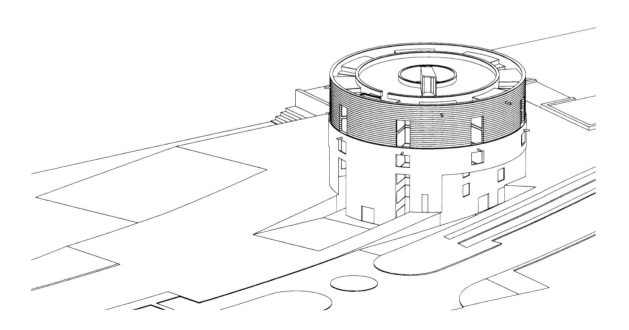

below axonometric

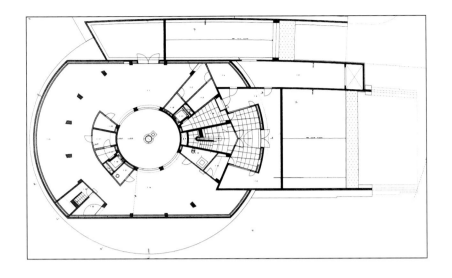
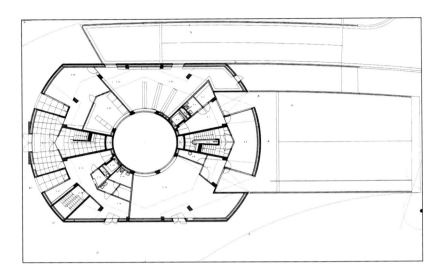
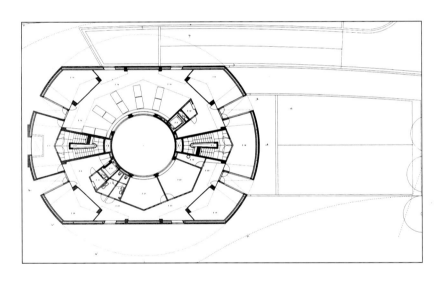
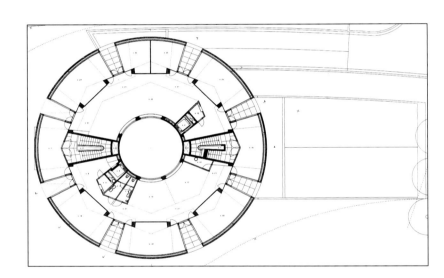
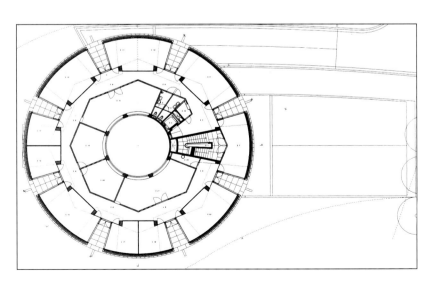
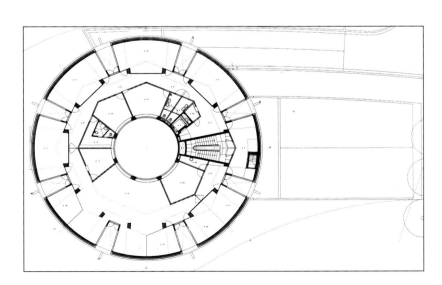

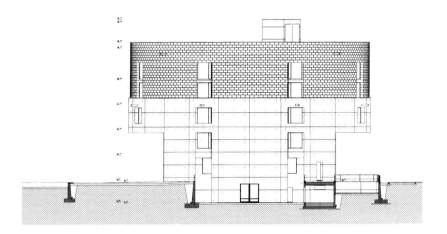
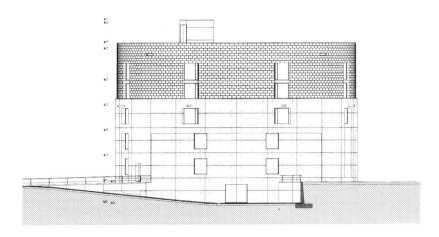
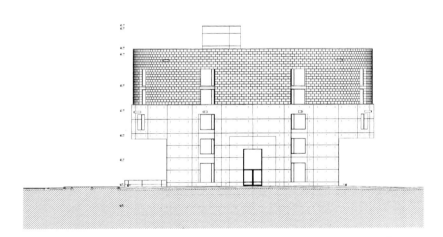
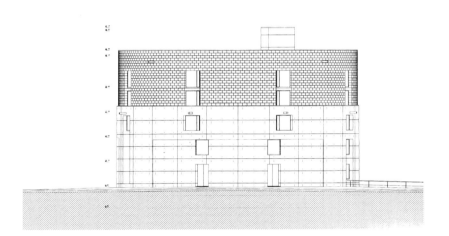
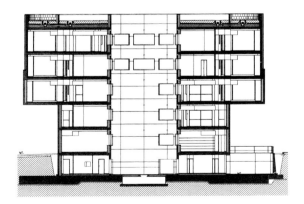

401   elevations and section

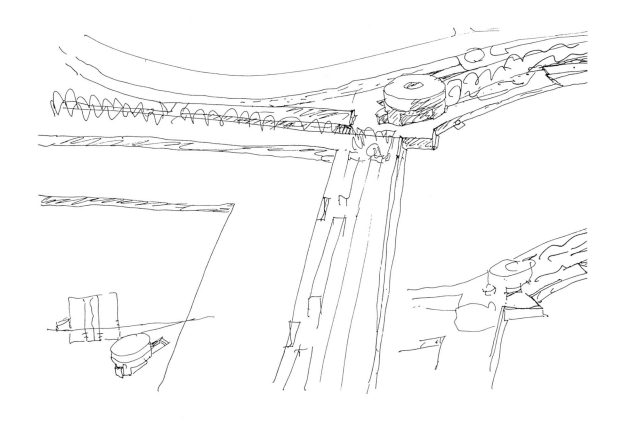

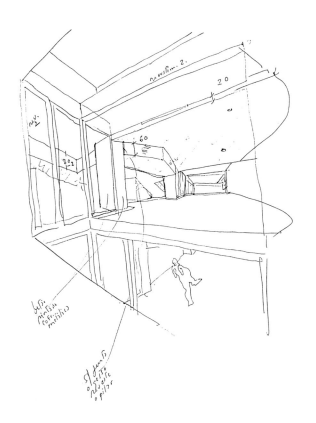

1990   Urban Design for Boulevard Brune, Cité de Jeunesse *Paris, France*

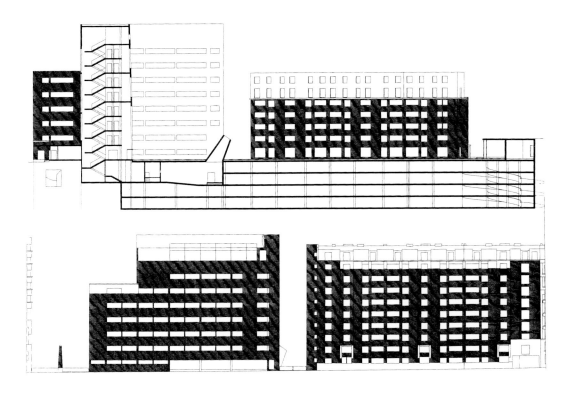

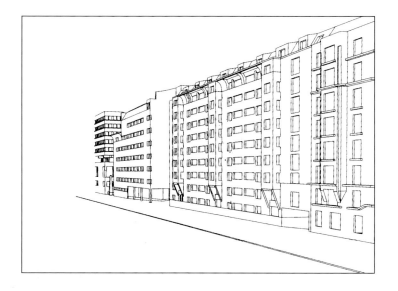

404   section, elevation and perspective

1990–2 Urban Plan for Avenida José Malhoa *Lisbon, Portugal*

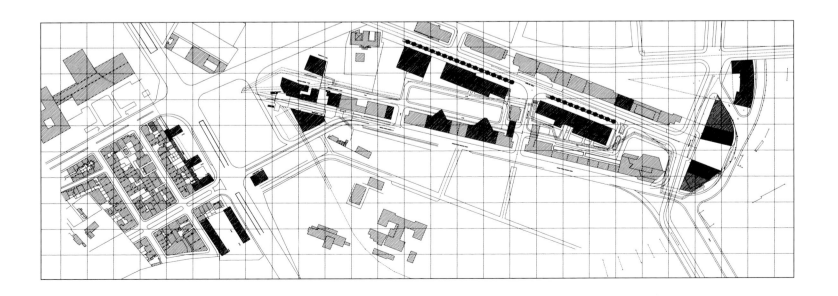

site plan

1990 Design of Rectory and Law Library, University of Valencia *Valencia, Spain*

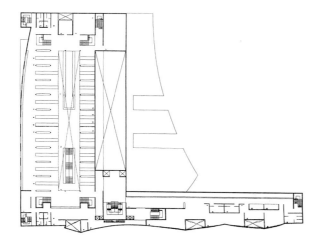
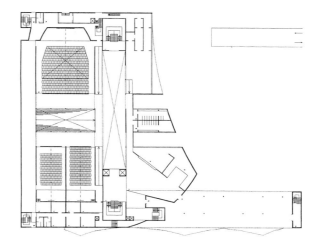
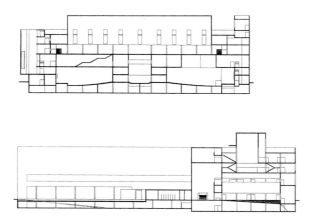
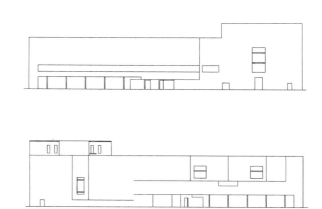

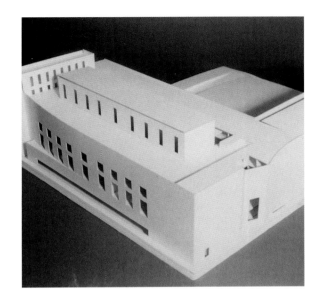
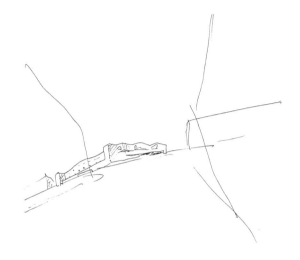
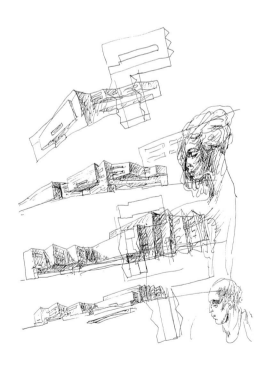
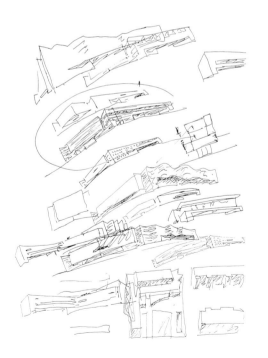

1990–8 Boavista Building *Porto, Portugal*

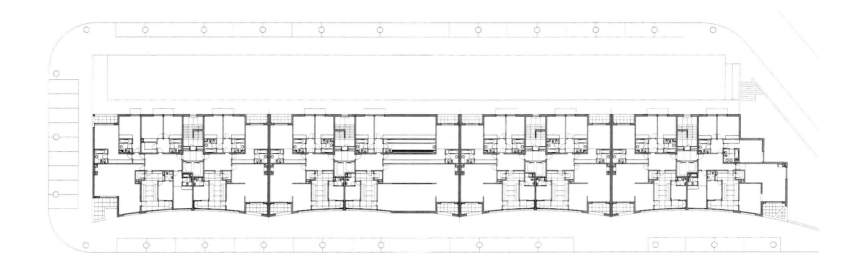
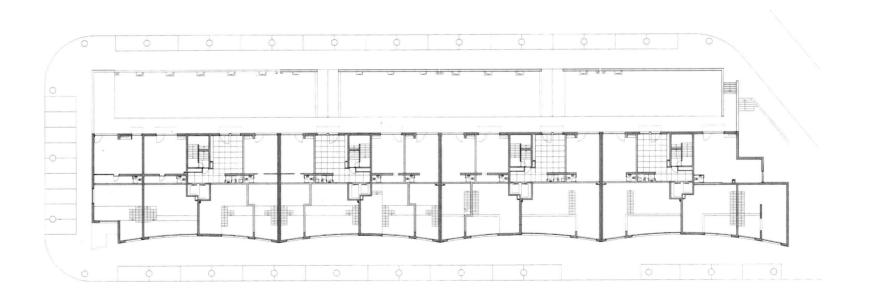

413   plans

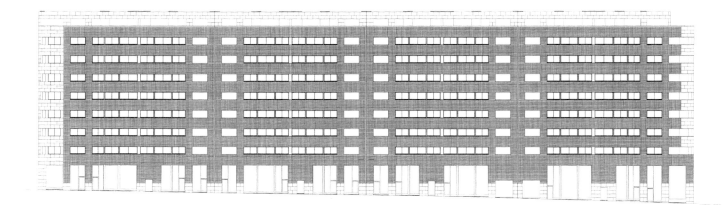
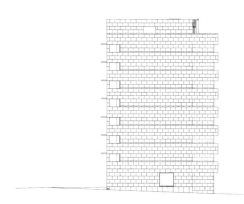

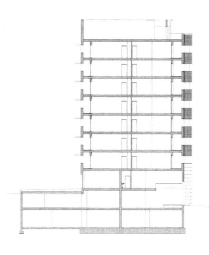
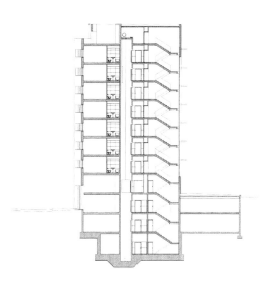

elevations and sections

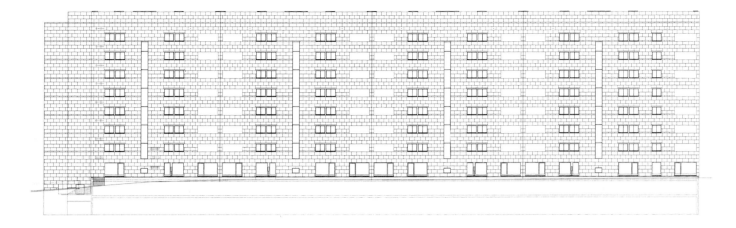

1991   Design for Office Building *Porto, Portugal*

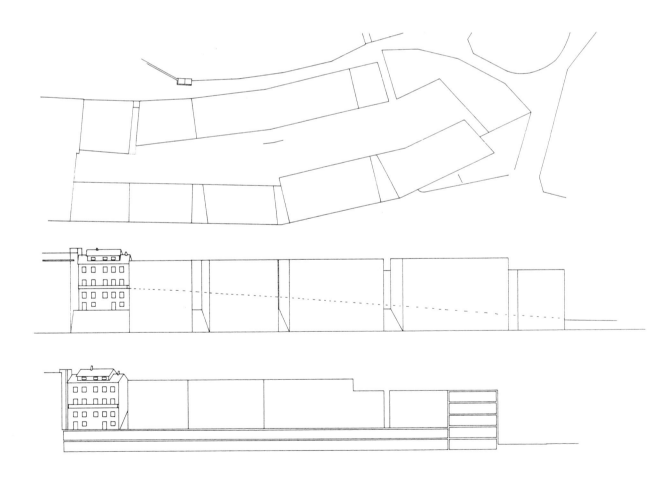

415   *above* Boa Vista elevation *below* plan, elevation and section

1991–9 Museum of Contemporary Art, Serralves Foundation *Porto, Portugal*

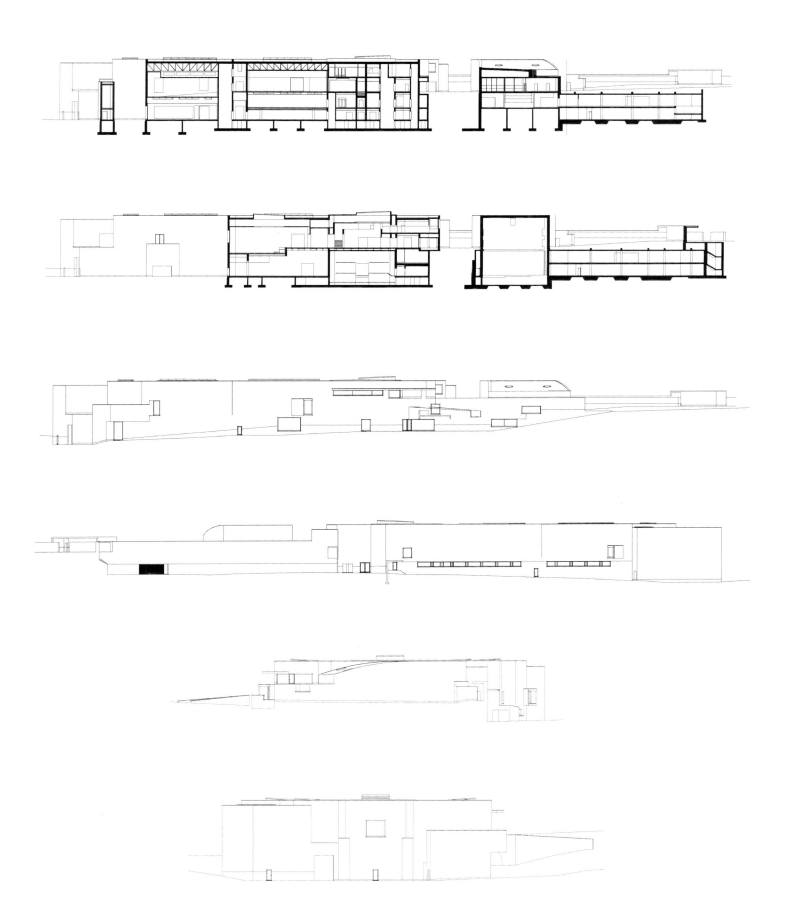

419 sections and elevations

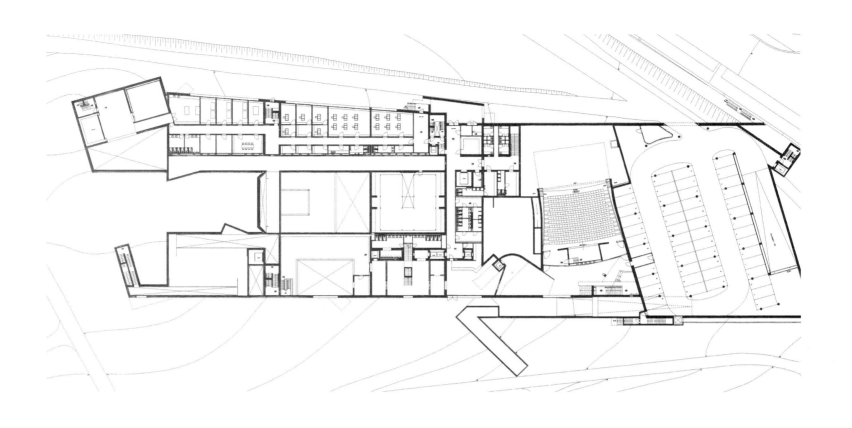
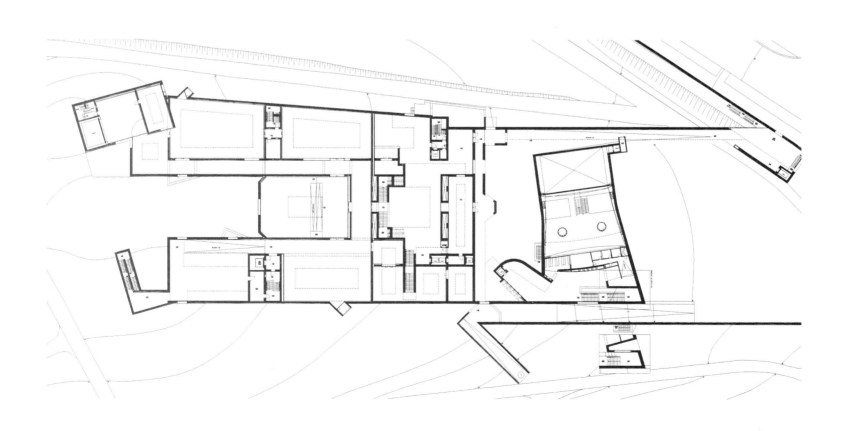

second and third floor plans

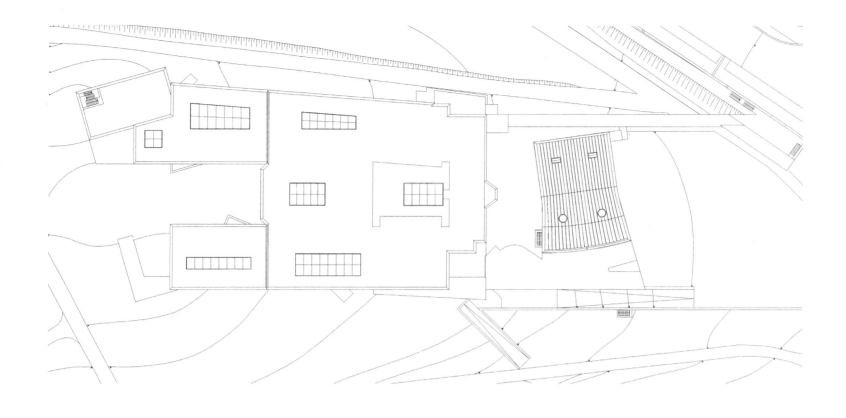

roof plan and site plan

1991–4 Restoration of Castro & Melo Building *Chiado, Lisbon, Portugal*

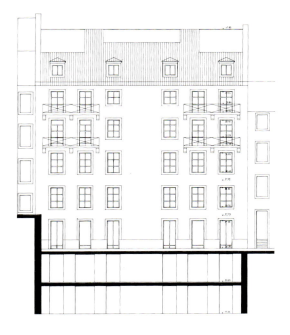

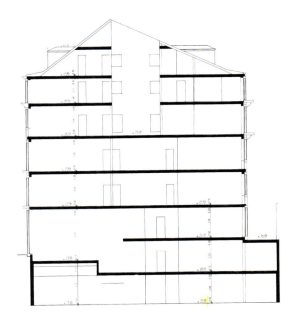
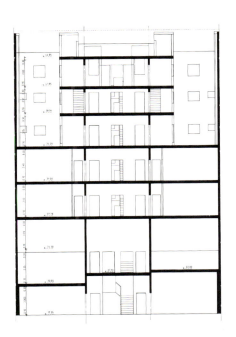

425   elevations and sections

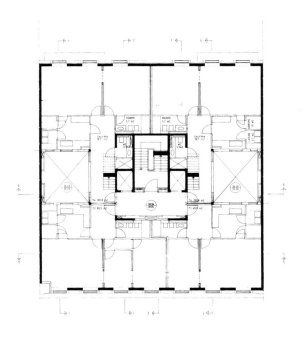
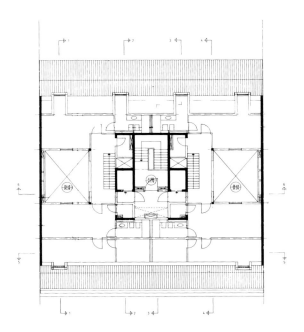
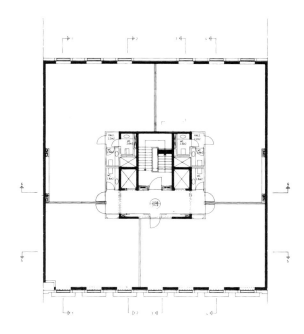
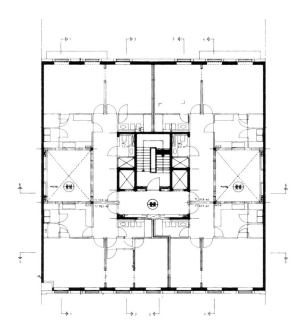

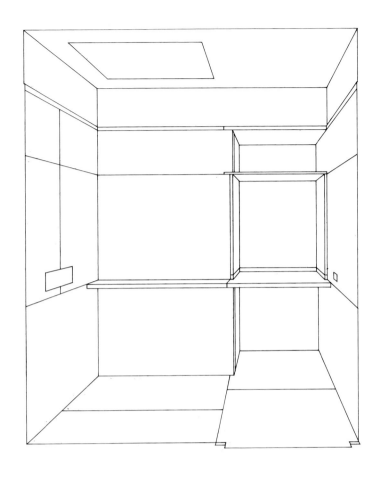
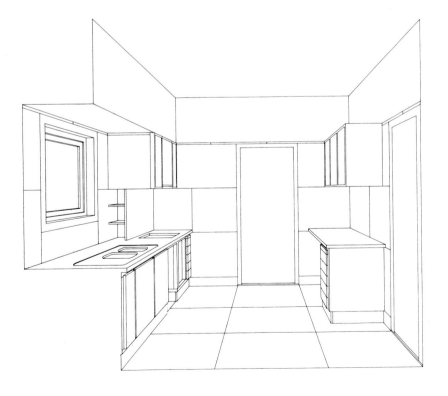
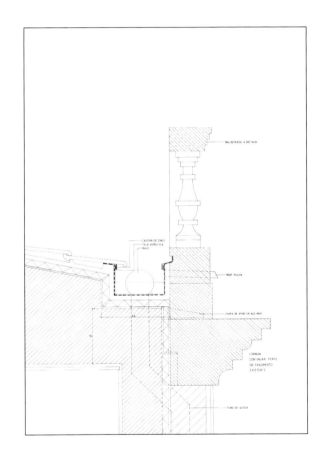

427 internal layouts and balustrade detail

1991–6 Restoration of Camara Chaves Building *Chiado, Lisbon, Portugal*

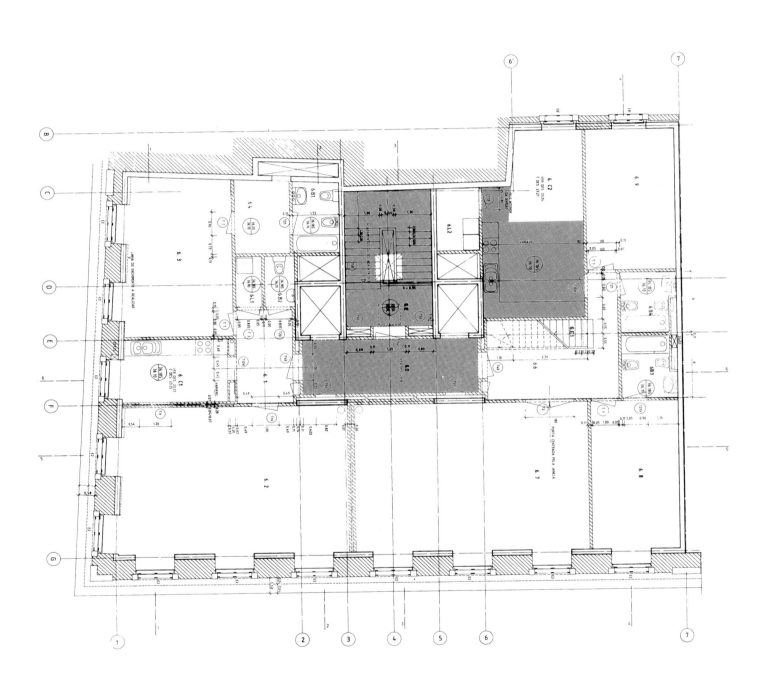

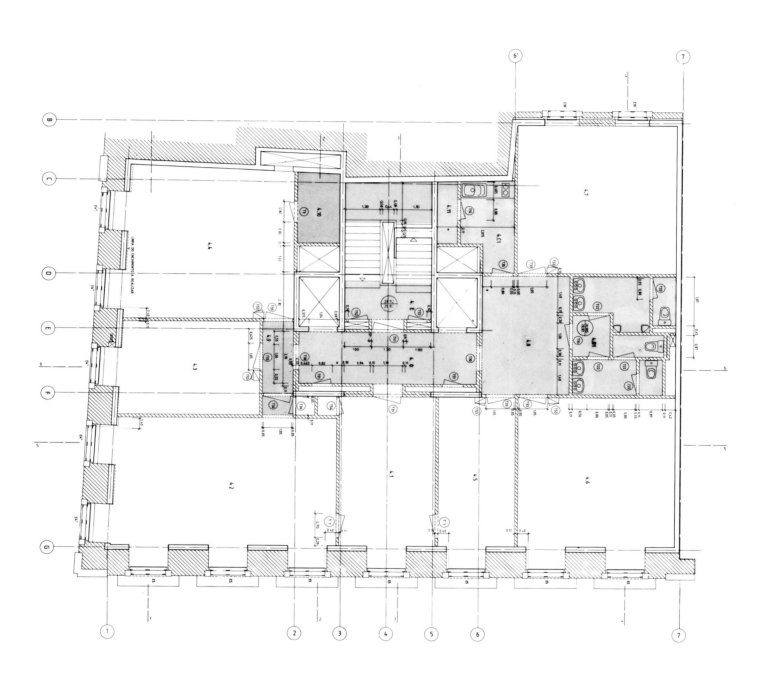

plan

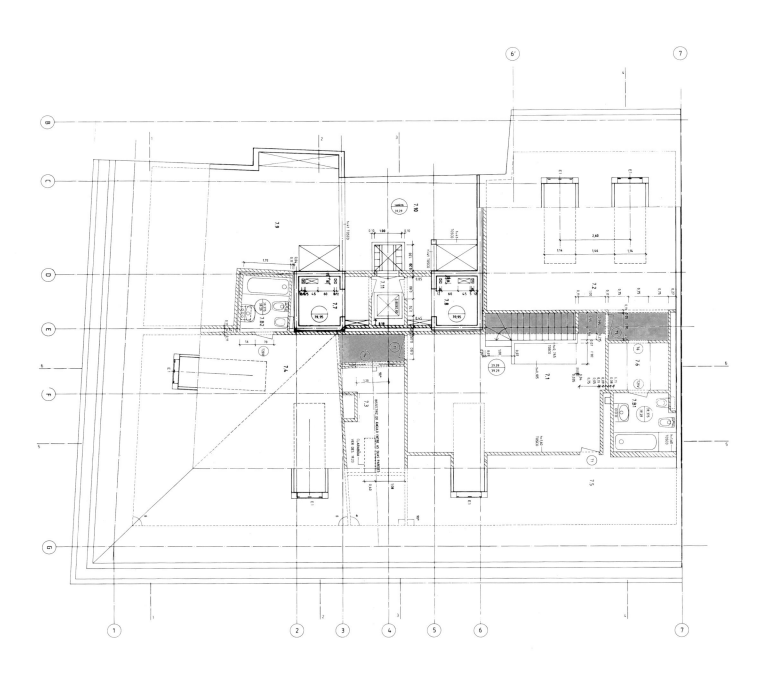

432 plan

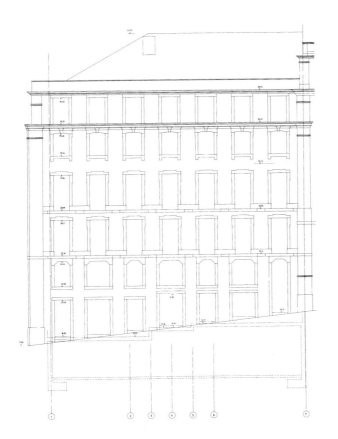
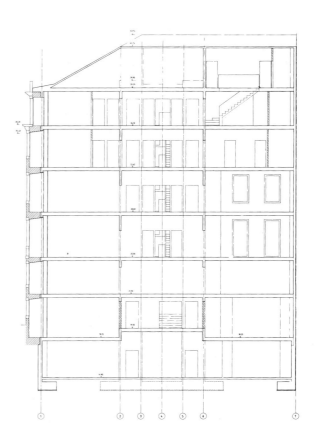
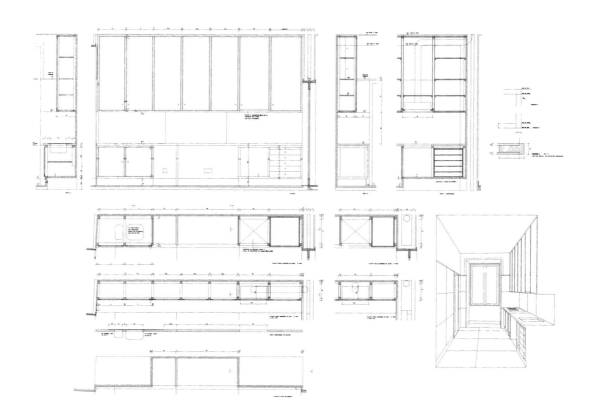

433   *above* elevation and section   *below* details of fittings

1991 Design for Restoration of Grandes Armazéns do Chiado Building *Lisbon, Portugal*

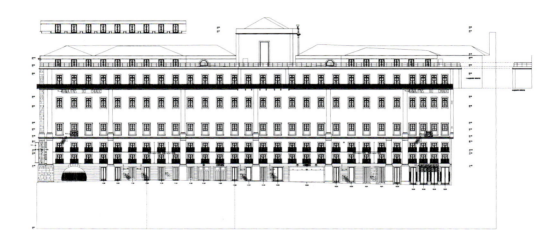

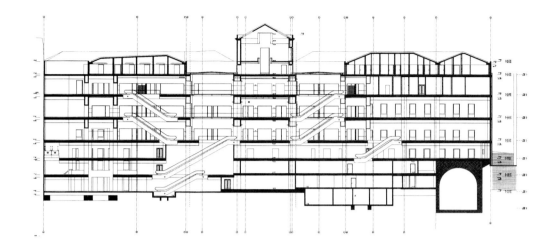
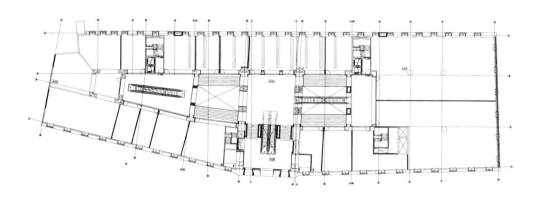
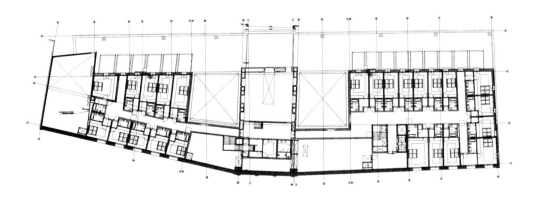

435   section and plans

1991–6   Restoration of Grandella Building *Chiado, Lisbon, Portugal*

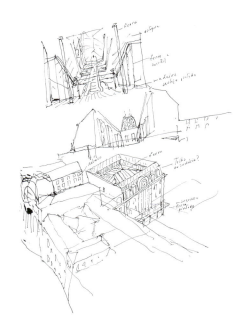

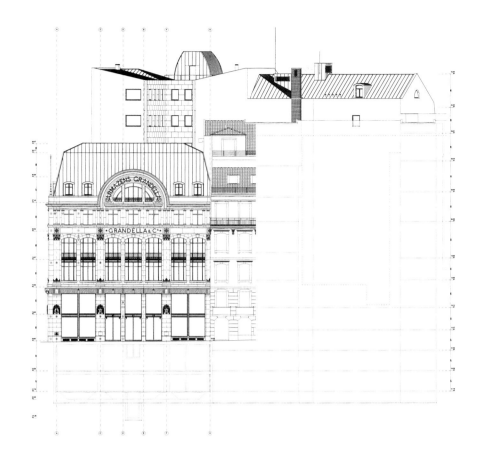

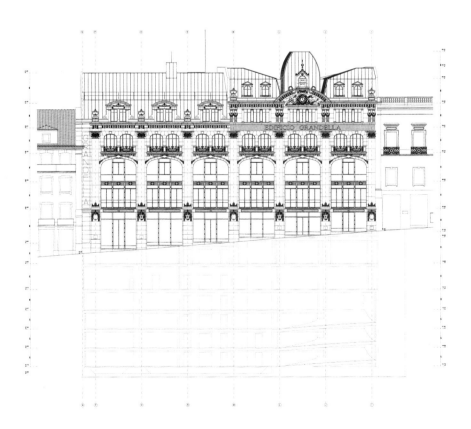

elevations

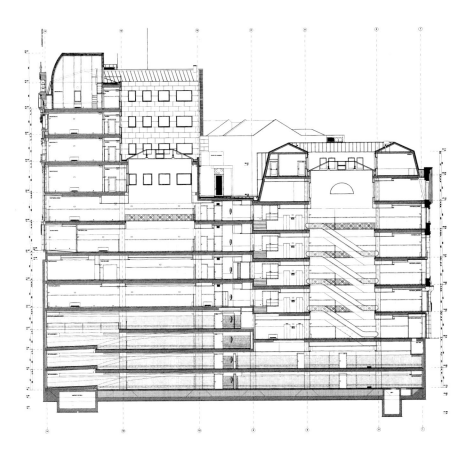
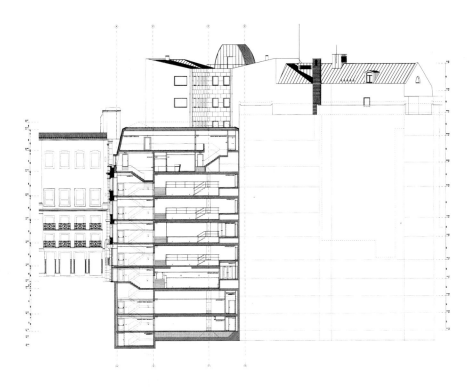

1991–3 Eurocentre Complex *Boavista, Porto, Portugal*

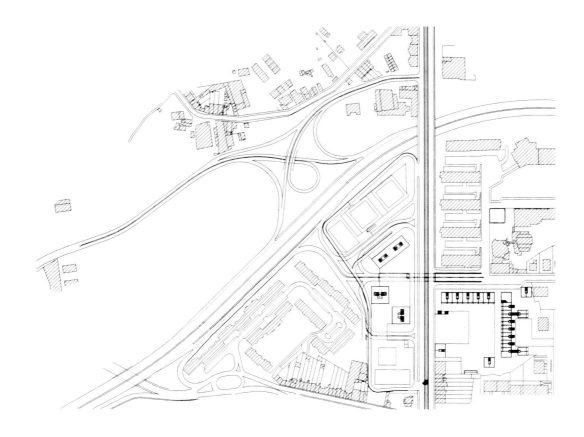

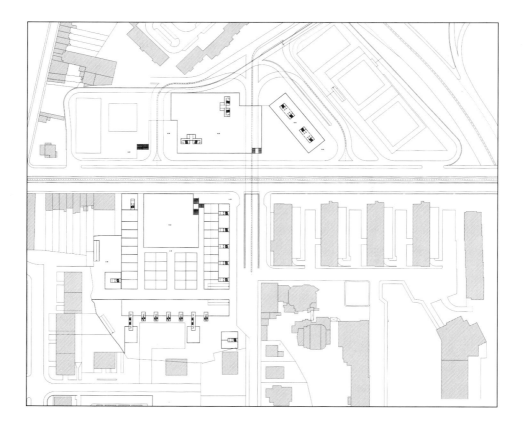

440 site plan and first floor plan

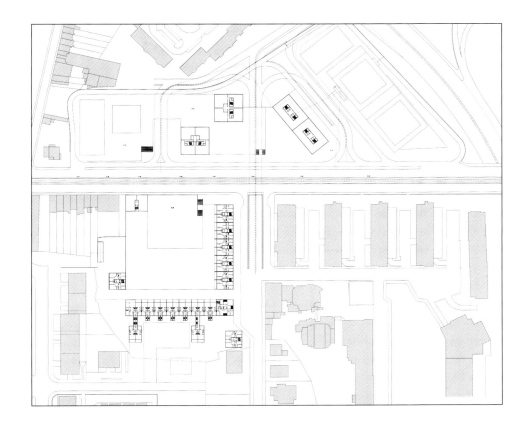
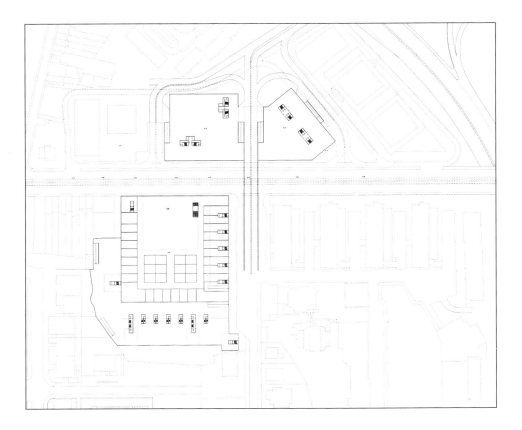

441   typical floor plan and second floor plan

1991–4 Vitra International Factory *Weil am Rhein, Germany*

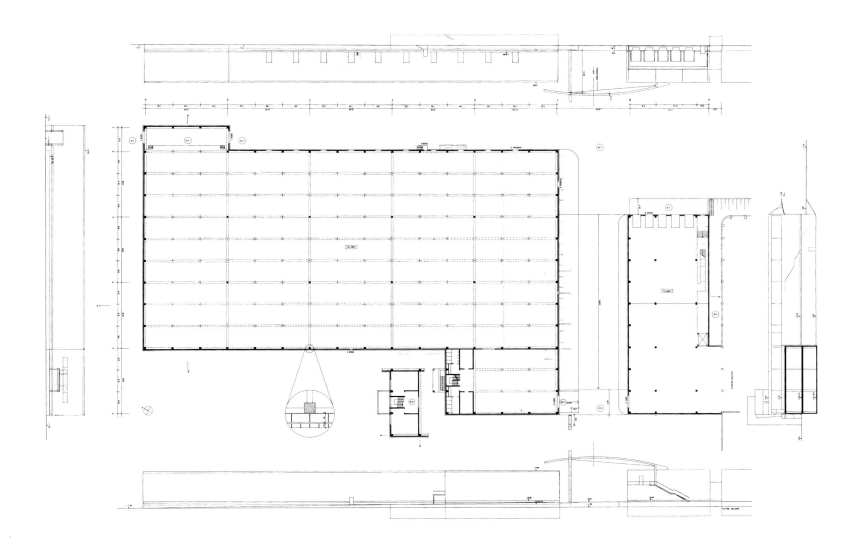
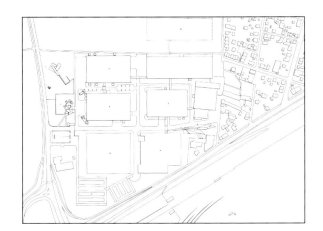

plan, elevations and site plan

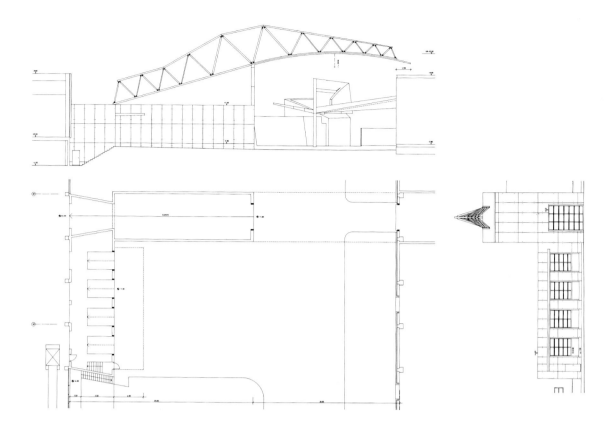
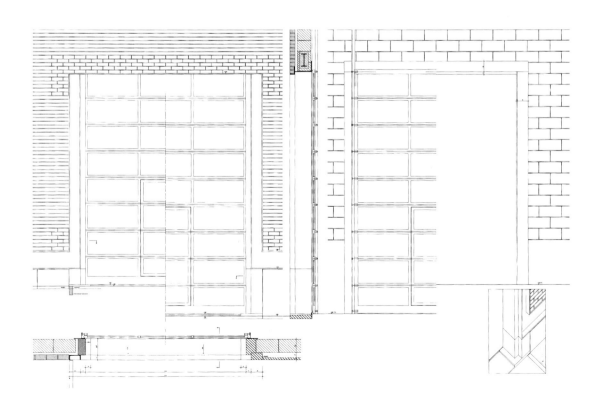

446 plan, elevations and construction details

1991–4 Design for Remodelling of Pai Ramiro Restaurant *Porto, Portugal*

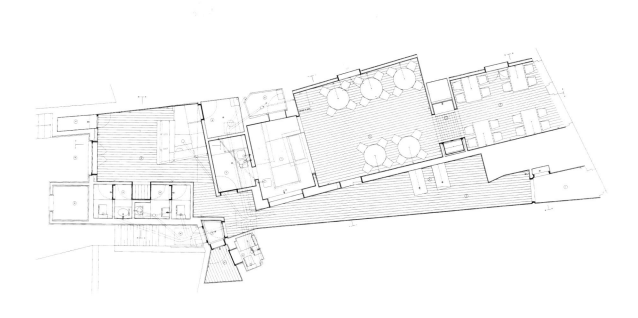

1991 Design for Remodelling of Condes Cinema *Lisbon, Portugal*

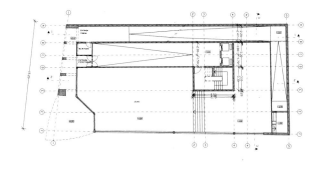
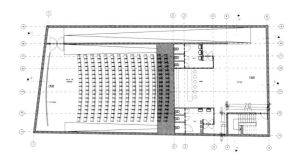
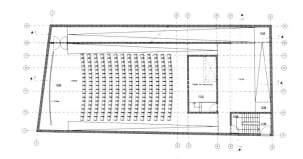
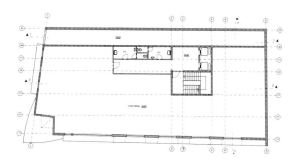
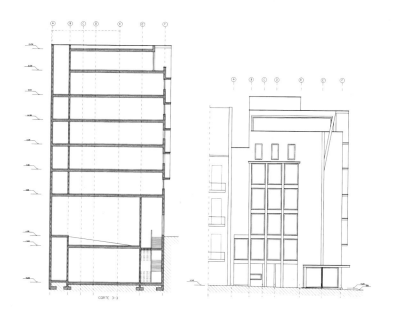
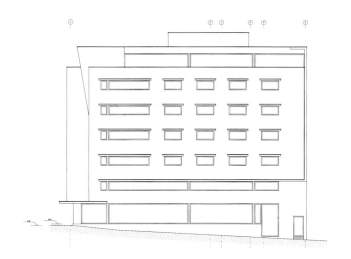

450   basement, lower ground, ground and second floor plans, section and elevations

1991–3   Design for Lusitânia Insurance Company Headquarters *Lisbon, Portugal*

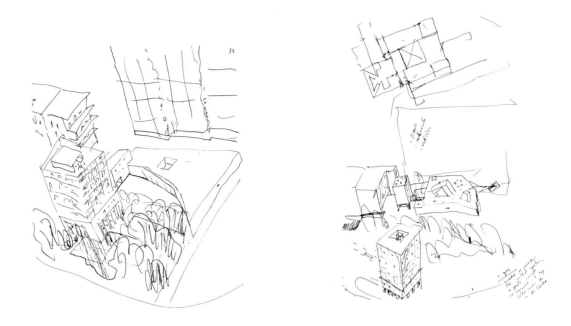

1991   Design for Terraços de Bragança Complex *Lisbon, Portugal*

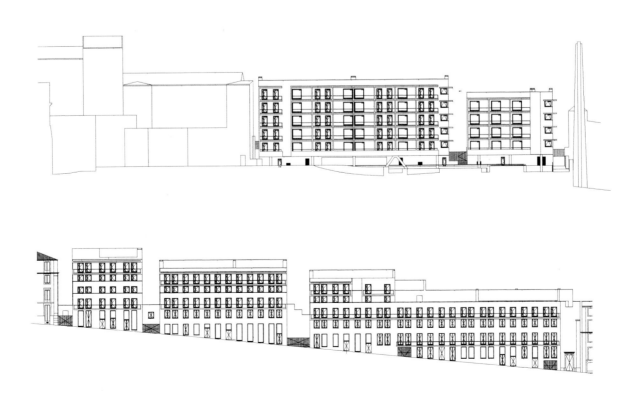

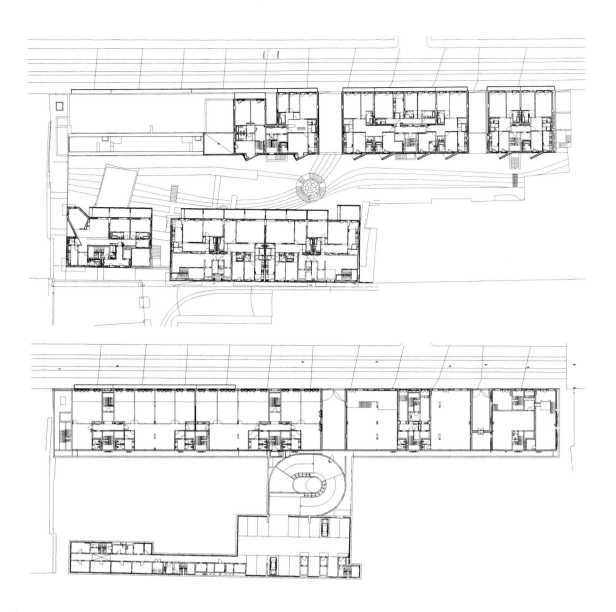
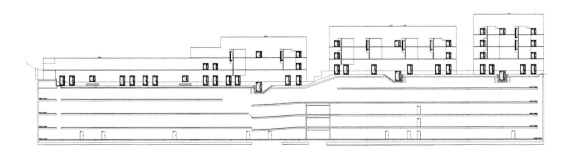

452   plans and long section

1991–5 Studies for Cargaleiro Foundation Headquarters *Lisbon, Portugal*

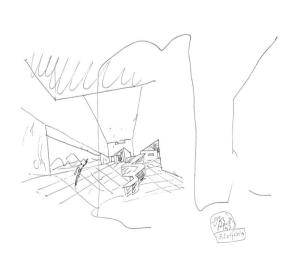
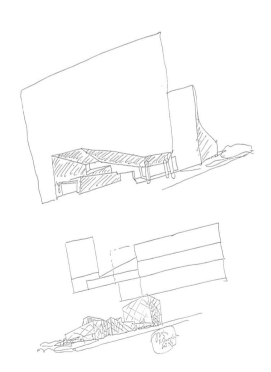

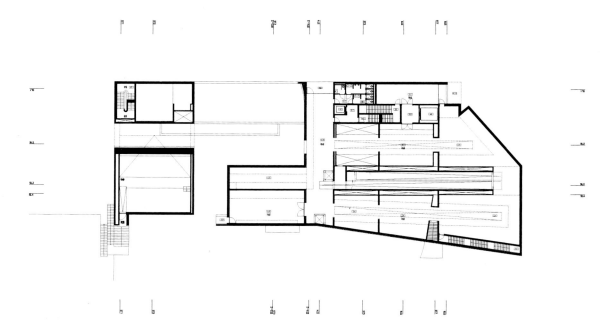
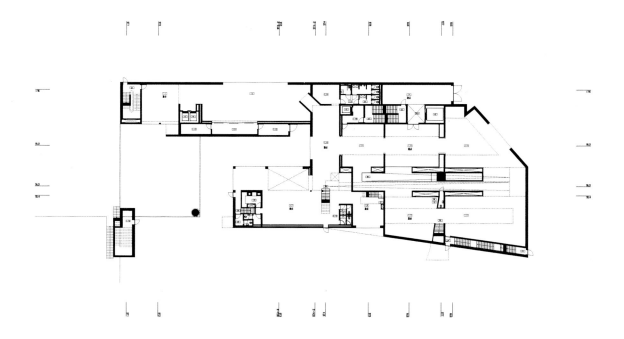

454　ground and first floor plans

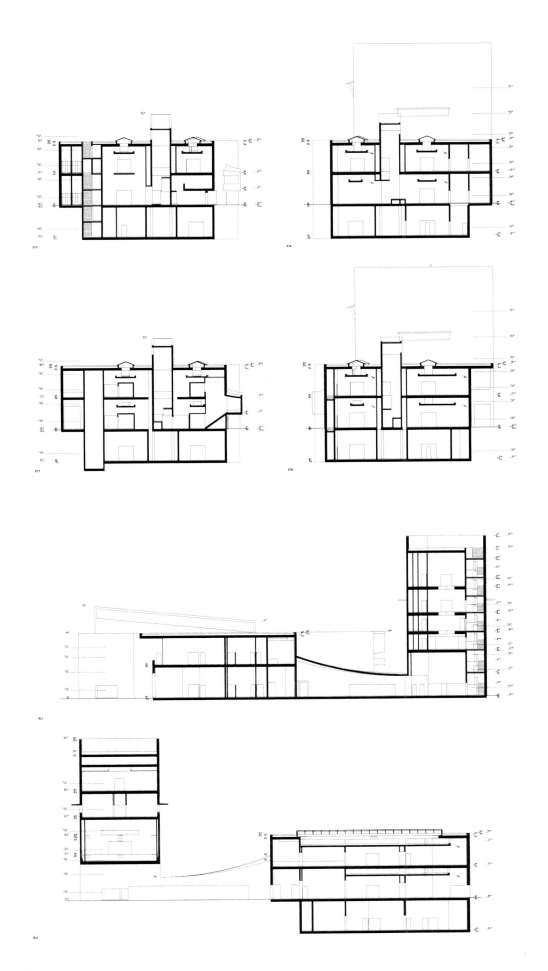

455 cross and long sections

1992 Design for Residential Complex *Malaga, Spain*

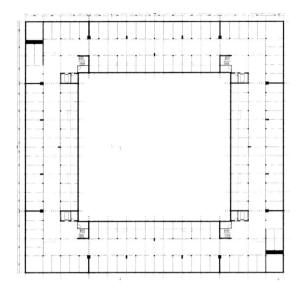
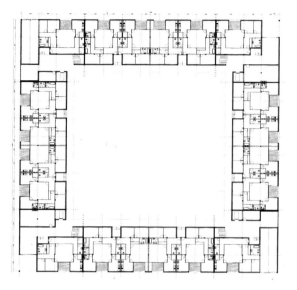
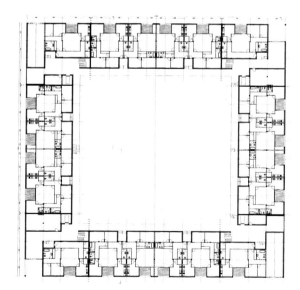
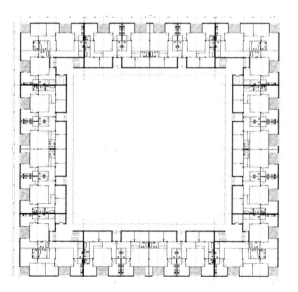

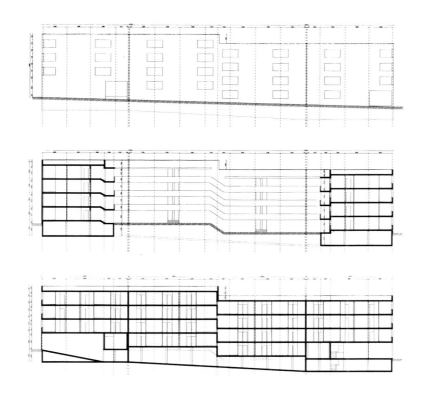
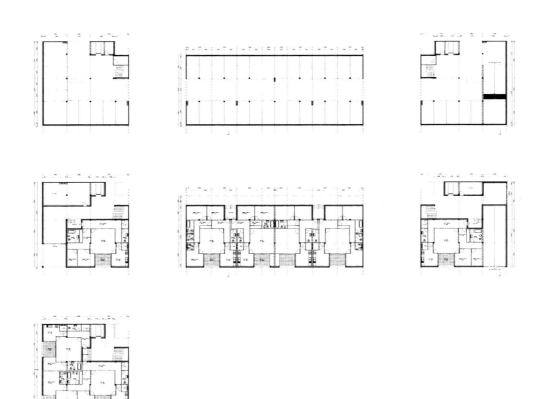

457   *above* sections and elevation *below* plans

1992–5 Headquarters of the Young Businessmen's Association (ANJE) *Oeiras, Portugal*

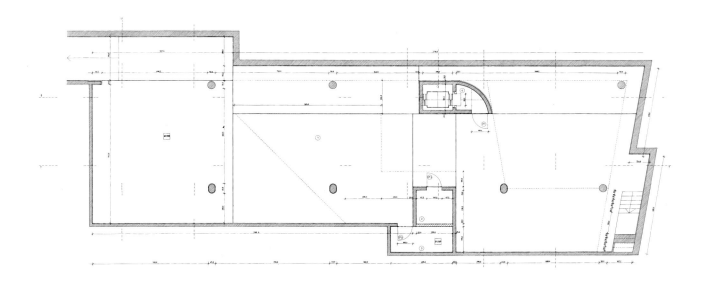
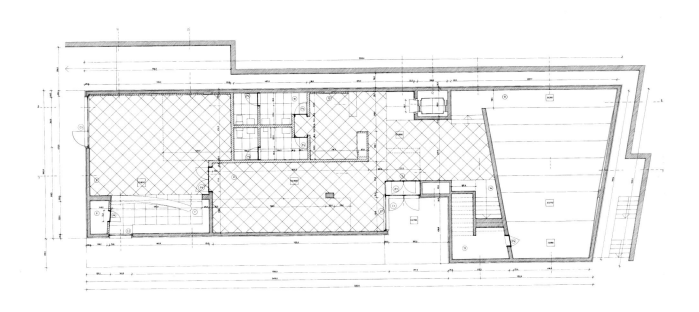

459 lower ground and ground floor plans

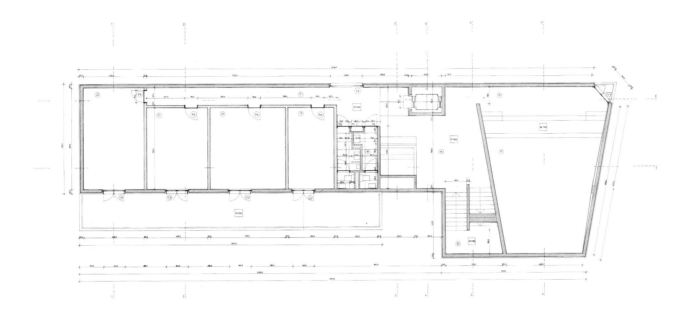
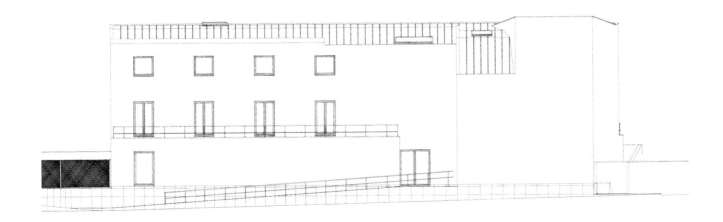

461　first floor plan and north-west elevation

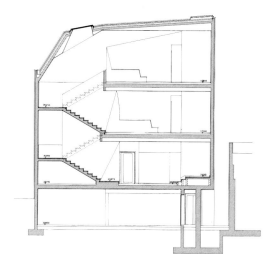
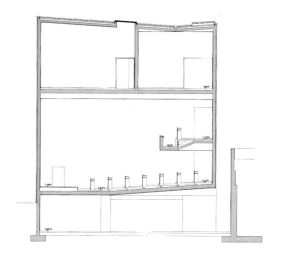

462 cross sections

1992 Restaurant and Tea Room *Malagueira, Évora, Portugal*

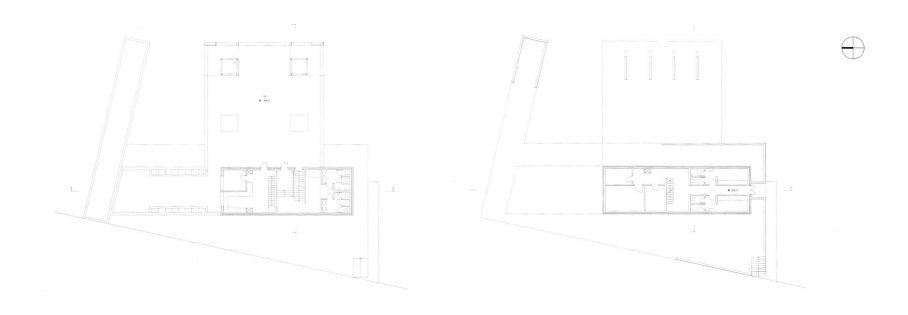

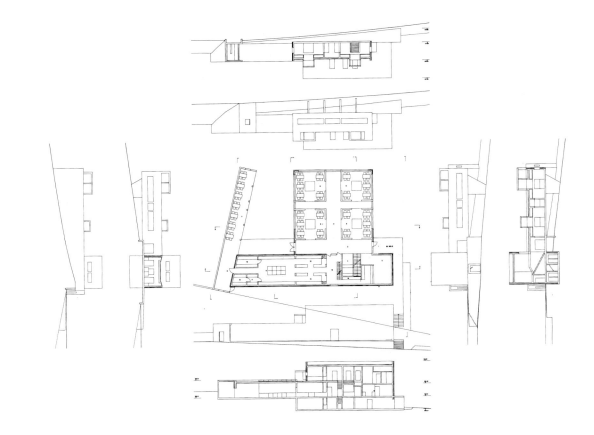
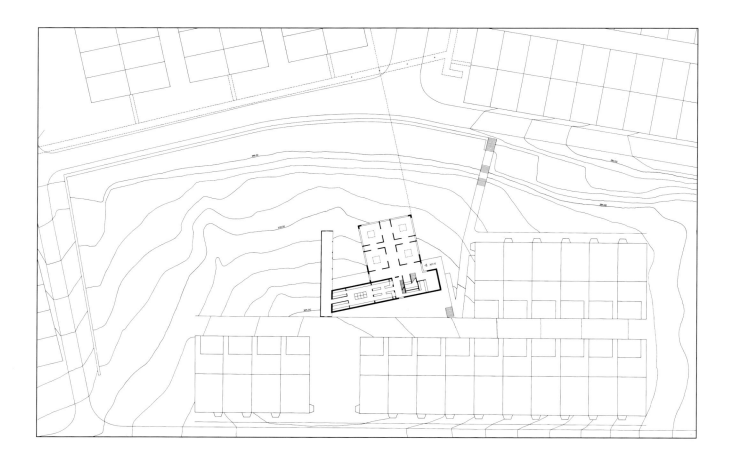

464 plan, sections, elevations and site plan

1992 Study for Language School *Malagueira, Évora, Portugal*

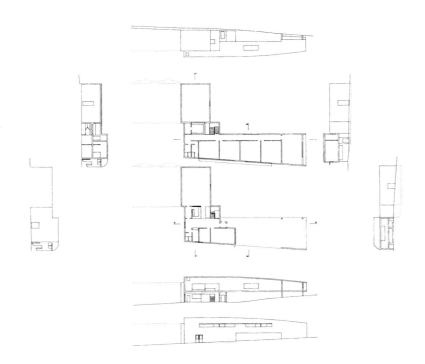

1992–8 Fermata Baixa/Chiado Underground *Lisbon, Portugal*

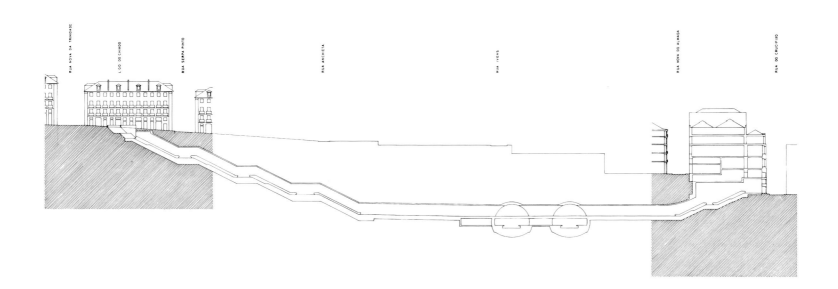

465   *above* ground and first floor plans, sections and elevations *below* section

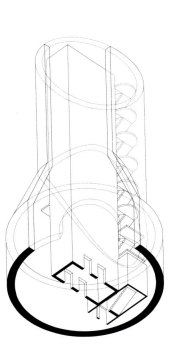

466 axonometric

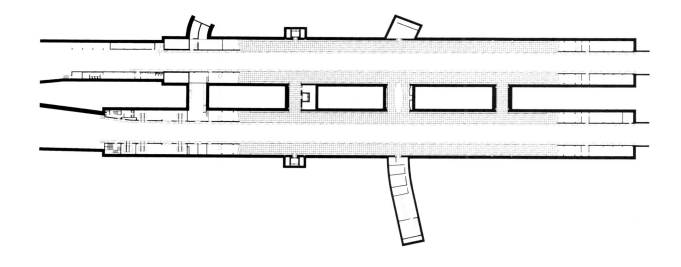
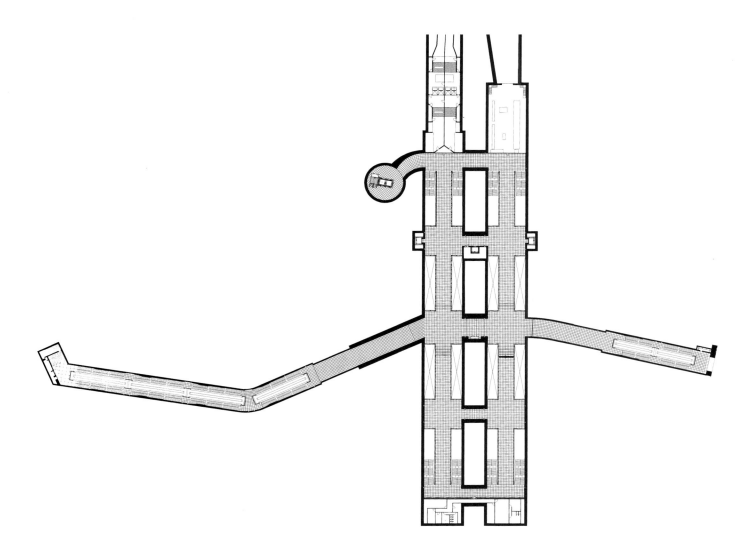

467　plans

1992 'Visions for Madrid' Exhibition *Madrid, Spain*

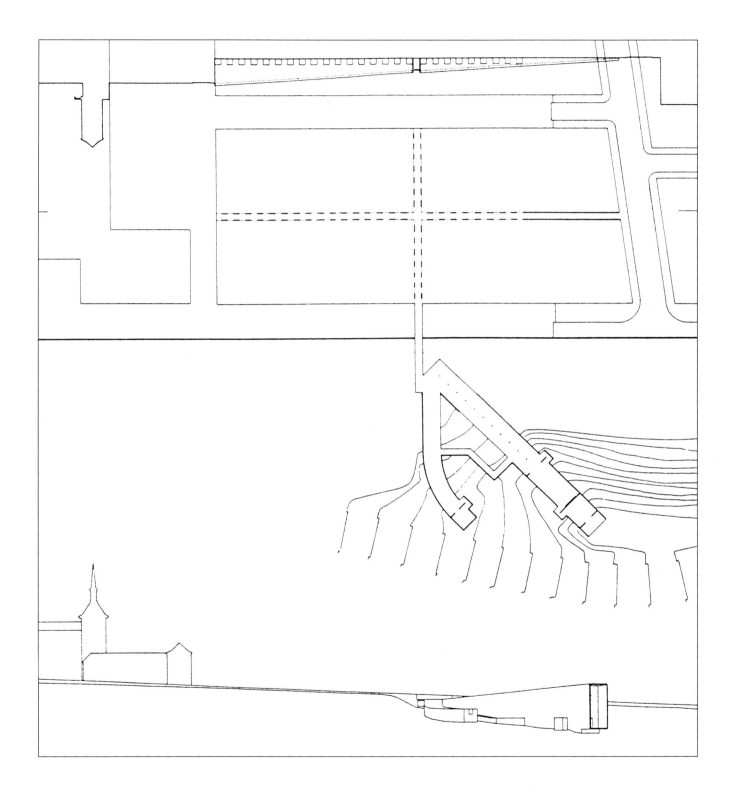

site plan and elevation

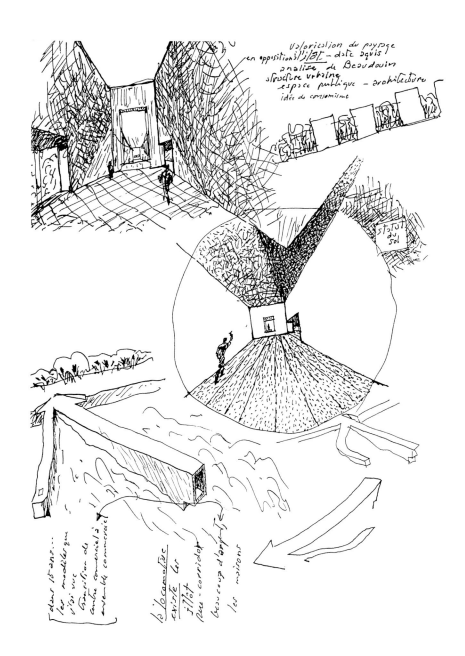

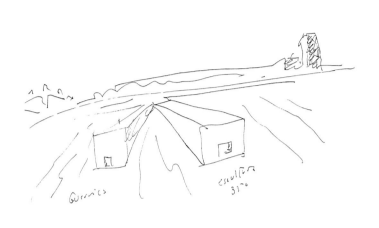

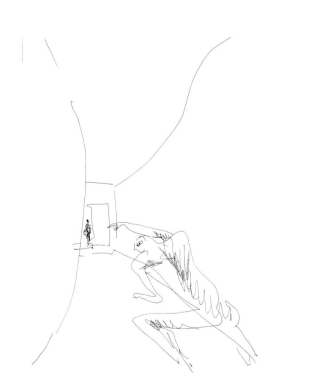

1992–3 Design for Museum of Contemporary Art *Helsinki, Finland*

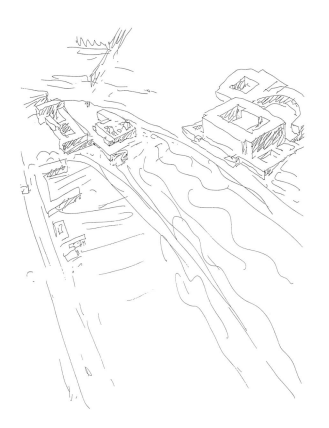

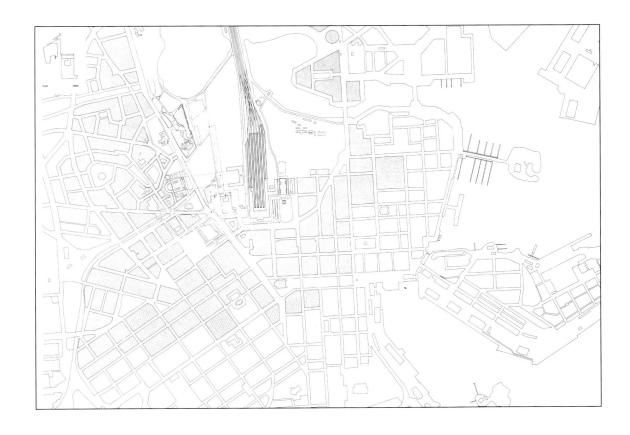
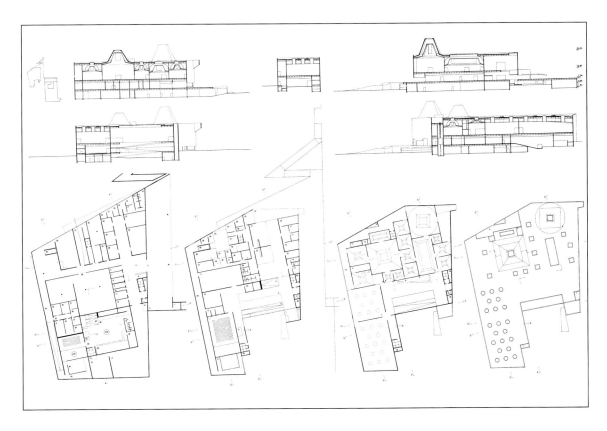

475   site plan, lower ground, ground, first floor and roof plans and sections

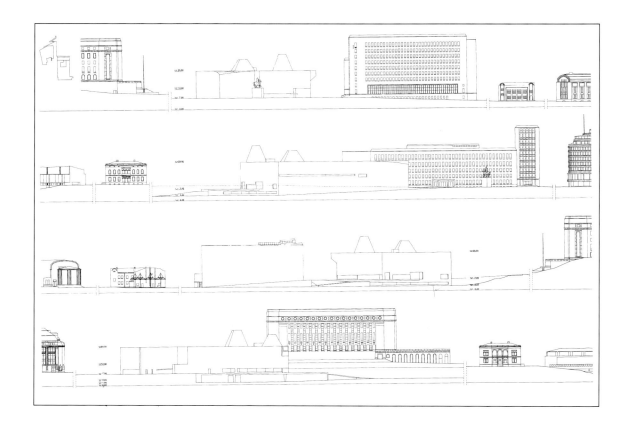
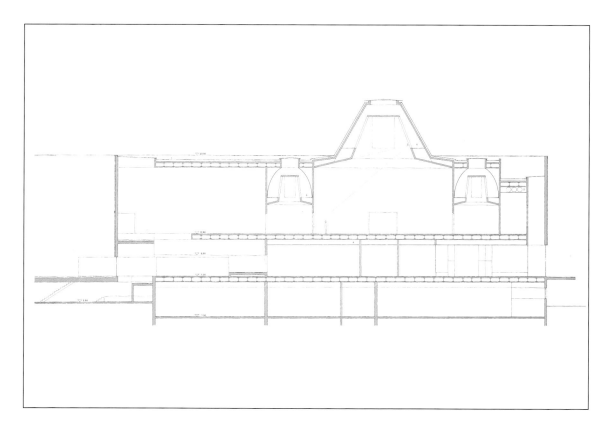

476 elevations and section

1993 Design for Restoration of Ludovice Building for the '25 April' Association *Lisbon, Portugal*

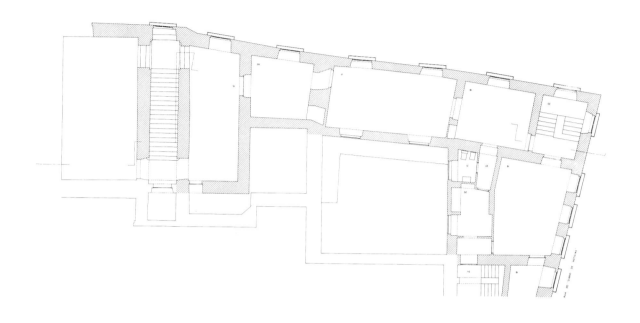

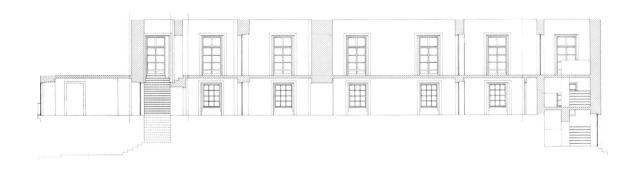

plan, section and model

1993   Urban Plan for São João *Costa da Caparica, Portugal*

1993   Design for Residential Complex *Setúbal, Portugal*

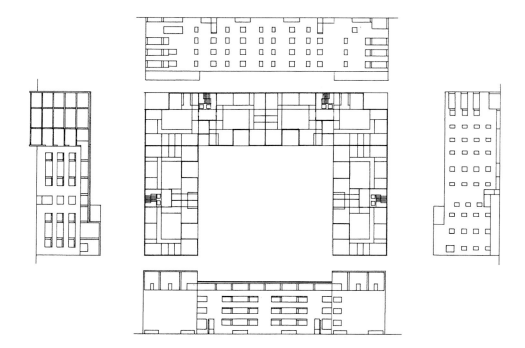

above site plan *below* plan, section and elevations

1993   Design for Housing and Office Complex *Matosinhos, Portugal*

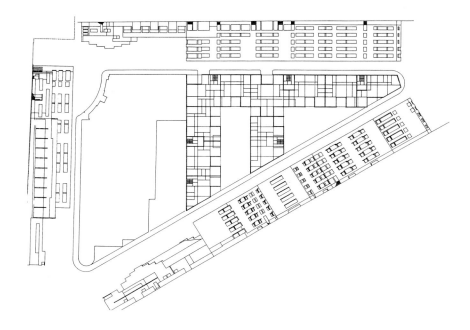

1993   Design for Ocean Swimming Pool Restaurant *Leça da Palmeira, Portugal*

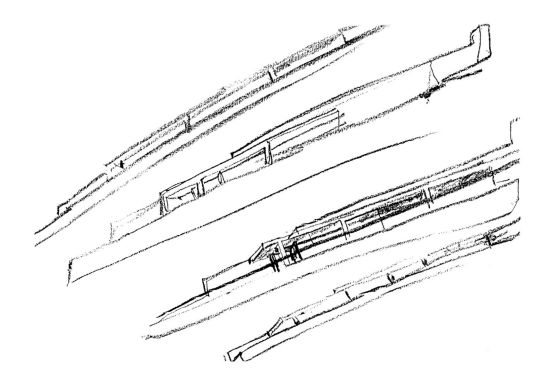

479   *above* plan and elevations

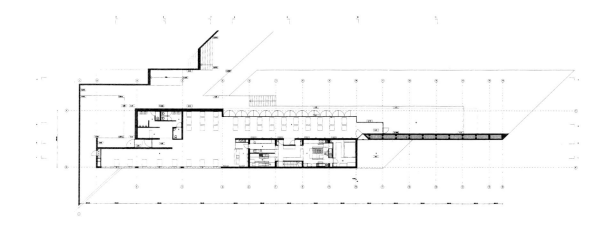
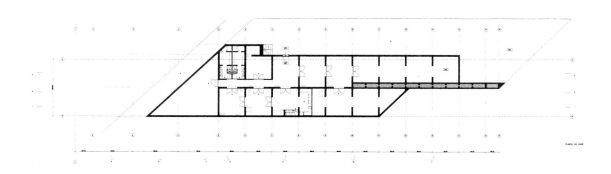
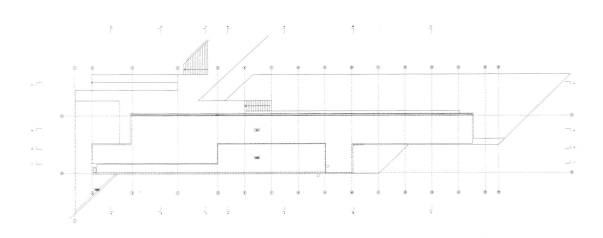

480 plans

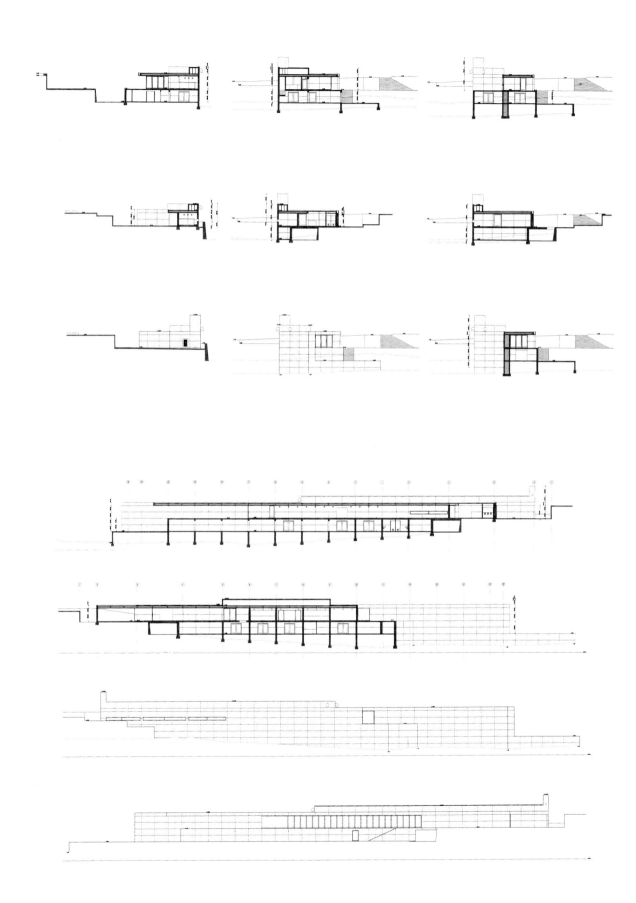

sections and elevations

1993–7 Restoration of Costa Braga Building, House of Youth and Pavilions *Matosinhos, Portugal*

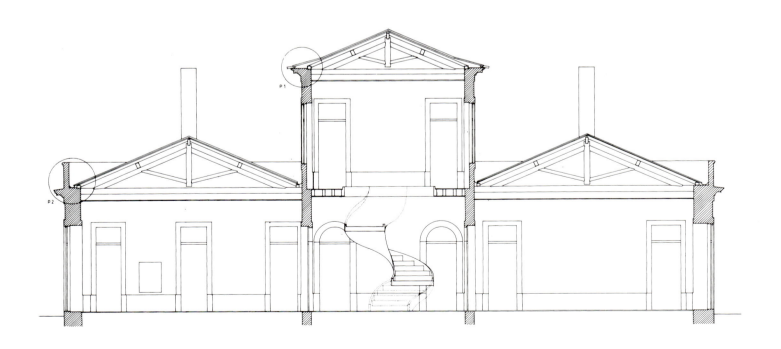

483   section

1993–7 Revigrés Showroom *Águeda, Portugal*

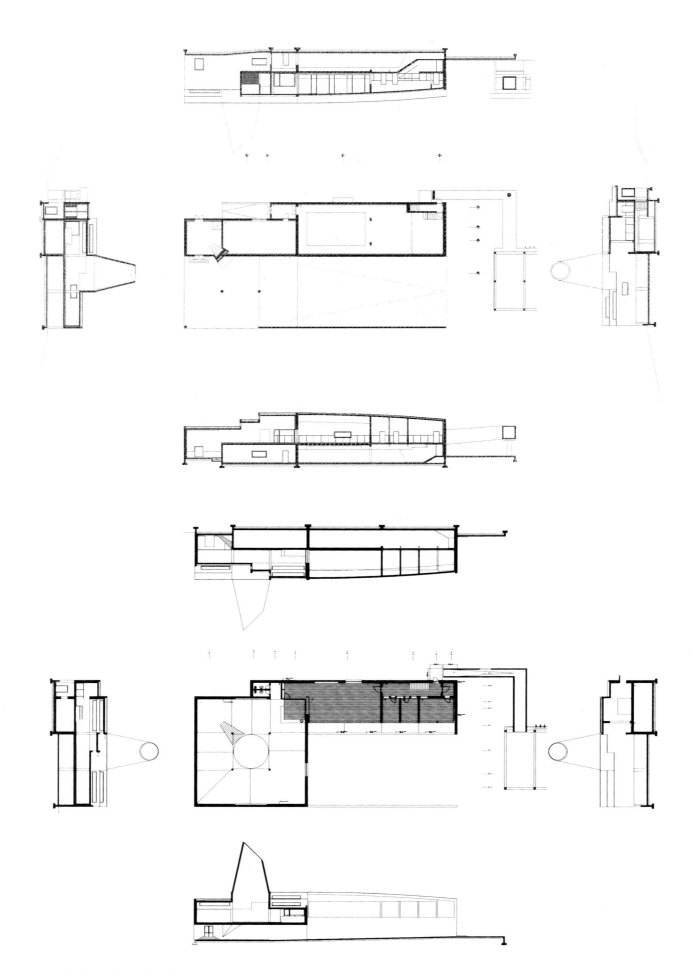

487 ground and first floor plans and sections

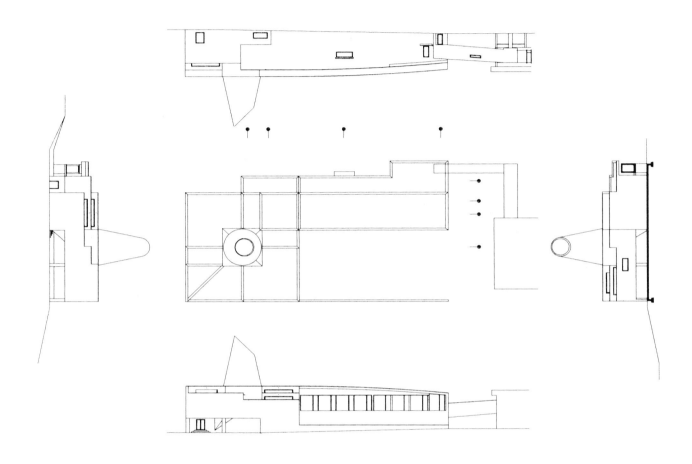

488   roof plan and elevations

1993–7　Office Building *Porto, Portugal*

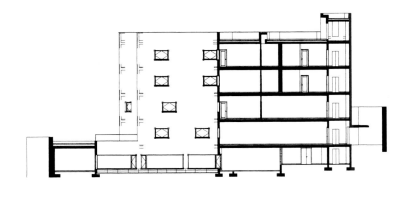

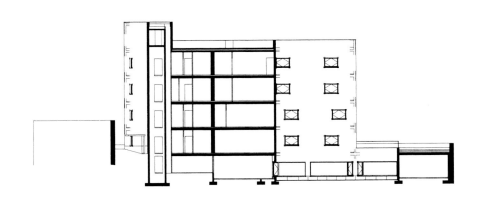

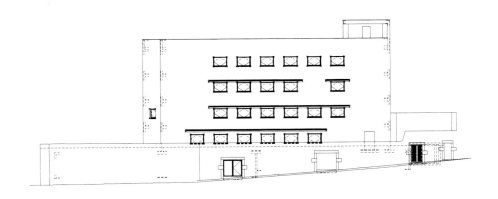

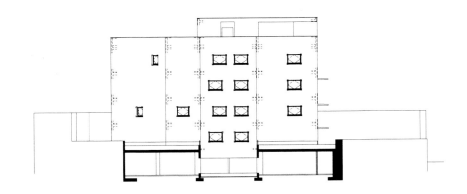

491   sections and elevations

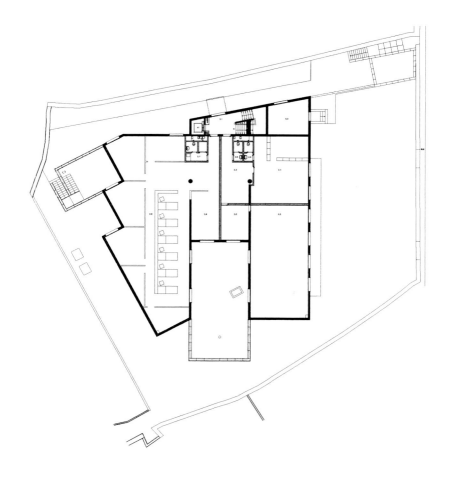
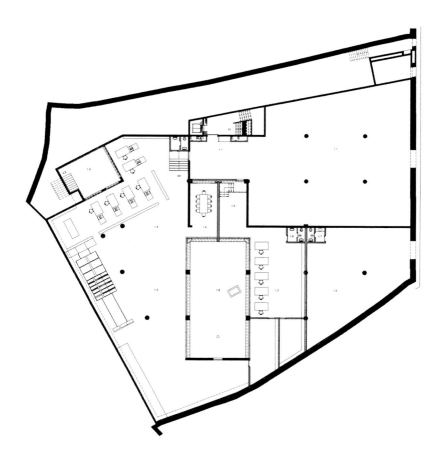

492　plans

1993 Study for Two Houses *Teixeira da Cunha, Felgueiras, Portugal*

1993   Urban Plan for City Centre *Montreuil, France*

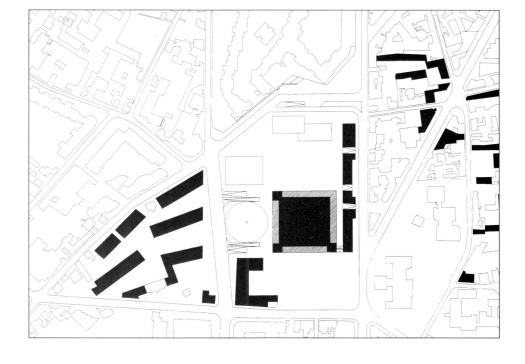
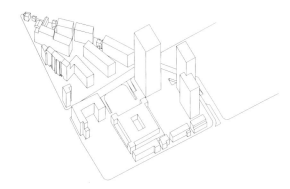

axonometric, site plan and model

1993 Design for Artists' Studios *Montreuil, France*

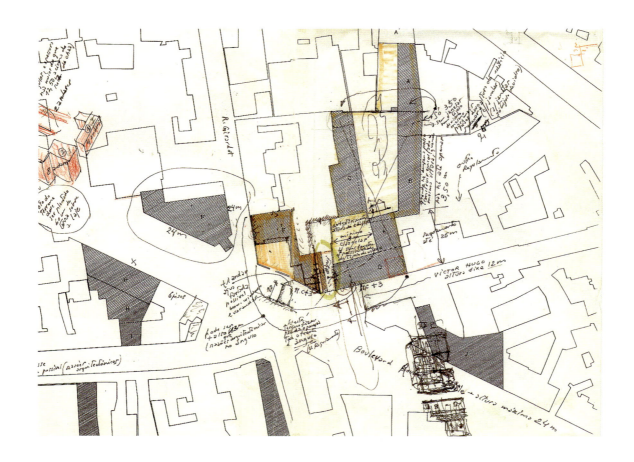

site plan

1993 Dimensione Fuoco Laboratory, Showroom and Housing *San Donà di Piave, Italy*

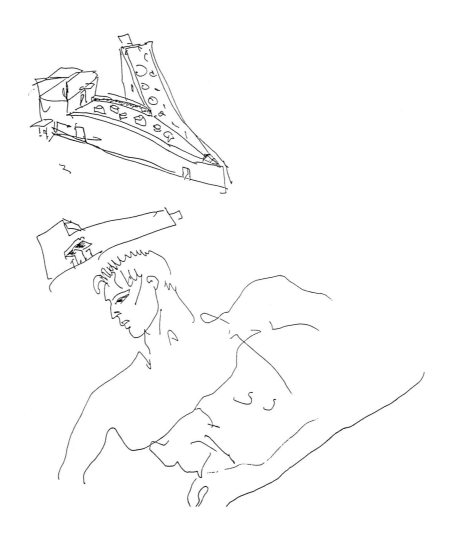

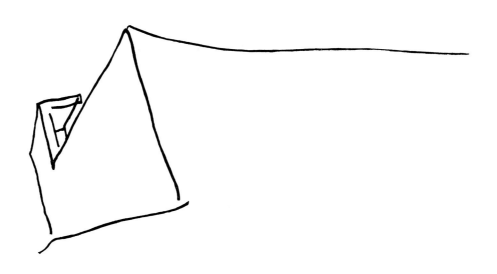

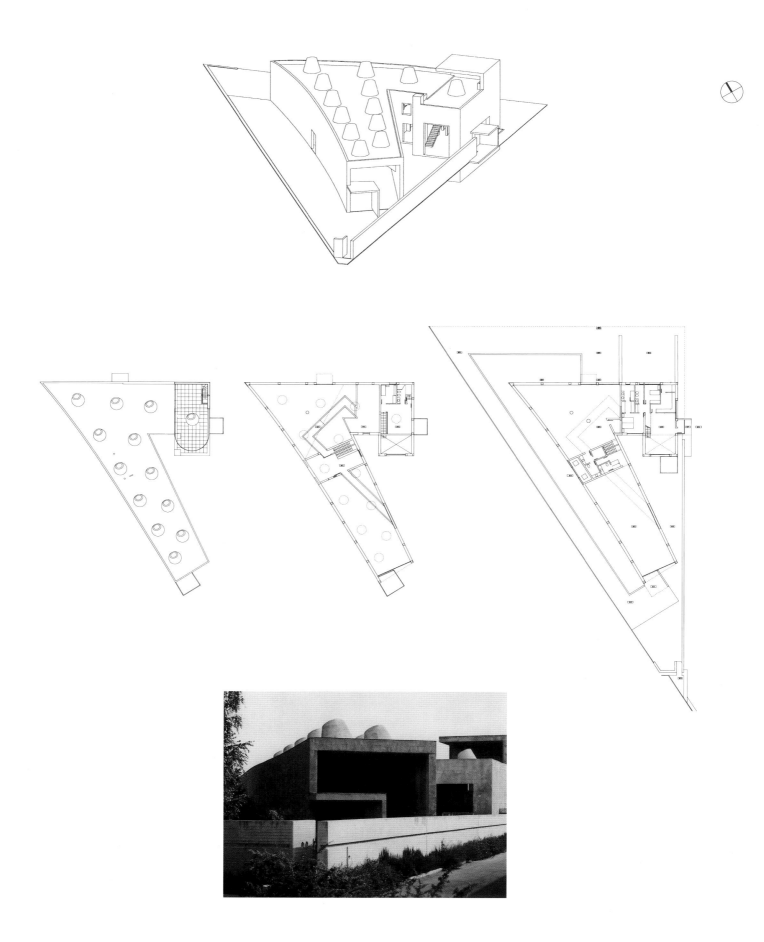

498 axonometric, ground, first floor and roof plans

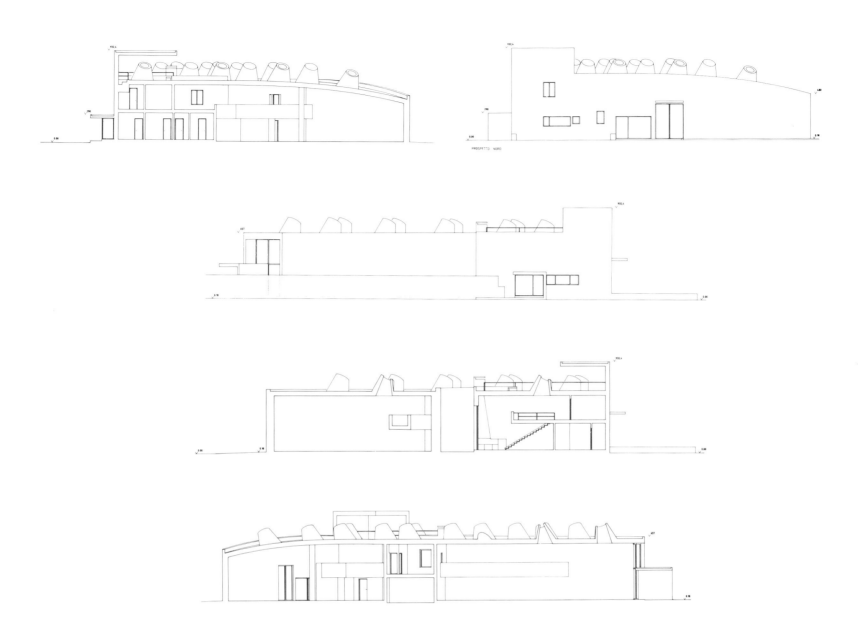

499 sections and elevations

1993 Design for J. Paul Getty Museum *Malibu, Santa Monica, USA*

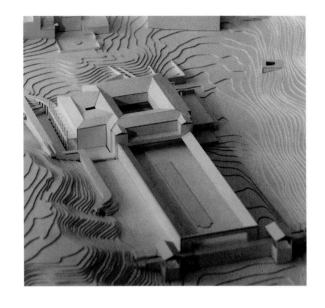

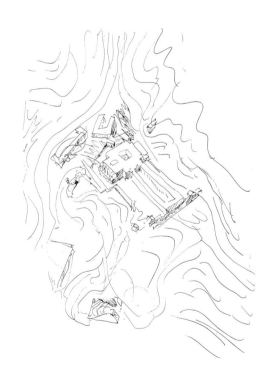

model

1993–5 Design for 'Puerta Real 1' Office Building and Restaurant *Granada, Spain*

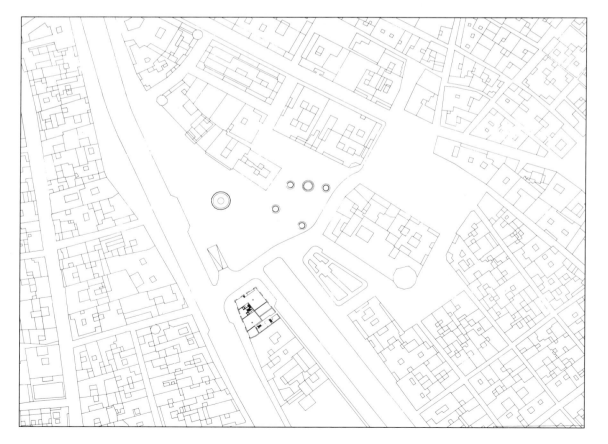

site plan

503   lower ground, first, third and fifth floor plans

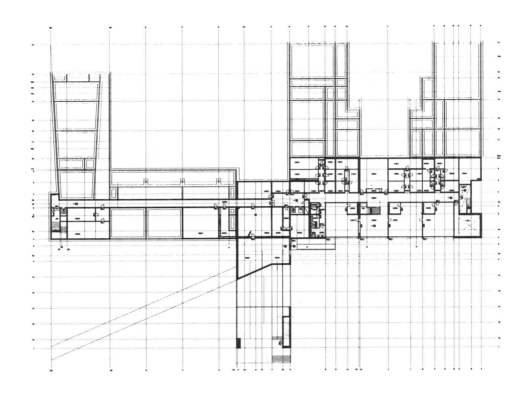
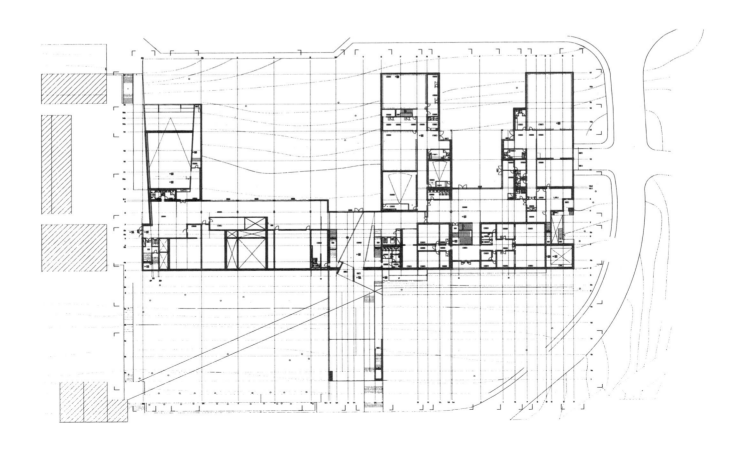

506 plans

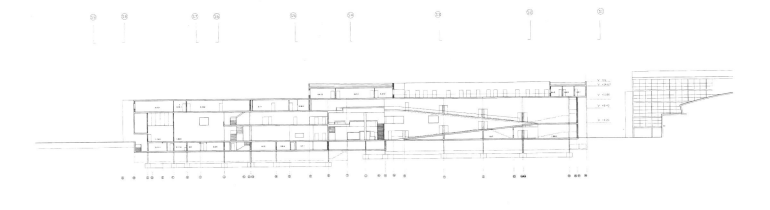
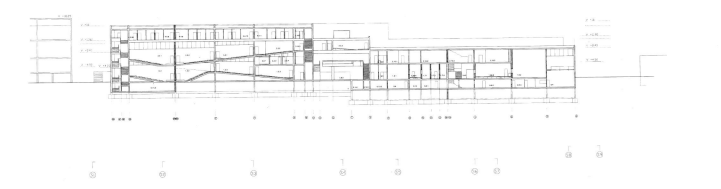
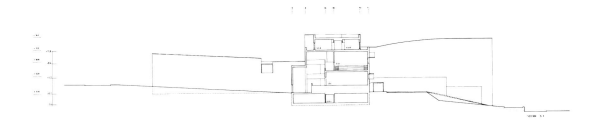
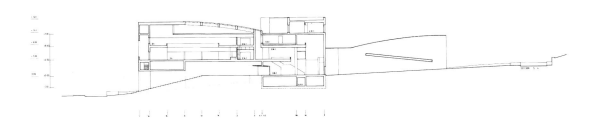

above long sections *below* cross sections

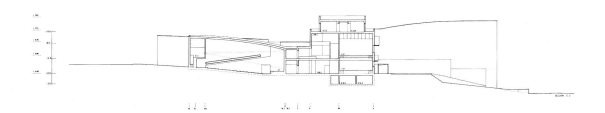
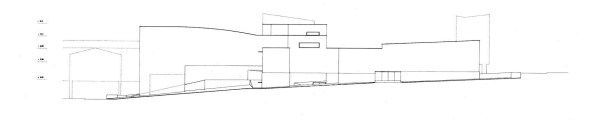
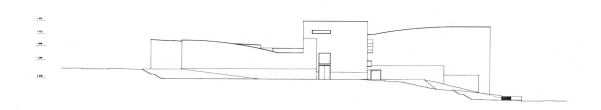

508　cross sections and elevations

1994 Casa Jovem Co-operative Social Housing Complex *Guarda, Portugal*

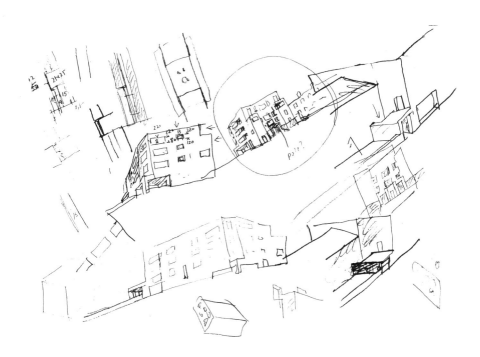

site plan

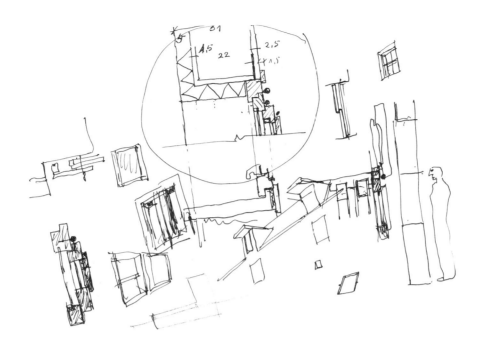

511 roof, third, second, first, ground and lower ground floor plans

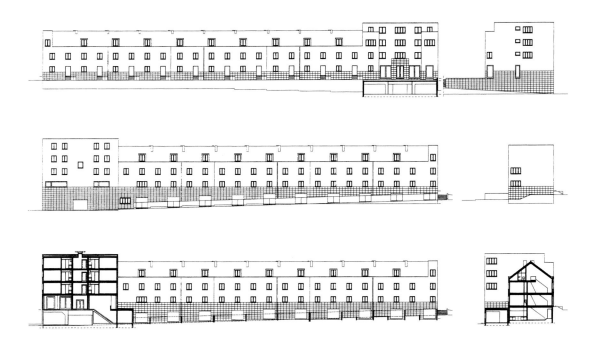

1994 Design for Children's Education Centre, Serralves Foundation *Porto, Portugal*

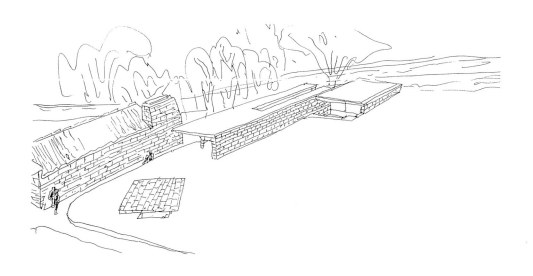

512 *above* Casa Jovem sections and elevations *below* sketch

1994 Design for Granell Museum *Santiago de Compostela, Spain*

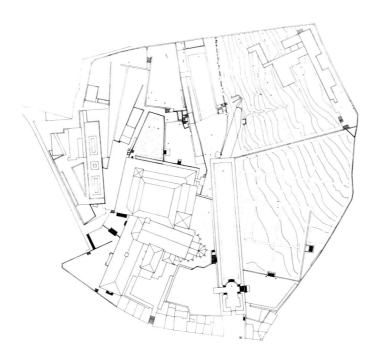

1994 Design for La Salle Parking *Santiago de Compostela, Spain*

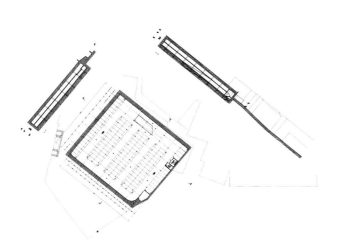
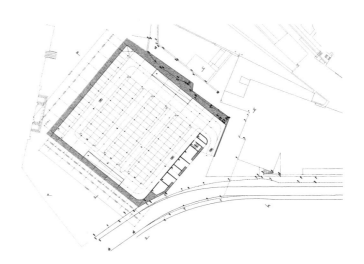

above site plan *below* lower ground and ground floor plans and sections

1994 Restoration of Bar in Serralves Foundation House *Porto, Portugal*

 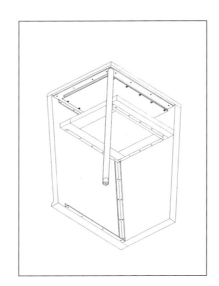 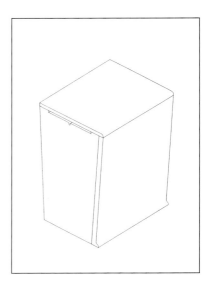

1994 Fountain Design for Vitra International *Weil am Rhein, Germany*

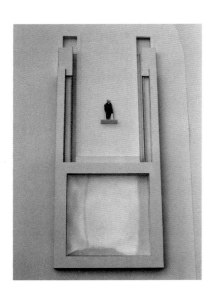 

1994 Master Plan for Rossio São Brás *Évora, Portugal*

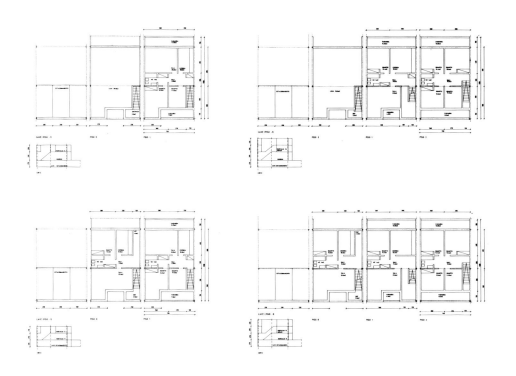

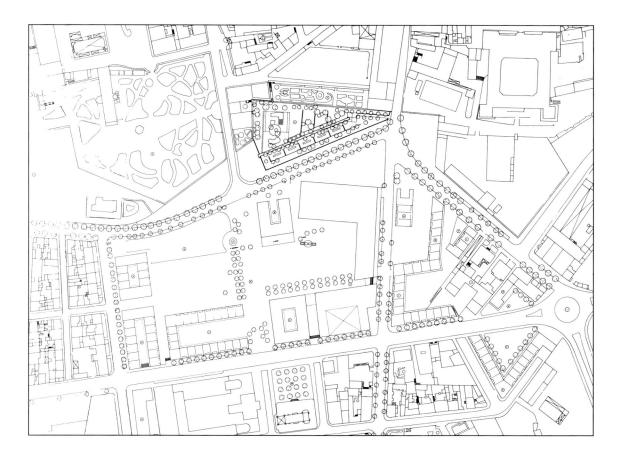

515 plans and site plan

1994 Design for Universiadi '97 Sports Complex *Palermo, Italy*

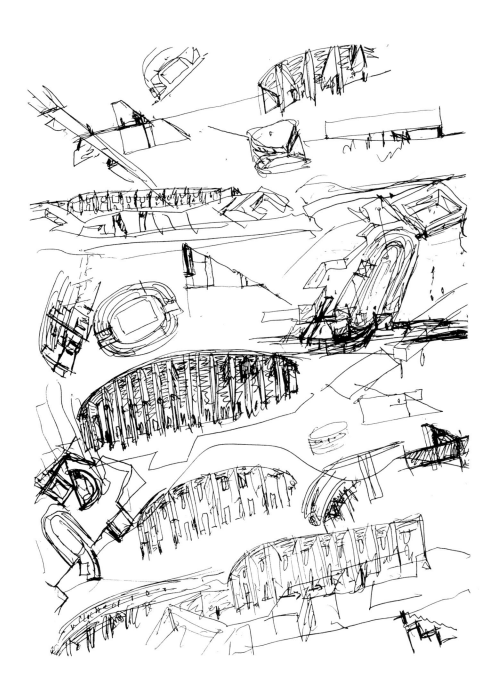

1994 Restoration of Ancient '2 de Maio' Market *Viseu, Portugal*

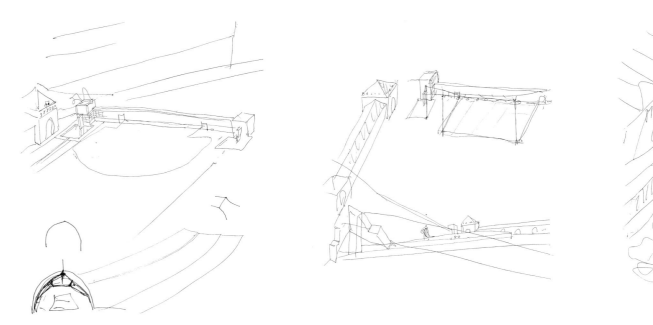

1994 Design for Restoration of Santa Justa Lift *Lisbon, Portugal*

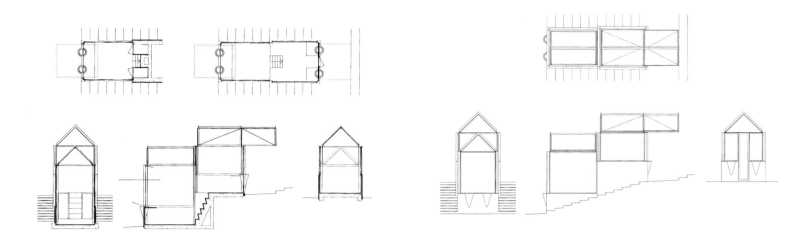

1993 Remodelling of '25 April' Association Building *Lisbon, Portugal*

above plans, sections and elevations *below* elevations and ground, second and third floor plans

1995 Design for Ishmaelite Centre and Aga Khan Foundation Headquarters *Lisbon, Portugal*

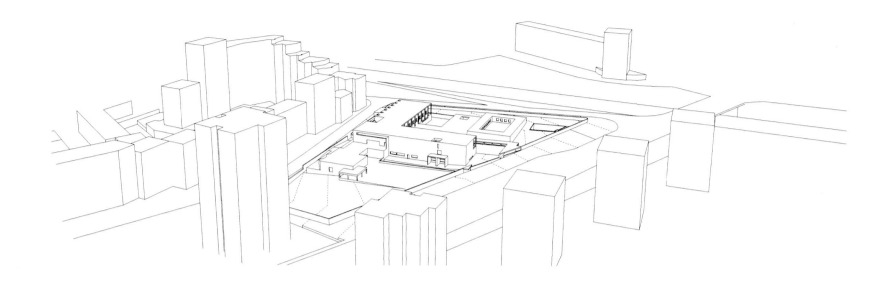
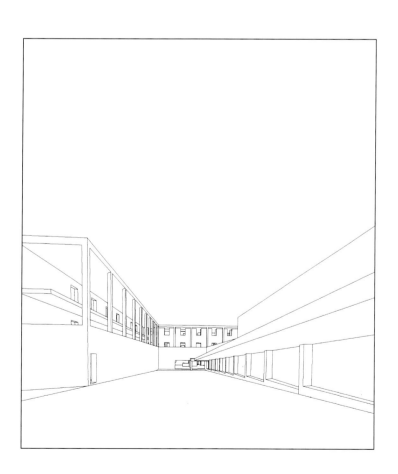
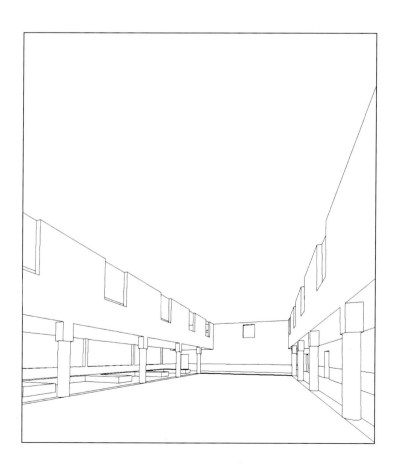

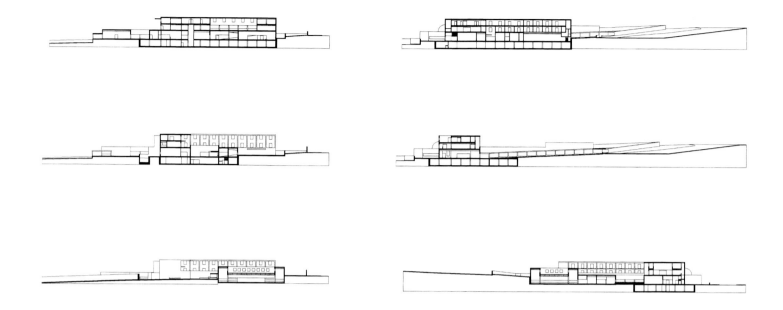
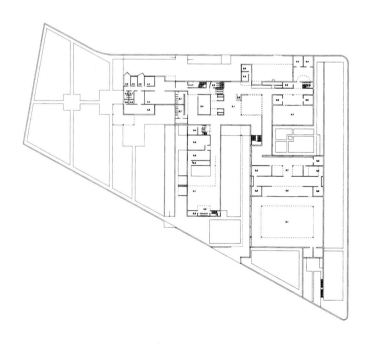
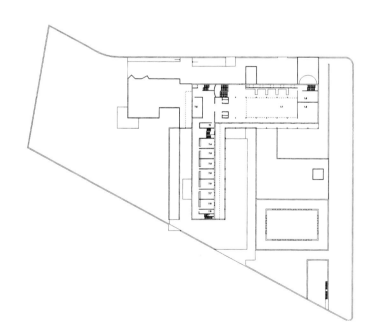

521   sections and lower ground and second floor plans

1995 Restoration and Extension of Stedelijk Museum *Amsterdam, The Netherlands*

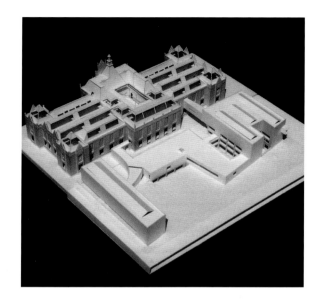

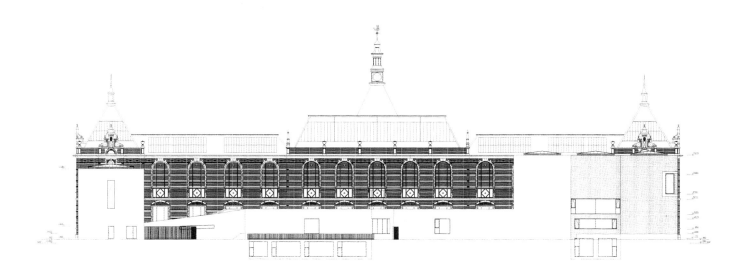

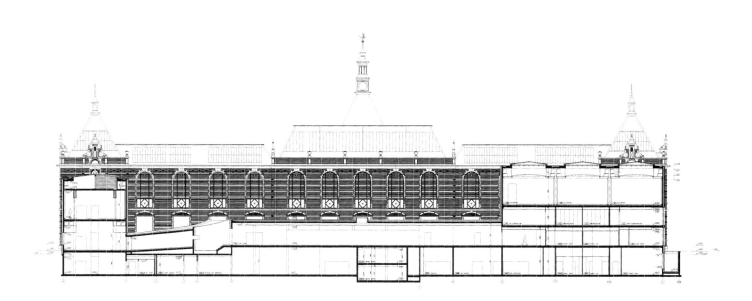

523　south elevation and long section

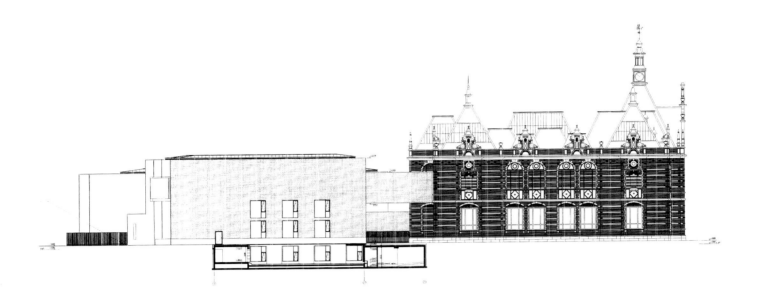

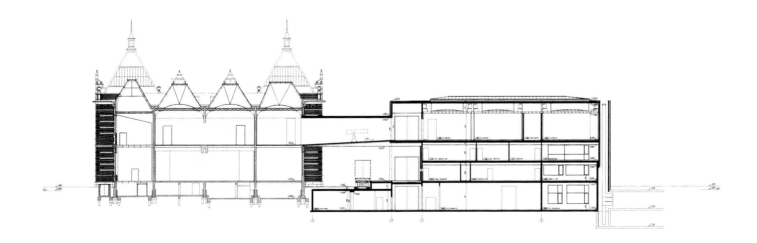

524 east elevation and cross section

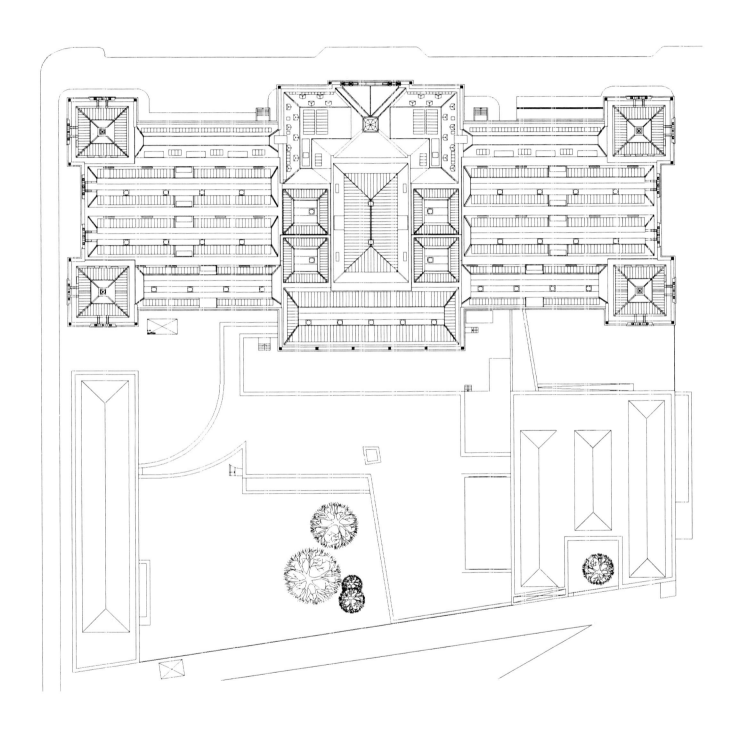

525   site plan

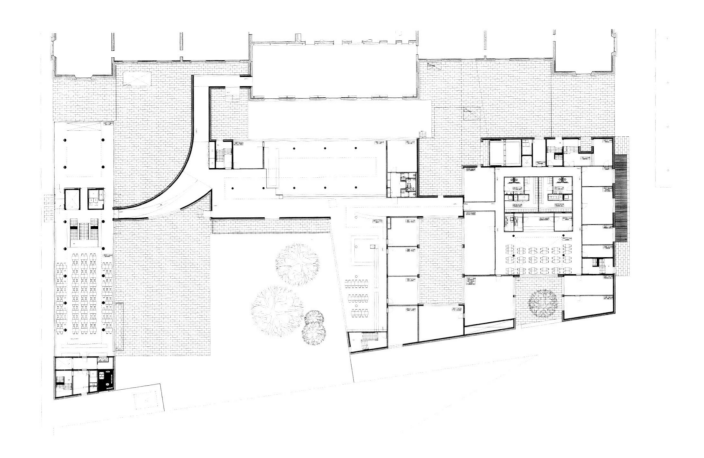
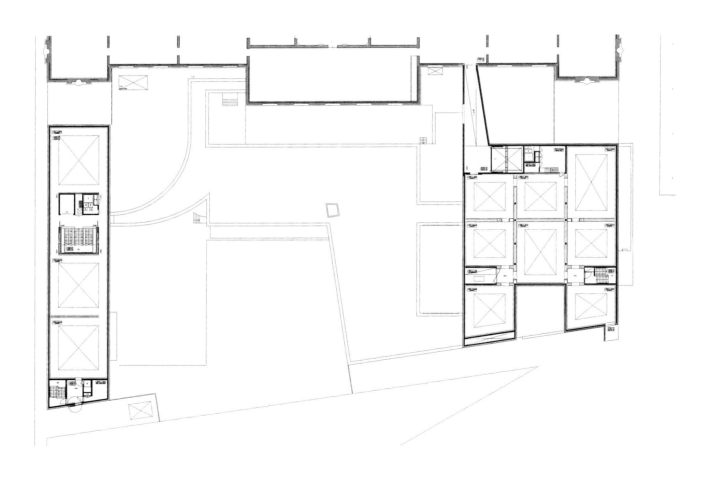

Villa Savoye
Álvaro Siza

Paris, December 1987

Picasso said that it takes ten years to learn to draw, and another ten years to learn to draw like a child. Nowadays, these last ten years seem to be missing from architectural training.

The delight to be had from a visit to the Villa Savoye comes from the encounter with a kind of naïveté and with the constant transformation of each idea: with constant invention. Each step alters the architectural order, which nonetheless remains ever present, and turns on its head the importance of the various different elements. These may be trivial in isolation; perceived or not, they will always accompany whoever lives there, never causing a surprise. Each invention generates another. The possibilities of discovery are endless – above and below, to the right and to the left, diagonally and at right angles.

There is nothing primitive or under-developed in the direct, almost crude expressiveness of detail. It is a second spontaneity, achieved with effort but also immediately discovered, the deployment, speeded up almost to the point of syncretism, of hypothesis and criticism, an approach towards essentiality.

Unlike Chareau, whose ingenious discoveries and use of new materials it would appear he continuously observed, Le Corbusier did not have a fixed clientele or a team of wonderful craftsmen. He pursued an idea in its depth and its breadth. Precise but not fully detailed drawings, open to conformism or adventurousness, shot through with doubts, intuitions and influences, in the declining world in which designer and craftsman understood one another directly, as happened to Chareau.

In his reading he seems to have been influenced by the ideas of Alexandre Vaneyre, who, in a gesture as broad as the journey to the East, suggested that Switzerland, a country of confluences and indecision, should adopt the vivid whiteness of the Mediterranean. He was not satisfied with the invented national style, a mixture of alpine architecture and the Medieval, for which Alfredo de Andrade's village at the Turin Exposition had served as a model.

The practice of painting, in the encounter with Ozenfant, seems to have been oriented towards a linear association of ordinary objects – a bottle, a guitar, a pipe, an everyday glass – purified forms in which straight lines and curves, forming an endless skein, develop within a frame: the foundations of the terrace of Poissy, from which they stretch to the sky.

This practice of association and extension puts down roots and reaches high levels; it will progress from the platforms of La-Chaux-de-Fonds to the far horizons of Chandigarh, passing through the serried plots of Paris, through the sprawling cities of South America – individual blocks of 144 x 144 metres, or large platforms between enormous rocks.

Linear and curved structures slide vertiginously between the mountains of Algeria or of Rio de Janeiro, making use of gorges and inlets to the sea. Compact cells are divided in the interstices of the blocks, fragmenting in the conquest of the possibility of building, in the Maison du Salut. In the 3 x 3 metre studio in the Rue de Sèvres, where the light from the top of the Venice Hospital was perhaps not necessary, Paris is imbued with an Esprit Nouveau. The quest is not always patient.

But the Villa Savoye appears, an encounter between investigation and a degree of freedom: a customer and a clearing.

It could be an object from another world; and this is what it looks like at first sight. It could be built of iron and aluminium and nothing more. But instead the plaster lends continuity to the syncopated forms, and the cracks which open each day expose the indecisions of the building process and of the hands which turn the design into reality.

Next to the road, half-hidden by a wall, the porter's lodge announces the language of the unseen house. A skilful path divides the two buildings, as perfectly and completely related to one another as though this were a little Parisian plot. Le Corbusier completely occupies the space: the house is a detail of this space.

Powerful forms, contained in a parallelepiped raised on pillars, proclaim themselves here and there through a continuous horizontal gap, either on the floor or on the terrace. The pillars around the edge practically coincide with the limits of the building. With the capital missing, the meeting with the horizontal plane is uncertain, a few square centimetres short. The box might fall, sliding on the pillars; the expanded forms on the terrace barely reach the elevation, tense and close to the break promised by the narrow architrave over a doorway.

The appearance of the house provokes a sensation of hardness, the pillars are fused to the first-floor wall. You have to go around them; on the remaining three sides the free-standing structure forms the edge of a covered corridor. A curve of calculated radius leaves two pillars outside; it indicates the entrance to the garage. A number of visible beams deflect any softness. The main door occupies a central position in the curved wall, coinciding with the axis of the structural mesh, of four connecting columns. Inside, the structure divides so as to frame the door and the way in, marked by the ramp.

This framing is reinforced with unimaginable economy: a wall, balanced on the opposite side by a fixed table and a standard wash basin; two lamps placed symmetrically close to the door.

The simple order is successively and continually taken apart: the sculptural staircase, the triangular opening over the courtyard, the asymmetry of the ramp, the light, twists in the wall. The second floor is built around a courtyard which illuminates it under perfect conditions. The asymmetry is controlled by the axial ramp, which is repeated on the outside up to the terrace; the violence of the route is contained there by the sumptuous curves of the walls, as though in an embrace.

Mysteriously there is calm, resulting from the saturation of tensions. The long development of the living room dominates multiplied diagonals, reflected on the mosaic flooring of the entrance-hall; the way through the main bedroom – another U shape – provides a sensation of depth, like in an old house; and once more it reveals the view of the courtyard and the open space.

Each element has an independent life, it suddenly goes out of focus, as happens in a town you go to every day. The meeting between elements is not absolutely perfect. The skirting boards hesitate when they meet obstacles or the water pipes; the frames of the doors or the curves of the stairs, or the bathroom wall do not have an indisputable control. Nothing is systematic. There are obvious errors in design and in the hands which executed it,

mutual indecisions intersect one another; and each error produces poetry, by showing us how to transform.

What impresses us in this Le Corbusier, and finally runs through all of his writings or designs, is the disconcerting rejection of what is already asserted, a sort of innocence, an unease which is not destroyed by his capacity for analysis and for synthesis and convictions, a certain insecurity, the rejection of self-sufficiency, underlying an apparent arrogance.

Much of the delight of the Villa Savoye – of its Architecture – comes from an ambiguous and precarious complicity between those who produced it: promoters, builders, design. Its continuous decay reflects the impossibility of maintaining this delightful balance, but also of not trying to. We do not know what gods inhabit it. Like a Japanese temple, it is remade before it fades away. It suggests health, youth, happiness, hygiene, the gilded box – the noble art – beneath the white. Here dwells an indefatigable and endless quest, carpets from Chandigarh designed on an aeroplane, sculptures modelled by correspondence, portraits of Josephine, the smile of Eve in Paradise.

1995–8   Portuguese Pavilion at Expo '98 *Lisbon, Portugal*

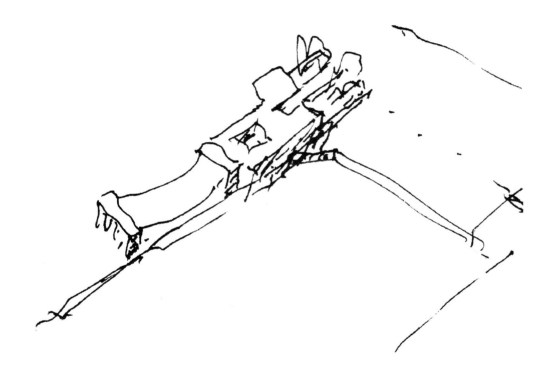

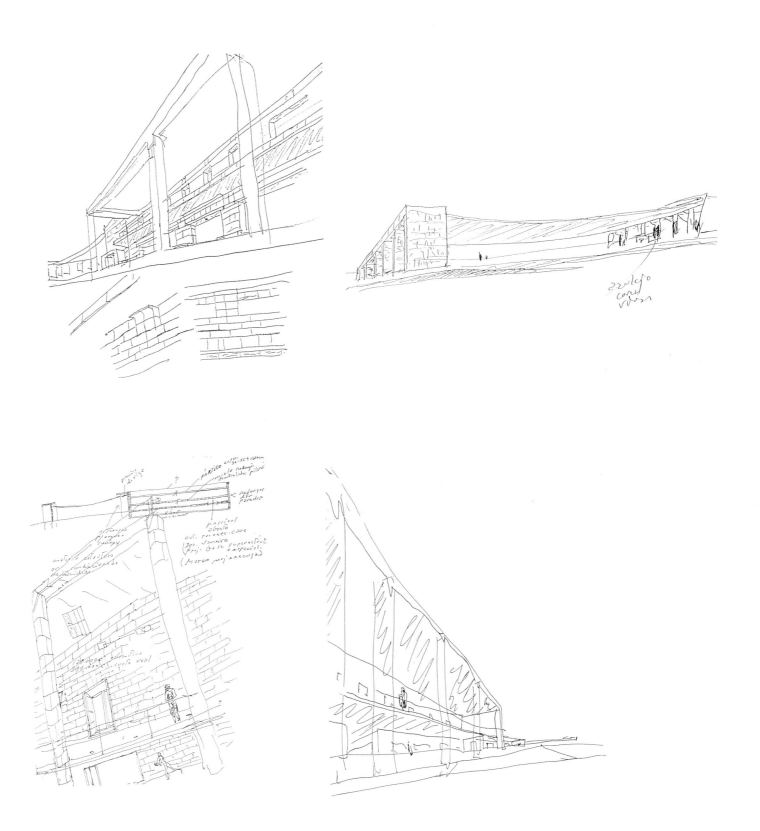

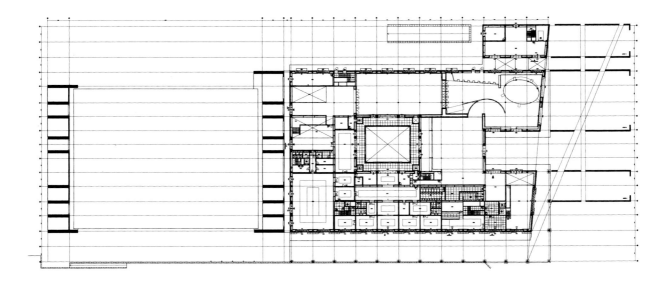
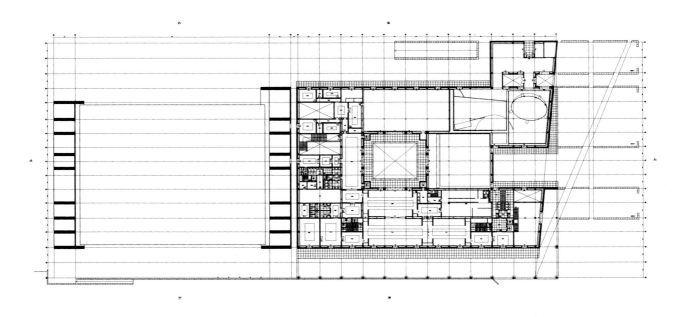
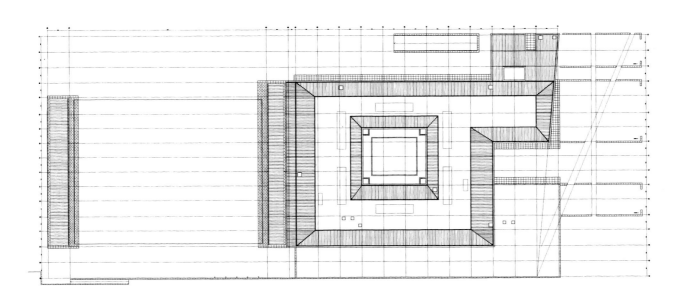

535 *opposite* ground, first floor and roof plans

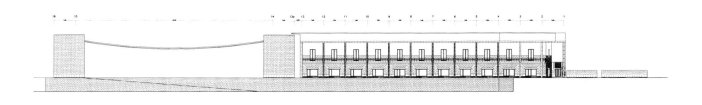

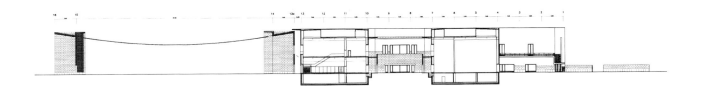

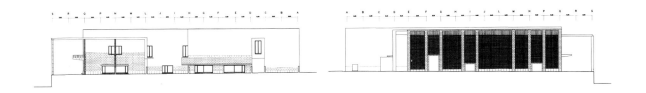

elevations and long section

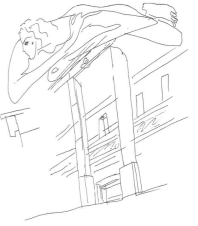

1995–8 Rectory, University of Alicante *Alicante, Spain*

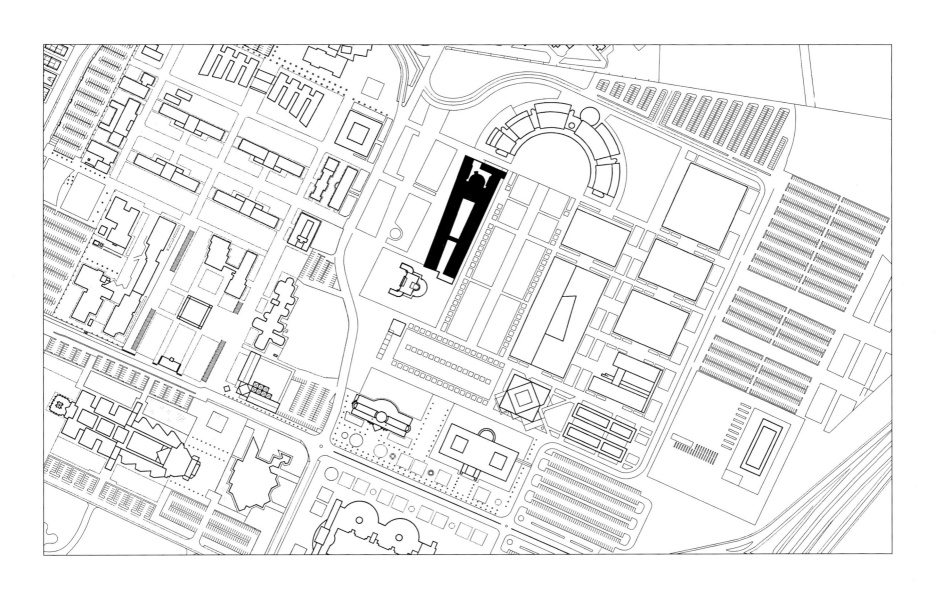

543　site plan

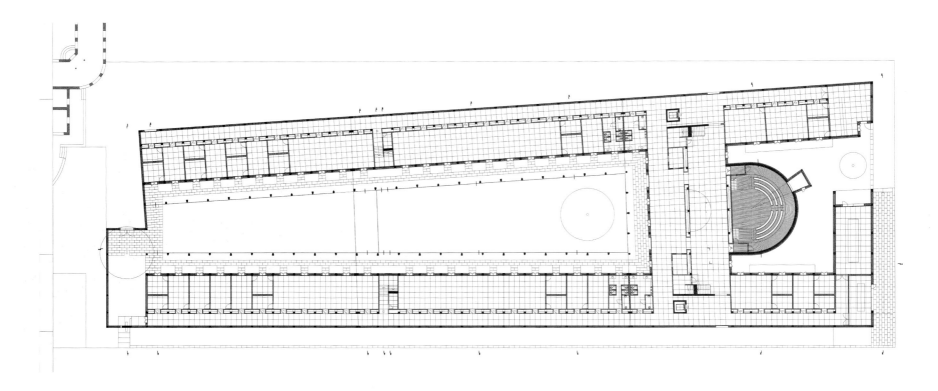
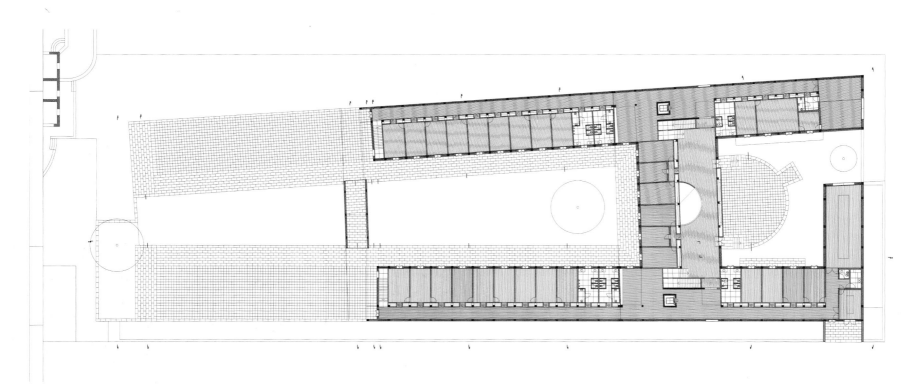

plans

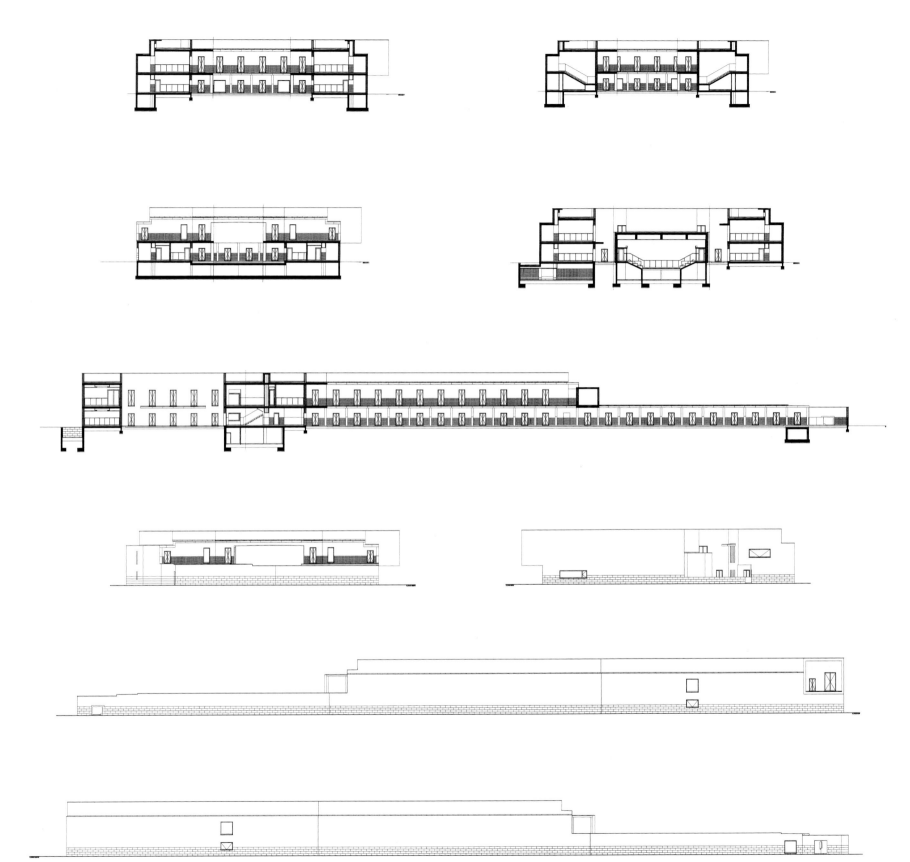

547 sections and elevations

1995 Douro and Leixões Port Authority Building *Matosinhos, Portugal* (under construction)

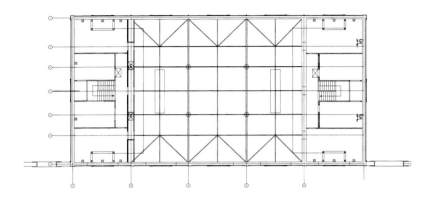

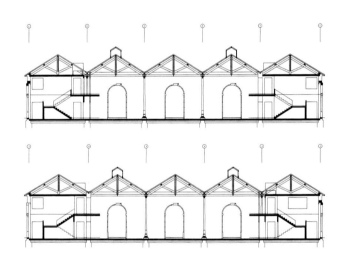

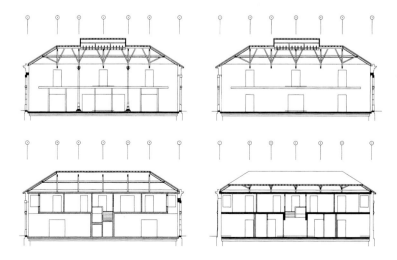

plan and sections

1995 Van Middelem-Dupont House *Oudenberg, Belgium*

553 site plan, sections and elevations

1995 Design for Pinto Sousa House *Oeiras, Portugal*

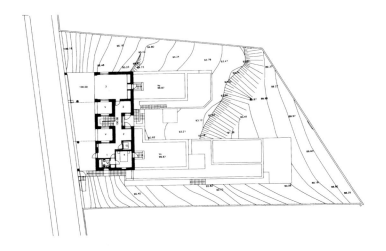
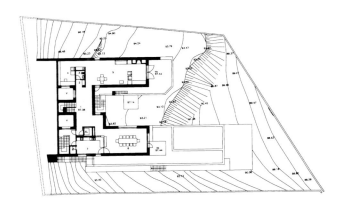
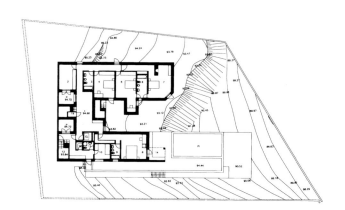
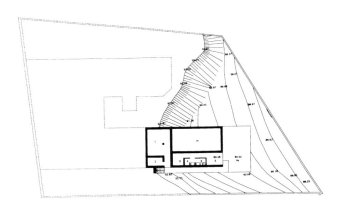

floor plans – below ground levels 3, 2 and 1 and ground floor

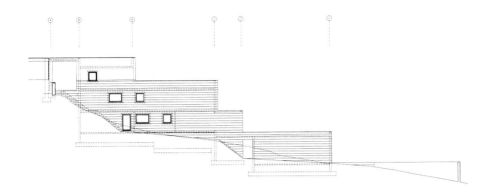

1995   Urban Plan for Lagoinha *Belo Horizonte, Brazil*

above Pinto Sousa House elevation

1995 Urban Plan and Restaurant, Palace of the Dukes of Braganza and Campo de São Mamade Area
Guimarães, Portugal

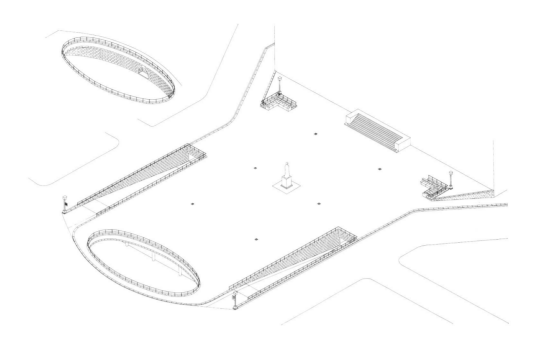

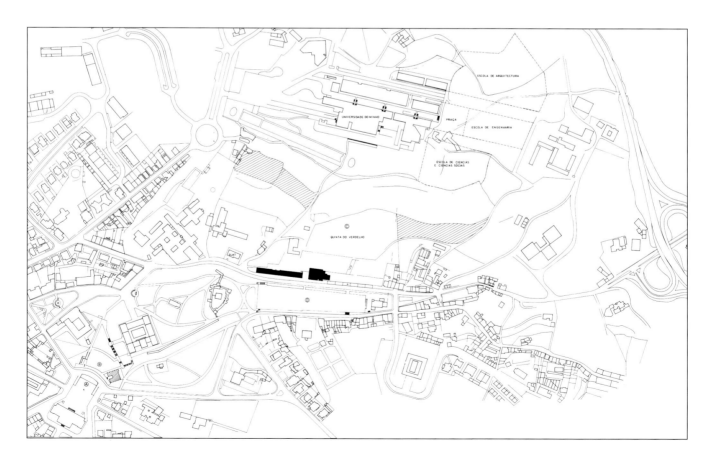

axonometric and site plan

1995 Town Hall *Caorle, Italy*

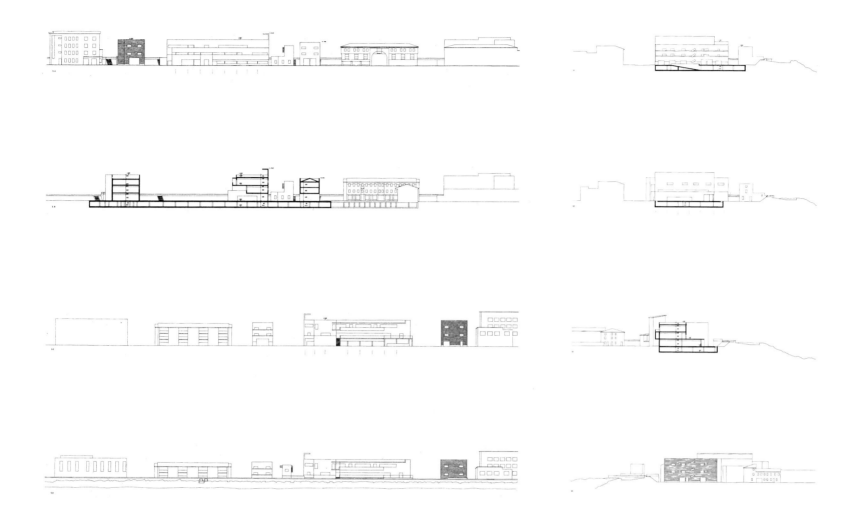

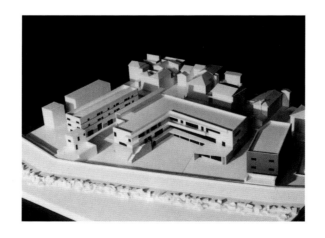

long sections, cross sections and elevations

1995 Residential Complex and Restoration of Two Houses *Palmeira, Évora, Portugal*

1995 Agostinho Vieira House *Baião, Portugal*

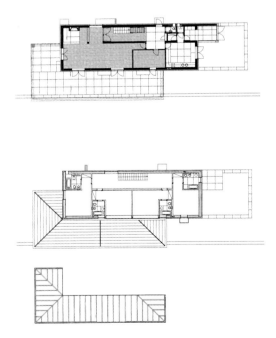
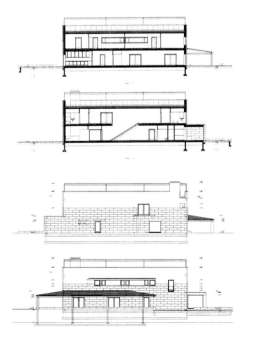

above site plan *below* ground and first floor plans, sections and elevations

1996 Set Design for Ballet, Gulbenkian Foundation *Lisbon, Portugal*

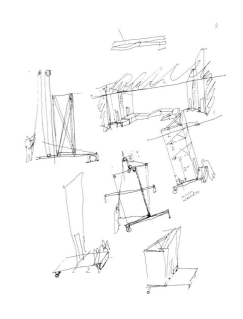 

1996 Kolonihaven, Open-Air Structure *Copenhagen, Denmark*

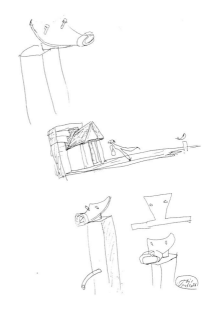 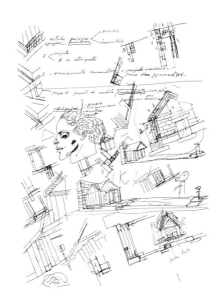 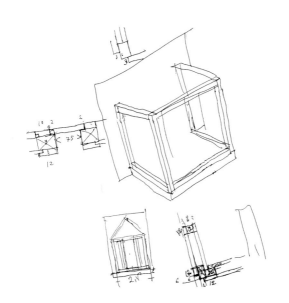

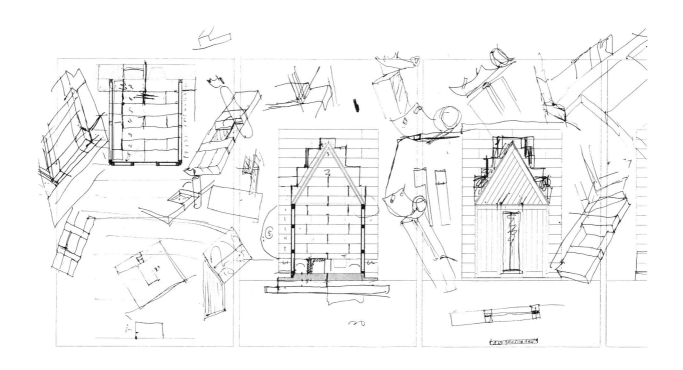
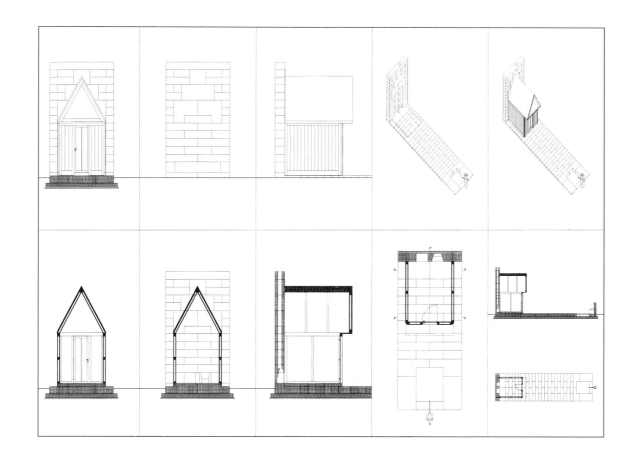

563   plan, sections, elevations and axonometrics

1996 Design for Underground *Porto, Portugal*

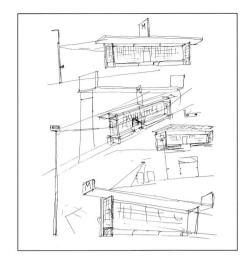
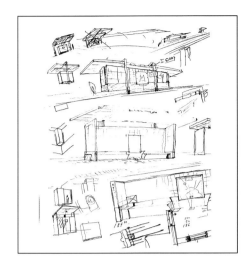

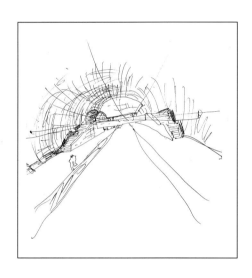
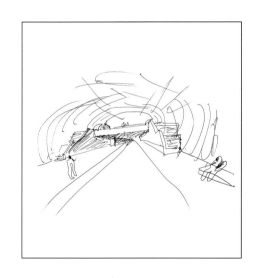
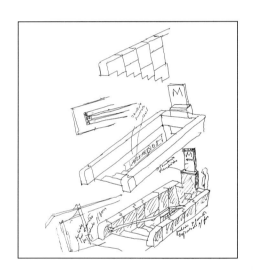
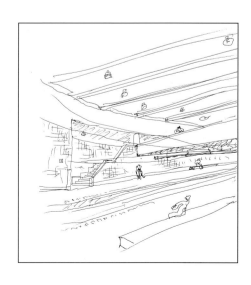
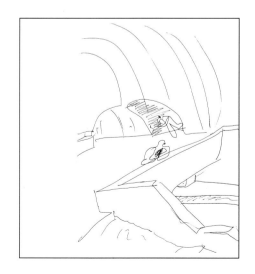
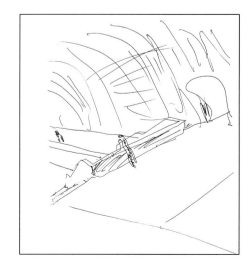

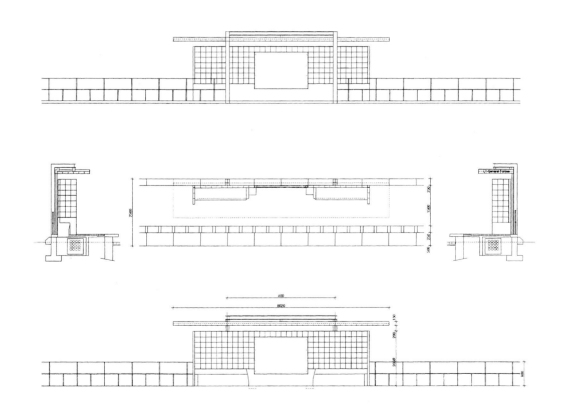

perspective, plan, sections and elevations

1996 Docking Pier, European Architects in Thessaloniki *Salonika, Greece*

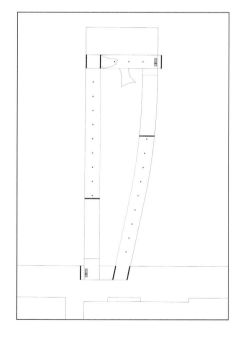 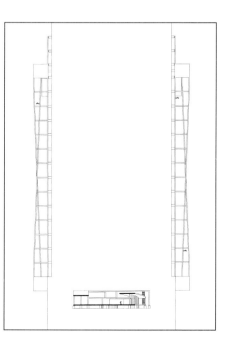

plan, cross section and elevations

1996 Urban Plan for South Matosinhos *Matosinhos, Portugal*

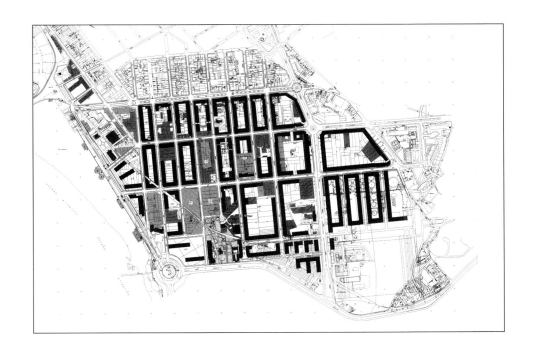

site plan

1996 Medical Clinic *Malagueira, Évora, Portugal*

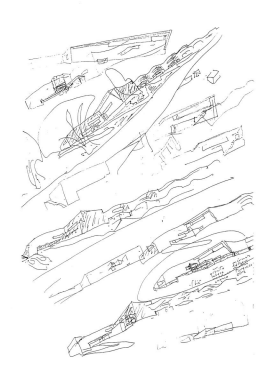
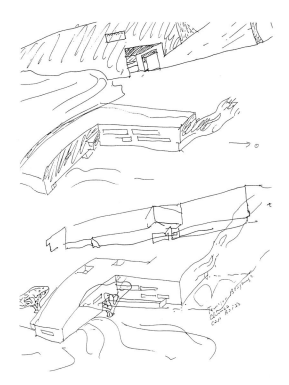

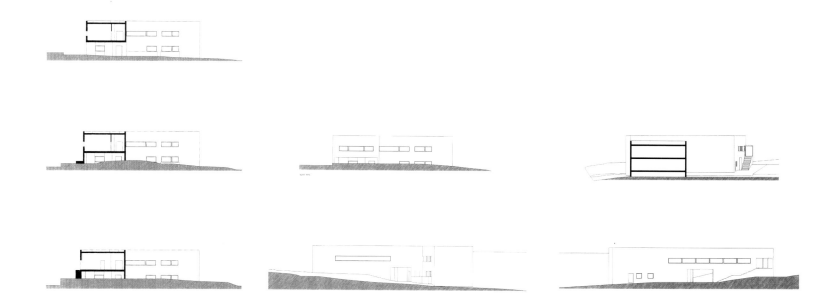
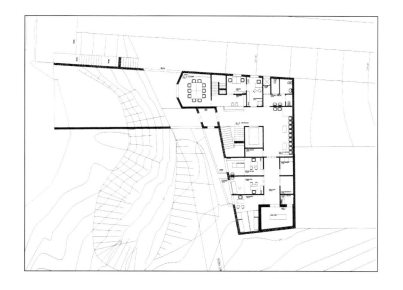

569　sections, elevations, ground and first floor plans

1996 Housing, Office and Shopping Complex *Raimundo Rotunda, Évora, Portugal*

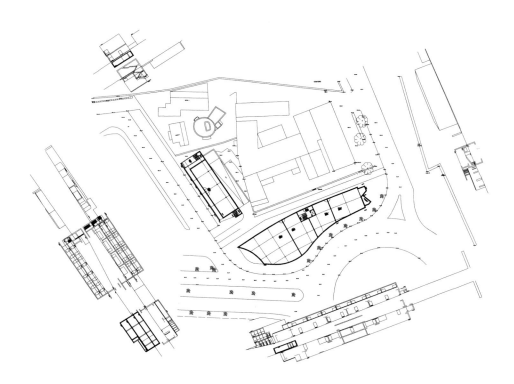

1997 Chiado Bar *Lisbon, Portugal*

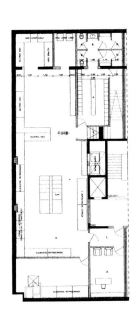
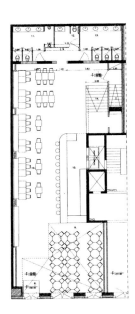

above site plan, sections and elevations *below* lower ground, ground and first floor plans

1997 Design for Sports Hall *Vigo, Spain*

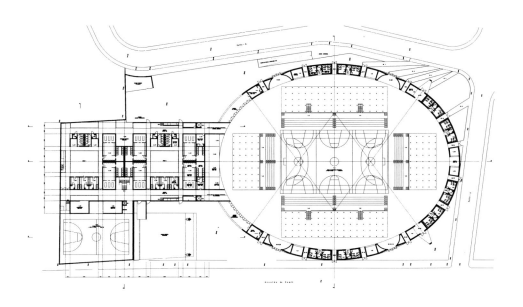

1997 Park and Cultural Centre *Caxinas, Vila do Conde, Portugal*

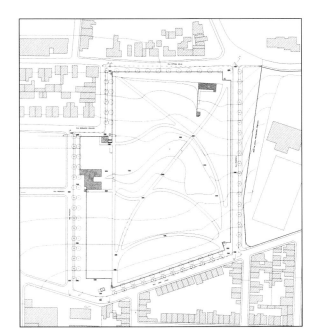

above plan *below* site plan

Alvar Aalto
Álvaro Siza

Finland became independent in 1917 and the following year Alvar Aalto produced his first work: the redesigning of his parent's house. There followed an enthusiastic involvement in the effort to achieve and assert national independence: buildings for co-operatives and for patriotic organisations, industrial buildings, and national and international exhibition pavilions. The activity of this period was interrupted, and also strengthened, by the Second World War.

Aalto became known internationally after the popularization of the Paimio Sanatorium (1929) and the Viipuri Library (1930), and particularly after the dazzling appearance of the New York pavilion (1938). In June 1940 he published the text 'Reconstruction in the Post-War Period' in the *Magazine of Art*, in which he set out problems and proposed solutions, advocating the universality of the responses: 'Finland should be the primary place for experimentation and research in the human activity now called reconstruction. It is this country's duty towards humanity.' In this text Aalto defends a third way, evolutionary and open, between the temporary shelter in response to the emergency and the new 'finished' city. His points of view are still up to date and are more obvious if we look at the consequences of reconstruction in the way it was carried out in France or Germany, or even in England.

Recent controversies, like the one going on in Berlin (in IBA '87) or the marginal outbreaks of post-modernism, and even and above all the disillusioned reaction of the populations, everywhere, lead us to think of the acknowledged quality of Finnish architecture, which owes such a great deal to Aalto.

'I don't think that I have any propensity for folklore', he stated in 1967; 'My own sense of tradition is related mainly to the climate, to the material conditions, to the nature of the tragedies and comedies which touch us. I do not produce an ostensibly "Finnish architecture", and I see no opposition between the Finnish and the international elements.'

In spite of his international success, which would have allowed him to follow other paths, Aalto stayed in Finland, that distant, sparsely populated and little known country, sliced by lakes and forest, where the roads have no markings and are covered in snow for much of the year. Pure surface which is drawn on by feet in the most natural way. The work he did after the war is strongly conditioned by restrictions in materials and the means of production and transport. Unlike what was happening in other countries, the lack of concrete and iron led to the use of local materials (bricks, wood, copper) and allowed craftsmanship to survive.

The work of Aalto is not defined in reaction to 'modernist mechanisation', and when he says anything on this subject he usually does so with moderation; he does not betray the CIAM or constructivist component of his training, nor the neo-classical, nor the romantic. These frontiers do not exist for him; and like in the landscape of Finland, the accidents constitute a fine, continuous and varied fabric. Even when this landscape guides his production, when the shape of the lakes is like that of the windows he designs, this is no more than one particular aspect of his aptitude to include everything in the design, to take everything as stimulus. A Finlander with a desire to travel (a traveller is a man with strong roots) draws on what most impresses him and becomes, like all great creators, an 'agent of cross-fertilisation' – the seed of transformation. What I mean by this is that, by mastering proven models (the model is universal), he transforms them, as he introduces them into different, distorted realities; he also interbreeds them, uses them in a surprising and luminous way: strange objects which come to earth and then put down roots. The MIT students' dormitory in Boston (1947) is an American building and at the same time an Aalto work. And whoever criticizes the marble of the Enso-Gutzeit building does not understand it. There is Morocco in Seinäjoki, Delphi in Otaniemi, London in Sunila, Venice in Helsinki – and there is Finland as well. But the transformation never depends solely on Morocco, or Delphi, or London, or Venice.

'A great number of demands and marginal problems stand in the way of the clear exposition of the basic architectural idea,' Aalto wrote in 1947. 'In such cases I often proceed in an entirely instinctive way. After absorbing into my subconscious the characteristics of the work and its infinite requirements, I try for a while to forget all the problems, and begin to draw in a manner that is very close to abstract art. I draw, guided solely by instinct, skipping architectural syntheses, sometimes ending up with sketches that look like children's compositions. In that way the main idea, based on abstract foundations, gradually takes shape, a sort of universal substance which enables the various problems and contradictions to harmonize with one another.' Reading these lines, it is really surprising to hear people say, 'Aalto, architect, Finn, didn't theorise, he didn't talk about method'. He did, brilliantly. And I know of no more accurate and penetrating analysis of the mental process of designing than what is summarized in this fragment and in Aalto's other writings and discourses, which are no less illuminating for being brief. What this discourse illuminates is not the way in which Aalto designed but rather the way in which design should be accomplished in our own time – a way that has been hidden for various reasons, as happens to 'the naked truth, which needs no words, hidden beneath the mantle of the imagination'. Architects are modest if anyone is. In one way or another they wrap mantles around their own work. These mantles, very intricate and occasionally elegant with a complex hang, stand up perfectly well when suitably starched and can be confused with the body of a theory, or of a method of action, in spite of the fact that the head cannot be seen, either disappearing into the darkness or into the glare of a brilliant light. And so thousands of architecture students run their fingers down the furrows and discover that all the runs lead to the ground or to the ether.

Aalto's architecture was only influential in Portugal after the second half of the fifties. And I think that it was only for a short time and more frequently in the forms (some of them) than in the content. But this influence is not accidental, nor does it come only from Italy, like almost everything does, nor is it only the forms which remain. The fact that it coincides with one of the few moments of collective professional action and of the breaking of the isolation between Porto and Lisbon is significant. I refer to the period after the *Inquérito à Arquitectura Portuguesa* and to the movement which followed it, involving students and architects from Lisbon and Porto, united around the magazine *Arquitectura*.

Studying Aalto may help us not to consider him as the ultimate great genius with whom communication is difficult but, on the contrary, to appreciate his capacity for generous communication. His influence must find expression above all in the reform of our schools of architecture, helping to open them up to the problems of the present day. It is in reacting to these problems that we may be able to find a way forward without placing our trust in post-war modernism, which is something that we in Portugal have not had.

1997 Designs for University Library *Évora, Portugal*

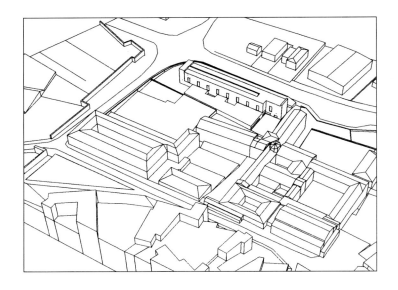
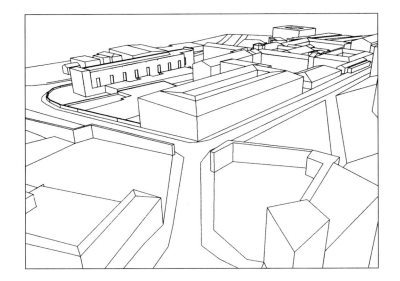
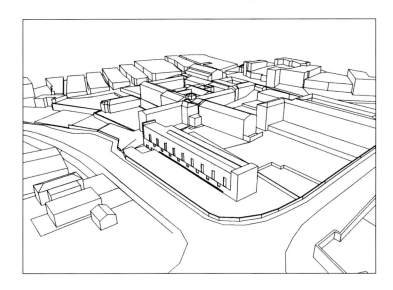
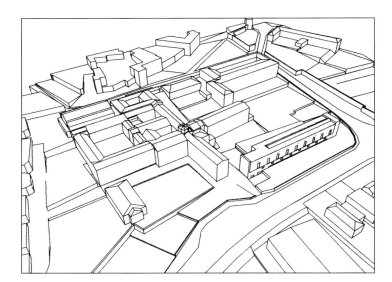

1997 Manzana dei Revellín Cultural Centre *Ceuta, Spain*

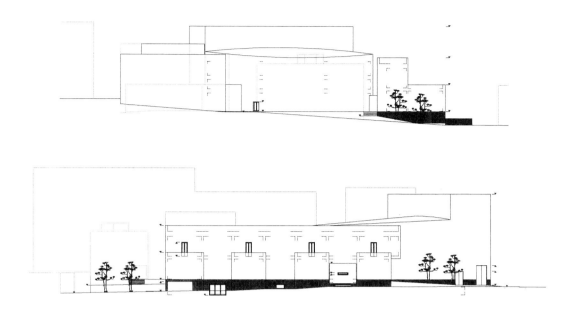

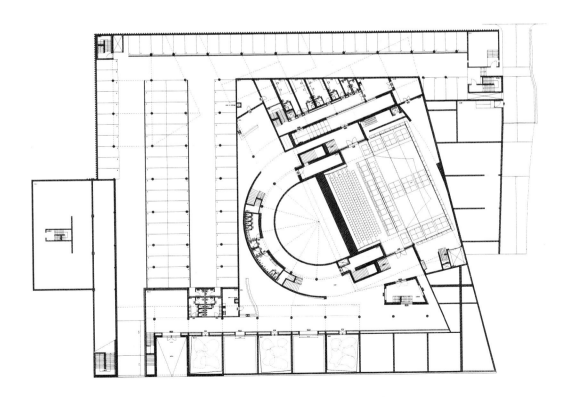

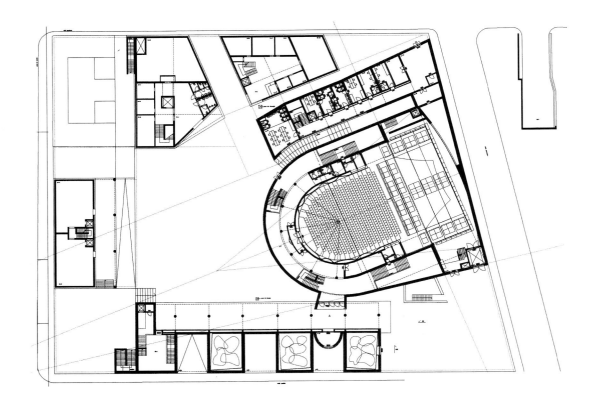
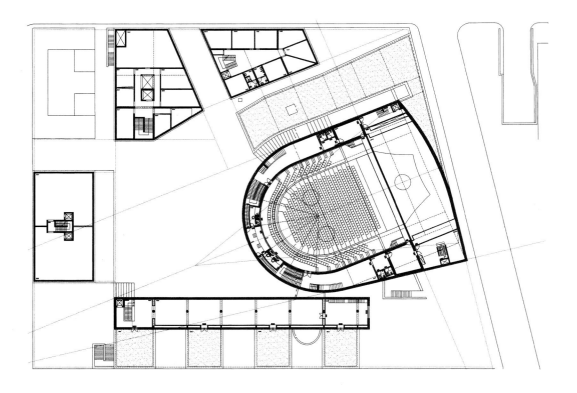

576　first and third floor plans

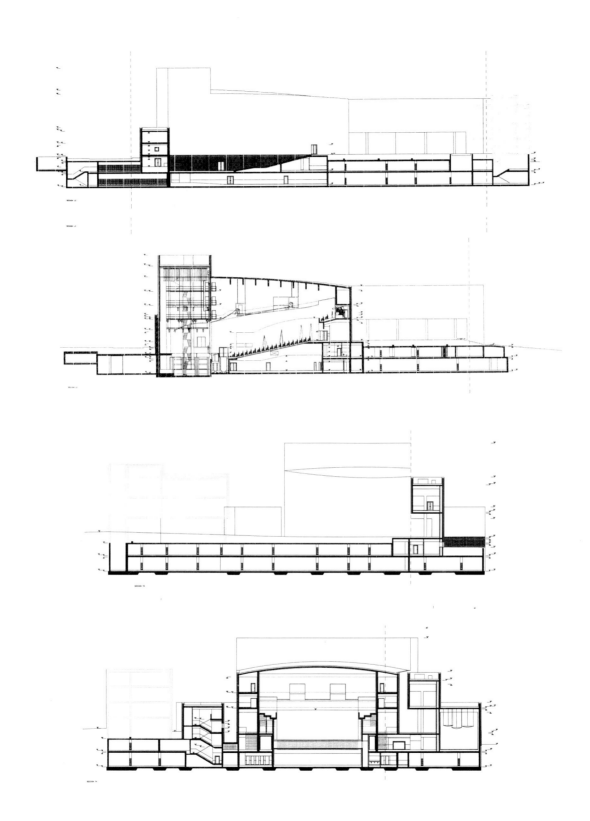

1997 Hotel *Almeria, Spain*

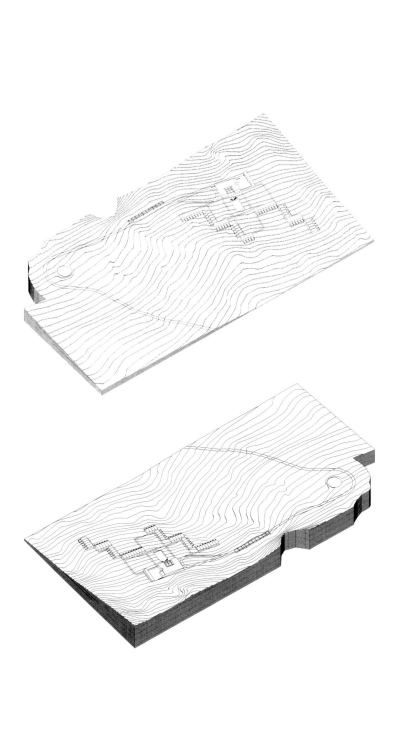

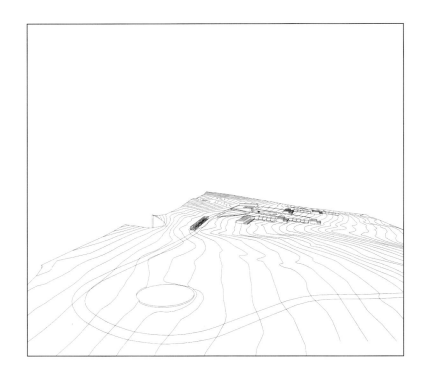

1997 Urban Design for Dr. Machado de Mantos Square *Felgueiras, Portugal*

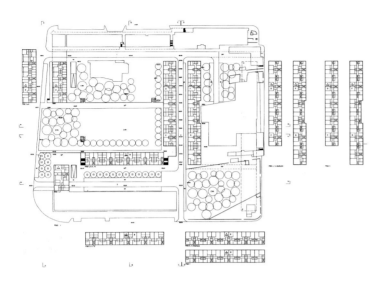
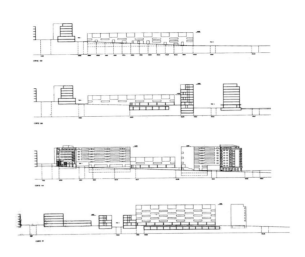

1997 Rectory and Auditorium, University Campus *Valencia, Spain*

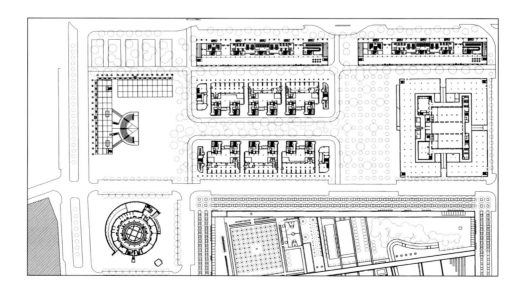

above plans, sections and elevations *below* site plan

1997 Renova Factory and Showroom *Torres Novas, Portugal*

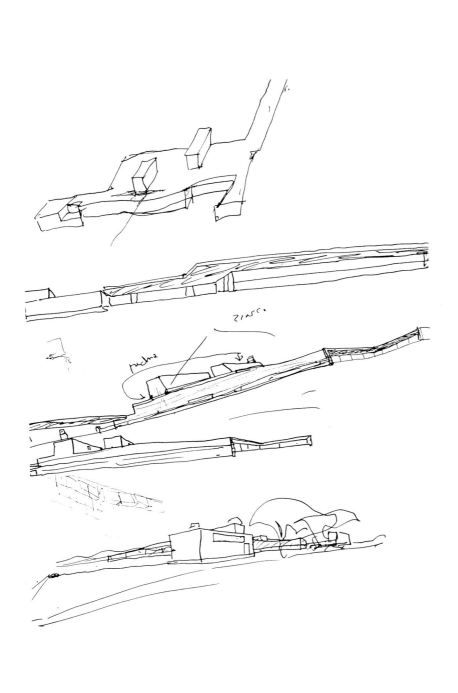
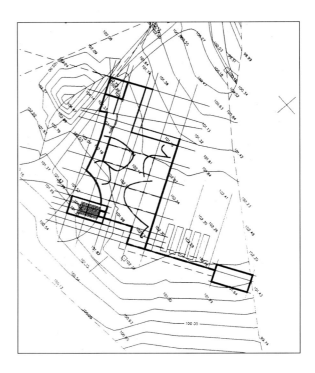
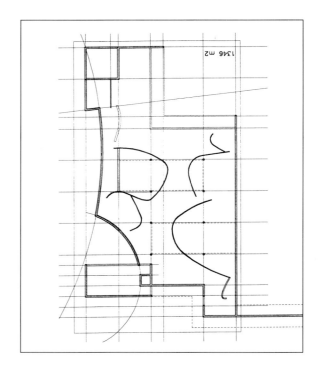

site plan and plan

1997 South District Town Hall *Rosario, Argentina*

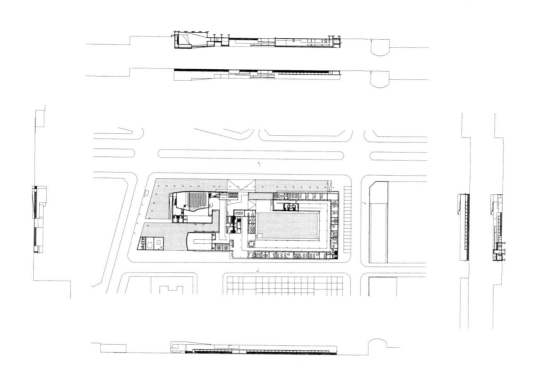

1998 Leonel Building *Chiado, Lisbon, Portugal*

581 *above* plan, sections and elevations *below* sections and plans

1998 Restoration of Villa Colonnese and Seven Houses *Vicenza, Italy*

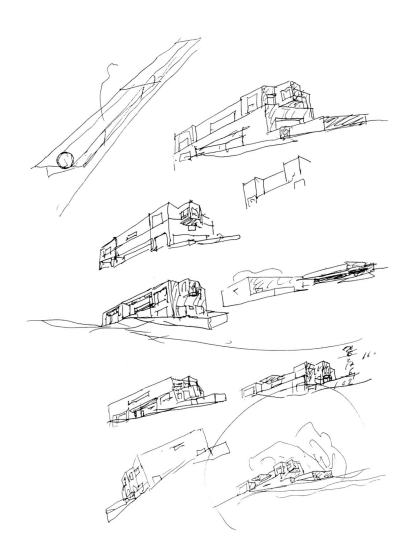

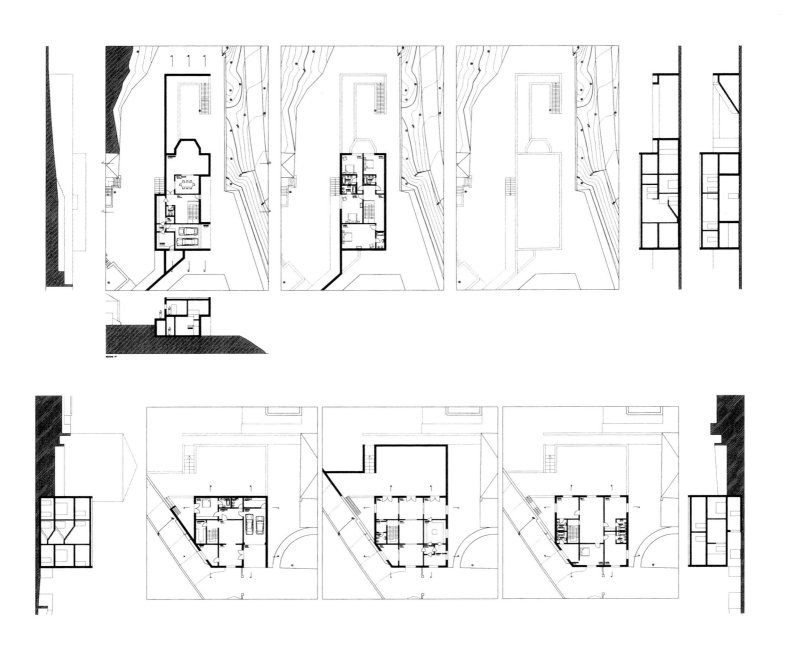
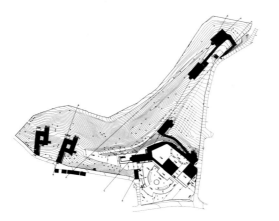

583 *above* ground, first floor and roof plans, sections and elevation of villa three *centre* ground, first and second floor plans and sections of villa four *below* site plan

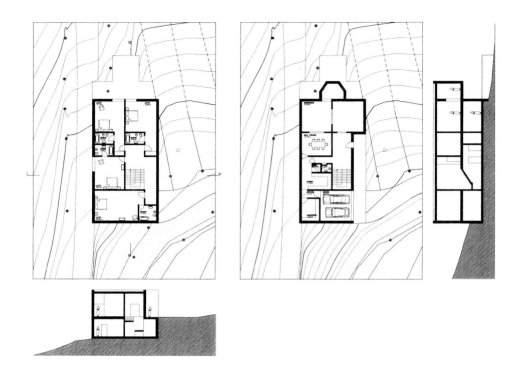
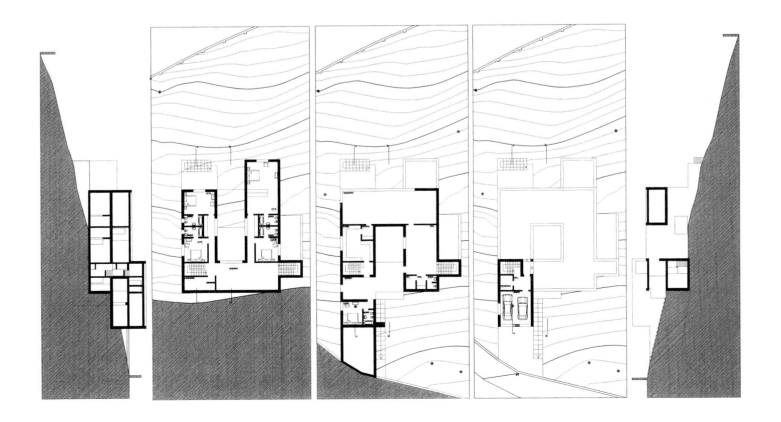

584   *above* ground and first floor plans, and sections of villa five *below* ground, first floor and roof plans, and sections of villa one

1998 Santa Maria de Rosario alla Magliana Church *Rome, Italy*

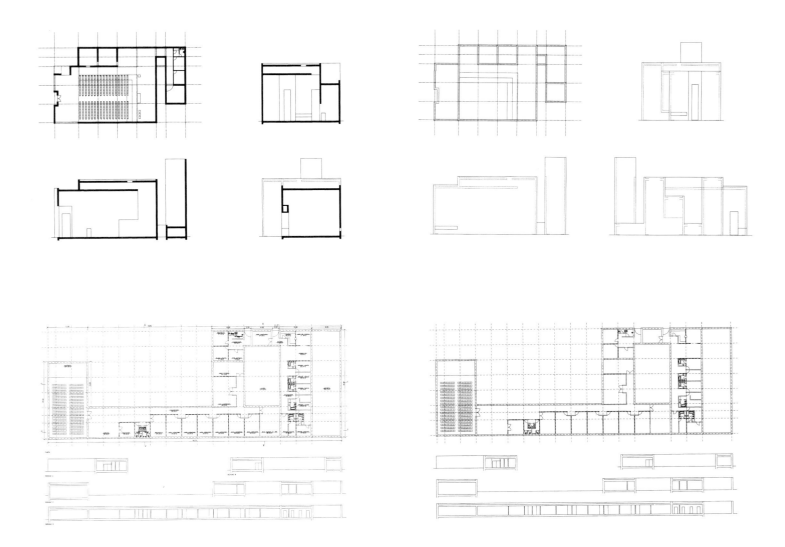

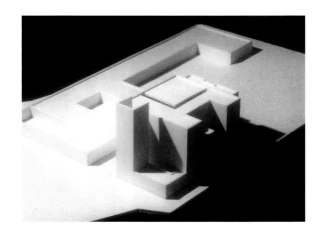

above plans, sections and elevations of church *centre* plans and sections of oratory and parish centre *below* model

1998 Housing and Shopping Complex *Porto, Portugal*

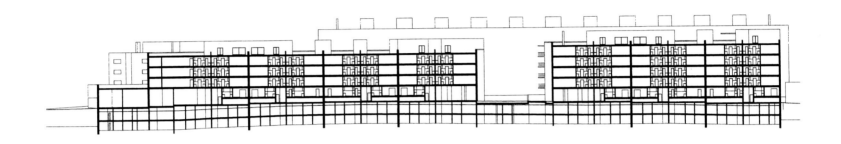

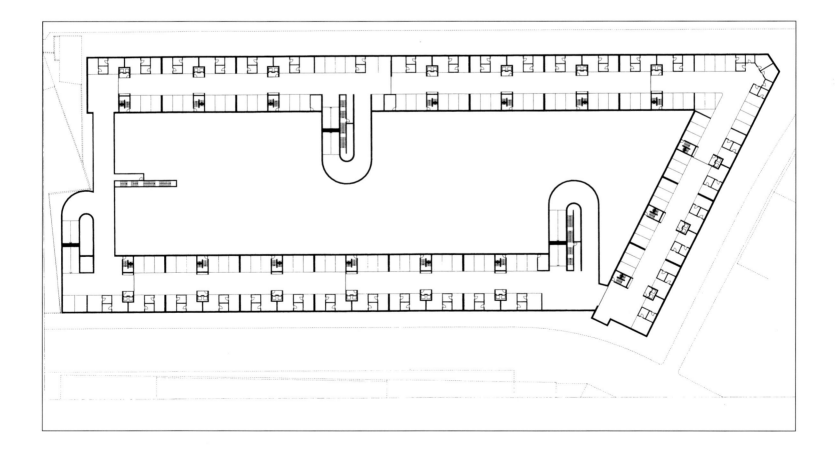

long section and plan

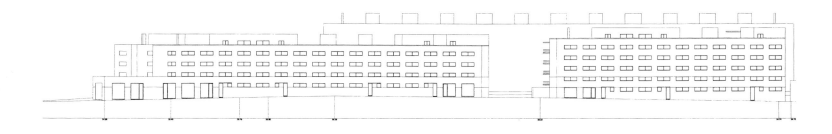

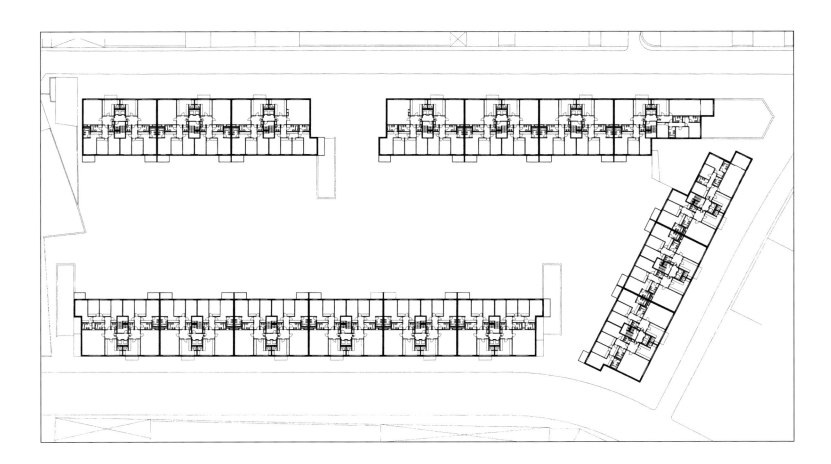

587　elevations and plan

1998 Zaida Building, Housing, Office and Shopping Complex *Granada, Spain*

floor plans (lower ground, ground, first, second, third, fourth, fifth and roof)

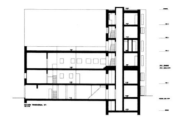   

sections and elevations

1998 Cape Verde National Bank Office *Praia, Cape Verde Island*

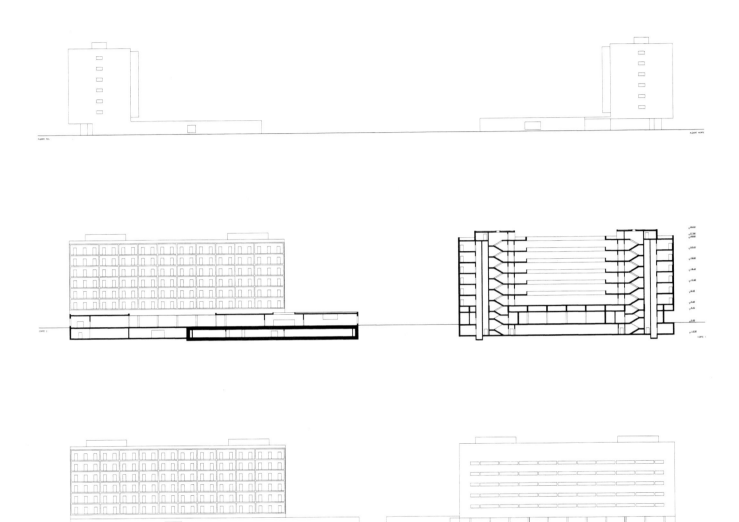

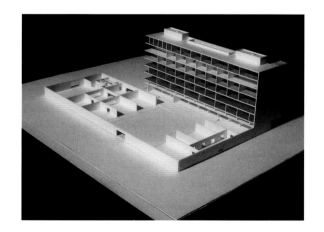

elevations and sections

1998 Design for Cultural Centre and Auditorium for Iberê Camargo Foundation *Alegre Port, Brazil*

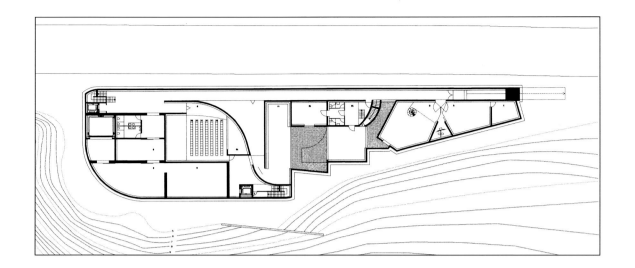
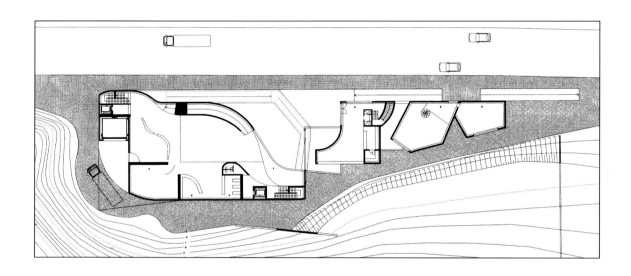
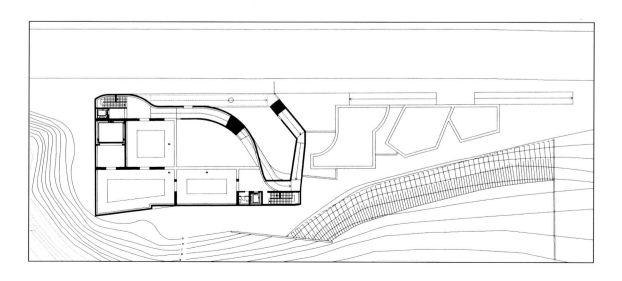

lower ground, ground and first floor plans

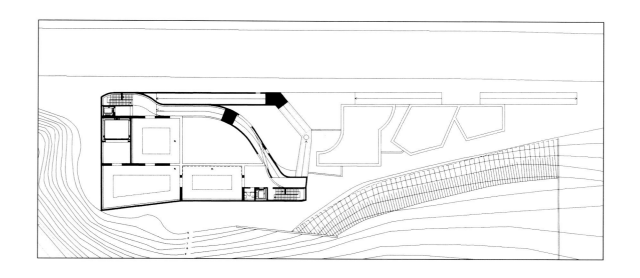
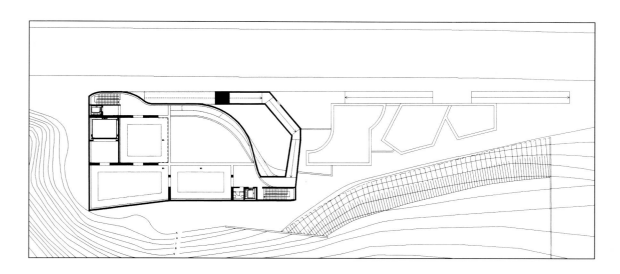
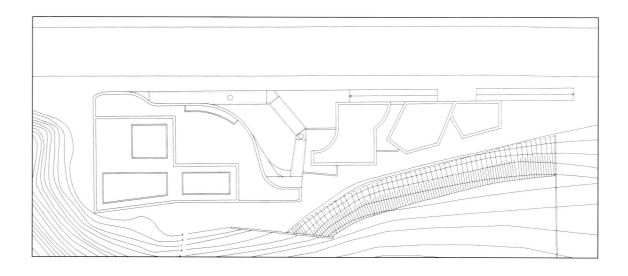

second, third floor and roof plans

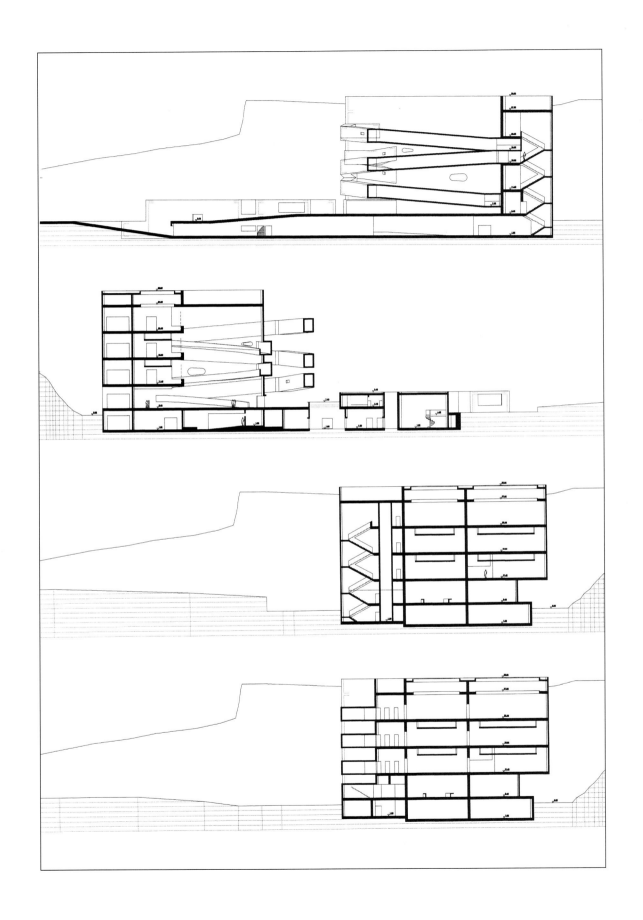

1999 Restoration of Solar Magalhães House for Afonso Henriques Foundation *Amarante, Portugal*

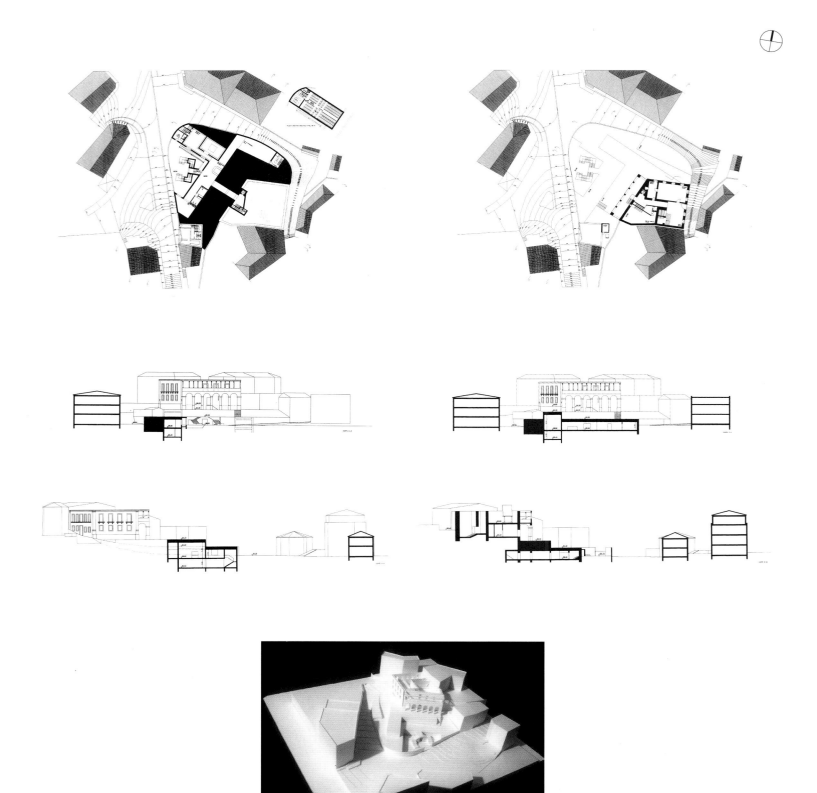

ground and first floor plans, sections and elevations

On Design
Álvaro Siza

I have begun to turn my attention towards furniture commissioned by the people I have designed houses for. My items of furniture, therefore, have been conceived for particular spaces. Nonetheless, just as the design of a building seeks to free itself progressively from its functional conditions, the design of a piece of furniture tends to configure an object that can be adapted to different situations. The difficulty lies in expressing its autonomy, which must not interfere with the autonomy of the space itself. For this reason, three exercises strike me as indispensable: imagining the town, imagining the building and imagining the piece of furniture – each depends on the others.

The first pieces of furniture that I designed were prototypes, conceived specifically for the interiors for which they were destined. The limits of approximation were relatively small and not a cause for concern. Subsequently, because of the demands of serial production, it struck me that this immediate and exclusive relationship with a particular space was a form of weakness. In fact, once a certain point in the process has been reached, the design must be freed from its dependent status so as to acquire greater autonomy and individuality. The quality of the results depends on the outcome of this quest for autonomy and, in the meantime, on connections with the environment. The important thing is to clarify the nature of each piece of furniture, to ask oneself what it is in essence. My chief concern in designing a chair, for example, is that it should look like a chair. That is the underlying problem, but nowadays people design chairs that look like other things and the quest for originality leads them to ignore the essence, so to speak, of each object. Every object has a history, and if we consider them in perspective they may appear slightly different: it is in these slight differences that they show their meaning in regard to time. Differences may be introduced, varying materials or proportions, but what must remain is the 'essence' of the chair, or rather its relationship with the body. For this reason, too, Adolf Loos' reflections on design are important and contemporary: they emphasize the fact that necessity, not art, is the spur for the design of a perfect object. The Thonet chair designed by Loos is wonderful. Looking at it, you can tell without further ado: 'That is a Thonet chair'. Nonetheless, there is something particular about its proportions and certain inconspicuous details and, although the overall result is an entirely unique object, at the same time it shows a certain banality. The fact remains that an object, some exceptional cases aside, cannot be a 'protagonist' in any absolute sense; it must express a great degree of moderation, or rather allow itself to be used to establish connections. I maintain that industrial design confronts this very problem. The furniture that has made its mark on history has a considerable level of moderation and a kind of banality – a word with a double meaning, which I use not in the sense of 'lacking in interest or quality', but rather of 'available for continuity'.

Observation is the most important exercise for an architect. The more we observe, the closer we come to the essence of things. When I design an object, I start off with a large number of ideas and sketch things that are very different and sometimes extravagant. The design slowly undergoes a process of reduction, leading to the essence and the gradual conquest of its substance. The stylized chairs that I drew as a child already had all the characteristics distinguishing this particular object from all others: four legs, a back, a seat. This remains the starting point: refining awareness then amounts to the conquest of a 'second spontaneity', involving a dangerous process of navigation in which shipwreck is always a possibility. Design implies a strong degree of contact with the work of the craftsman and also with industrial production. In order to exploit its potential, we must first understand the possibilities that it offers. In the course of the production process, particularly when one is using a provincial craftsman, a close link must be established between the design and the person carrying it out. At the moment I am designing a set of cutlery. The fork will have specially inserted tines and the weight of the blade of the knife will be compatible with that of the handle, avoiding imbalance. Many solutions come from experience, from considering how objects have been transformed and improved over time. In this case too, I have only made sketches which have enabled me to produce a number of prototypes. Observing these, I have begun to add modifications to them, and then to discuss them with architect friends and with members of my family, who have fewer preconceptions. This 'learning process' supports the design, which absorbs hypotheses and criticism, and thus the responses to that criticism.

Returning to the design of the chair: in order to express a certain uniqueness, without betraying its essence, it is important to ensure that the design does not run the risk of being too obvious. In this way it can assume a touch of originality that might be discreetly attractive, while remaining 'banal' at the same time. Starting out obsessed with originality shows an uncouth and superficial attitude.

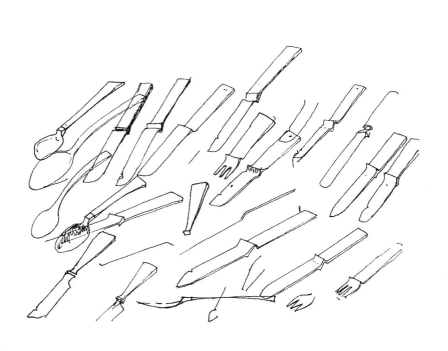

above silverware (1993–7) *opposite* Havana ashtray (1994), Jarras vases (1995), fruit bowl (1996), Álvaro mirror (1975)

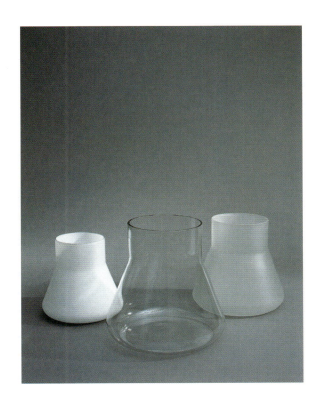
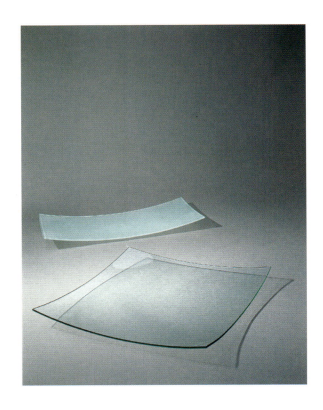
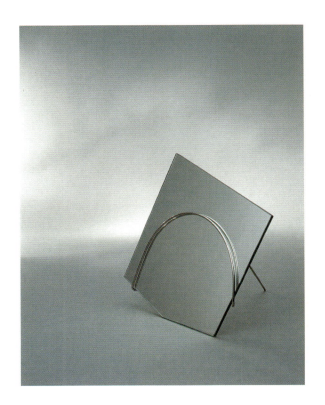

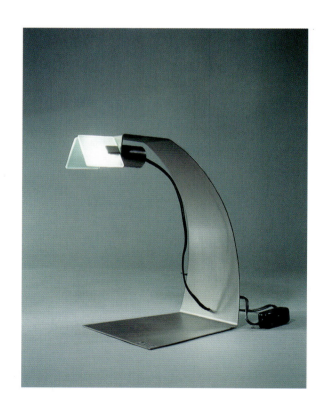

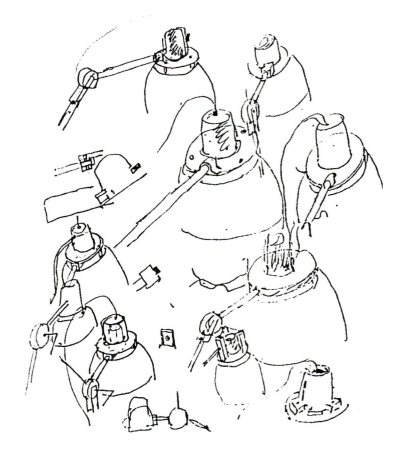

opposite lamps: Mecânica (1997), Falena (1994), Fil (1990), 3 (1995) *above* bookcase (1987), book stands (1990)

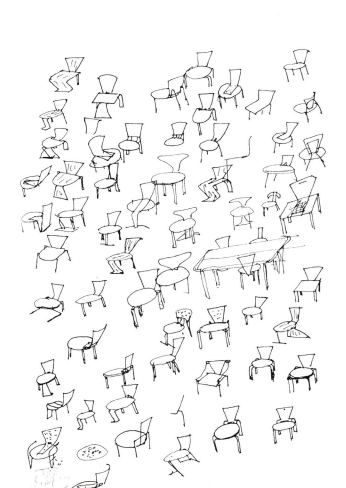

602 *above* chairs: C1 (1985), Marco (1996) *opposite* Mare table and chair (1997), folding chairs (1973), C2 arm chairs (1992), Boa Nova armchair (1956)

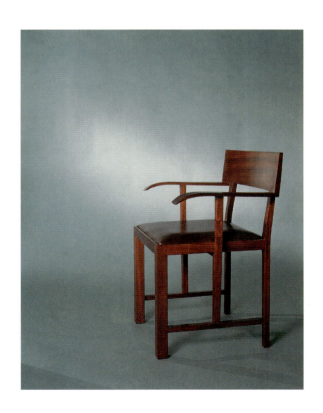

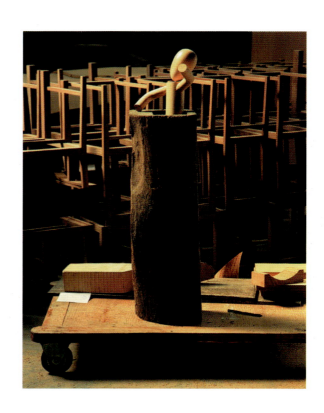

605   *opposite* door fittings (1993), chest of drawers 1 (1985), *the navigator* sculpture (1998), other sculptures *above* garden chaise-longue (1990)

Biography

Álvaro Siza Vieira was born in Matosinhos (Porto) in 1933. After attending the School of Fine Arts in Porto (1949–55), he joined the architecture faculty of the same town (ESBAP) where, in the sixties, he became a teacher immediately after graduation. After spending some time working with Fernando Távora, from 1955 to 1958, Siza opened his professional studio in Porto, where he still works. Siza has also taught in various universities in the United States, Switzerland, South America and elsewhere. His works have been shown at exhibitions organized throughout the world, including at the Venice Biennale, the Milan Triennale, the Centre Georges Pompidou in Paris, the Helsinki Museum of Architecture, and at venues in Germany, Holland, Spain, Portugal, England, Brazil and the United States. Invited to take part in various major international competitions, in particular at the end of the seventies, and after working for the IBA in Berlin, Siza has built many prestigious works including his most recent works, the Portuguese Pavilion at the Lisbon Expo '98 and the Museum of Contemporary Art in Santiago de Compostela. His buildings and designs have been published by the most important architectural magazines in the world and have been the subject of various monographs. Since the early eighties, Siza has received many major international awards and prizes, including the 'European Award for Architecture' from the Economic European Community/Mies van der Rohe Foundation, the Gold Medal of the Alvar Aalto Foundation, the Harold W. Brunner Memorial Prize, the Pritzker Prize and the Praemium Imperiale. The universities of Valencia, Lausanne, Palermo, Santander, Lima and Coimbra have also awarded him honorary degrees.

Bibliography

1957 'Paintings and Sketches', in E. Lapa Carneiro (ed.), catalogue, *Exposição Individual de Pintura e Desenho no Club Naval Povoense*, Póvoa de Varzim

1959 'Paintings and Sketches', in catalogue, *I Exposição dos Alunos das Escolas Superiores de Belas Artes do Porto e Lisboa*, Coimbra
A. Real, 'Álvaro Siza na Galeria Dominguez Alvares', in *Diário de Noticias*, June
H. Tavares, 'Arte e Artistas-Siza Vieira Expõe na Galeria Alvarez, aguarela e desenho', in *Jornal Feminino*, June

1960 E. Lapa Carneiro, 'Exposição de pintura do Arqt. Siza Vieira', in *Fanqueiro*, October
N. Portas, 'Tres Obras de Álvaro Siza Vieira', in *Architectura*, no. 68
'Centro Paroquial de Matosinhos', in *Boletim Paroquial de Matosinhos*
'66.º Aniversário da Cooperativa de Lordelo, número 1', Inauguration of the headquarters building, Lordelo, October

1964 N. Portas, 'Álvaro Siza Vieira', in *Arquitectura para Hoje*
'Álvaro Siza Vieira', in *World Arquitecture One*

1965 N. Portas, V. Rosa, 'Álvaro Siza Vieira – Casa de Chá da Boa Nova', in *Architectura*, no. 88, May/June

1966 *Ver*, no. 2

1967 C. Flores, 'La obra de Álvaro Siza Vieira', in *Hogar y Arquitectura*, no. 68, January/February
N. Portas, 'Sobre la joven generación de arquitectos portugueses', in *Hogar y Arquitectura*, no. 68, January/February
P. Vieira de Almeida, 'Un análisis de la obra de Álvaro Siza Vieira', in *Hogar y Arquitectura*, no. 68, January/February
P. Vieira de Almeida, 'Uma Análise da Obra de Álvaro Siza Vieira', in *Arquitectura*, no. 96, March/April

1969 A. Krafft, 'Álvaro Siza Vieira', in *Architecture, Formes et Fonctions*, Lausanne
N. Portas, 'Álvaro Siza Vieira', in *A Cidade como Arquitectura*, Lisbon

1970 N. Portas, 'Arquitecturas Marginadas em Portugal', in *Cuadernos Summa-Nueva Visión*, no. 49
L. Sabater (ed.), *Diccionario Ilustrado de la Arquitectura Contemporánea*, Barcelona
B. Zevi, J. Augusto França, *História da Arquitectura Moderna*, Lisbon
'Álvaro Siza Vieira', in *Arte Moderna em Portugal, 1911–1961*, Lisbon

1972 V. Gregotti, 'Architetture recenti di Álvaro Siza', in *Controspazio*, no. 9, September
N. Portas, 'Note sul significato dell'architettura di Álvaro Siza nell'ambiente portoghese', in *Controspazio*, no. 9, September

1973 'Álvaro Siza Vieira', in *Boletim Cooperativista*, Lisbon

1974 'Álvaro Siza Vieira', in *Lotus*, no. 8, September

1975 'Casa unifamiliare a Oporto, Gruppo di abitazione a Caxinas, Studio per abitazioni economiche a Oporto', in *Lotus*, no. 9
'Siza – en overlevende arkitekt fra Porto', in *Arkitekten*, no. 4, April

1976 *Álvaro Siza*, catalogue, exhibition at the School of Architecture, Aarhus
O. Bohigas, 'Álvaro Siza Vieira', in *Arquitecturas Bis*, no. 12
O. Bohigas (ed.), 'Álvaro Siza Vieira', in *Once Arquitectos*, Barcelona
B. Huet, 'La Passion d'Álvaro Siza', in *L'Architecture d'Aujourd'hui*, no. 185, May/June
F. Marconi, 'Portogallo, Operação SAAL', in *Casabella*, no. 419, November
C. Matos (ed.), 'Álvaro Siza Vieira', in *Boletim Cultural*, no. 2
R. Moneo, 'Arquitecturas en las márgenes', in *Arquitecturas Bis*, no. 12
F. Raggi, 'Álvaro Siza Vieira', in *Europa-America*, catalogue, Venice Biennale, Venice
'Stadtstruktur-Stadtgestalt', in *Jahresberich 1976*, Berlin
'Tres intervenciones en la ciudad de Oporto', in *Projecto y ciudad histórica*, International Seminar of Architecture, Santiago de Compostela
'Linee di azione dei tecnici. La zona di S. Victor', in *Lotus*, no. 13, December
'Álvaro Siza Vieira', in *Entwurfswoche zur Integration moderner Architektur in Altbaustrukturen*, Berlin

1977 'I.D.Z. Symposium-Ideen zur Stadtgestalt', in *Bauwelt*, no. 2, January

1978 V. Gregotti, 'Oporto', in *Lotus*, no. 18, March

1979 F. Burkhardt, 'Álvaro Siza, Portugal: Bauen zwischen Tradition und Moderne', in *Regionalismus im Bauen: Inspiration oder Imitation?*, Darmstadt
M. Düttmann, 'Analyse und Kommentar', in *5 Architekten zeichnen für Berlin*, Berlin
Álvaro Siza architetto, 1954–1979, catalogue, Padiglione d'Arte Contemporanea, Milan
Bauwettbewerb Görlitzer Bad, Berlin
'Débat synthèse', in *Construire incu u populu*, bulletin, Chambre de Métier de Haute-Corse, May
'Görlitzer Bad', in *Aktuelle Wettbewerbe*, August
'Görlitzer Bad', in *Bauwelt*, no. 33, September
'Plano de pormenor para a zona da Malagueira, Évora', in *Arquitectura*, no. 132, March

1980 M. Komonen, 'Neilikkatwallanku. Mousken arkkitehti', in *Arkkitehti*, no. 7, July
V. Magnago Lampugnani, *Architektur und Städtebau des 20. Jahrhunderts*, Stuttgart
J. P. dos Santos, 'Two projects by Álvaro Siza, one for West Berlin and one for Vila do Conde, in Portugal', in *9H*, no. 3
E. Souto de Moura, 'An 'amoral' architect', in *9H*, no. 3
'Kreuzberg, Schlesisches Tor', in *Erste Projekte zur behutsamen Stadterneuerung*, Berlin
'Álvaro Siza. Interview', in *PAN*
'Wohnungsquartier S. Victor', in *Architektur 1940–1980*, Munich
A+U, no. 123 (special issue)
L'Architecture d'Aujourd'hui, no. 211 (special issue)

1981 J. Abrams, 'Name to reckon with', in *Building Design*, no. 532, 13 February
H. Beck (ed.), 'Álvaro Siza Vieira's Guggenheim transformation', in *UIA International Architect*, no. 4
A. Cagnardi, 'Luoghi problemi progetti dodici anni dopo il terremoto', in *Polis*, no. 25
E. Casagrande, P. Val, '…einen Palast durch die Hintertür betreten', in *Stadtbauwelt*, no. 44
B. Cassirer, *Bürgerbeteiligung in Portugal, die SAAL-Projekte in Porto 1974–1976*, Berlin
F. Couto Gulin, 'Álvaro Siza Vieira, la lección de un maestro', in *Boletín del Consejo Superior de los Colegios de Arquitectos*, March
J. P. Guerra, 'A força organizada da população é a base da transformação da cidade', in *O Diário*, 13 April
R. Maillard (ed.), 'Álvaro Siza Vieira', in *Diccionario de Arquitectos*, Barcelona
P. Nicolin, 'Álvaro Siza Vieira: Tre progetti per Kreuzberg, Fränkelufer-Kottbusserstrasse, Schlesisches Tor', in *Lotus*, no. 32
M. A. Pina, 'Siza Vieira, arquitectura, arquitectura', in *Jornal de Letras, Artes e Idéias*, no. 14
J. Vilas, 'Avenida da Ponte ou avenida dos projectos? Que alternativa realista ao trabalho do Álvaro Siza?', in *Jornal de Notícias*, 15 May
M. Waisman, 'El rigor poético de Álvaro Siza', in *Summarios*, April
'Architecture Portugaise: Portrait d'Álvaro Siza Vieira', in *BIP – Urbanisme, Architecture, Arts Plastiques*, no. 113, May
'Entwicklungsplanung und Kindertagstätten', *Wettbewerb Block 133*, in *Bauwelt*, no. 34, September
'Álvaro Siza Vieira en Madrid', in *Arquitectura*,

January/February
'The Malagueira Project in Évora', in *Excursion to Portugal*, Rotterdam

1982 F. Burkhardt, 'Arcadia von Póvoa', in *Bauwelt*, no. 47, December
B. Pinto Almeida, 'Siza Vieira: mergulhar na confusão com un pé em terra firme', in *Expresso*, 28 August
N. Portas, 'Arquitecturas Marginadas en Portugal', in *Cuadernos Summa-Nueva Visión*, Buenos Aires
J.-P. Rayon, 'Introduzione al metodo di Álvaro Siza. Quartiere Malagueira', in *Casabella*, no. 478, March
L. Sabater (ed.), 'Álvaro Siza Vieira', in *Diccionario Ilustrado de la Arquitectura Contemporánea*, Barcelona
'Kreuzberg SO, 36 Block, 121 (Nord)', in *Internationale Bauausstellung 1984–1987*, catalogue, IBA, Berlin
'Four architects and their contribution to the work of the Faculty of Architecture at the University of Bogata', in *Proa*, no. 305, April

1983 A. Alves Costa, 'Oporto and the young architects; some clues for a reading of the works', in *9H*, no. 5
L. Beaudouin, C. Rousselot, 'Berlin, un reimmeuble d'angle', in *AMC*, no. 2, October
D. Boassen, 'Interview met Álvaro Siza', in *Wonen TABK*, no. 9, May
B. Cassirer, 'Entretien avec Álvaro Siza', in *AMC*, no. 2, October
R. Collovà, 'Álvaro Siza: Action Building'; F. Venezia, 'Costruito in loco; Álvaro Siza e Évora', in *Lotus*, no. 37
F. Ferreira, 'Álvaro Siza e a Arquitectura Portuguesa Actual', in *Vertical*, The Hague
V. Gregotti, 'Recent architecture of Álvaro Siza', in *Design + Art*, no. 14
H. van Dijk, 'De kwetsbare transformaties van Siza', in *Wonen TABK*, no. 9, May
E. Hubeli, 'Álvaro Siza Vieira', in *Werk, Bauen und Wohnen*, no. 7/8, July
M. Komonen, 'Portugalilaisen kaupunkitradition keijastuksia. Álvaro Siza uusi suunitelma historiallisessa Evorassa', in *Arkkitehti*, no. 8, August
M. Lawenby, 'Álvaro Siza. Malagueira Cooperative Housing', in *Ten New Buildings*, London
P. Nicolin, *Dopo il terremoto*, Milan
J. Paciéncia, 'A Propósito de uma Exposição', in *Jornal dos Arquitectos*, no. 16/18, March/May
N. Portas, 'The contextual interpretation and the importation of models', in *9H*, no. 5
M. Robalo, 'O Bairro arabe de Álvaro Siza', in *Expresso*, 2 July
C. Rousselot, L. Beaudouin, 'Interview with Álvaro Siza', in *Design + Art*, no. 14
P. Rumpf, 'Internationales Gutachtverfahren für das Kulturforum in Berlin', in *Bauwelt*, no. 46/47
F. Vanlaethem, 'Álvaro Siza, le nouveau Quartier Malagueira a Évora', in *ARQ*, August
F. Vanlaethem, 'Pour une architecture épurée et rigureuse', in *ARQ Architecture/Quebec*, 14 August
'A Casa do Dr. Fernando Machado; A Casa Interrompida', in *Obradoiro*, no. 8
'Het Malagueira-Projekt, Zelfbeuwrest Architektuur (Bouça, S. Victor, Lapa, Antas)', in *Drie Steden in Portugal*, July
'Old-New: Ancient-Modern', in *Parametro*, no. 121
'Álvaro Siza a Évora ou l'urbanité d'un paysage', in *Techniques et Architecture*, no. 351
'Álvaro Siza Vieira: casa di vacanze a Moledo do Minho', in *Parametro*, no. 121
'Siza', in *Internationales Gutachten Kulturforum*, Berlin
Quaderns, no. 159 (special issue)

1984 P. A. Croset, 'Berlin 87: la costruzione del passato', in *Casabella*, no. 506
M. De Giorgi, A. Torricella, 'Atlante comparato dell'architettura contemporanea: le otto posizioni emergenti e le loro teste di serie', in *Modo*, no. 69, May
M. De Michelis, 'Case d'affitto a Berlin negli anni ottanta', in *Lotus*, no. 41
D. Mackay, 'Ultimas tendencias en arquitectura de transición', in *La casa unifamiliar*, Barcelona
P. Rumpf, 'L'Ultimo Concorso IBA', in *Casabella*, no. 500, March
P. Testa, 'The Architecture of Álvaro Siza', in *Thresholds Working Paper 4*, Cambridge, Mass.
D. Vitale, 'Portogallo', in *Domus*, no. 655, November
W. Wang, 'Berlin Game', in *Building Design*, 14 February
'Edificio per appartamenti a Kreutzberg', in *Abitare*, no. 226, July/August
'L'Effet réglementaire: Habitation particulière', in *L'Architecture d'Aujourd'hui*, no. 235
'Álvaro Siza', in *Bauwelt*, no. 40, October
'Neuordnungskonzept Berlin. Kreuzberg Fränkelufer', in *Zwischenbericht, Internationale Bauausstellung Berlin*, February
'San Leucio: cinque proposte per un territorio', in *Casabella*, no. 505, September
'Zentrum des Berliner Kulturforums', in *Baumeister*, January

1985 M. Bedarida, 'Portugal: l'École de Porto', in *AMC*, no. 7, March
M. Celani, P. D'Ugo, 'La vicenda di Bouça e Malagueira: Álvaro Siza', in *Spazio e Società*, September/December
K. Frampton, R. Collovà, 'Álvaro Siza Vieira: casa Duarte e appartamento Teixeira', in *Casabella*, no. 514, June
C. Magnani, C. Trevisan, 'Il Concorso dello IACP di Venezia per il Campo di Marte alla Giudecca', in *Casabella*, no. 518, November
C. Magnani, C. Trevisan, 'Italian Job: Competition for Housing in the Campo di Marte alla Guidecca', in *Architect's Journal*, no. 45, November
J. Salgado, *Álvaro Siza em Matosinhos*, Matosinhos
Álvaro Siza. Projekte für Berlin, catalogue, Galerie Aedes, Berlin
W. Wang, 'House in Ovar, Portugal', in *9H*, no. 7
'Liaison: Restructuration du Campo di Marte, Giudecca, Venise', in *L'Architecture d'Aujourd'hui*, no. 242, December

1986 P. A. Croset, 'Banca a Vila do Conde', in *Casabella*, no. 526, July/August
F. Irace, 'Il quartiere Malagueira a Évora', in *Abitare*, no. 252, March
L. M. Mansilla, 'Álvaro Siza Vieira', in *Arquitectura*, no. 261, July/August
M. Petranzan, D. Schiesari, 'Intervista-dialogo con Álvaro Siza', in *Architettura, cronache e storia*, no. 363, January
Y. Safran, 'City Segment', in *Building Design*, no. 792, June
M. Tebaldi, 'Siviglia: concorso di idee per l'Esposizione Universale 1992', in *Domus*, no. 677, November
P. Teixifor, 'Álvaro Siza: Siza et interview', in *Skala*, 6 October
W. Wang, 'Arquitectos de Oporto: Távora, Siza, Souto de Moura', in *Arquitectura*, no. 261, July/August
W. Wang, 'House in Ovar, Portugal', in 'A+U', no. 191, August
W. Wang (ed.), *Álvaro Siza: Recent Work*, exhibition catalogue, 9H Gallery, London
'E un gesto completo, rico, sinples', in *Arquitectura Portuguesa*, no. 6, March/April
'Terrain de Campo di Marte sur la Giudecca', in *L'Architecture d'Aujourd'hui*, no. 248, December

1987 J. D. Besch, 'Elogio della trasformazione, Álvaro Siza Vieira: Progetti per l'Aia', in *Casabella*, no.

538, September
V. Consiglier, J. Teixeira Lopes, 'Álvaro Siza e Tomás Taveira, dois arquitectos portugueses', in *Projecto*, no. 98, April
M. De Michelis, 'New projects on the Giudecca', in *Lotus*, no. 51
H. van Dijk, 'Het wegontserpen van coflictisituaties: Siza's projecten en de Haage Schilderswijk', in *Archis*, no. 7, July
J. P. dos Santos (ed.), *The Architecture of Álvaro Siza*, Milan
P. Testa, 'Tradition and Actuality in the António Carlos Siza House', in *Journal of Architectural Education*, no. 40
P. Testa, 'Unity of the Discontinuous: Álvaro Siza's Berlin Works', in *Assemblage*, no. 2, February
F. Venezia, 'Nuovo padiglione universitario, Porto', in *Domus*, no. 679, January
M. Zardini, 'Dalla città alla rocca', in *Casabella*, no. 534, April
'Agència Bancària', in *Quaderns*, no. 169–170, April/September
'Casino 'Winkler' in Salzburg', in *Baumeister*, July
'Álvaro Siza, Casino de Salzburgo', in *Obradoiro*, no. 13

1988 K. Frampton, 'On Álvaro Siza', in *Arkkitehti*, no. 4
J. R. Moreno, 'Arquitectos viajeros. El riesgo de lo foráneo (Kreuzberg)', in *Arquitectura y Vivienda*, no. 16
B. Secchi, 'Il Concorso per l'area di Piazza Matteotti – La Lizza a Siena', in *Casabella*, no. 552, December
Á. Siza, 'Esquissos de Viagem', in *Documentos de Arquitectura 1*, Porto
W. Wang, 'Álvaro Siza Vieira. La nuova Facoltà di Architettura di Porto', in *Casabella*, no. 547, June
W. Wang (ed.), *Álvaro Siza. Figures and Configurations*, Cambridge, Mass.
'Edificio per abitazione, L'Aia', in *Domus*, no. 696, July/August
'Facultad de Arquitectura de Oporto', in *Quaderns*, no. 176, January/March
'Ultimate le due case di Álvaro Siza all'Aia', in *Casabella*, no. 548
'Álvaro Siza premiatissimo', in *Casabella*, no. 552, December
'Álvaro Siza Vieira: 106 habitatges a la Haia', in *Quaderns*, no. 178, July/September
'Álvaro Siza Vieira', intervista di M. Periel, in *Quaderns*, no. 178, July/September
'Álvaro Siza Vieira: dos habitatges unifamiliars', in *Quaderns*, no. 178, July/September
'Álvaro Siza é o escolhido: vai reconstruir o centro de Lisboa', in *Projeto*, no. 115, October
'Viviendas y Locales en La Haya, 1985–1988. Álvaro Siza', in *Arquitectura*, no. 271/272

1989 U. Barbieri, 'Álvaro Siza Vieira: due isolati residenziali. L'Aia', in *Domus*, no. 705, May
C. Batán, '¿Será un monumento? Concurso para el Centro Cultural de la Defensa', in *Arquitectura Viva*, no. 5, March
E. Ginés, 'Álvaro Siza o el dulce encanto de la obra en penumbra. El soporte geométrico de un poeta de la arquitectura', in *Arte y Cemento*, no. 7, March
J. Glusberg, 'Conversa com Álvaro Siza', in *Projecto*, no. 124, August
A. R. di Marcoi, 'Álvaro Siza em destaque', in *Projecto*, no. 120, April
M. Montuori, 'Un architetto portoghese: le piccole opere sono le più difficili', in *Modo*, no. 113, April
F. Peña, 'Álvaro Siza. El proyecto de Museu Galego de Arte Contemporáneo y el Retorno de Santo Domingo de Bonaval', in *Obradoiro*, no. 15
F. Peña, 'Álvaro Siza. Centro Galego de Arte Contemporanea', in *Obradoiro*, no. 15
'Álvaro Siza. Contrapunto poético', in *A+U*, December/January
F. Peña, 'Álvaro Siza: O Portugues de Bonaval', in *Luzes*, no. 13, Spring
A. Sousa Oliveira, 'Tres chás. Pico do Areeiro, Madeira. Proposta de Álvaro Siza Vieira', in *Arquitectos*, no. 1, January/February
P. Testa, P. Brinckert, 'Il piano di Macao: progetti di Álvaro Siza Vieira', in *Casabella*, no. 559, July/August
'Lisbona, proposta per il recupero del Chiado incendiato', in *Casabella*, no. 558, July
'Proposta para a recuperaçao da Zona Sinistrada do Chiado, Álvaro Siza', in *Engenharia & Arquitectura*, no. 114/115, April/June
'Concurso de Ideas. Centro Cultural de la Defensa. Madrid 88', in *Arquitectura*, no. 275/276, November/December
'El valor de la memoria. Remodelación en el sur de La Haya', in *Arquitectura y Vivienda*, no. 19
'Siza, un Portugais a l'Haye; Maître et Modèles; Deux maisons à leur place', in *L'Architecture d'Aujourd'hui*, no. 261, February
'Álvaro Siza, anteproyecto do Complexo Polideportivo na illa de Arosa', in *Obradoiro*, no. 15
Architécti, no. 3 (special issue)
A+U, June (special issue)

1990 A. Angelillo, 'Plano de Urbanização de Macau. Descrição de Álvaro Siza a Fernando Tavora', in *Architécti*, no. 5, June
G. Borella, 'Álvaro Siza. Progetto di recupero per l'area del Chiado a Lisbona', in *Domus*, no. 714, March
M. Bottero, 'Álvaro Siza: tre opere – Casa Duarte a Ovar, 1981–1985; il ristorante Boa Nova a Leça da Palmeira, 1958–1963; piscina a Leça da Palmeira, 1961–1966', in *Abitare*, no. 286, June
G. Byrne, 'Lisbona; una città vulnerabile. Il Chiado di Álvaro Sizà', in *Lotus*, no. 64
J. M. Hernández León, 'Un paso en frente. El Centro Cultural de la Defensa', in *Arquitectura Viva*, no. 11, March/April
M. Reig, 'La idea feliz. Todo sobre Álvaro Siza', in *Casa Vogue España*, no. 17, September
M. de Solá Morales, 'Quartiere Pendino a Napoli. Un'altra tradizione moderna', in *Lotus*, no. 64
J. M. Montaner, 'Centro Galego de Arte Contemporáneo. Santiago de Compostela. Álvaro Siza Vieira 1988', in *Nuevos Museos, Espacios para el arty y la cultura*, Barcelona
Á. Siza, 'Quello che è', in *Lotus*, no. 64
'Barcelona 92. Centro Meterológico. Geometrías macladas. Álvaro Siza Vieira', in *Arquitectura y Vivienda*, no. 22
'Centro Galego de Arte Contemporáneo en Santiago de Compostela', in *Geometría*, no. 7
'Farmacia Moderna. Álvaro Siza Vieira', in *Lápiz*, no. 70, Summer
Bauwelt, no. 29/30 (special issue)

1991 M. Barda, 'Schilderswijk Centrum, Holanda, projecto de Álvaro Siza', in *A+U*, January
L. Beaudouin, 'Álvaro Siza', in *L'Architecture d'Aujourd'hui*, no. 278, December
E. Comas, 'Casa e cidade: Reflexão gaúcha, realizações europeias', in *A+U*, January
P. A. Croset, A. Angelillo, 'Scuola in Portogallo di Álvaro Siza: la svolta di Penafiel; Álvaro Siza: recenti lavori in Portogallo', in *Casabella*, no. 579, May
K. Frampton, 'Il disegno veloce. Le annotazioni di Álvaro Siza', in *Lotus*, no. 68
J. M. Montaner, *La continuidad del contextualismo cultural*, in *Documentos de Arquitectura. Arquitectura Europea 1977–1990*, no. 14
J. M. Montaner, 'L'idea del villaggio Olimpico di Barcelona: tipi e morfologie', in *Lotus*, no. 67
A. L. Nobre, 'Entrevista Álvaro Siza', in *A+U*, no. 37
S. Rosa de Carvalho, 'De avantgardistische kracht van het verleden. Wederopbouwplan van Siza voor Lissabon', in *De Architect*, March
Y. Simeoforidis, 'Cultural Oases or Refuges'; E. Tzirtzilake, 'Malagueira 1991', in *Tefchos*, no. 6
W. Wang, 'Álvaro Siza: Some remarks on his architecture', in *Forum International*, no. 8, May/August

'2º Congreso Internacional de Urbanismo – Maringá', in *A+U*, no. 39, December/January
C. R. dos Santos, 'Álvaro Siza, una arquitectura que pensa e faz pensar, Jardim Escola João de Deus'; M. Toussaint, 'Tradiçao, modernidade e violència criativa', in *Projeto*, no. 146, December
Á. Siza, A. Madureira, 'Complexo da Boavista no Porto', in *Architécti*, no. 11/12
'Álvaro Siza 1954–1988', *A+U*, June
'Siza Vieira. A futura Praça de Espanha', in *Decisão. Propriedade & Investimento*, no. 1, March
AQ – Arquitectura de Andalucía Oriental, Spring/Summer (special issue)
Architécti, no. 8 (special issue)

1992 J. A. Ballesteros, 'Insomnios', in *Arquitectura*, no. 294, December
C.A. Boyer, 'Álvaro Siza: le prix Pritzker pour le plus sensible des architectes', in *Jardin des Modes*, no. 162, September
P. Figueiredo, 'Siza Vieira – A arquitectura ao encontro de si própria', in *Atlantis (Air Portugal)*, no. 5, September/October
B. Fleck, *Álvaro Siza*, Basel
J. M. Fort, 'Centro Meteorológico de la Villa Olímpica', in *Diseño Interior*, no. 18, September
J. Isasi, 'El corredor de fondo – Álvaro Siza, premio Pritzker', in *Arquitectura Viva*, no. 24, May/June
D. Lengart, A. Vince, *Univerités-Ècoles Supérieures*, Paris
A. Milheiro, 'Um Siza Vieira na Catalunha – Uma obra para Barcelona', in *Sábado*, no. 237, December
M. Romanelli, 'Lampada da tavolo FIL', in *Domus*, no. 740, July/August
J. Rodrigues, 'Álvaro Siza – Obra e Método', in *Editora Civilização*, December
Á. Siza, 'Centro di controllo meteorologico e costiero a Barcelona', in *Casabella*, no. 593, September
Á. Siza, 'Torre Vigía. Centro Meteorológico', in *A & V Monografías de Arquitectura y Vivienda*, no. 37, September/October
Á. Siza, 'Chiado', in *Tefchos*, no. 9, Autumn
Á. Siza, 'Reiseskizzen', in *Bau Art*, no. 3
M. Thorne, 'Visiones para Madrid', in *Arquitectura Viva*, no. 27, November
W. I. Verzjil, 'Interview with Álvaro Siza', in *Archidea*, Autumn
'Facultade de Arquitectura, Segunda Fase', in *Constructora San Jose*, December
'Ponto e Virgula. Schilderwijk-Centrum 5, La Haya, Álvaro Siza, Carlos Castanheira, 1984–1991', in *Bloques de Viviendas*, Barcelona
'Untimely Notes', in *Tefchos*, no. 7
Anales de Arquitectura, no. 4 (special issue)

1993 E. and L. Beaudouin, 'Noi siamo il paesaggio di tutto quanto abbiamo visto', in *Casabella*, no. 605, October
L. Biondi, 'Progetto per gli spazi pubblici di Malagueira', in *Casabella*, no. 597/598, January/February
B. Colenbrander, 'Chiado, Lissabon, Álvaro Siza und die Strategie der Erinnerung'; C. Devillers, 'Le Centre-Ville', in *AMC*, no. 40, April
C. Gaeshirt, 'Der Chiado im Angust 1993', in *Bauwelt*, no. 36, September
C. Machabert, 'Une Production Artistique Manifeste. Álvaro Siza', in *Techniques & Architecture*, no. 406, February/March
R. Maillinger, 'Ein Portugiese in Barcelona. Meteorologische Station im Olympischen Dorf', in *Baumeister*, no. 1, January
C. Magrini, E. Roncalli, 'Álvaro Siza e i bagni in Portogallo', in *Il bagno*, no. 124, April
S. Milesi, 'Montreuil: strategie di politica urbana', in *Casabella*, no. 605, October
E. Morteo, 'Álvaro Siza: il progetto come esperienza', in *Domus*, no. 746, February
G. Polin, 'La Chiesa di Salemi. Il Teatro di Salemi', in *Abitare*, no. 320, July/August
A. J. Rodrigues, 'A Arte na Arquitectura de Álvaro Siza', in *Obradoiro*, no. 22, April
J. P. Santos, *Álvaro Siza. Obras y Proyectos 1954–1992*, Barcelona
Á. Siza, 'Centro Galego de Arte Contemporánea. Santiago de Compostela. 1988–1993', in *Jornal dos Arquitectos*, no. 128, November/December
Á. Siza, 'Faculdade de Arquitectura, Universidade do Porto', in *Architécti*, no. 126/127, August/September
Á. Siza Vieira, 'Faculdade de Arquitectura', in *Obradoiro*, no. 22, April
F. Tranfa, 'La Rinascita del Chiado', in *Costruire*, no. 123, September
'Detachment and involvement. The work of Álvaro Siza for the Schilderswijk area The Hague', in *Dr. H. P. Berlagestichting*, The Hague
'Il Campus della Vitra; F. O. Gehry, Á. Siza, T. Ando, Z. Hadid, A. Citterio e T. Dwan', in *Abitare*, no. 321, September
'Il concorso per il Casinò Winkler', in *Quaderni di Lotus*, no. 19
'Educational High School', in *Archidea*, VII, Spring
'Galician Centre for Contemporary Art', in *GA*, April
'Prémios de Arquitectura em Portugal', in *Jornal dos Arquitectos*, no. 129, December
The Pritzker Prize 1992 Álvaro Siza, Chicago
'New Vitra Factory Building, Weil am Rhein', in *Zodiac*, no. 10, December
'Álvaro Siza, Tejido de Piedra – Centro Gallego de Arte Contemporáneo', in *Arquitectura Viva*, no. 33, November/December
Portugalska stirje vidiki, Ljubljana

1994 A. Angelillo, 'Álvaro Siza appronta una galleria di architettura e design in Italia', in *Casabella*, no. 617, November
A. Angelillo and C. Quintans Eiras, 'Santiago de Compostela: una politica di progetti. Parco di San Domingo di Bonaval e Museu Granell', in *Casabella*, no. 618, December
C. Bobenbach, 'Vitra Produktions-Gebäude in Weil am Rhein', in *Bauwelt*, no. 24, June
'Álvaro Siza. Un museo in Spagna, una scuola in Portogallo'; R. Collovà, 'Sul Centro di Arte Contemporanea di Galizia'; A. Angelillo, 'Santiago e Setúbal: conversazione con Álvaro Siza', in *Casabella*, no. 612, May
P. L. Cerri, L. Gazzaniga, 'Álvaro Siza – Un laboratorio di mobili 1987–1994', in *Domus*, no. 759, April
D. Cohn, 'Pilgrimage to Santiago', in *Architectural Record*, no. 10, October
D. Cohn, 'Siza in Granite', in *Bauwelt*, no. 19, May
K. Frampton, 'En busca de una línea lacónica. Notas sobre la Escuela de Oporto', in *Arquitectura Viva*, no. 47, May/June
J. Giovannini, 'Siza Misses at Vitra', in *Architecture*, no. 9, September
R. Henmi, R. van Nostrand, T. Fraser, *Envisioning Architecture: An Analysis of Drawing*, St. Louis
C. Muro, 'Álvaro Siza. Escrits', in *Aula d'Arquitectura*, no. 7, December
A. Okabe, 'Museum em Santiago', in *Nikkei Architecture*, no. 503, October
R. Ray, 'Cloistered Creativity', in *Architectural Review*, no. 1172, October
R. Ray, 'Monastic Modern (Centre for Contemporary Art)', in *Architecture*, no. 9, September
R. Santos and S. Cabral de Mello, 'E fez-se luz', in *Casa Cláudia*, no. 79, October
G. C. da Silva, 'Álvaro Siza Vieira. Uma Aula de Arquitectura', in *Galeria de Arte*, no. 1
W. Wang, 'Álvaro Siza. Centro d'Arte Galiziana Contemporanea a Santiago di Compostela', in *Domus*, no. 760, May
W. Wang, 'Álvaro Siza. Kunstzentrum in Santiago

de Compostela', in *Baumeister*, no. 9, September
W. Wang, 'Transformaties en referenties; vier recente projecten van Álvaro Siza', in *De Architect*, no. 11
F. Zanco, 'Álvaro Siza. Centro di Arte Contemporanea, Santiago de Compostela', in *Domus Dossier*, no. 2
M. G. Zunino, 'Università dalla A alla Z', in *Abitare*, no. 332, September
F. I., 'Saggio d'estetica industriale', in *Abitare*, no. 333, October
'Anos 60, Anos de Ruptura. Arquitectura Portuguesa nos anos sesenta. Lisboa '94', in *Livros Horizonte,* catalogue, Sala do Risco-Piscina de Marés, Lisbon
'Centro de Arte Contemporánea, Santiago', in *Arquitectura Viva*, no. 45/46
'Chiado', in *Jornal dos Arquitectos*, no. 134, April
'I classici di domani', in *Architektur und Wohnen*, no. 759
'Lisbonne per Álvaro Siza', in *Philips*, no. 94/95
'Santiago + FAUP', in *GA*, March
'Viviendas y Oficinas en Boavista, Oporto – Álvaro Siza Vieira y António Madurerira', in *Arquitectura Viva*, no. 47, May/June
Diseño Interior, no. 33, March (special issue)
'Álvaro Siza', *El Croquis*, no. 68/69 (special issue)

1995 P. Aido, 'Olhar as ruínas, 1990', in *Livros do Oriente*, Lisbon
L. Aquino, 'Álvaro Siza. Arquitecto do Mundo', in *Revista de Matosinhos*, no. 10, November
M. Brausch, M. Emery, *Fragen zur Architektur. 15 Architekten im Gespräch*, Basel
I. Bravo, 'Álvaro Siza Vieira. Escuela Superior de Educación en Setúbal', in *Diseño Interior*, no. 48
A. Bussel, 'Searching for Siza', in *Progressive Architecture*, no. 4, April
M. Cannatà, F. Fernandes, 'Álvaro Siza a Santiago de Compostela', in *Abitare*, no. 345, November
F. Cardoso de Menezes, 'A aposta numa casa impar', in *Expansão*, no. 35/36, February/March
C. Cordeiro, 'Nos Campo de Moledo', in *Casa Cláudia*, no. 82, January
M. Dubois, 'In de naam van de schelp. Siza's Museum in Santiago', in *Archis*, no. 1, January
B. Fleck, *Álvaro Siza*, London
K. Frampton, 'Seis puntos sobre los dilemas de la vivienda', in *Arquitectura Viva. Monografias*, no. 56, December
L. Gazzaniga, 'Edificio della Facoltà di Architettura dell'Università di Porto', in *Domus*, no. 770, April
M. Graça Dias, 'Los ojos de Minerva. Biblioteca de la Universidad de Aveiro', in *Arquitectura Viva*, no. 40, January/February
G. Gresleri, 'Fuori dalle leggi del peso', in *Parametro*, no. 208, May/June
G. Hammer, 'Chiado in Lissabon', in *Baumeister*, no. 2, February
R. Hollenstein, 'Die Architekturburg über dem Fluß', in *NZZ-Folio*, July
F. Irace, 'Scuola Superiore di Educazione', in *Abitare*, no. 338, March
L. Kelly, 'Álvaro Siza. Der Architekt als Künstler', in *Architektur & Technik*, no. 4
P. de Llano, C. Castanheira (eds.), *Álvaro Siza. Opere e progetti*, Milan
C. Quintans, 'Centro Gallego de Arte Contemporáneo', in *Diseño Interior*, July
R. Riederhof, 'Siedlung in Schilderswijk', in *Bauwelt*, no. 13, April
V. Riso, 'Il modo di costruire nell'architettura di Álvaro Siza', in *Parametro*, no. 208
Á. Siza, 'Centro de Arte Contemporáneo de Galicia en Santiago de Compostela', in *Informes de la Construcción*, vol. 47, no. 439, September/October
Á. Siza, *Professione poetica*, Milan
Á. Siza, R. Collovà, 'Vivere una casa', in *Domus*, no. 771
L. Trigueiros (ed.), *Álvaro Siza 1986–1995*, Lisbon
'Contemporáneo', in *Diseño Interior*, no. 6, July
'Álvaro Siza Library, Faculty of Architecture, University of Oporto, Portugal', in *GA*, no. 108
'Álvaro Siza in mostra a San Marino', in *Casabella*, no. 626, September
Pietra su pietra. Premio internazionale Architetture di pietra, exhibition catalogue, Fiere di Verona, Verona
'Álvaro Siza. The Window in History', in V. Magnano Lampugnani (ed.), 'The Architecture of the Window', in *YKK Architectural Products + Domus, International Design Review*, December
'PP do Pólo III da Universidade do Porto', in *Jornal dos Arquitectos*, no. 154, December
W. Wang, 'Álvaro Siza: pass one e fede in architettura', in *Domus*, no. 770, April
'Álvaro Siza Vieira. Reitoria da Universidade de Alicante; Centro de Educação Infantil e Escola Primária em Alcoi', in *Architécti*, no. 31, December 1995–January 1996
'Design. Por conta e risco', in *Casa Cláudia*, no. 85, April
'Porto, a spasso con l'architetto', in *Weekend viaggi*, March
'Álvaro Siza. Casa Luis Figuereido', in *Anuário da Decoraçao. Interiores e Design*
'Álvaro Siza. Galician Center of Contemporary Art', in *A+U*, no. 297, June
'From the Drawing Board to the Building', in *Acanthus*, no. 3
'Álvaro Siza e Isabel Aguirre. Parque de Santo Domingo de Bonaval, Santiago', in 'Álvaro Siza. Museumgarten in Santiago de Compostela', in *Topos*, no. 11, June
Arquitectura Viva Monografias, no. 51/52, January/April

1996 A. Armesto, Q. Padró, *Casas Atlánticas / Atlantic Houses. Galicia y norte de Portugal / Galicia and northern Portugal*, Barcelona
A. Angelillo, 'Opinioni e progetti di Álvaro Siza', in *Casabella*, no. 630/631, January
G. Benavides, 'Siza en el Perú', in *Arkinka*, no. 5, April
G. Borella, 'Itinerario n. 127. Siza e il Portogallo', in *Domus*, no. 786, October
P. Brandão, F. Jorge, *Lisboa do Tejo, a Ribeirinha. The Riverside*, Lisbon
V. Cruz, 'Passado e Futuro (Quinta de Santiago)', in *Casa Cláudia*, no. 94, Spring
J. M. Fernandes, 'Álvaro Siza Vieira. Ristorante "Piscina de Marés"', *Leça, Oporto, Matosinhos*, in *Il Portogallo del mare, delle pietre, delle città*, catalogue, Milan Triennale
J. M. Fernandes, 'Portugal em Milão e a Herança Moderna. Juntos ao mar', in *Jornal dos Arquitectos*, no. 158, April
B. Fleck, *Álvaro Siza. City Sketches*, Basel
D. Machabert, 'Saint-Jacques de Compostelle. Siza dialogue avec la ville', in *D'Architecture*, no. 62, January
D. Machabert, 'Álvaro Siza à Montreuil', in *Techniques & Architecture*, no. 427, August/September
C. Muro, 'Nicht entworfen, nicht konstruiert', in *Bauwelt*, no. 37
H. Osório, 'Escola do Porto. Com a marca de Siza', in *Casa Cláudia*, no. 94, Spring
M. Perez Bodegas, 'Protagonistas 1991–1996. Hace cinco años y cinquenta numeros', in *Diseño Interior*, no. 50, January
G. Polazzi, 'Álvaro Siza. Biblioteca di Aveiro', in *Area*, no. 27, July/August
R. Ryan, 'Álvaro Siza. Centro de Arte Contemporánea. Santiago de Compostela', in *A+U*, no. 64, February/March
J. P. dos Santos, 'Casa a Valbom nella valle del Douro', in *Domus*, no. 778, January
V. Tatano, 'Álvaro Siza Vieira. Un architetto lusitano', in *Modulo*, no. 226, November
P. Testa, 'Una chimera a Porto: la Facoltà di

Architettura', in *Lotus*, no. 88, April
M. Toussaint, 'O CCB em transição. Artistas / Arquitectos. Álvaro Siza. Obras e projectos', in A. Meireles, 'O Siza e eu; Visita à futura Casa da Juventude', in *Revista da Câmara Municipal de Matosinhos*, April
M. C. Tronconi, 'Centro Galego di Arte Contemporanea: un padiglione sul giardino', in *Lotus*, no. 88, April
M. C. Tronconi, 'Öffnung eines Hortus conclusus', in *Bauwelt*, no. 37, October
W. Wang, 'Álvaro Siza Vieira. Architektur Fakultät in Porto', in *Baumeister*, no. 11, November
A. Zabalbeascoa, *Álvaro Siza, Oporto, Portugal, 1996. El taller del arquitecto*, Barcelona
'Álvaro Siza. Rio de Janeiro', in *Revista de Arquitectura*, no. 5, May/June
'Álvaro Siza Vieira, La Faculdad del Equilibrio', in *ABC de las Artes*, June
Architécti, no. 34, August/October
Jornal dos Arquitectos, no. 163, September
Between Sea & City. Eight Piers for Thessaloniki, Rotterdam
Contemporary European Architects, vol. 4, Cologne
'Naturstein. Building with Stone. Kunstzentrum für zeitgenössische Kunst in Santiago de Compostela', in *Detail*, no. 1, January/February
'Crosscurrents: Fifty-one World Architects', in *Contemporary Architects. Ideas and Works*, January
Esquisson de Álvaro Siza, catalogue, Sezon Museum of Art, Tokyo-Hiroshima-Kamakura
'Projecto di Marte de Álvaro Siza Vieira', in *Jornal dos Arquitectos*, no. 164, October
'Prémio Secil. BUA, ESE, Castro & Melo', in *Jornal dos Arquitectos*, no. 165, November
Sensing the Future. The Architect as Seismograph. Sixth International Architecture Exhibition, catalogue, Venice Biennale, Venice
'Álvaro Siza. Casa do Lagoal', in *Architécti*, no. 35

1997 A. Angelillo (ed.), *Álvaro Siza. Architecture Writings*, Milan
A. Angelillo, 'Álvaro Siza. Chiesa a Marco de Canavezes', in *Casabella*, no. 640/641, December 1996/January 1997
C. Baglione, 'Álvaro Siza in Veneto', in *Casabella*, no. 646, June
M. A. Baldellou, 'Mano a mano con Álvaro Siza', in *Oro*, no. 40, December
X. Casabella Lopez, C. G. Seoane, 'Centro Galego di Arte Contemporanea e as suas monstruosas transformaciones', in *Obradoiro*, no. 26, May
M. Dubois, 'Het kerkgebouw op het einde van het millenium. De sacraliteit van het licht', in *Vlannderen*, no. 265
M. Faiferri, 'Álvaro Siza: opere recenti', in *L'industria delle costruzioni*, no. 313/314
L. Fernandez Galiano, 'Álvaro Siza y Rafael Otero. Viviendas sociales, Cádiz; 1996, Doce meses y quatro estaciones. Septiembre, iglesias de autor', in *Arquitectura Viva Monografias*, no. 63/64, January/April
C. Gaenshirt, 'Orientierung an der Peripherie. Kirche in Marco de Canavezes', in *Bauwelt*, no. 8, February
E. A. Gárcia, 'La magia del demiurgo', in *BAU*, no. 16
A. Graf, 'Universitätsbibliothek in Aveiro', in *Baumeister*, no. 11, November
G. Gresleri, 'Progetto del quartiere Malagueira raccontato da Vincenzo Riso', in *Parametro*, no. 219, May/June
H. Leiprecht, 'Álvaro Siza: die Poetik des Raums. Das Centro Galego de Arte Contemporánea in Santiago de Compostela', in *DU*, no. 4, April
D. Machabert, 'Rencontre avec Álvaro Siza', in *Mégapole*, no. 16
P. Nicolin, 'Osservazioni sull'intervento di Álvaro Siza al Chiado', in *Lotus*, no. 92
L. Peretti, M. Clement, 'Álvaro Siza, Torre dell'acqua, Biblioteca', in *Casabella*, no. 643, January
F. Schneider (ed.), *Grundißatlas. Wohnungsbau / Floor Plan Atlas Housing*, Basel
A. R. Ramos, 'Uma Casa com Arte', in *Exame*, no. 103
L. Trigueiros (ed.), *Álvaro Siza, 1954–1976*, Lisbon
'Church of Marco de Canavezes near Porto, Portugal; University of Aveiro, Main Library, Aveiro, Portugal', in *GA*, no. 50, April
'Piers für Thessaloniki; Hombroich', in *Bauwelt*, no. 14, April
Kenchiku Bunka, no. 607, May
'Santa Maria's Church. Parochial Centre of Marco de Canavezes', in *Dialogue*, no. 10, December
'Álvaro Siza Vieira. Facultad de Arquitectura Universidad de Oporto', in *Arquitectura*, no. 312
'Álvaro Siza, obras y proyectos', in *BASA*, no. 19, June
'Álvaro Siza. Rectory of the University of Alicante', in *GA*, no. 51, May
'Esquisso de Ponte Carlos, Praga', in *Abitare*, no. 363, June
Álvaro Siza Móveis e Objectos, exhibition catalogue, ICEP, Porto
Portugal. Architektur im 20. Jahrhundert. Architektur und Wandlung, catalogue, Monaco

1998 B. Arriola, 'Iglesia Santa Maria – Premio IberFAD 98', in *Arte y Cemento*, no. 15, September
O. Boissière, 'Vieira de Castro house, Vila Nova de Famalicão, Portugal, 1988–1997', in *Twentieth Century Houses. Europe*, Paris
J. de Castro, 'Um mês antes da abertura (Expo '98 Antevisão)', in *Casa Arquitectura e Construção*, no. 4
M. Dubois, *Álvaro Siza. Inside the City*, New York
M. Faiferri (ed.), *Álvaro Siza. Progetti e opere*, Rome
L. Fernandez Calisto, 'Álvaro Siza. De Oporto a Lisbona', in *Arquitectura Viva*, no. 59, March/April
C. Gaenshirt, 'Fragile Monumentalität. Der Portugiesische Pavillon von Álvaro Siza', in *Bauwelt*, no. 26, July
Y. Futagawa, 'Interview with Álvaro Siza', in *GA Document Extra*, no. 11
A. Graf, *Die Skulptur im Park. Zwei Häuser in den Haag, Holland*, in *Einfamilienhäuser aus Backstein. Über 40 individuelle Bauten aus Ziegel und Klinder*, Monaco
A. Guiheux (ed.), *Álvaro Siza*, catalogue, Centre Georges Pompidou, Paris
H. Hoffmann, 'Wasserspiele. Expo '98 in Lissabon: "Die Ozeane. Ein Erbe für die Zukunft"', in *AIT*, no. 7/8
R. Lewitt, 'Ritual Modification. Church Marco de Canavezers, Portugal. Architect Álvaro Siza', in *The Architectural Review*, August
S. Luz Afonso, 'The Portuguese Pavillion', in *Connaissance des Arts*, June
F. Rambert, 'Entretien avec Álvaro Siza', in *Connaissance des Arts*, October
V. Riso, *Álvaro Siza. La facoltà di Architettura di Porto*, Florence
C. Sat, 'Expo Lisbona 98. A Lisbona l'ultima Esposizione Mondiale del Novecento', in *Casabella*, no. 654
Á. Siza, *Immaginare l'evidenza*, Rome-Bari
L. Spinelli, 'Álvaro Siza, Rolando Torgo. Chiesa del complesso parrocchiale di Marco de Canavezes', in *Domus*, no. 802, March
P. Trétiack, 'Les Utopies (Océans) de Lisbonne', in *Beaux Arts*, no. 170, July
Vassalo Rosa, 'Il piano urbanistico e ambientale della zona est di Lisbona, Le realizzazioni'; in *Casabella*, no. 654
'Baixa-Chiado Station. Access ivens, Álvaro Siza, Porto, Portugal', in *Hiroba*, January
Intorno alla fotografia. Trentasette cornici per trentasette fotografi (Álvaro Siza / Roberto

Collovà), catalogue, Association Jaqueline Vodoz et Bruno Danese, Paris-Milan
'Lisbon Expo Reviewed. Portuguese Pavilion. Álvaro Siza', in *The Architectural Review*, no. 1217, August
'Obras finalistas y seleccionadas. Premios Iberfad 1998. Iglesia de Santa Maria, Marco de Canavezes, Portugal. Álvaro Siza con Rolando Torgo', in *On Diseño*, no. 194, August
'Álvaro Siza', in *Arquitectura Viva Monografias*, no. 69/70
'Álvaro Siza. Complesso di edilizia popolare a Schilderswijk War, den Haag', in *Lotus*, no. 96, June
'Luminosa abstracción. Centro paroquial, Marco de Canavezes', in *Arquitectura Viva*, no. 58
'Álvaro Siza. Maison van Middelem-Dupont, Ourdenburg, Belgium', in *GA*, no. 55
'Álvaro Siza. Marienkirche in Marco de Canavezes bei Porto, Portugal', in *Architektur & Wettbewerbe*, no. 174, June
'Álvaro Siza. Portuguese Pavilion', in *Kenchiku Bunka*, no. 621, July
'Nuno Portas conversa con Siza Vieira. Chiado: o fim do mito – 10 anos depois, Chiado em lume brando', in *Vida Mundial*, no. 7, August
Techniques & Architecture, no. 439, September (special issue)

1999 J. A. Aldrete-Haas, 'Álvaro Siza. Serralves Museum of Contemporary Art', in *Bomb*, no. 68, Summer
U. Brickmann, 'Ein Heim für Architekten', in *Bauwelt*, no. 1/2, January
F. Burkhardt, 'Álvaro Siza Vieira e Roberto Collovà. Ricostruzione della Chiesa Madre e ridisegno di Piazza Alicia e della strada adiacente, Salemi, Trapani', in *Domus*, no. 813, March
D. Chon, 'Mikrochirurgische Eingriffe. Metrostation Chiado in Lissabon', in *Deutsche Bauzeitung*, no. 2, February
R. Collovà, 'Una piazza coperta', in *Lotus*, no. 99
C. Fuchs, 'Santa Maria in Marco de Canavezes. Álvaro Siza Vieira mit Edite Rosa', in *Baumeister*, no. 6, June
C. Gaenshirt, 'Kunstmuseum. Neubau der Fundação de Serralves in Porto', in *Bauwelt*, no. 32, August
J. M. Hernández León, 'Placeres de la Memoria. Álvaro Siza, Museo Serralves en Oporto', in *Arquitectura Viva*, no. 66, May/June
P. Jodidio, *Álvaro Siza*, Cologne
M. C. Loriers, 'Intimité Topographique. Piscine à Matosinhos, Portugal', in *Techniques & Architecture*, no. 441, February/March
P. McGuire, 'Hail Siza. House, Vila Nova de Famalicão, Portugal', in *The Architectural Review*, no. 1228, June
L. Melis, 'Rectoraat in Alicante door Álvaro Siza', in *De Architect*, no. 8, April
J. Navarro Baldeweg, 'Esculturas de Álvaro Siza en la Fundación ICO', in *Guadalimar*, no. 145, January
G. Polazzi, 'Rettorato dell'Università, Alicante. Álvaro Siza Vieira', in *Area*, no. 44, May/June
J. Puig i Batalla, D. Osuna Páez, *The Multifunctional Library. London, April 20–24, 1998*, exhibition catalogue, Barcelona
I. de Solà-Morales, 'Barcelona', in *Area*, no. 42, January/February
V. Riso, 'Álvaro Siza. La muratura armata del padiglione della Facoltà di Architettura di Porto', in *Costruire in Laterizio*, no. 67, January/February
J. Salgado, 'Álvaro Siza: l'interminabile disegnare'; in *Casabella*, no. 667, May
M. Suárez, 'Anotaciones ImpreSizas', in *041. Revista de Arquitectura y Urbanismo*, no. 2, March/May
F. P. Testa, 'Á. Siza Vieira, Edificio per studi di architetture, Porto, Portogallo', in *Domus*, no. 813, March
M. Toussaint, 'Por entre o olhar de Laurent Beaudouin sobre Álvaro Siza', in *Arquitectos*, no. 190, May/June
'Habitar el paisaje. Casa Vieira de Castro, Vila Nova de Famalicão, Portugal', in *Arquitectura Viva*, no. 65
'Álvaro Siza. Alicante', in *Architectural Design*, no. 75/76
'Álvaro Siza. Arquitecto', in *Dialogue*, no. 27, July
'Álvaro Siza. Fundação Iberê Camargo, Porto Alegre, Brazil', in *GA*, no. 58, April
'Álvaro Siza Vieira. Vieira de Castro House, Vila Nova de Famalicão, Portugal 1998', in *A+U*, no. 345, June
'Álvaro Siza Vieira and Roberto Collovà. The Rebuilding of the Cathedral and Piazza Alicia. Salemi, Sicily, Italy, 1982–', in *A+U*, no. 347, August
'Álvaro Siza. Rectory of the University of Alicante', in *GA*, no. 57, January
'Álvaro Siza 1995–1999', *El Croquis*, no. 95/96, May (special issue)

Chronology of Works

Buildings and projects are listed according to their start date.

1952 Kitchen for Grandmother's House, Matosinhos, Portugal

1954 Four Houses, Matosinhos, Portugal (1954–7)

1956 Parish Centre, Matosinhos, Portugal (1956–9)
Design for Low-Cost Housing Complex, Matosinhos, Portugal

1957 Carneiro de Melo House, Porto, Portugal (1957–9)

1958 Tea House, Boa Nova Restaurant, Leça da Palmeira, Portugal (1958–63)
Quinta da Conceição Swimming Pool, Matosinhos, Portugal (1958–65)

1959 Design for Monument to Aos Calafates, Foz, Porto, Portugal

1960 Design for Restaurant, Perafita, Matosinhos, Portugal
Martins Camelo Family Grave at the Sendim Cemetery, Matosinhos, Portugal
Angola Oil Refinery Cafeteria, Matosinhos, Portugal
Remodelling of Parents' House, Matosinhos, Portugal
Design for Tennis Court, Senhora da Hora, Matosinhos, Portugal
Luís Rocha Ribeiro House, Maia, Portugal (1960–9)
Lordelo Co-operative, Porto, Portugal (1960–3)

1961 Design for Doctor Júlio Gesta House, Matosinhos, Portugal
Ocean Swimming Pool, Leça da Palmeira, Portugal (1961–6)

1962 Ferreira da Costa House, Matosinhos, Portugal (1962–5)

1963 Design for Rui Feijo House, Moledo do Minho, Portugal
Siza Family Tomb, Matosinhos, Portugal

1964 Alves Costa House, Moledo do Minho, Portugal (1964–71)
Alves Santos House, Póvoa de Varzim, Portugal (1964–70)

1965 Antonio L. Ribeiro House, Vila do Conde, Portugal
Design for Marlã Shop, Matosinhos, Portugal
Studies for Sacor Housing Complex, Matosinhos, Portugal
Leça and Boa Nova Coastal Development Plan, Leça da Palmeira, Portugal (1965–74)

1966 Design for Adelino Sousa Felgueira House, Marco de Canavezes, Portugal
Design for Sacor Petrol Station, Matosinhos, Portugal (1966–70)
Warehouse, Matosinhos, Portugal
Study for Ocean Swimming Pool Restaurant, Leça da Palmeira, Portugal

1967 Design for Hotel, Vale de Canas, Coimbra, Portugal
Monument to Antonio Nobre (poet), Leça da Palmeira, Matosinhos, Portugal (1967–80)
Manuel Magalhães House, Porto, Portugal (1967–70)

1968 Urban Development Plan for Avenida D. Afonso Henriques, Porto, Portugal
Studies for Carlos Vale Guimarães House, Aveiro, Portugal
Design for Office Building in Avenida D. Afonso Henriques, Porto, Portugal (1968–74)

1969 Borges & Irmão Bank I, Vila do Conde, Portugal (1969–74)
Shop Facade Remodelling and Interior Design, Porto, Portugal

1970 Interior Design for Domus Co-operative, Porto, Portugal
Study for Álvaro Bonifacio Housing Scheme, Ovar, Portugal (1970–2)
Villa Cova Housing Complex, Caxinas, Vila do Conde, Portugal (1970–2)

1971 Alcino Cardoso House, Lugar da Gateira, Moledo do Minho, Portugal (1971–3)
Pinto & Sotto Mayor Bank, Oliveira de Azeméis, Portugal (1971–4)
Study for Mobil Oil Housing Complex, Matosinhos, Portugal (1971–2)

1972 Domus Co-operative Supermarket, Porto, Portugal
Design for Marques Pinto House, Porto, Portugal
Studies for Barbara de Sousa Housing Scheme, Ovar, Portugal
Pinto & Sotto Mayor Bank, Lamego, Portugal (1972–4)
Lamego Club, Lamego, Portugal
Design for Pinto & Sotto Mayor Bank, Régua, Portugal (1972–3)

1973 Study for Chapel in Rio Tinto, Gondomar, Portugal
Design for House in Azeitão, Setúbal, Portugal (1973–4)
Art Gallery, Porto, Portugal (1973–4)
Studies for Residential Complex for Housing Development Office, Bouça, Porto, Portugal
Beires House, Póvoa de Varzim, Portugal (1973–6)

1974 SAAL Residential Complex, São Victor, Porto, Portugal (1974–9)

1975 External Staircase and Remodelling of Cálem House, Foz do Douro, Porto, Portugal
Design for Paula Frassineti School, Porto, Portugal
Design for Pico do Areeiro Restaurant, Madeira Island, Portugal
SAAL Social Housing, Bouça II, Porto, Portugal (1975–7)

1976 Studies for Ribeira Market Stall, Porto, Portugal
Design for Reconstruction of Two Houses in the Barredo Quarter, Porto, Portugal
Urban Development Plan for Lada Square and Redevelopment of Barredo Quarter, Porto, Portugal
Design for Francelos House, Vila Nova de Gaia, Portugal
António Carlos Siza House, São João de Deus, Santo Tirso, Portugal (1976–8)

1977 Malagueira Residential District, Évora, Portugal (1977–97)
Design for Borges & Irmão Bank, Vila do Conde, Portugal

1978 Borges & Irmão Bank, Vila do Conde, Portugal (1978–86)

1979 J. M. Teixeira Apartment, Póvoa de Varzim, Portugal (1979–86)
Maria Margarida Aguda House, Arcozelo, Vila Nova de Gaia, Portugal (1979–87)
Design for Fränkelufer Residential Complex, Berlin, Germany
Design for Görlitzer Bad Swimming Pool, Berlin, Germany

Design for Habiflor/Florbela Espanca
Co-operative Residential Complex, Villa Viçosa,
Portugal (1979–81)
Design for A Riconquista Co-operative
Residential Complex, Aviz, Portugal (1979–81)

1980 Design for Caixa Geral de Depósitos,
Matosinhos, Portugal
Competition Design for Schlesisches Tor
Residential Complex, Berlin, Germany
Bonjour Tristesse, Schlesisches Tor Residential
Complex, Berlin, Germany (1980–4)
J. M. Teixeira House, Taipas, Guimarães, Portugal
(1980–91)
Design for Dom Company Headquarters,
Cologne, Germany
Apartment Building, 11–12 Kottbusser Dam,
Kreuzberg, West Berlin, Germany
Avelino Duarte House, Ovar, Portugal (1980–4)
Kindergarten and Senior Citizens' Clubhouse,
Schlesisches Tor Recreational Centre, Berlin,
Germany (1980–90)

1981 Design for Fernando Machado House, Porto,
Portugal
Design for Hotel and Restaurant in Monte Picoto,
Braga, Portugal

1982 Design for Cultural Centre, Sines, Portugal
(1982–5)
Study for Coach Station, Guimarães, Portugal
Design for Aníbal Guimarães da Costa House,
Trofa, Portugal
Shopping and Office Complex, Guimarães,
Portugal (1982–8)

1983 Design for Mário Bahia House, Gondomar,
Portugal (1983–93)
Nina Shop, Porto, Portugal
Macau City Expansion Plan, China (1983–4)
Design for Kulturforum, Berlin, Germany
Design for Restoration of Church, Salemi, Italy
(1983–97)
Design for Monument to Gestapo Victims, Berlin,
Germany
Design for Hotel in Malagueira, Évora, Portugal
(1983–9)
Design for Extension of French Institute, Porto,
Portugal
Urban Plan, Schilderswijk-West, The Hague, The
Netherlands (1983–4)
De Punkt and De Komma Social Housing,
Schilderswijk-West, The Hague, The Netherlands
(1983–8)

1984 Urban Redevelopment Plan, Caserta, Italy
Design for Erhard Josef Pascher House, Sintra,
Portugal
David Vieira de Castro House, Famalicão,
Portugal (1984–94)
Luís Figueiredo House, Gondomar, Portugal
(1984–94)
João de Deus Nursery School, Penafiel, Portugal
(1984–91)
Restoration of Póvoa House, Faculty of
Architecture, Porto, Portugal (1984–6)
Housing and Shopping Complex, Schilderswijk,
The Hague, The Netherlands (1984–8)

1985 Van der Vennepark Garden, Schilderswijk-West,
The Hague, The Netherlands (1985–8)
Restoration of Campo di Marte, Guidecca,
Venice, Italy
Study for Espertina Housing Scheme, Águeda,
Portugal
Carlos Ramos Pavilion, Faculty of Architecture,
Porto, Portugal (1985–6)

1986 City Park Design, Salemi, Italy
Expo '92 Master Plan – Competition, Seville,
Spain
Design for Hydrographic Institute, Lisbon,
Portugal
Urban Plan, Monterusciello, Naples, Italy
(1986–7)
Design for Extension of Winkler Casino, Salzburg,
Austria
Urban Plan for Pendino Quarter, Naples, Italy
(1986–7)
Teacher Training College, Setúbal, Portugal
(1986–94)
Faculty of Architecture, University of Porto, Porto,
Portugal (1986–96)

1987 César Rodrigues House, Porto, Portugal
(1987–96)
Design for Remodelling of Miranda Santos House
(Ferreira da Costa), Matosinhos, Portugal
(1987–96)

1988 Design for La Defensa Cultural Centre, Madrid,
Spain (1988–9)
Design for Matteotti Piazza, Siena, Italy
Design for Malagueira Housing, Évora, Portugal
Piezometric Tower, University of Aveiro, Aveiro,
Portugal (1988–9)
Library, University of Aveiro, Aveiro, Portugal
(1988–95)
Galician Centre of Contemporary Art, Santiago de
Compostela, Spain (1988–93)
Design for Sports Complex, Villanueva de Arosa,
Spain
Design for Alcino Cardoso House, Moledo do
Minho, Portugal (1988–91)
Carvalho Araújo Shop, Lisbon, Portugal (1988–9)
Design for Guardiola House, Seville, Spain
Reconstruction of the Chiado Area, Lisbon,
Portugal (1988–)
Design for Reconstruction of Portal di Riquer,
Alcoi-Valencia, Spain

1989 Housing in Concepción Arenal, Cádiz, Spain
Competition Design for National Library of
France, Paris, France
Residential Settlement, Schilderswijk, The Hague,
The Netherlands (1989–93)
Design for S. João Bosco Church and Parish
Centre, Malagueira, Évora, Portugal
Ferreira de Castro Office Building, Oliveira de
Azeméis, Portugal (1989–95)
Urban and Circulation Study for Praça de
Espanha, Lisbon, Portugal
Ana Costa and Manuel Silva House, Santo
Ovidio, Lousada, Portugal (1989–95)

1990 Design for Pereira Ganhão House, Tróia, Portugal
Santa Maria Church and Parish Centre, Marco de
Canavezes, Portugal (1990–6)
Ceramic Terrain Housing and Offices, Maastricht,
The Netherlands
Design for Santo Domingo de Bonaval
Restaurant, Santiago de Compostela, Spain
(1990–3)
Olympic Village Meteorological Centre and
MOPU Delegation Headquarters, Barcelona,
Spain (1990–2)
Urban Design for Boulevard Brune, Cité de
Jeunesse, Paris, France
Urban Plan for Avenida José Malhoa, Lisbon,
Portugal (1990–2)
Design of Rectory and Law Library, University of
Valencia, Valencia, Spain
Boavista Building, Porto, Portugal (1990–8)
Santo Domingo de Bonaval Garden, Santiago de
Compostela, Spain (1990–4)

1991 Design for Office Building, Porto, Portugal
Museum of Contemporary Art, Serralves
Foundation, Porto, Portugal (1991–9)
Restoration of Castro & Melo Building, Chiado,
Lisbon, Portugal (1991–4)
Restoration of Camara Chaves Building, Chiado,
Lisbon, Portugal (1991–6)

Design for Restoration of Grandes Armazéns do Chiado Building, Lisbon, Portugal
Restoration of Grandella Building, Chiado, Lisbon, Portugal (1991–6)
Eurocentre Complex, Boavista, Porto, Portugal (1991–3)
Vitra International Factory, Weil am Rhein, Germany (1991–4)
Design for Remodelling of Pai Ramiro Restaurant, Porto, Portugal (1991–4)
Design for Remodelling of Condes Cinema, Lisbon, Portugal
Design for Lusitânia Insurance Company Headquarters, Lisbon, Portugal (1991–3)
Design for Terraços de Bragança Complex, Lisbon, Portugal
Studies for Cargaleiro Foundation Headquarters, Lisbon, Portugal (1991–5)

1992 Design for Residential Complex, Malaga, Spain
Headquarters of the Young Businessmen's Association (ANJE), Oeiras, Portugal (1992–5)
Restaurant and Tea Room, Malagueira, Évora, Portugal
Study for Language School, Malagueira, Évora, Portugal
Fermata Baixa/Chiado Underground, Lisbon, Portugal (1992–8)
'Visions for Madrid' Exhibition, Madrid, Spain
Design for Museum of Contemporary Art, Helsinki, Finland (1992–3)

1993 Design for Restoration of Ludovice Building for the '25 April' Association, Lisbon, Portugal
Urban Plan for São João, Costa da Caparica, Portugal
Design for Residential Complex, Setúbal, Portugal
Design for Housing and Office Complex, Matosinhos, Portugal
Design for Ocean Swimming Pool Restaurant, Leça da Palmeira, Portugal
Restoration of Costa Braga Building, House of Youth and Pavilions, Matosinhos, Portugal (1993–7)
Revigrés Showroon, Águeda, Portugal (1993–7)
Office Building, Porto, Portugal (1993–7)
Study for Two Houses, Teixeira da Cunha, Felgueiras, Portugal
Urban Plan for City Centre, Montreuil, France
Design for Artists' Studios, Montreuil, France
Dimensione Fuoco Laboratory, Showroom and Housing, San Donà di Piave, Italy
Design for J. Paul Getty Museum, Malibu, Santa Monica, USA
Design for 'Puerta Real 1' Office Building and Restaurant, Granada, Spain (1993–5)
Faculty of Journalism, Santiago de Compostela, Spain
Remodelling of '25 April' Association Building, Lisbon, Portugal

1994 Casa Jovem Co-operative Social Housing Complex, Guarda, Portugal
Design for Children's Education Centre, Serralves Foundation, Porto, Portugal
Design for Granell Museum, Santiago de Compostela, Spain
Design for La Salle Parking, Santiago de Compostela, Spain
Restoration of Bar in Serralves Foundation House, Porto, Portugal
Fountain Design for Vitra International, Weil am Rhein, Germany
Master Plan for Rossio São Brás, Évora, Portugal
Design for Universiadi '97 Sports Complex, Palermo, Italy
Restoration of Ancient '2 de Maio' Market, Viseu, Portugal
Design for Restoration of Santa Justa Lift, Lisbon, Portugal
Design for Residential Complex, Malagueira, Évora, Portugal

1995 Design for Ishmaelite Centre and Aga Khan Foundation Headquarters, Lisbon, Portugal
Restoration and Extension of Stedelijk Museum, Amsterdam, The Netherlands
Portuguese Pavilion at Expo '98, Lisbon, Portugal (1995–8)
Rectory, University of Alicante, Alicante, Spain (1995–8)
Douro and Leixões Port Authority Building, Matosinhos, Portugal
Van Middelem-Dupont House, Oudenberg, Belgium
Design for Pinto Sousa House, Oeiras, Portugal
Urban Plan for Lagoinha, Belo Horizonte, Brazil
Urban Plan and Restaurant, Palace of the Dukes of Bragança and Campo de São Mamede Area, Guimarães, Portugal
Town Hall, Caorle, Italy
Residential Complex and Restoration of Two Houses, Palmeira, Évora, Portugal
Agostinho Vieira House, Baião, Portugal
Design for Primary School, Alcoi-Alicante, Spain
Design for Biophysics Institute on Hombroich Island, Düsseldorf, Germany (1995–6)
Fehlbaum Family Tomb, Weil am Rhein, Germany (1995–6)
Design for Extension of Hotel Ritz, Lisbon, Portugal

1996 Set Design for Ballet, Gulbenkian Foundation, Lisbon, Portugal
Kolonihaven, Open-Air Structure, Copenhagen, Denmark
Design for Underground, Porto, Portugal
Docking Pier, European Architects in Thessaloniki, Salonika, Greece
Urban Plan for South Matosinhos, Matosinhos, Portugal
Medical Clinic, Malagueira, Évora, Portugal
Housing, Office and Shopping Complex, Raimundo Rotunda, Évora, Portugal

1997 Chiado Bar, Lisbon, Portugal
Design for Sports Hall, Vigo, Spain
Park and Cultural Centre, Caxinas, Vila do Conde, Portugal
Design for University Library, Évora, Portugal
Manzana dei Revellín Cultural Centre, Ceuta, Spain
Hotel, Almeria, Spain
Design for Dr. Machado de Mantos Square, Felgueiras, Portugal
Rectory and Auditorium, University Campus, Valencia, Spain
Renova Factory and Showroom, Torres Novas, Portugal
South District Town Hall, Rosario, Argentina
Design for Social Centre, Malagueira, Évora, Portugal

1998 Leonel Building, Chiado, Lisbon, Portugal
Restoration of Villa Colonnese and Seven Houses, Vicenza, Italy
Santa Maria de Rosario alla Magliana Church, Rome, Italy
Housing and Shopping Complex, Porto, Portugal
Zaida Building, Housing, Office and Shopping Complex, Granada, Spain
Cape Verde National Bank Office, Praia, Cape Verde Island
Design for Cultural Centre and Auditorium for Iberê Camargo Foundation, Alegre Port, Brazil

1999 Restoration of Solar Magalhães House for Afonso Henriques Foundation, Amarante, Portugal

Index of Works

Italics denotes pictures and **bold** denotes project pages.

'2 de Maio' Market restoration, Viseu **517**
'25 April' Association Building remodelling, Lisbon **518**

Adelino Sousa House, Marco de Canavezes **111**
Agostinho Vieira House, Baião **559**
Alcino Cardoso House, Lugar da Gateira, Moledo do Minho (1971–3) 19, *19*, *21*, *23*, **127–30**
Alcino Cardoso House, Moledo do Minho (1988–91) **354**
Álvaro Bonifacio Housing Scheme, Ovar **123**
Alves Costa House, Moledo do Minho 16, *18*, 19, **104–5**
Alves Santos House, Póvoa de Varzim 16, **106–7**
Ana Costa and Manuel Silva House, Santo Ovidio, Lousada **374–5**
Angola Oil Refinery Cafeteria, Matosinhos **93**
Aníbal Guimarães da Costa House, Trofa **223**
António Carlos Siza House, Santo Tirso 19, 20, **159**
Antonio L. Ribeiro House, Vila do Conde **108**
A Riconquista Residential Complex, Aviz **195**
Art Gallery, Porto 42 **139**
Artists' Studios, Montreuil **496**
Avelino Duarte House, Ovar 28–31, *31*, *33*, 46, 50, **211–16**
Avenida José Malhoa urban plan, Lisbon **405**
Avenida D. Afonso Henriques urban plan, Porto **117**

Barbara de Sousa Housing Scheme, Ovar **136**
Barredo Quarter (reconstruction of houses), Porto **157**
Beires House, Póvoa de Varzim 19, 23, **141–5**
Biophysics Institute, Hombroich Island, Düsseldorf **560**
Boa Nova Tea House and Restaurant, Leça da Palmeira 7, 8, *10*, 12–14, *13*, *14*, 16, 82, **83–8**
Boavista Building, Porto **408–15**
Bonjour Tristesse, Schlesisches Tor Residential Complex, Berlin 8, *9*, *9*, 31, 32, *35*, **196**, **197–203**
Borges & Irmão Bank I, Vila do Conde (1969–74) 20, *24*, *25*, **121**
Borges & Irmão Bank, Vila do Conde (1978–86) 23, *179*, **180–5**
Boulevard Brune, Cité de Jeunesse urban design, Paris **404**

Caixa Geral de Depósitos, Matosinhos **196**
Cálem House remodelling, Foz do Douro, Porto **150**
Camara Chaves Building restoration, Chiado, Lisbon **428–33**
Campo di Marte restoration, Guidecca, Venice **278–9**
Cape Verde National Bank Office, Praia **590**
Cargaleiro Foundation Headquarters, Lisbon 55, **453**
Carlos Ramos Pavilion, Faculty of Architecture, Porto 34, 37, 40, **280–4**
Carlos Vale Guimarães House, Aveiro **117**
Carneiro de Melo House, Porto **81**

Carvalho Araújo Shop, Lisbon **354**
Casa Jovem Social Housing Complex, Guarda **510–12**
Caserta urban redevelopment plan **251**
Castro & Melo Building restoration, Chiado, Lisbon **424–7**
Ceramic Terrain Housing and Offices, Maastricht **392–6**
César Rodrigues House, Porto **318**
Chapel in Rio Tinto, Gondomar **138**
Chiado Area reconstruction, Lisbon 356, **357–64**
Chiado Bar, Lisbon **570**
Children's Centre, Serralves Foundation, Porto **512**
Church restoration, Salemi **236–7**
City Park design, Salemi **285**
Coach Station, Guimarães **223**
Condes Cinema remodelling, Lisbon **449–50**
Costa Braga Building, House of Youth and Pavilions restoration, Matosinhos **482–3**
Cultural Centre and Auditorium for Iberê Camargo Foundation, Alegre Port **591–4**
Cultural Centre, Sines 37, **222**

David Vieira de Castro House, Famalicão **253–60**
De Punkt and De Komma Social Housing, Schilderswijk-West, The Hague 32, *39*, **242–50**
Dimensione Fuoco Laboratory, Showroom and Housing, San Donà di Piave **497–9**
Docking Pier, Salonika **566–7**
Dom Company Headquarters, Cologne 28, **209–10**
Domus Co-operative interior design, Porto **122**
Domus Co-operative Supermarket, Porto **136**
Douro and Leixões Port Authority, Matosinhos **552**
Dr. Machado de Mantos Square, Felgueiras **579**

Erhard Josef Pascher House, Sintra **251**
Espertina Housing Scheme, Águeda **279**
Eurocentre Complex, Boavista, Porto **440–1**
Expo '92 Master Plan – Competition, Seville **286–7**

Faculty of Architecture, University of Porto, Porto 8, 32, 34, 40–2, *43*, *44*, *45* **302–17**
Faculty of Journalism, Santiago de Compostela 55, **505–9**
Fehlbaum Family Tomb, Weil am Rhein **561**
Fermata Baixa/Chiado Underground, Lisbon **465–70**
Fernando Machado House, Porto **221**
Ferreira da Costa House, Matosinhos 16, **103**
Ferreira de Castro Office, Oliveira de Azeméis **373**
Francelos House, Vila Nova de Gaia **158**
Fränkelufer Residential Complex, Berlin 28, 31–2, **190–2**
French Institute extension, Porto **239**
Furniture **602–5**

Galician Centre of Contemporary Art, Santiago de Compostela 8, 34, 42–9, *46*, *47*, *48*, *49*, 336, **337–49**

Görlitzer Bad Swimming Pool, Berlin 28, **193–4**
Grandella Building restoration, Chiado, Lisbon **436–39**
Grandes Armazéns do Chiado Building restoration, Lisbon **434–35**
Granell Museum, Santiago de Compostela **513**
Guardiola House, Seville **355**

Habiflor/Florbela Espanca Co-operative Residential Complex, Villa Viçosa **195**
Headquarters of the Young Businessmen's Association (ANJE), Oeiras **458–62**
Hotel, Almeria **578**
Hotel, Vale de Canas, Coimbra **112**
Hotel and Restaurant in Monte Picoto, Braga **221**
Hotel in Malagueira, Évora **239**
Hotel Ritz extension, Lisbon **561**
House in Azeitão, Setúbal **138**
Houses, Matosinhos (four family houses) 7, **73–5**
Housing and Office Complex, Matosinhos **479**
Housing and Shopping Complex, Porto **586–7**
Housing in Concepción Arenal, Cádiz **366**
Housing, Office and Shopping Complex, Raimundo Rotunda, Évora **570**
Hydrographic Institute, Lisbon **288**

Ishmaelite Centre and Aga Khan Foundation Headquarters, Lisbon **519–21**

J. Paul Getty Museum, Malibu, Santa Monica **500–1**
J. M. Teixeira Apartment, Póvoa de Varzim **186–7**
J. M. Teixeira House, Taipas, Guimarães **204–8**
João de Deus Nursery School, Penafiel 46, *50*, **265–7**
Júlio Gesta House, Matosinhos 16, **94**

Kindergarten, Schlesisches Tor Recreational Centre, Berlin 32, *36*, *37*, **217–20**
Kitchen for Grandmother's House, Matosinhos **70**
Kolonihaven, Open-Air Structure, Copenhagen **562–3**
Kreuzberg Apartment Building, West Berlin **210**
Kulturforum, Berlin **233–35**

Lada Square urban development plan and redevelopment of Barredo Quarter, Porto **158**
La Defensa Cultural Centre, Madrid **320**
Lagoinha urban plan, Belo Horizonte **556**
Lamego Club, Lamego **137**
Language School, Malagueira, Évora **465**
La Salle Parking, Santiago de Compostela **513**
Leça and Boa Nova Coastal Development Plan, Leça da Palmeira **109–110**
Leonel Building, Chiado, Lisbon **581**
Library, University of Aveiro 8, 34, 49–50, *51*, *52*, *53*, **326–35**
Lordelo Co-operative, Porto **96**

Low-Cost Housing Complex, Matosinhos **81**
Ludovice Building restoration, Lisbon **477**
Luís Figueiredo House, Gondomar 31, *34*, **261–64**
Luís Rocha Ribeiro House, Maia 16, 23, **95–6**
Lusitânia Company Headquarters, Lisbon **451**

Macau City expansion plan, China **232**
Malagueira Residential District and Housing, Évora 7, 25–6, *27*, *29*, *30*, 160–2, **163–76**, 322
Manuel Magalhães House, Porto 16–19, **114–116**
Manzana dei Revellín Cultural Centre, Ceuta 55, **575–7**
Maria Margarida Aguda House, Vila Nova de Gaia 37, **188–9**
Mário Bahia House, Gondomar 31, **227–30**
Marlã Shop, Matosinhos **108**
Marques Pinto House, Porto **136**
Martins Camelo Family Grave, Matosinhos **92**
Matteotti Piazza, Siena **321**
Medical Clinic, Malagueira, Évora **568–9**
Miranda Santos House (Ferreira da Costa) remodelling, Matosinhos **319–20**
Mobil Oil Housing Complex, Matosinhos **123**
Monterusciello urban plan, Naples **288**
Montreuil City Centre, urban plan **495**
Monument to Antonio Nobre, Leça da Palmeira **113**
Monument to Aos Calafates, Foz, Porto **92**
Monument to Gestapo Victims, Berlin 28, **238**
Museum of Contemporary Art, Helsinki **474–76**
Museum of Contemporary Art, Serralves Foundation, Porto 8, 55, 336, **416–23**

National Library of France competition design, Paris **367**
Nina Shop, Porto **231**

Ocean Swimming Pool, Leça da Palmeira 8, 14–16, *17*, 82, **97–102**
Ocean Swimming Pool Restaurant study, Leça da Palmeira (1966) **112**
Ocean Swimming Pool Restaurant design, Leça da Palmeira (1993) **479–81**
Office Building in Avenida D. Afonso Henriques, Porto 20, **118–120**
Office Building, Porto (1991) **415**
Office Building, Porto (1993–7) **490–93**
Olympic Village Meteorological Centre and MOPU Delegation Headquarters, Barcelona 28, **398–403**

Pai Ramiro Restaurant, Porto **449**
Palace of the Dukes of Bragança and Campo de São Mamede Area urban plan and restaurant, Guimarães **557**
Parents' House remodelling, Matosinhos **94**
Parish Centre, Matosinhos 14, **76–80**
Park and Cultural Centre, Caxinas, Vila do Conde **571**

Paula Frassineti School, Porto **150**
Pendino Quarter urban plan, Naples **291**
Pereira Ganhão House, Tróia **376**
Pico do Areeiro Restaurant, Madeira Island **150**
Piezometric Tower, University of Aveiro **322–5**
Pinto & Sotto Mayor Bank, Lamego 23, **137**
Pinto & Sotto Mayor Bank, Oliveira de Azeméis 20–3, *25*, **131–35**
Pinto & Sotto Mayor Bank, Régua **137**
Pinto Sousa House, Oeiras **555–6**
Portal di Riquer reconstruction, Alcoi-Valencia **365–6**
Portuguese Pavilion at Expo '98, Lisbon 8, 50, 52–5, *56*, *58*, *59*, *60*, **529–41**
Póvoa House restoration, Faculty of Architecture, Porto **268–9**
Praça de Espanha urban study, Lisbon **373**
Primary School, Alcoi-Alicante **560**
Product Designs **598–601**
'Puerta Real 1' Office Building and Restaurant, Granada **502–4**

Quinta da Conceição Swimming Pool, Matosinhos 14, *15*, 16, **89–91**

Rectory and Auditorium, University of Valencia **579**
Rectory and Law Library, University of Valencia **406–7**
Rectory, University of Alicante 8, 40, **542–51**
Renova Factory and Showroom, Torres Novas **580**
Residential Complex and Restoration of Two Houses, Palmeira, Évora **559**
Residential Complex for Housing Development Office, Bouça, Porto **140**
Residential Complex, Malagueira, Évora **177**
Residential Complex, Malaga **456–57**
Residential Complex, Setúbal **478**
Restaurant and Tea Room, Malagueira, Évora **463–64**
Restaurant, Perafita, Matosinhos **92**
Revigrés Showroom, Águeda **484–89**
Ribeira Market Stall, Porto **157**
Rossio São Brás Master Plan, Évora **514**
Rui Feijo House, Moledo do Minho **103**

S. João Bosco Church and Parish Centre, Évora **372**
SAAL Residential Complex, São Victor, Porto 7, 25, **146–9**
SAAL Social Housing, Bouça, Porto 7, 23–5, *26*, **151–6**
Sacor Housing Complex, Matosinhos **108**
Sacor Petrol Station, Matosinhos **111**
Santa Justa Lift restoration, Lisbon **518**
Santa Maria Church and Parish Centre, Marco de Canavezes 8, 50–2, *54*, 377–8, **379–91**
Santa Maria de Rosario Church, Rome **585**
Santo Domingo de Bonaval Garden, Santiago de Compostela 42, **350–53**

Santo Domingo de Bonaval Restaurant, Santiago de Compostela **397**
São João urban plan, Costa da Caparica **478**
Schilderswijk Housing and Shopping Complex, The Hague 32, *38*, **270–5**
Schilderswijk Residential Settlement, The Hague (1989–93) 8, 32, **368–71**
Schilderswijk-West urban plan, The Hague **240–1**
Schlesisches Tor Redevelopment Project, Berlin 8, 9, *9*, 31, 32, *35*, *36*, 37, **197–203**, 217–20
Sculptures **604**
Senior Citizens' Clubhouse, Schlesisches Tor Recreational Centre, Berlin 32, *36*, **217–20**
Serralves Foundation House Bar, Porto **514**
Set Design for Gulbenkian Foundation Ballet, Lisbon **562**
Shop Facade remodelling and interior design, Porto **122**
Shopping and Office Complex, Guimarães **224–6**
Siza Family Tomb, Matosinhos **104**
Social Centre, Malagueira, Évora **178**
Solar Magalhães House, Amarante **595**
Sports Hall, Vigo **571**
Sports Complex, Villanueva de Arosa **354**
Stedelijk Museum restoration and extension, Amsterdam **522–6**
South Matosinhos urban plan, Matosinhos **567**

Teacher Training College, Setúbal 31, 32, 34–40, *40*, *41*, 52, 55, **292–301**
Teixeira da Cunha Houses, Felgueiras **494**
Tennis Court, Senhora da Hora, Matosinhos **94**
Terraços de Bragança Complex, Lisbon **451–52**
Town Hall, Caorle **558**
Town Hall, South District, Rosario **581**

Underground, Porto **564–5**
Universiadi '97 Sports Complex, Palermo **516**
University Library, Évora **574**

Van der Vennepark Garden, Schilderswijk-West, The Hague 32, **276–7**
Van Middelem-Dupont House, Oudenberg **553–4**
Villa Colonnese and Seven Houses restoration, Vicenza **582–4**
Villa Cova Housing Complex, Caxinas, Vila do Conde 20, *22*, **124–6**
'Visions for Madrid' Exhibition, Madrid **471–3**
Vitra International Factory, Weil am Rhein 8, 46, **442–8**
Vitra International Fountain Design, Weil am Rhein **514**

Warehouse, Matosinhos **111**
Winkler Casino extension, Salzburg **289–90**

Zaida Building, Housing, Office and Shopping Complex, Granada **588–9**

Publishers' Acknowledgements

The publishers wish to thank: Shaun Whiteside for translations from Italian into English (pp. 7–9, 66–7, 82, 336, 377–8, 597 and 607); Marion Mayer for translations from Portuguese into English (pp. 160–2); Alvaro Siza's Office for granting permission to publish The Chiado essay (p. 356); and Skira, Milan for granting permission to reproduce Siza's writings in English (pp. 71–2, 252, 527–8, 572–3).

Photographic Credits

Front cover:
Rectory, University of Alicante, Spain (1995–8) © Roland Halbe/artur

Back cover:
Álvaro Siza sketch, 'Puerta Real 1' Office Building and Restaurant, Granada, Spain (1993–5)

Book photographs:
Alessandra Chemollo
Roland Halbe
Maria Chiara Porcu
Uwe Rau
Álvaro Siza Office
Teresa Siza
Francisco Vidinha

The selection of material provided by Siza's office was edited by Carlos Castanheira

Álvaro Siza Collaborators

Andreia Afonso
Susana Afonso
Petra Katarina Alankoja
Carolina Albino
Anna Aí
Sara Almeida
Antonic Angelillo
Luís Antas de Barros
Daniela Antonucci
Maira José Araújo
Alfredo Jorge Ascensão
Maria Clara Bastai
Matthew Becker
Gonzalo Benavides
Tatiana Berger
Matthew Betmalek
Giacomo Borella
André Eraga
Luisa Brandão
Peter Brinkert
Maite Brosa
Jorge Carvalho
José Luis Carvalho Gomes
Carlos Castanheira
Edgar Castro
Rui Castro
Mario Caccio
Peter Cody
Roberto Collovà
Jane Considine
Mateo Corrales
Alexandre Alvez Costa
Guilherme Páris Couto
Roberto Cremascoli
Francisco José Cunha
Maurice Custers
Alessandro D'Amico
Adalberto Dias
António Dias
Luis Diaz-Mauriño
Zahra Dolati
Joan Falgueras
Tiago Faria
Cristina Ferreirinha
Rudolf Finsterwalder
Brigitte Fleck
Teresa Fonseca
John Friedman
Christian Gaenshirt
Michele Gigante
Jean-Gerard Giorla
Teresa Godinho
João Gomes da Silva
Ramiro Gonçalves
Teresa Gonçalves
José Fernando Gonçalves
Anton Graf
Karine Grimaux
Jotta van Groenewoud
Hughes Grudzinski
Cristina Guedes
Francisco Guedes
Francisco Guedes de Carvalho
Miguel Guedes de Carvalho
Filipa Guerreiro
Angela Jimenez
Jun Shuang Kim
Hana Kassem
Bradford Kelley
Lia Kidalis
Ulrich Krauss
Cecilia Lau
Daria Laurentini
Raffaele Leone
Robert Levit
Nuno Ribeiro Lopes
Francisco Lucena
Roger Lundeen
Ulrike Machold
António Madureira
Beatriz Madureira
Bruno Marchand
Oreste Marrone
Eduardo Marta da Cruz
Luis Filipe Mendes
Chantal Meysman
Pier Paolo Mincio
Elisiário Miranda
Maria Moita
Francesca Montalto
Anabela Monteiro
Jorge Nuno Monteiro
Abílio Filipe Mourão
Carles Muro
Colm Murray
Mitsunori Nakamura
Miguel Nery
José Manuel Neves
Graça Nieto
Antónia Noites
Joelke Offringa
Edison Okumura
Vitor Oliveira
Pascale Pacozzi
V. De Pasquale
Luisa Penha
Maria Chiara Porcu
Angela Princiotto
Marco Rampulla
Bárbara Rangel Carvalho
José Eduardo Rebelo
Ashton Richards
Dinora Rodrigues
Pedro Rogado
Edite Rosa
João Sabugueiro
José Salgado
Maria Manuela Sambade
José Paulo dos Santos
Paul Scott
Dirk Sehmsdorf
Clemente Menéres Semide
Carlos Seoane
Fariba Sepehrnia
Avelino Silva
Andrea Smaniotto
Sabina Snozzi
Joana Soares Carneiro
Ivone Sobral
Eduardo Souto de Moura
Yves Stump
Ameet Sukhthankar
Peter Testa
Sofia Thenaisie Coelho
Taichi Tomuro
Helena Torgo
Viviana Trapani
Mona Trautman
Jan van de Voort
Orlando Varejão
Salvador Vaz Pinto
Humberto Vieira
Sandra Vivanco
Wilfried Wang
Pascale de Weck
Ana Williamson
João Pedro Xavier